CODE
BREAKERS

Other books by Craig Collie

Nagasaki: The massacre of the innocent and unknowing (2011)

The Path of Infinite Sorrow: The Japanese on the Kokoda Track (2009)
co-written with Hajime Marutani

*The Reporter and the Warlords: An Australian at large
in China's republican revolution* (2013)

CODE BREAKERS

Inside the shadow world of signals intelligence
in Australia's two Bletchley Parks

CRAIG COLLIE

ALLEN&UNWIN
SYDNEY·MELBOURNE·AUCKLAND·LONDON

First published in 2017

Copyright © Craig Collie 2017

All rights reserved. No part of this book may be reproduced or transmitted in any form or by any means, electronic or mechanical, including photocopying, recording or by any information storage and retrieval system, without prior permission in writing from the publisher. The Australian *Copyright Act 1968* (the Act) allows a maximum of one chapter or 10 per cent of this book, whichever is the greater, to be photocopied by any educational institution for its educational purposes provided that the educational institution (or body that administers it) has given a remuneration notice to the Copyright Agency (Australia) under the Act.

Allen & Unwin
83 Alexander Street
Crows Nest NSW 2065
Australia
Phone: (61 2) 8425 0100
Email: info@allenandunwin.com
Web: www.allenandunwin.com

Cataloguing-in-Publication details are available
from the National Library of Australia
www.trove.nla.gov.au

ISBN 978 1 74331 210 0

Maps by Keith Mitchell
Set in 12/16.5 pt Bembo by Post Pre-press Group, Australia
Printed and bound in Australia by Griffin Press

10 9 8

MIX
Paper from responsible sources
FSC® C009448

The paper in this book is FSC® certified. FSC® promotes environmentally responsible, socially beneficial and economically viable management of the world's forests.

Contents

List of maps		vi
Abbreviations		vii
Diagram of Allied code-breaking units		ix
Chapter 1	Burn the codes and ciphers	1
Chapter 2	Pioneer of the code breaker's craft	18
Chapter 3	Special Intelligence Bureau	42
Chapter 4	The road to Corregidor	65
Chapter 5	Scramble to safety	82
Chapter 6	The turning of the tide	109
Chapter 7	Midway	136
Chapter 8	Central Bureau	168
Chapter 9	The Water Transport Code broken	202
Chapter 10	The admiral's itinerary	221
Chapter 11	Buried treasure	247
Chapter 12	The front line and the back room	283
Chapter 13	A new world, a new enemy	321
Coding and decoding Japan's military messages		333
Glossary of technical terms		335
Cast of characters		337
Acknowledgements		343
Notes		345
Bibliography		363
Index		380

List of maps

Map 1:	Manila Bay	76
Map 2:	The Battle of the Coral Sea, 1942	130
Map 3:	Allied advances along the northern New Guinea coast, 1943	255
Map 4:	Allied assault on Hollandia and its airfields, 1944	275
Map 5:	No. 6 Wireless Unit landings in support of the Allied invasion of Leyte, 1944	291
Map 6:	No. 6 Wireless Unit landings in support of the Allied invasion of Luzon, 1945	313

Abbreviations

AIF	Australian Imperial Force
ASIO	Australian Security Intelligence Organisation
ATIS	Allied Translator and Interpreter Section
AWAS	Australian Women's Army Service
AWS	Aircraft Warning Service (Philippines)
BRUSA	Britain–United States (Agreement)
CGS	Chief of General Staff (Australian Army)
CNS	Chief of Naval Staff
COIC	Combined Operational Intelligence Centre (Australia)
CSO	Chief Signal Officer
DCO	District Communications Office (US)
D/F	direction finder
DNI	Director of Naval Intelligence
DSB	Defence Signals Branch (Australia)
FECB	Far East Combined Bureau (Hong Kong, Singapore)
FRUMEL	Fleet Radio Unit Melbourne (US, Australia)
GCCS	Government Code and Cipher School (UK)
GHQ	General Headquarters
HQ	headquarters
IJA	Imperial Japanese Army
IJN	Imperial Japanese Navy
MI5	Military Intelligence, Section 5 (UK)
MI6	Military Intelligence, Section 6 (UK)
POW	prisoner of war

RAAF	Royal Australian Air Force
RAN	Royal Australian Navy
RFP	radio fingerprinting
RN	Royal Navy (UK)
SIB	Special Intelligence Bureau (Australia)
sigint	signals intelligence
SIS	Signal Intelligence Service (US)
SWPA	Southwest Pacific Area (US/Australia)
SWS	Special Wireless Section (Australia)
TICOM	Target Intelligence Committee
USAAF	United States Army Air Force
USN	United States Navy
WAAAF	Women's Auxiliary Australian Air Force
WAC	Women's Army Corps (US)
WRANS	Women's Royal Australian Naval Reserve
WU	Wireless Unit

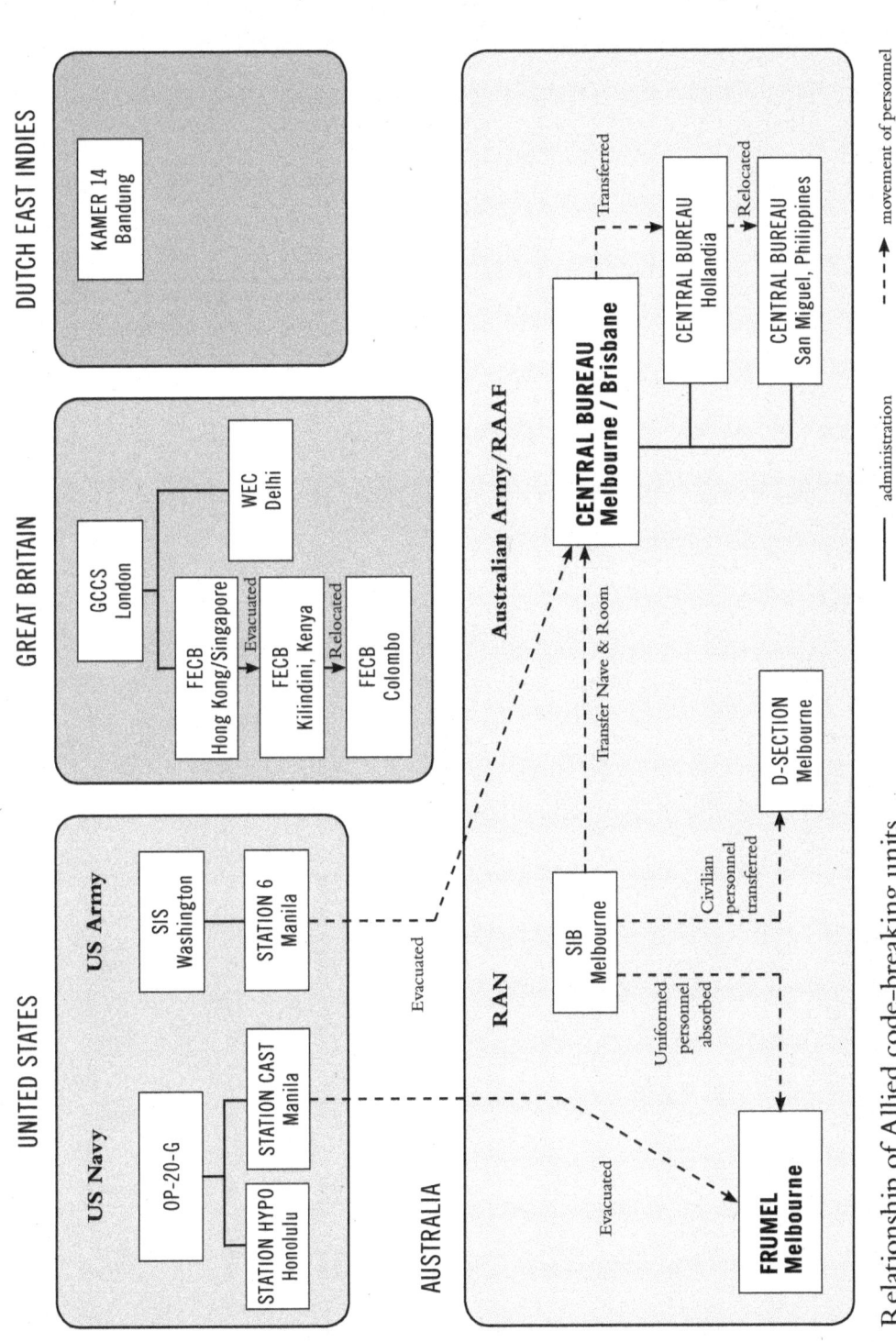

Relationship of Allied code-breaking units

Chapter 1

Burn the codes and ciphers

Like a messenger from the dark side, a lone despatch rider roars out of Park Orchards, a trail of dust from the gravel road settling slowly behind him in the early-morning glow. Cottages vacated for the military, and untended apple and pear orchards, are left behind. The growling motorcycle with its oversized headlamp winds downhill through scrubby eucalypt bushland towards central Melbourne, some 30 kilometres away. It is November 1941, and Europe has been at war for two years.

Now trouble is brewing closer to home, with a belligerent Japan chided by the United States over its military incursions into China. Word is that the handwritten notes inside the sealed bag strapped to the man's chest have something to do with that, but this Don R—jargon for despatch rider—has no idea what he is carrying and doesn't really care. Anonymous in goggles, helmet and dark jacket, he has been ordered to deliver the package to an office in Victoria Barracks, on St Kilda Road, and that is what he does.

Built in the mid-nineteenth century to house British troops, the imposing main building now houses the Defence Secretariat and the War Cabinet room. The new Prime Minister, John Curtin, has an office there, too. When Australia's federal government moved to Canberra in 1927, the Department of Defence and the administrations of all three armed forces remained in Melbourne.

With the war too distant for security measures to be any more than cursory, the despatch rider is allowed to enter the fortress-like complex with minimal scrutiny. In any case, he's a familiar figure there, and he heads straight for the new red-brick headquarters of Australia's navy and air force. The sealed bag from Park Orchards is delivered to an office tucked out of the way. A wooden plaque on its door announces the occupant as Commander T.E. Nave, but there's no indication of what position he holds. In fact, Eric Nave is head of a compact unit of ten people, the newly formed Special Intelligence Bureau (SIB). Only a handful of people in the military and the government know of its existence, and only a select few of those understand its function.

Trim and erect, with sharp features and receding grey hair, 42-year-old Nave is every inch a naval officer. Standoffish and formal, perhaps from shyness, he has a steely determination that will shape his career for better or worse. Transferred from the Royal Australian Navy (RAN) to the Royal Navy (RN), for which he worked in signals intelligence in Hong Kong and Singapore, he returned to Australia after developing tropical sprue, a debilitating digestive disease. Continuing the secretive work he was doing in Singapore, in June 1940, Nave set up a cryptographic group dedicated to breaking Japan's diplomatic and commercial codes. Melbourne is too far from Japanese military operations to consistently intercept their communications, but a diplomatic corps has missions all around the world.

The wireless intercept station at Park Orchards is operated by the Australian Army. It has agreed to supply the Special Intelligence Bureau with copies of any radio messages it intercepts from Japan, whether voice transmissions or signals in the Japanese version of Morse code.

BURN THE CODES AND CIPHERS

Written characters in Japanese can represent either whole words (*kanji*) or syllables (*kana*). Radio operators have established a system for converting *kana* syllables into Morse-style dots and dashes, or in radio transmissions, 'dits' and 'dahs'. Instead of representing individual letters, as in International Morse Code, the dit-dah combinations represent *kana*. Numbers are the same in both codes. There is nothing particularly secret about *kana* Morse. It's just a convenient way of telegraphing messages without the need to first romanise Japanese words for translation into International Morse.

To keep messages from prying eyes and ears, they have to be encrypted before they are transmitted. A common encryption method involves substitution: individual *kana* and common words and phrases are replaced with groups of two to four kana or up to five digits that may be changed at regular intervals. These groups are contained in codebooks given only to intended recipients of the message. Anyone else would have to find some ingenious way of cracking the cipher without that assistance.

Eric Nave has spent the last fifteen years cracking various Japanese code systems for the British; now he is doing it back in his own country. On this day, going through the newly delivered intercepts from Park Orchards, he notices one that seems to be in J-19 code, used for secret diplomatic messages. Nave, along with British, Dutch and American code breakers, has been decrypting J-19 for some time, but even when most of the code is known, producing a clean message is a long and tedious process.

Different Japanese words are often represented by the same sets of *kana* symbols. These words can be distinguished in spoken Japanese by intonation, but when written in *kana*, they are difficult to tell apart except by context. Often, a whole string of words has to be decoded and translated before the ambiguities can be resolved. But Eric Nave has patience and perseverance on his side. After converting the message from Morse to coded *kana* to decoded *kana*, he translates it into English, a task that also requires interpretation of diplomatic vernacular. After a week of concerted effort, he finally deciphers and translates the message, which has been broadcast to Japanese embassies and consulates around the world:

CIRCULAR #2353: REGARDING THE BROADCAST OF A SPECIAL MESSAGE IN AN EMERGENCY

IN CASE OF AN EMERGENCY AND THE CUTTING OFF OF INTERNATIONAL COMMUNICATIONS, THE FOLLOWING WARNING WILL BE ADDED IN THE MIDDLE OF THE DAILY JAPANESE LANGUAGE SHORTWAVE NEWS BROADCAST.

1. IN CASE OF JAPAN–US RELATIONS: EAST WIND, RAIN [*Higashi no kaze ame*].
2. JAPAN–USSR RELATIONS: NORTH WIND, CLOUDY [*Kita no kaze kumori*].
3. JAPAN–BRITISH RELATIONS: WEST WIND, CLEAR [*Nishi no kaze hare*].

THIS SIGNAL WILL BE GIVEN IN THE MIDDLE AND AT THE END OF A WEATHER FORECAST, AND EACH SENTENCE WILL BE REPEATED TWICE. WHEN THIS IS HEARD, PLEASE DESTROY ALL CODE PAPERS, ETC. THIS IS A COMPLETELY SECRET ARRANGEMENT. FORWARD AS URGENT INTELLIGENCE.

Although Nave is not entirely surprised to read this message, the fact of its transmission is alarming. Since Japanese forces invaded Manchuria ten years earlier, international concern about its intentions in the region has been growing. The Allies' attempts at appeasement have done little to moderate Japan's behaviour.

Expressing outrage at the sustained bombing of the southwestern Chinese city of Chungking (Chongqing) and at the Japanese occupation of French Indochina, in July this year the United States embargoed the sale of aviation fuel and high-quality scrap metal to Japan. These are key to Japan's dream of a Greater East Asia Co-prosperity Sphere, an Asian empire in which it will call the shots. Tokyo has sent an emissary, Saburo Kurusu, to Washington to join Ambassador Kichisaburo Nomura for talks with US Secretary of State Cordell Hull, but the adversaries' positions are poles apart. The decrypted message suggests that the Japanese have scant hope of a favourable outcome in Washington and are standing by to move onto a war footing.

Eric Nave takes the decoded message to Commodore John Durnford, the RAN's acting Chief of Naval Staff. In September, Nave took to the same office a decoded message from Tokyo that instructed Japan's consul-general in Melbourne to find another neutral country that could represent Italian interests. This was a role that Japanese diplomats had filled since its ally Italy entered the war in Europe. The Naval Board's secretary, Captain James Foley, did not think this request reflected an expectation that Japan would soon be at war. He took no action.

This time, Foley can see the significance of the decoded signal, and it is passed on to Frederick Shedden, Secretary of the Defence Department. The letter attached to it, dated 28 November 1941 and headed 'MOST SECRET AND PERSONAL', recommends that 'the contents should be brought to the notice of the Prime Minister', and notifies him that an increased number of operators are monitoring Japanese overseas news broadcasts. Prime Minister Curtin is handed the letter that same day.

The letter concludes: 'As this information has been obtained by most secret methods it is essential that it should not be compromised in any way.' 'Most secret methods' is code for signals intelligence. Australia and its allies are making significant progress in these methods, although the Japanese are largely unaware of this.

The 'Winds message', as it will come to be known, is also picked up by the British in Singapore and by the Dutch in Bandung,

Java. Intercepted by a US Navy station in Seattle, it is also sent to Washington for decryption, but the code breakers there have other priorities, notably a diplomatic cipher machine they call Purple, a Japanese adaptation of Germany's notorious and equally vulnerable Enigma machine. The Americans are so pleased with their success in deciphering Purple-encrypted messages that they have limited interest in other codes.

The Park Orchards radio intercept station is on high alert. Operators fluent in Japanese listen in on Japan's shortwave news broadcasts and other transmissions. This isolated locale was being developed as a country club before the Depression. The operators work in shifts over 24 hours in two huts built near the club house, known as The Chalet, and sleep in tents on the football ground.

On 4 December, the 'execute' weather forecast is picked up by the Park Orchards antenna, an intercept station in Hong Kong, and a US Navy facility in Cheltenham, Maryland. The regular Japanese news broadcast includes the forecast of *higashi no kaze ame*, east wind rain, indicating an expected diplomatic break with the United States. However, this message only confirms what the Allies already know: that Japanese missions are standing by to sever relations with the US. In any case, the 'execute' message soon takes second place to a more specific and more urgent one.

Broadcast two days earlier, on 2 December, and picked up at Park Orchards, this coded message is one of several brought in with the routine motorcycle despatch to the cryptographic unit in Victoria Barracks. Recognising one of the messages as J-19 code and anticipating a follow-up to the Winds message, Nave works on it with particular intensity in his small, cluttered office. Poring over the complex puzzle, he is in his element. As the message emerges like a photograph in developer bath, a mixture of excitement and tension rises in the outwardly reserved officer. The Pacific region is on the precipice of war.

BURN THE CODES AND CIPHERS

CIRCULAR #2448: ORDERS FOR DESTRUCTION OF DOCUMENTS

TO: JAPANESE CONSUL, MELBOURNE
FROM: FOREIGN MINISTER, TOKYO   2 DECEMBER 1941
        URGENT   MOST SECRET

TAKING CARE THAT OUTSIDERS ARE UNAWARE OF IT, PLEASE SEE THAT THE FOLLOWING MEASURES ARE CARRIED OUT.

- KEEPING ONE COPY OF EACH OF THE 'C' CODE AND (TU?) CODE, BURN ALL CODES INCLUDING THE THREE SERVICES SPECIAL CODE AND THE CODE FOR COMMUNICATION WITH THE ARMY.
- WHEN THE ABOVE HAS BEEN COMPLETED CABLE THE ONE WORD 'HARUNA'.
- DESTROY BY FIRE ALL FILES OF INWARD AND OUTWARD TELEGRAMS.
- TAKE THE SAME ACTION WITH OTHER DOCUMENTS, BEING CAREFUL TO AVOID THE SUSPICION OF OUTSIDERS.
- FURTHER, AS THIS IS A PREPARATION FOR THE WORST EVENTUALITY, PLEASE SEE THAT YOUR STAFF PROCEED WITH THEIR DUTIES CALMLY AND CIRCUMSPECTLY AND REFRAIN FROM UNLAWFUL ACTION.

Transmission of the one-word message 'HARUNA', the name of a scenic mountain in central Honshu, is detected on 4 December. Whatever uncertainties there might have been in the Winds message, for Nave they have now been erased. War is about to break out, he is sure, even if he has no clues about how or where. The burning of codes is a classic step on the eve of war. Having spent some time living in Japan, Nave also understands the symbolic importance of such gestures in that nation's culture.

Nave takes the fruit of his speedy decryption to another part of Victoria Barracks. He shows it to Commodore Durnford, who is in charge of the Navy's administration while Admiral Sir Guy Royle, the Chief of Naval Staff, is at a meeting of the War Cabinet in Canberra. Like Royle, Durnford has been seconded from the Royal Navy, which supplies all the senior staff for the RAN.

'Important piece of information, Nave,' says Durnford.

'Very important, sir!'

Durnford immediately rings Canberra on the Secraphone, which scrambles the voice at one end of the call and unscrambles it at the other. The contents of Nave's decrypted message are passed to the War Cabinet, which is meeting at that moment.

When the Secraphone's distinctive green handset is returned to its cradle, Durnford asks, 'How long do you think we've got?'

'Well, it's a matter of days, sir. Probably at the weekend, I would think. The Japanese imagine all Americans have fuzzy heads on Sunday mornings, and that's probably when they'll strike.'

— • —

Early on 7 December 1941—at 7.55 a.m., to be precise—353 Japanese fighters, bombers and torpedo planes launched from six aircraft carriers struck the US naval base at Pearl Harbor in Hawaii. It was a Sunday, as Eric Nave had guessed it might be. All eight of the US Navy's battleships were damaged, and four of them were sunk, along with eight smaller warships. One hundred and eighty-eight aircraft were destroyed, and 2402 Americans were killed. Japan's losses were extremely light: 65 killed or wounded and one Japanese sailor captured. However, none of the aircraft carriers of the US Pacific Fleet were in Pearl Harbor at the time of the attack.

In a speech to a joint session of Congress the next day, President Franklin Roosevelt described 7 December as 'a date which will live in infamy'. Congress passed a formal declaration of war against Japan and officially brought the United States into the Second

BURN THE CODES AND CIPHERS

World War. Roosevelt's speech of just over seven minutes decried the 'dastardly' strike, which he characterised as a sneak attack on an unsuspecting victim.

If Nave's decrypted intercepts had been passed to Washington, it seems that they hadn't been given much credence. However, they weren't lone clues lost in a sea of successful subterfuge, and the US wasn't an unsuspecting victim. As the economist Thomas Schelling put it: 'It is not true that we were caught napping at the time of Pearl Harbor. Rarely has a government been more expectant. We just expected wrong.'

Since the 1920s, both Japan and the United States had been developing contingency plans in case war broke out between them. As Japan continued to expand into China, the US moved its Pacific Fleet from San Diego to Honolulu and increased its military presence in the Philippines to discourage further Japanese aggression. When the US imposed its oil embargo in July 1941, it cut off 80 per cent of Japan's oil imports. By November, the Japanese were offering to withdraw their troops from most of China and Indochina, provided the US, Britain and the Netherlands ceased aiding China and lifted their sanctions against Japan. An American counter-proposal required Japan to evacuate all of China unconditionally and make pacts of non-aggression with the Pacific powers. This was designed to aggravate the Japanese.

By late 1941, many observers believed open hostilities between America and Japan were inevitable. A Gallup poll just before Pearl Harbor found that 52 per cent of Americans expected war with Japan and most expected Japan to start it. This was hardly a climate in which, when it did so, the attack could be characterised as 'sneak'. In any case, signals intelligence had unearthed a number of clues, in addition to the Winds and Haruna messages, pointing not only towards a Japanese attack, but also to Pearl Harbor as a plausible target. The problem was that the significance of these messages, clear in retrospect, was obscured by a clutter of counter-indications and a failure to distribute intelligence to those who needed it most.

Early in the year, US military planners had been concerned about the possibility of an air attack on Pearl Harbor. The Pacific Fleet, under Admiral Husband E. Kimmel, developed an operational plan that envisaged the enemy's initial actions being 'raids or straight attacks on Wake, Midway and other United States outlying possessions'. The Army's General Walter Short was advised that the most probable approach by a Japanese carrier force would be from the north-west, but by August the danger of an attack on Pearl Harbor was fading in the minds of those responsible for America's Pacific defence. A Japanese push southward from China and Indochina had begun to seem more likely. Japan was thought to not have the capacity to attack on more than one front, so Southeast Asia replaced Hawaii as the most expected target.

Yet there were still signs pointing to Pearl Harbor. On 24 September, over two months before the Japanese strike, a coded radio transmission from Tokyo to Japan's consul in Honolulu was intercepted in Hawaii by the US Army. The subject was vessels in Pearl Harbor. The message instructed that 'REGARDING WARSHIPS AND AIRCRAFT CARRIERS, WE WOULD LIKE YOU TO REPORT ON THOSE AT ANCHOR, TIED UP AT WHARVES, BUOYS AND IN DOCK (DESIGNATE TYPES AND CLASSES BRIEFLY. IF POSSIBLE, AND WHERE THERE ARE TWO OR MORE VESSELS ALONGSIDE THE SAME WHARF).'

The Army ordinarily sent its Hawaiian station's coded intercepts to Washington by a scheduled Pan American passenger service, but as the weekly flight was delayed by weather, this particular message—the radio operator had no idea of its content—was sent instead by surface mail. It reached the Signal Intelligence Service (SIS) in the national capital on 6 October and decryption was completed four days later.

The intercept was circulated among those cleared to receive such intelligence, codenamed 'Magic', but that did not include the military commanders in Hawaii. An indication of Japanese intent might have prompted increased vigilance had it been shared with the islands' defenders. Thomas Schelling has commented that, in the thinking of the time, 'intelligence, like a string of pearls too precious to wear, [was] too sensitive to give to those who need it'.

With the benefit of hindsight, the Japanese request divided the naval base at Pearl Harbor into a grid of target areas for aerial attack. Different strategists in Washington had different views of its purpose: it was an example of Japan's obsession with amassing detailed information, no matter how trivial; it was a plan for local sabotage; it was to get an idea of how quickly an American task force could put to sea. No one guessed right.

Japan had a looming fuel crisis. Its solution was to seize the oil fields of Borneo and Sumatra controlled by the Netherlands. The American expectation of a southward drive was correct, but Japanese strategists were convinced that aggressive military action in the south would inevitably involve the Philippines. That would draw the United States, those islands' colonial governor, into the conflict. A preemptive attack on the US fleet in Honolulu was thought necessary to forestall an expected retaliatory strike.

Fleet Commander Admiral Isoroku Yamamoto ordered a carrier task force to depart from bases in Japan on 15 November and proceed as single vessels or in small groups to Hitokappu Bay in the Kurile Islands, between Japan and the eastern end of Siberia. The assembled fleet was to prepare for the coming offensive and await the order to proceed. Strict radio silence was maintained, and Morse sending keys were sealed or disabled. The ships could still listen to encrypted instructions from Tokyo, but they couldn't message back. Communications between ships were by signal flags or blinker lights. With no signals from the carrier fleet, American eavesdroppers assumed the ships were at their home base, where they would have phone lines to shore and no need to communicate by radio. The Japanese encouraged this misconception with dummy radio traffic from the Inland Sea and Kyushu.

On 1 December, a request from Tokyo in J-19 code to its Honolulu consulate was intercepted by the US Army at Fort Shafter, Hawaii: 'WIRE ME IN EACH CASE WHETHER OR NOT THERE ARE ANY OBSERVATION BALLOONS ABOVE PEARL HARBOR OR IF THERE ARE ANY INDICATIONS THAT THEY WILL BE SET UP. ALSO ADVISE WHETHER OR NOT THE WARSHIPS ARE PROVIDED WITH ANTI-TORPEDO NETS.'

The balloons in question were barrage balloons, tethered by steel cables to moorings in the ground and set up to cripple low-flying aircraft. It was a defensive measure already used by the British against the Luftwaffe. The intercepted message was sent by surface mail to Washington to be decrypted and translated. It arrived on 23 December, sixteen days after the attack took place.

The Honolulu consulate replied on 6 December in PA-K2 code, the J-19 codebooks having been destroyed on Tokyo's instruction. There were no torpedo nets and no barrage balloons, it reported, noting that this could provide an opportunity for a 'surprise attack'. That phrase might have raised American eyebrows if there had been an opportunity to ponder it, but the response—intercepted by the US Army in San Francisco and forwarded to the War Department by fast teletype—was not decrypted until 8 December because of the low priority given to consular radio traffic. It would have taken less than an hour to decode a message in PA-K2 code.

Meanwhile, with no radio signals from the Imperial carrier fleet, there was no reason to think it was anywhere but sitting safely at its base in Japan's Inland Sea. Commander Joe Rochefort, head of the US Navy's radio intelligence unit in Hawaii, noted in his log on 2 December, 'Almost a complete blank on information on the carriers today,' and a day later, 'No information on submarines or carriers.' The lack of signals was regarded by signals intelligence as reassuring, not ominous, but Admiral Kimmel was not reassured.

BURN THE CODES AND CIPHERS

Ed Layton, the intelligence officer of the Pacific Fleet, told his commander about Rochefort's notes.

'What, you don't know where the carriers are?' asked Kimmel.

'No, sir.'

'You mean to say that you, the intelligence officer, don't know where they are?'

'No, sir, I don't,' replied Layton.

'For all you know, they could be coming around Diamond Head and you wouldn't know it?'

'Yes, sir, but I'd hope they'd have been sighted by now.'

— ● —

On 6 December, the US Navy station at Bainbridge Island, near Seattle, intercepted a message from Japan's Foreign Minister, Shigenori Togo, to his negotiators in Washington, telling them a formal response to Cordell Hull's ten-point note was coming. It would be in fourteen parts and was to be kept secret until they were instructed to present it. In the afternoon, the first thirteen parts of message No. 902 were intercepted. It contained nothing new except the final sentence of Part 13: 'THEREFORE, VIEWED IN ITS ENTIRETY, THE JAPANESE GOVERNMENT REGRETS THAT IT CANNOT ACCEPT THE PROPOSAL AS A BASIS OF NEGOTIATION.' Part 14 of the message came through at 3 a.m., east-coast time: 'IT IS IMPOSSIBLE TO REACH AN AGREEMENT THROUGH FURTHER NEGOTIATIONS.'

A couple of hours later, two more messages were intercepted and sent to the Army for decoding, since no Navy cryptanalysts were on duty. The first was: 'NO. 907 (URGENT—VERY IMPORTANT). RE MY NO. 902. WILL THE AMBASSADOR PLEASE SUBMIT TO THE US GOVERNMENT (IF POSSIBLE TO THE SECRETARY OF STATE) OUR REPLY TO THE UNITED STATES AT 1:00 PM ON THE 7TH, YOUR TIME.'

The second concluded with the Haruna instruction: 'NO. 910 (EXTREMELY URGENT). AFTER DECIPHERING PART 14 OF MY NO. 902... PLEASE DESTROY AT ONCE THE REMAINING CIPHER MACHINE

AND ALL MACHINE CODES. DISPOSE IN LIKE MANNER ALSO SECRET DOCUMENTS.'

The Office of Naval Intelligence's Commander Al Kramer delivered the decrypted fourteen-part message to the Secretary for the Navy, Frank Knox, pointing out that 1300 EST was 0730 in Hawaii and 0300 in Malaya. Colonel Rufus Bratton of the War Department tried to locate the US Army Chief of Staff, General George Marshall, to pass on the intercepts, but was told he was out horse riding. It was 10.30 a.m. on the 7th by the time the general rang back.

The Army's intelligence chief, General Sherman Miles, had agreed with Bratton that a target in the Pacific or the Far East was going to be hit, but he believed incorrectly that all Pearl Harbor's ships had gone to sea. When Marshall arrived at his office just before 11.30, he was given the night's intercepts by Miles and Bratton. Disturbed by the implications of the 1 p.m. deadline, he phoned his Chief of Naval Operations, Admiral Harold Stark, to find that although Kramer had suggested notifying the Pacific commanders, Stark was worried about information overload and felt a warning he had sent on 27 November was sufficient.

Soon after, the admiral changed his mind and told Marshall he thought they should tell the Pacific commanders about the intercepts. The general scribbled a hasty message to his Hawaii commander for Bratton to take to the War Department Signal Centre.

'Japanese are presenting at 1 p.m. Eastern Standard Time today what amounts to an ultimatum,' Marshall wrote. 'Also, they are under orders to destroy their code machines immediately. Just what significance the hour set may have we do not know but be on alert accordingly. Inform naval authorities of this communication.'

At this point, the United States military was overtaken by its unpreparedness for war. Bratton was told the message should reach Fort Shafter, Hawaii, in twenty minutes. Atmospheric interference, however, had broken the Signal Centre's contact with Honolulu since 11.30 and the despatch for General Short was sent instead by Western Union telegram. Transmitted to San Francisco and then Honolulu, it arrived at about 7.30 a.m. local time. Unknown to any of those involved in this fumbling communication, Japan's audacious opening move was then only 25 minutes away.

The teletype receiver at Fort Shafter, in the middle of Oahu, was not operating at that hour, so the message—it had no priority designation—was taken by a Japanese-American named Tadeo Fuchikami on his motorcycle rounds. At that hour, most residents of Honolulu were either still asleep, eating breakfast or getting ready for church. As Fuchikami set out, the first wave of attack planes was seen on army radar at the northern end of the island, but the blips were presumed by the newly assigned duty officer to be six US B-17 bombers that were scheduled to arrive.

At 7.55, taking full advantage of surprise, torpedo bombers attacked the battleships in Pearl Harbor. Many of the locals mistook the early explosions for an industrial accident of some sort, but bursts of gunfire, continuing loud booms, pillars of smoke and low-flying aircraft made clear that something more serious was happening. Admiral Kimmel watched the start of the attack in horror from his front lawn. An armour-piercing bomb smashed through the deck of the USS *Arizona*, exploding the forward magazine. The noise was deafening and the reaction chaotic. All hell had broken loose, but it was not immediately clear what was happening or why.

Smoke rising from burning ships created an eerie, dusky light. Warplanes flew in all directions like angry wasps. Most civilians would not have recognised the rising-sun insignia that would soon become so familiar. As grim realisation dawned on history's witnesses, confusion turned to pandemonium. Courier Fuchikami's delivery routine was disrupted by traffic jams. The message from Washington to be on the alert, still encoded for security, didn't reach Fort Shafter until 11.45, by which time the last Japanese plane had disappeared over the horizon. When General Short finally read the decoded message, he threw it into his waste-paper basket in disgust.

— ● —

It wasn't long before the American public began to clamour for scapegoats. They were easy to find. Ten days after the devastating attack, Admiral Kimmel and General Short were removed from their commands. The general was ordered back to Washington. The admiral retired from the Navy a few months later.

Taking it very personally, a despondent Joe Rochefort considered the event a failure of intelligence. He hadn't warned his commander of the Japanese attack before it happened, a violation of what he regarded as the prime purpose of his and his Hawaii unit's existence. But the problem wasn't a failure of intelligence so much as a failure to use it intelligently, along with poor distribution of the information that was available. Because of the secrecy that surrounded signals intelligence, its shortcomings were not held responsible for Pearl Harbor. No one knew what was happening there, but the surprise attack gave little confidence that signals intelligence would become a vital tool in the war that had just begun.

Progress by the United States and its allies in the arcane science of code breaking would steadily accelerate as the Pacific War ground on. In particular, American and Australian radio operators, cryptographers and translators, thrown together by circumstance, would contribute to some remarkable successes. Overcoming interservice rivalries, demarcation squabbles, personal enmities and cultural misunderstandings, they changed the course of the war. Theirs is a story of highly gifted people working anonymously in the shadowy half-light of signals intelligence. People sworn to secrecy fed off the mistakes and compromises made by an enemy

BURN THE CODES AND CIPHERS

under pressure. Untangling a maze designed to be impenetrable, they pounced on faults in the design of code systems and human errors in their use. Yet their triumphs too were secret, sealed away in a clandestine world, out of sight of the enemy and the public alike.

Chapter 2

Pioneer of the code breaker's craft

Born in Adelaide nine months before the turn of the century and single until he was forty, Eric Nave long enjoyed the social life of an unmarried officer of the Royal Navy, a mix of obligation and privilege in a largely carefree existence. His family has pictures of him in the 1920s, dressed to the nines and standing stiffly for the photographer with friends and acquaintances in the grounds of stately English homes. But such images gave no hint of his other, more secretive existence.

His start was plain enough. Nave's parents were of British-German-Swedish stock, his father responsible for timetables and train-driver rosters at South Australian Railways. As a young man, Eric was slim and fit, gregarious and charming. A natural left-hander, he was compelled to write with his right hand, a common practice at the time, but he played sport left-handed and with skill. He had powers of concentration and memory that would serve him well in his later career. He dreamed of studying law, but the cost was beyond his family's means. At the age of sixteen, he left school, passed the exams for the public service, and joined his father at the railways, working in accounts.

PIONEER OF THE CODE BREAKER'S CRAFT

In 1916, with Europe embroiled in war, the Royal Australian Navy called for midshipmen to carry out administrative duties. Nave applied, passed the RAN exam and was posted to the training ship HMAS *Tingira*. A midshipman when the war ended, he stayed in the RAN. He aimed for promotion to sub-lieutenant, a prerequisite for which was competence in a foreign language. The Royal Military College in Canberra had introduced Japanese into its curriculum to help improve Australia's political and military relations with that country. The RAN was prepared to pay an extra five shillings a day to naval personnel proficient in Japanese, a more attractive offer to the nineteen-year-old than the sixpence paid daily for French or German.

The Naval Board funded lessons with Mineichi Miyata, who had been brought from Japan to start a language course at Sydney's Fort Street Boys High School. Early in 1919, the teacher reported that his pupil was 'making remarkable progress' and could speak, read and write basic sentences with fluency. In the September exam, Nave scored 90 per cent and was sent for assessment at the University of Sydney. Impressed with the newly promoted sub-lieutenant's aptitude, the assessor recommended that he be posted to Japan for two years' further language training. Nave was attached to the British Embassy in Tokyo, and in February 1920 sailed for Japan on the SS *Eastern* with 26 gold sovereigns as advance pay and expenses in a money belt around his waist.

Not met on arrival nor given any instructions, Nave had to find his own way to the British Embassy. He made contact with its Japanese counsellor, Harold Parlett, who suggested he stay with two Australian Army officers at Shizuoka, in the tea-growing district near Mount Fuji. The young Australian would sit for an exam at the embassy at the end of the year, but as there was no prescribed course, he would have to buy textbooks and a dictionary and take advantage of the greater opportunities for study and conversation outside the city. He did so, and was able to insert himself into his Army housemates' weekly lessons with a local teacher, using Japanese characters drawn on cards.

With the arrival of spring, cherry trees burst into blossom, their pastel glow giving the gardens and streets a delicate beauty. Sundays and festive days were for *sakurami*, or cherry-blossom viewing. Whole families would picnic in nearby parks to enjoy nature's stunning display. Children, dressed in brightly coloured kimonos, carried flags and ran around happily, while adults immersed themselves in the beauty of the seasonal fairyland. It was a powerful memory, starkly at odds with the reality that would later shape his life.

As summer approached, American tea buyers returned to reoccupy the house and the Australians had to move on. The Army boys went to more distant parts of Japan, Nave 50 kilometres north to Hakone, a lakeside resort with a different view of Mount Fuji and no Europeans. Taking a room in an inn, he lived in pure Japanese style, sleeping on a *futon* on the floor, dining with chopsticks and bathing in a round wooden tub. His conversations were necessarily in Japanese. He would study each day until about four, then go for a walk. On these daily rambles, he got to know three salmon farmers and played tennis with them regularly on a gravel court.

As the end of the year approached, Nave came back to Shizuoka to prepare for the first-year exam. A language student from the Royal Navy wrote to him, enquiring about accommodation, and Nave offered him the spare room in the house he was renting from some American tea buyers. Lieutenant-Commander Harry Shaw RN moved in with his supply of duty-free gin and cigarettes, but Nave was not an imbiber of either. Shaw was older and something of a tearaway, but a friendship grew between the two dissimilar personalities that would weave through their professional lives.

Instructed to attend the British Embassy for an examination at the end of his first twelve months, Nave caught the train to Tokyo. His examiner was Harold Parlett, and his mark was again 90 per cent.

A second year passed with Nave immersed in Japanese language and town life, in Shizuoka in winter and Hakone in summer. For the last two months of his residency he boarded at the Church of England Mission House in Tokyo. Finding different social and cultural opportunities in the capital, Nave asked for his name to be placed on the list for the Emperor's Chrysanthemum Garden Party, to which members of foreign embassies were invited. All naval officers were put on the books of the China Station flagship, HMS *Hawkins*, for the occasion. The railway supervisor's son was inching his way up the social staircase.

On the other side of the coin, he found evidence that his mail was being opened by the censor of foreign mail and that his movements in Tokyo were being monitored. One day, as he was about to leave the embassy compound, he was warned that a person sitting opposite the embassy gate would probably follow him. Nave walked around the block a few times. The man indeed followed. But Nave was sanguine about the surveillance, feeling the Japanese had a right to keep an eye on the unrestricted movements of a foreign naval officer in their country.

After two years in Japan, Nave had become fluent in the language and developed a feeling for and understanding of the Japanese people, as well as a sense of connection to the land and culture. He returned briefly to Shizuoka to prepare for his final exam and, while there, gave a talk at the local girls' high school. Shortly afterwards, he was visited by the British naval attaché in Tokyo. On their way back to the station, they passed a line of schoolgirls, who giggled and bowed deeply to the Australian.

'What have you been up to here?' joked the attaché.

The final examination, in April 1923 and again set by Parlett, was a thorough test based on a popular Japanese novel, *Botchan*, the story of a young teacher sent to a provincial school. Nave's mark of 91 per cent put him ahead of the three Royal Navy language students in Japan at that time, one of them his Shizuoka housemate,

Harry Shaw. Parlett commented in his written report that 'this officer's knowledge is on a higher plane of practical utility than is usually obtainable in two years'. Clearly, Eric Nave was going to be a valuable asset somewhere, but exactly where was still unclear.

Unbeknown to Nave at the time, in 1914 the Australian government had approved the establishment of a Naval Intelligence Branch at the Navy Office. Wireless telegraphy was the new thing in military intelligence, and the British Navy was already intercepting and deciphering German naval signals. The first recovery of a codebook of the Imperial German Navy had actually taken place in Melbourne's Port Phillip Bay.

When Britain declared war, German merchant ships in Australia's ports were seized and searched for codebooks and other secret documents, but none were found. They had probably been destroyed. On learning four days later that the German-Australian Steamship Co.'s SS *Hobart* was on the way to Melbourne, and guessing that the captain was probably unaware of the outbreak of war, Australian authorities had radio traffic jammed. *Hobart* arrived outside Port Phillip Bay still ignorant of hostilities, and was met by an armed RAN boarding party whose members were disguised as quarantine officials. They seized control of the ship before the captain could destroy any documents and found a copy of the *Handelsverkehrsbuch*, the German mercantile code. It was copied and sent to the Admiralty in London. A fake telegram using the code played a major part in the 1914 defeat of Admiral Maximilian von Spee in the Battle of the Falkland Islands.

After the war, intelligence in Australia drifted; little attempt was made to capitalise on its promising start. By the time Eric Nave returned from Japan, the Admiralty had expressed concern at the lack of postwar intelligence coming from Australia and had offered a Royal Navy officer to set up an intelligence centre. He had proposed combining naval and military intelligence, but both chiefs of staff rejected the idea. It wasn't the last time that service leaders would ignore the advantages of combining resources.

Now a lieutenant, Nave returned to Australia in May 1923 and was recalled for duty as supply officer on the cruiser HMAS *Brisbane*, patrolling the Pacific islands. His fluency in Japanese was of little use there, but at the end of the year he was attached to Vice-Admiral Shichigoro Saito, commander of a Japanese training squadron, on a goodwill visit to Australia and New Zealand to thank them for their generosity after a devastating earthquake in Japan. Nave interpreted for Saito in his meeting with Lord Jellicoe, the Governor-General of New Zealand. The Japanese commander was a great admirer of Jellicoe, the victor over the German navy in the 1916 Battle of Jutland.

Nave was impressed with the skill and professionalism of the Imperial Japanese Navy, commenting, 'They could be most valuable allies or alternatively formidable adversaries.' He was able to organise a souvenir photograph of three Japanese captains, but couldn't tell another officer where the 'red light district' was. It wouldn't have been hard for a navy man to find that out, but he chose not to.

On his return, Nave was posted to HMAS *Sydney*, where he trained telegraphists in reading Japanese *kana* Morse code. 'After reading plain language messages,' he wrote to his commodore, 'I propose attempting to decode ordinary Japanese economic code messages with a view to later breaking down the ciphers.' He had started down the path on which he would remain for the next twenty years.

— • —

In May 1925, the Admiralty asked a reluctant RAN to lend Lieutenant Nave to the Royal Navy's China Station as an interpreter on the commander-in-chief's staff. Word of his mastery of Japanese had filtered through to the RN. Two months later, Nave travelled by Japanese steamer, English warship and Yangtze River tug to join the cruiser HMS *Hawkins*, anchored off Shanghai. The presiding admiral, Sir Edwyn Sinclair Alexander-Sinclair, a dour northern Scot, had been instructed that the newcomer was 'not to be employed in the Admiral's office nor on ship duties, details will be forwarded by safe hand'. Japanese naval wireless traffic was to be intercepted and given to Nave for examination.

The Government Code and Cipher School (GCCS) had been set up in London in 1919 as a civilian agency under Admiralty control. Its public function was to advise government departments about the security of their codes, but it had a covert role of studying the ciphers of foreign powers. Twenty-five code breakers were recruited to the unit, based on The Strand under Alistair Denniston, who had been relocated from the Royal Navy's wartime decryption agency, Room 40. An amendment of the Official Secrets Act compelled telegraph companies to give GCCS copies of messages passing along their wires. These provided a wealth of raw material.

GCCS was transferred to the Foreign Office and moved into the MI6 offices near St James Park. By 1924, with the Anglo-Japanese alliance formally ended and Britain planning a major naval base at Singapore, a naval section was added to it. The RN intercept station in Hampshire was too distant to monitor Far East traffic, so British ships in east Asian waters were co-opted to intercept signals for a small cryptographic unit set up on HMS *Hawkins*. It was this unit that Eric Nave joined the following year. He was to gather information about Japanese radio traffic and call signs, and send intercepted messages to the Admiralty for passing on to GCCS. As to exactly what information and how he was to assess it, he was given no instructions.

For an office, the Australian was given a cabin cluttered with piles of red-printed intercepts. His quarters became unbearably hot despite awnings and a wind scoop through the porthole. Cooped up in his poorly ventilated room, bent over the red print and trying to focus on its content, Nave worked six or seven hours a day. At night, he could lie on the deck and be attacked by insects or sweat it out in the cabin. Relief from such uncomfortable working conditions was found in regular sport on shore—cricket, tennis, golf—and amusement among the expatriates of Shanghai.

Finding that Tokyo radio switched hourly from a commercial call sign (JJC) to a naval call sign (AB), Nave was able to identify the individual signal addresses for Japan's main naval bases—Yokosuka, Kure and Sasebo—followed by lesser bases, then operational authorities and squadrons. He made significant inroads into naval codes thanks to the stream of increased radio traffic after the death of Emperor Yoshihito in 1926 and the succession of his son, Hirohito, to the Chrysanthemum Throne. Nave realised that every word the new emperor was said to have uttered would be broadcast unaltered. Going through the long coded messages of Hirohito's statements and matching them to quotes in Japan's mainstream press, he made substantial progress in deciphering the codes.

All decrypts, along with red forms with any material he'd been unable to decode, were passed to GCCS in London, where Harry Shaw, his former housemate in Japan, was in charge of breaking Japanese naval codes. By 1927, Nave had decoded all Japan's naval ciphers then in use.

He returned to Australia at the end of his two-year attachment to the Royal Navy to be told that the Admiralty—without providing a reason—had asked for him to be transferred to London. Arriving there in January 1928, he was told he would be working for the Government Code and Cipher School, not the Admiralty. Nave was unaware that Commander William 'Nobby' Clarke, of GCCS's Naval Section, had lobbied the Admiralty for his secondment to the Royal Navy in the first place. Nave knew little about the organisation except that his material from the Far East ended up there. Harry Shaw was still at GCCS but in a few months would be going to the China Station.

For the first time in his life, Nave was in London, a mecca for Australians travelling overseas. Enchanted by surroundings he'd previously seen only in magazines, he crossed Horse Guards Parade to the Broadway Buildings near St James Park underground station. A plaque at the entrance identified the occupant as the 'Minimax Fire Extinguisher Company', but he'd been told it was actually GCCS. He took a lift to the fourth floor. After he met with the bureau head and Clarke, the latter took Nave to his new Naval Section office, small and shabby with an old desk, two chairs, a cupboard and a secure cabinet. A pile of intercepted red-print messages waited on the desk for the new occupant of this dingy, charmless room.

'It's small, old chap,' Clarke, who had been a barrister in a past life, assured him cheerfully, 'but quite cosy.'

Telegrams between Tokyo's Admiralty and Japanese naval attachés across Europe appeared daily on Nave's desk for deciphering. They had passed through the lines of a British cable company somewhere in their journey from Asia to Europe and had been routinely copied. Taps on telephone lines to the Japanese Embassy in London led into a small booth in GCCS where Nave listened in. What he heard, however, was mostly trivial. It was solitary work. Nave missed the camaraderie of ship life, having already forgotten the discomfort of the tropics.

Guessing that the London attaché would be sending home articles of interest from English newspapers, Nave hunted down sources and, by comparing their length and identifying known elements of the code, he was able to fill in more gaps. Messages sent in the attaché code revealed details of new military technology in Japan, orders placed with naval suppliers, and arrangements between Tokyo and its missions in Europe. Nave also worked on the Imperial Japanese Navy's main operational code, called JN-1

PIONEER OF THE CODE BREAKER'S CRAFT

by the Allies. By the end of 1928, over 800 code values had been recovered.

Work was isolating, but Eric Nave found relief in English society. He shared a suite of rooms in nearby Ravenscourt Park with two Australian civilians who worked in a city bank. Always on the lookout for congenial company, he was invited by old China Station contacts to spend weekends at stately homes. He and a Shanghai acquaintance toured Scotland in a Fiat open roadster, playing golf and catching salmon. Enjoying the privileges of the Surrey Cricket Club, he played village cricket with West Kent as a middle-order batsman and spin bowler.

The Australian Naval Board asked the Admiralty when it could expect its officer on loan, now promoted to lieutenant-commander, back in Australia. It wanted to appoint Nave secretary to the commander-in-chief of the Australian Fleet. The Admiralty responded by offering Nave a permanent transfer to the Royal Navy with a full RN pension backdated to when he joined the RAN, and later promotion to commander. Someone in the British service had been doing his research. The Australian navy didn't have a pension scheme, only a lump sum on retirement, and Nave had already written to his Naval Board asking about the protocol for promotion to commander. This would be jumping ship, almost literally. He gave it long and hard thought before accepting. The transfer was announced in the *London Gazette* on 2 December 1930.

Nave returned from a visit home to be told he would be stationed on the heavy cruiser HMS *Kent*, earmarked to join the China Station. While he was pleased to be part of a ship's company again and not immersed in piles of papers in a secret room, he was less enthusiastic about returning to the tropics. Embarking on the three-funnelled *Kent* in July under cover as deputy supply officer, he sailed to Hong Kong via the Suez Canal.

Early in 1931, *Kent* was made the flagship of Vice-Admiral Sir Howard Kelly, commander-in-chief of the China Fleet, now expanded to over 100 ships. The fleet was there to discourage Japanese expansion in east Asia. It was supposed to be backed up by the naval base at Singapore, but after ten years of stop-start construction the base was still not in operation. Not much discouragement of the Japanese was evident.

As commander in a far-flung corner of the British Empire, Kelly was an absolute ruler. Tall, with thick white hair, he was a domineering man engaged in intense rivalry with his older brother, also an admiral in the Royal Navy. They hadn't spoken for years. When a ship he was on struck a rock in the Formosa (Taiwan) Strait, his older brother cabled, 'GLAD YOU ARE SAFE.' The reply was a curt 'GLAD YOU ARE GLAD.'

When *Kent* went to sea again, the ship's flag lieutenant said to Nave, 'What about a game of bridge tonight?' Nave cheerfully agreed, only to find that he'd been recruited for the admiral's contract bridge game. His protest that he only played auction and didn't know the conventions of contract bridge fell on deaf ears. The players cut for partners, and the Australian drew Admiral Kelly.

'Nice play, Nave,' commented his commander at the end of the game. 'You'll do fine.'

For two years, he was co-opted as this demanding senior officer's nightly bridge partner, leaving little time for personal relaxation or for meeting the extra demands of his combined supply and intelligence roles.

The Imperial Japanese Navy had replaced its operational code, the one Nave had worked on at GCCS, with a new code super-encrypted from additive tables. It was, in effect, a double code with two codebooks, the first for converting the message into code, the second for re-encoding the coded message. The intense concentration required to break this double code, the demands of his supply duties, his semi-official role as the admiral's bridge partner and the suffocating humidity all played on Nave's health. He lost his appetite and grew noticeably thinner.

But he persevered and managed occasionally to break through the fog of encryption.

The occupation of Manchuria by Japan's Kwantung Army in late 1931 had generated a massive increase in Japanese military radio traffic. Nave managed to decode enough of a message sent to a Japanese naval commander to learn that the Kwantung Army had been instructed not to extend its operations south of the Great Wall. Although Britain wasn't directly involved in this conflict, the radio messages provided useful information for the China Fleet's strategic planning. After handing his decrypt to the Fleet Intelligence Officer, Nave was summoned by Kelly's chief of staff and told that the admiral had ordered that the message be signalled to the Admiralty to pass on to the War Office and the Foreign Office.

'He shouldn't send this by wireless, should he?' said the chief of staff.

The admiral wanted to impress his superiors in London. The problem was that although the British transmission would be coded, if the Japanese intercepted and decoded it, they would know that progress was being made in penetrating their own codes.

'No, sir,' was the junior officer's reply.

'Will you go and tell him so?'

Nave obeyed the implied command. When the snowy-headed admiral saw his bridge partner at his door with the signal he'd authorised for despatch, he coloured slightly.

'I think, sir . . . ,' started Nave hesitantly.

'And who asked you to think, Nave?'

Unnerved, he mumbled, 'I thought you expected me to, sir.'

Kelly was from a military family in which rank was all, but this young man was both his bridge partner and an expert in decryption. He allowed Nave to suggest that the message go by landline so it could not be intercepted by the Japanese. The admiral accepted the suggestion.

In January 1932, Japanese aircraft bombed Shanghai from carriers moored on the Yangtze River. Troops then stormed the districts outside the International Settlement, and fierce fighting broke out with local forces. American and British warships, including HMS *Kent*, moved to the trouble spot and steamed between Chinese and Japanese naval ships on the river, briefly defusing hostilities there.

The flotilla arrived at Shanghai about midnight, and various foreign naval commanders made a courtesy call on Admiral Kelly as the senior naval officer in the port. A Japanese staff lieutenant came on board to present the apology of his commander, Rear-Admiral Yugoro Hori, and, with Nave translating, asked if it would be convenient for him to call on Admiral Kelly in the morning, as he was very busy at that moment.

Indeed he was. The Japanese had resumed aerial bombing of the city once the foreign ships had moved on and into port.

Caution was needed in British dealings with the Japanese. English traders had profited from the anti-Japanese boycotts in Shanghai that had triggered the Japanese attack, provoking anti-British feeling in Japan. The country was a pariah in many Japanese eyes, but caution was a stranger to the imperious Kelly.

'Tell this officer,' he barked at Nave, 'I have important matters to discuss with the Japanese admiral and I wish to see him now.'

An hour later, the commander of the Japanese navy's 3rd Battleship Division—a man with a gaunt face, close-cropped hair and a small, neat moustache—came on board. He was taken directly to Admiral Kelly's cabin. Trained at an English naval college, Admiral Hori had no need of Nave as an interpreter.

Stunned by the stubborn resistance of the Chinese defenders and continuing to make little progress in eliminating them, the Japanese bombed Chinese areas along the Whangpo (Huangpu) River, where *Kent* was moored. An angry Admiral Kelly huffed, 'If those aircraft continue to fly over my flagship, I'll shoot them down.' Nave was relieved he didn't have to take that message to the Japanese.

The British commander instead called a conference on *Kent* of all foreign senior officers present, having been assured that the Chinese would accept a settlement if both sides withdrew from the battle zone. Nave was sent to summon them.

Among those at the meeting was Admiral Kichisaburo Nomura, the same Nomura who a decade later would be negotiating with the Americans while Japan prepared for the Pearl Harbor attack. The Japanese were told their military operation was so close to Shanghai's International Settlement that it was a serious threat to foreign life and property. Nomura argued that he had to protect Japanese residents and property there, but agreed that if the Chinese withdrew from the area, there would be little need for that protection. The Japanese commander undertook to withdraw his marines if and when the Chinese withdrew a specified distance.

The Imperial Japanese Army had joined the fray and feared mutual withdrawal would deprive the Japanese of the appearance of victory. Japan's foreign and army ministers both believed diplomacy should follow decisive victory, and authorised a renewed effort in Shanghai. Despite increased Japanese bombing, the Chinese fought on for several days before they withdrew the required distance. A ceasefire was agreed on 3 March.

Nave was despatched to the Japanese flagship to remind senior officers of their promise and to request a copy of the signal ordering the withdrawal. He was told not to return until he had it. After some delay, he was given a carbon copy of the order on flimsy rice paper. Returning in triumph, like British Prime Minister Neville Chamberlain from Munich seven years later, Nave handed the message to his commander-in-chief, to be told to translate it while the admiral had lunch.

In his freezing cabin, Nave grappled with a difficult translation of hand-written Japanese characters, many of which were faint and indistinct. The result was imperfect, but the best he could do. Having handed his effort to Kelly and about to start a lunch that was getting cold, he was summoned back by the admiral's orderly.

Kelly waved the translation at him and handed it back. 'Nave, put this into understandable English!'

The Australian was beginning to feel the strain of his multiple roles, along with the effects of the climate. After another struggle, he produced an improved but still imperfect translation and returned it via the orderly. He resumed his uninviting lunch, now quite cold, and heard no further complaint—but no thanks, either.

Although this was translation, not cryptography, its subtext contained information that would prove valuable. No warning of the initial Japanese assault on Shanghai had been evident in intercepted signals. Clearly, the Japanese navy was capable of keeping communications highly secure when it needed to.

At the time, though, little attention was given by the armed forces to signals intelligence. Admiral Kelly regarded Nave more as an on-call interpreter with plenty of spare time. Kelly was generally neither recipient nor beneficiary of Nave's decoding work, so he placed little value on it, and the unreasonable demands on Nave's time continued unabated.

The fleet moved on to the British concession of Weihaiwei in northern China. Japanese radio traffic had escalated and, with no easing of his supply duties, Nave withdrew from the admiral's bridge nights. He worried that this might create problems for him, but there were changes afoot anyway. After long and unfruitful lobbying, the lone cryptographer was finally provided with a telegraphist to handle all intercepts. Soon after, with Kelly leaving for a Whitehall posting, the fleet came back to Hong Kong so his successor could board the flagship. There was no opportunity for reprisals against card-game deserters.

Lieutenant-Commander Nave's two-year posting with the China Fleet finished in 1933. After leave in Australia, he returned to London in October to rejoin the Government Code and Cipher School. Harry Shaw was sent out to replace him. After the 'Shanghai Incident', more intercept stations in the Far East were proposed, and more Japanese linguists were put to work at GCCS in London. Nave was given an assistant who had completed a language course in Japan the year before, and the Royal Navy built an intercept station on Stonecutters Island in Hong Kong to pick up transmissions from Japan. The Land of the Rising Sun had been moved up the list of nations on which the British wanted to keep a watchful eye and ear.

The British were beginning to recognise both the enormous potential of cryptography in naval intelligence and the limitations of the small teams then working on it. Late in 1934, the Y Committee, in charge of intercepting foreign communications, met in London. Nave was invited to the gathering, which would address concerns about Japan's increased espionage in the Far East. In his opening address, the chief of MI6, Admiral Sir Hugh Sinclair, said, 'We have agents in all the important cities and ports in the world and yet 90 per cent of the reliable information we get comes from Nave here and a few people like him. What are we going to do about that?'

The outcome was a decision to establish the Far East Combined Bureau (FECB) as a Hong Kong outpost of GCCS. Located in an office block in the colony's naval dockyard, it was separated from nearby buildings by iron grilles and guards armed with revolvers. Little effort was made to disguise its presence, although its function was kept quiet.

Most of the code breakers, headed by Harry Shaw, were experts in Japanese, a few in Chinese and Russian. Initially navy and ex-navy men, they were to concentrate their efforts on three Japanese naval codes: the general code, the Flag Officers' code, used by very senior ranks, and a basic code for reporting ship departures. Messages the team couldn't decode were sent to

London in a diplomatic bag. The signal interceptors were navy and air force ratings, who lived and worked on Stonecutters Island, 6 kilometres across the harbour from the dockyard. Couriers took their intercepts across the harbour on the public ferry, then brought them to the dockyard offices.

FECB also had an Intelligence Section where intercepted and decoded material was evaluated and passed on. Its chief, Captain John Waller, was also head of the bureau. Shaw had been used to dealing directly with GCCS, but Waller wanted everything to go through him and made little effort to conceal the fact that Japanese codes had been broken. Shaw was resentful at being corralled and aghast at the chief's cavalier approach to secrecy about sources. Within a year, the two most senior officers in FECB were barely speaking to each other. Morale in the bureau was low. Divisions between code breakers and intelligence analysts and between the three component services—army, navy and air force—seriously hampered the exchange of ideas and results. It was a problem that would continually plague radio intelligence organisations, which suffered from mutual isolation and lack of effective oversight.

— ● —

Since 1932, GCCS had been intercepting naval attaché messages it couldn't decrypt. It guessed the Japanese were using a cryptographic machine like the German Enigma, at that time a commercial cipher machine. GCCS was right. The M-1 cipher, called Orange by the Americans, used a machine-encrypted code of four *kana* syllables. In London, Nave helped break the code when the Japanese naval attaché in Rome sent a long coded message to Tokyo and repeated it verbatim in plain text. The attaché had been having a passionate affair with a local girl and had discovered she was actually a plant by Italian intelligence. He cabled his superiors that he intended to pay for his shame with his life. It made useful but heart-rending reading for the eavesdropper.

PIONEER OF THE CODE BREAKER'S CRAFT

The naval attaché code was broken late in 1934, but its keys were changed monthly so the system had to be broken again each month. Nave found himself becoming so familiar with the code and its changes that he could often anticipate the introduction of new variants. They were the same revisions he would have made if he had been responsible for maintaining the code's security.

To relieve the tedium of endlessly sorting messages, he and his London colleagues tried to replicate the Orange machine's function using a brown foolscap file folder, a collar stud rescued from a laundry parcel, and a piece of string. Slots were cut in the folder for *kana* characters to be inserted. It was a clumsy model, rather like a primary school project, but it worked after a fashion, well enough to prompt a search for experts to make a more accurate model. The Signal School at Portsmouth was asked to take on the task and produced a Bakelite device with twin wheels, like the Orange machine itself, allowing decrypters to solve monthly key changes more readily.

A side benefit of penetration of the attaché code was the tracking of collaborators with the Japanese, starting with an RAF war hero. Squadron Leader Fred Rutland had been awarded a DSC as a seaplane pilot in the First World War. He had been recruited by Japan after the war as an adviser on naval flying. After he resigned from the RAF, it came to the notice of MI5 through a 'very reliable source' codenamed 'BJ'—for bluejacket (sailor), after the colour of the UK folder for diplomatic radio intelligence—that he'd had secret talks with the Japanese. By the early Thirties, Rutland had agreed to spy for the Japanese navy and set up dummy companies in California and Hawaii as a cover for future Japanese agents.

Nave was aware from earlier decoding that an Englishman was working for the Japanese under the cover name of Shinkawa (new river). On HMS *Kent* an intercept had contained notice of Shinkawa's arrival in Shanghai. On passing it to GCCS, Nave had been told all future messages regarding this person were to be sent directly to the Admiralty for the attention of the Director of Naval Intelligence.

MI5's surveillance of a clandestine meeting between Rutland and the Japanese naval attaché in London's Richmond Park had not worked out. The war hero and the diplomat drove in through different entrances, left their cars in the middle of the park and wandered off, out of listening range. However, the attaché's report to Tokyo of his meeting with Shinkawa was intercepted. Nave, now back with GCCS, decrypted it, although he didn't know Shinkawa's real identity. Tokyo was told that a passage to America had been booked for Shinkawa and his family, and booking details were given.

When Sinclair saw the decrypted message, he called a meeting with his deputy and Nave. The deputy wanted to pass the information to MI5.

'No, they'll only make a balls of it,' said the admiral. 'If he's arrested now, the Japs will suspect their codes are being read and change them. Then we won't get anything until Nave cracks the new code.'

Most likely the MI6 chief knew MI5 was already on the case but saw no reason to share that with anyone without a 'need to know'. As it was, an MI5 agent was booked on the same ship as the Rutlands and in a cabin close to theirs. He made friends with the family, bought chocolates for the children and chatted to the former airman about work opportunities in the US. Things were so bad in Britain, the MI5 agent said, that he was hoping to find a job in the 'land of opportunity'. Rutland commented that he might have something for him if he was interested, as he would be needing a man in Oregon. The MI5 man was eventually given a position in Rutland's Portland office, from where he briefed London on comings and goings at the company while the company passed on to the Japanese the whereabouts of US naval vessels.

PIONEER OF THE CODE BREAKER'S CRAFT

It was a season for unmasking spies. A Nave decrypt of an intercept from the Berlin–Tokyo circuit revealed that a German, given a Japanese name for cover, was sailing from Hamburg to Honolulu via Yokohama with his wife and two children. The cable set out the German's salary and expenses, a life insurance policy in favour of his wife, and details of the ship booked to Honolulu. Under cover of a furniture business there, he was to back up Rutland's operation in San Diego. From the booking details, the man was identified as 41-year-old Otto Kuehn, a First World War naval officer and former POW in Britain. With these two plants, Japan was keeping a close eye on both major US naval bases on the Pacific. Now the spies were themselves under observation.

Nave was struggling to fathom the changes in a country where he had spent two formative years. He was horrified to hear that Admiral Saito, for whom he had interpreted on the goodwill visit to Australia and New Zealand thirteen years before, had been assassinated by young Turks of the Imperial Japanese Army. The Japan he thought he knew, no longer existed. Whether he liked it or not, he was on a collision course with this new Japan.

Eric Nave was promoted to commander as promised, then posted to the newly established Far East Combined Bureau in Hong Kong, arriving in the chaotic aftermath of a typhoon in October 1937. Working in the dockyard offices and replacing Harry Shaw as head of the cryptography section, he was listed as an interpreter on the commander-in-chief's staff, to disguise his actual role.

Japanese diplomatic and commercial cables passing through a British telegraph company in Hong Kong were routinely 'borrowed' by FECB and delivered to Nave daily in a wicker basket. In one of the decrypted messages, he found in the consul-general's report to Tokyo that a fluent speaker of Japanese had arrived in the colony and joined the British intelligence section. Nave's stomach sank. It was a reference to him.

Brain alight, adrenaline surging, Nave tried to guess how this information might have been leaked. As he frantically raced through the possibilities, a prime suspect emerged. An Italian woman, a friend of the new wife of Captain E.G.N. Rushbrooke, China Station's Chief of Intelligence, had sat next to him at a dinner given by the Rushbrookes. She had shown considerable interest in his work in the colony, and asked just what it was that he was doing.

'Oh, just wearing out the seat of my pants in the dockyard, as far as I can tell,' Nave had answered airily.

'But what kind of work do you do?' the woman persisted.

'Well, I've just arrived, so I hardly know myself.'

'But what is your actual position?'

'I do some translation when it's called for.'

On a different occasion, the wife of an army officer, another of the Italian's friends, had grilled him on the same subject. In hindsight, their persistence had the smell of orchestration. Nave decided to feed into the FECB system a 'barium meal', giving plausible information to his suspects to see if it returned in Japanese consular signals. It did. Decrypted messages pointed to the Italian, who was a French banker's wife. Nave noted that the leaks stopped when she went to Europe on leave.

At first, Rushbrooke refused to believe the evidence, but when the leaks resumed on the return of his wife's friend, he had no alternative. He had learned the hard way to be more discreet in what he told his new wife. No action was taken, however, as FECB did not want to reveal that it could read the consul's cables. It was later discovered that the Italian woman had been recruited by Edda Ciano, daughter of Mussolini and wife of the Italian consul in Shanghai, a few years before.

The leak was an irritating sideshow to the main task of staying on top of Japan's evolving ciphers. Late in 1938, the Imperial Japanese Navy replaced its codes with a new four-*kana* General

Operational Code. Soon after, it was referring in its messages to yet another new code, Naval Code D, that was about to be introduced. While Nave worked on the older code, reserved now for use by flag officers, and a new Dockyard Code, Code D messages intercepted at Stonecutters Island were sent to GCCS, newly moved to a mansion at Bletchley Park, 80 kilometres north of London. There they were worked on by the eccentric but brilliant John Tiltman, a tall, dignified man who was always resplendent in tartan trousers.

Dubbed JN-25 by the Americans, Code D was a five-digit code double-encrypted using additive tables. Many of the messages reported ships' positions, and Tiltman found how to recognise coded numbers, of which zero would always be the most common. Within a few weeks, he had worked out how to strip off the additives and within a year he had penetrated JN-25's underlying code. The JN-25 code was in two parts: a dictionary of over 30,000 words and phrases, each assigned a five-digit number, and a 100-page book of additive tables with random five-digit numbers. More sophisticated than its predecessors, JN-25 was thought by the Japanese to be so complex it could not be broken.

Eric Nave was meanwhile working seven days of most weeks in the high humidity of Hong Kong's summer. Sweating so heavily he had to change his shirt two or three times a day, he began to suffer severe bouts of vomiting and was admitted to hospital. Since the relevant specialist was away on holiday, he was discharged without any diagnosis of his condition, but there was a consolation. Her name was Helena Gray. Introduced by Lou, a mutual friend, she was an English nurse at the hospital.

— ● —

By 1939, with Japan becoming more bellicose in the wake of its faltering occupation of China, the Hong Kong intelligence facility was vulnerable. FECB moved lock, stock and barrel to 'impregnable' Singapore and was re-established in the naval barracks at Selatar, on the island's north side. A radio intercept station was set up at Kranji, 10 kilometres away, to augment, and later replace, Stonecutters Island. Its intercepts were carried by despatch motorcyclists until a teleprinter link could be installed.

FECB staff and twenty truckloads of secret files were transferred to Singapore by ship, arriving on 28 August. About the same time, a close friend of Nave from GCCS days flew in from England. Lieutenant-Commander Malcolm 'Bouncer' Burnett brought the dictionary and additive tables unmasked by Tiltman so that FECB could decode messages in JN-25 that it intercepted at the new facility.

Now 40, Nave had been mixing with the English elite for many years, both at home and in their far-flung empire. Always part of a group of naval officers, a pleasant fellow and good at sport, he fitted in easily as the invitee from the Antipodean middle class. Fun-seeking, well-heeled young women joined in the weekend parties, but Nave—conservative and upright, his rectitude shaped by the navy—had formed no long-term attachments. His romances were few, fleeting and disappointing.

Then he met Helena. Ten years his junior, she soon followed him from Hong Kong to Singapore. On 2 September 1939, the day before war broke out in Europe, they were married in the colony's St Andrew's Cathedral. Bouncer Burnett was the best man; Harry Shaw, who had returned from England, gave the bride away. The newlyweds spent their honeymoon at an acquaintance's house in the cool of Malaya's Cameron Highlands, but all too soon Nave was back at work in an equatorial climate even more oppressive than the one FECB had left. The Naves lived in a bungalow on the naval base, and Helena, with other wives of FECB staff, worked on the punched-card tabulators that were used to sort through coded messages.

Soon after his return, Nave broke the Dockyard Code. He'd

made a little progress with the Flag Officers' Code, but FECB's main focus was on JN-25, used widely in Japanese naval communications. Both British agencies were now reading the new code, taking three or four weeks to uncover the new additives introduced every six months or so. With many more intercepts to work through and increasingly complex codes, code breaking had become team work: it was no longer the domain of lone-wolf experts.

The workload, the climate and frustration at the apparent complacency about Japanese intentions all seemed to affect Nave's health, and his bouts of sickness became more frequent. After a series of tests, he was finally diagnosed with the tropical digestive illness sprue and sent on leave to Australia. He and Helena, by then four months pregnant, left on a Dutch ship for Fremantle in February 1940. Eric travelled in civilian clothes and with a civilian passport, presenting himself as an accountant.

Lou, the friend through whom Helena had met Eric, was repatriated to England when war with Japan broke out two years later. Soon after leaving Hong Kong, her ship was bombed by the Japanese. It sank and Lou went down with it. Had she not married Eric Nave, Helena would have been on that ship too.

Chapter 3

Special Intelligence Bureau

Short, stockily built and constantly cheerful, 'Cocky' Long was a charmer and a skilled manipulator of people. A good listener with a wide circle of acquaintances, he appealed to people to do him personal favours with the unstated promise that they would be returned sometime in the future. His nickname was a remnant of school days: when his voice broke, the register going up and down, his conversation was punctuated by squawks that made him sound like a cockatoo.

Lieutenant-Commander Rupert Long had risen at the age of forty to Director of Naval Intelligence (DNI) in the Royal Australian Navy, taking the post in 1939 after a somewhat bumpy journey. The son of a school teacher, he had joined the RAN's new Naval College before the First World War, and later been posted as torpedo officer on the China Fleet's HMS *Dauntless*. In 1934, he was made District Intelligence Officer in Sydney, where he recruited agents and gathered random information. Overlooked for promotion to commander at that time, he was still the most senior naval officer working in intelligence, a specialty whose time was yet to come.

Long cultivated a network of informal sources—airline pilots, customs agents and businessmen who travelled regularly—and, through clubs and social functions, people who could do him favours: politicians, senior police, and a wealthy Pacific entrepreneur, Walter Carpenter, whose daughter became his second wife. In 1936, he was appointed Assistant Director of Intelligence with the Navy Office in Melbourne, overseeing more than 150 undercover agents and sharing intelligence with Britain's Foreign Office and MI6. His intelligence analysts liaised with the Far East Combined Bureau, giving access to some signals traffic, but the RAN had no cryptographic section because at the time it had no skilled cryptographers.

As DNI, Long combined forces with the RAN Director of Signals and Communications, Lieutenant-Commander Jack Newman, to lobby for an Australian signals intelligence organisation. The same age as Long, Newman too was a graduate of the RAN college, and had been a radio specialist on submarines before going to Britain's Naval Signalling School. Though strikingly different in temperament and appearance—Newman was tall, thin and brooding; Long thick-set and extroverted—the two men soon forged a useful alliance.

Not expecting war with Japan, Long had in mind interception of German radio traffic. He persuaded the Chief of Naval Staff, Admiral Ragnar Colvin, to propose to his counterparts in the army and the air force that a dedicated signals intelligence unit be set up. The Chief of Air Staff thought it unnecessary, but the army's Chief of General Staff could see some value in a unit watching enemy communications around Australia and its territories.

The Colvin proposal was considered by the Defence Committee in early 1940 and passed to Prime Minister Robert Menzies in April. Menzies was unconvinced. Most enemy—that is, German—messages were transmitted in Europe and the Atlantic, and he saw FECB as already covering Asia. Nonetheless, he wrote to the Dominions Office seeking the views of the British government. It was in no rush to provide them.

By this time, Eric Nave had returned to Australia. His diagnosis of tropical sprue confirmed, he was put on a diet of strawberries, liver extract, Melba toast and oranges. After three months' convalescence, he reported for duty at the Navy Office in Melbourne, insisting that his health prevented him from returning to Singapore. The Navy Office advised FECB that Commander Nave was medically unfit to return, and was told in reply that if he was unfit for the Far East, his services were required in Britain. The RAN stuck to its guns, getting a medical ruling that Nave was not even fit enough to travel through the tropics. This was not just out of concern for his wellbeing. The Australian Navy had a plan.

Cocky Long, in conjunction with Jack Newman, had decided to go ahead and set up a naval signals intelligence unit without waiting for London's reply to Menzies, and despite having no cryptographer on hand. When he heard that Nave was back in the country and wanting to stay, Long saw an immediate solution to his problem. Their paths had crossed when they were both serving in the China Station in the 1920s, and he had a broad idea of Nave's more recent work. Asked to set up a small cryptographic unit in Victoria Barracks, Nave jumped at the opportunity. He and Helena, now seven months pregnant, moved into a suite in a hotel in the bayside suburb of St Kilda.

Long had recruited Nave, but he preferred to do the glad-handing and leave ongoing management to others—in this case, Newman. As his first step towards a full-fledged Signals Division, Newman installed Nave and a couple of clerks in a space set aside under the Victoria Barracks roof. With the Australian Navy's radio stations in Canberra and Darwin scanning the waters north of Australia, Nave sifted out the Japanese messages, decrypted them, and translated the results into English.

In October 1940, Britain's Secretary of State for Dominion Affairs, Lord Cranbourne, finally replied to Prime Minister

SPECIAL INTELLIGENCE BUREAU

Menzies, saying he saw no reason to set up a large-scale intelligence body in Australia. It was 'inadvisable' to duplicate GCCS, but he suggested that the Australian connection through Nave with FECB in Singapore could be expanded, and that Australia could intercept signals from 'fixed commercial stations'—not military transmissions.

Nave was now well enough to manage short visits to the tropics. Attending a naval conference in Singapore with Jack Newman, he showed the FECB some of his early work and outlined the potential they both saw in an Australian unit. Japan was using South America for espionage bases away from FBI scrutiny, and Nave's group was well placed to intercept consular traffic from there. FECB was very interested.

Returning to Melbourne, Newman told Admiral Ragnar Colvin that British delegates at the conference had been keen for Australia to develop a cryptanalysis capacity, and that the Dutch East Indies (now Indonesia) and New Zealand had agreed to cooperate. Nave's involvement strengthened Newman's hand in dealing with the admiral. Colvin had been Britain's naval attaché in Japan when Nave was the outstanding language student there and had spent a day with him in Shizuoka. He was the attaché who had been delighted by Japanese schoolgirls giggling and bowing to Nave. Newman's report was forwarded to Menzies with Colvin's warm support, and the government approved the establishment of an Australian cryptographic organisation under Commander Nave, building on the small RAN unit already at Victoria Barracks.

The new body was called the Special Intelligence Bureau. FECB wanted SIB to be under its control, but offered no extra resources or personnel. Agreeing to cover consular and commercial traffic, SIB first decrypted material sent by airmail from Singapore. Soon it was working on codes in Australian intercepts of commercial traffic from Japanese merchant ships and traffic from former German territories such as the Caroline, Mariana and Marshall islands. Known as the Mandated Territories, they had been placed under Japanese administration after the First World War.

FECB passed to the Melbourne unit any relevant material that it decrypted. Overlooking the Garden Island naval base, Japan's Sydney consulate in Elizabeth Bay was notifying Tokyo of British warships in the harbour, and providing details of the power line between Sydney and Newcastle and of Newcastle's floating dock. The ominous signs of a nation preparing for war were also picked up in Australia. Nave decoded the instruction to Japan's Melbourne consulate to find another country to represent Italian interests.

At a Singapore conference in March 1941, Newman suggested that a range of high-level Japanese codes, including its navy's JN-25, be made available to Nave. The Australians were keen to expand their activities, but their British counterparts poured cold water on that, fearing that the new unit was trying to run before it could walk. The higher-level codes were so complicated, Newman was told, that 'a large staff of experts is required to obtain results'. Nevertheless, anything interesting would be forwarded to the Naval Board in Australia.

The British had a point. In December 1940, the Japanese had replaced the JN-25 code with a more intricate code, dubbed JN-25B by the Allies. However, in a far-reaching blunder, they failed to replace the additive table. The old table remained in use for two more months. FECB had resolved a substantial amount of it, enabling cryptographers to work backwards and identify values in the new code until the new additive table was implemented. Codes were becoming increasingly complex, and a coordinated team was more effective in breaking them. Nave's single-handed, start-to-finish method of working suited his temperament, but it was becoming untenable.

— ● —

SPECIAL INTELLIGENCE BUREAU

Following Admiral Colvin's proposal late in 1939 of an Australian signals intelligence capacity, the army started discreetly down that path, setting up a small cipher unit in Sydney. Someone in the army heard that two University of Sydney mathematicians, T.G. Room and R.J. Lyons, were playing around with decryption as an academic hobby. Military Intelligence approached the pair in January 1940 and invited them to form an 'unofficial group', developing expertise in cryptography and Japanese with old coded messages supplied by the army's Eastern Command.

English-born Gerry Room had come to Sydney in 1935 at the age of 32 to take up a professorship at the university. Marrying a year later, he had a house built on the edge of a bluegum forest in the outlying suburb of St Ives. Reserved, with a wiry build and a love of the outdoors, the bespectacled Room was a bushwalker and avid gardener, laying out his own grounds and digging a swimming pool. He was already making a study of number matrixes, but he understood no Japanese. Together with his friend from the Mathematics Department, lecturer 'Dickie' Lyons, he took a two-term crash course in the language with a private tutor.

Gerry Room recruited two more academics to complete the team, both from the University of Sydney's Greek Department: 31-year-old Professor Dale Trendall, only recently arrived from New Zealand, and a younger lecturer, Athanasius Treweek. Trendall was a classical archaeologist, a world authority on south Italian pottery. That was not much use in solving codes—but he was also a gifted linguist.

Not yet thirty and brimming with quiet self-assurance, 'Ath' Treweek had taught himself to read Japanese in anticipation of war with Japan. He was already serving in the militia as a captain in the Sydney University Regiment. When war broke out with Germany he had tried to join the AIF, but the university had refused to release him.

CODE BREAKERS

The informal group of four studied the few textbooks available on cryptography and set problems for each other in their spare time, meeting mostly at weekends and trying out various coding systems. Early on, they solved a simple Japanese code from scratch without even knowing the language.

Every few days, a Military Intelligence officer came from Sydney's Victoria Barracks to give the group raw Japanese consular traffic, much of it in low-level LA code. With its repetitive patterns, this substitution cipher was easily broken: though it required some knowledge of Japanese, it took the quartet only a weekend. Named after the first two letters of every message sent in it, LA code was used for financial and staffing reports, rarely anything important. The Japanese knew it wasn't very secure, but it served to conceal message content from inquisitive postal workers. It was ideal for cryptography beginners.

By October 1940, the Sydney group had identified three diplomatic codes commonly used by Japanese missions in Australia. For variety, they were sometimes given coded overseas mail from the District Censor, including one piece of correspondence sent through a Sydney forwarding address. The letter, from a British official in Shanghai, the Inspector-General of Customs, to a married woman in Melbourne, had another short letter inside and a newspaper clipping with certain words underlined in ink. The four men cracked the code in 24 hours to reveal an intimate poem:

> Ever think of Cathay?
> Blissful afternoon with prec[*ious*]
> Naked in my arms.
> Long caress k[*iss*] and s[*trokin*]g of
> Hand alluring shy hole.
> Many k[*isses*]
> Much l[*ove*].

SPECIAL INTELLIGENCE BUREAU

Three more salacious letters were intercepted and decoded, but were deemed no threat to security and forwarded to the intended recipient. The amateur code breakers considered inserting into a letter the coded words 'Beware! District Censor', but thought better of it.

Early in 1941, Eric Nave became aware of the University of Sydney group and decided he should go to Sydney and meet them. Impressed, he invited them to a Melbourne meeting with senior army and navy intelligence officers. The meeting on 2 May was attended by six service personnel, including Nave, with Room and Treweek representing the four academics. The military men praised the progress of the Sydney team and offered them positions within Nave's unit in Melbourne. They readily accepted on their own and their colleagues' behalf—the offer had been anticipated and discussed in advance—and the university authorities agreed to let them go.

With the four Sydneysiders due to arrive, Special Intelligence Bureau continued to build through 1941. Two experienced linguists joined the unit: Lieutenant A.B. 'Jim' Jamieson, back in Australia after eight years in Japan; and Lieutenant Ian Longfield Lloyd, an army translator back from Fiji, the son of a diplomat posted to Japan before the war. Thirty-year-old Jamieson, an RAN reservist, had taught at a Japanese university, edited textbooks, and worked on an English-language newspaper. On returning, he was told, with no further explanation, 'We have an officer who would like to see you.'

A meeting was arranged. Nave wore plain clothes, as he often did at this time, and was at first evasive about the reason for the meeting. As its purpose became clearer, the potential recruit's interest grew. Although Nave wasn't working on high-level codes, Jamieson felt quite positive about the unit and was sure that his linguistic ability could be part of something very useful.

Ath Treweek moved to Melbourne in June to join Nave's SIB. Already in the militia and promoted to major, he encountered minimal red tape in moving from academia to the armed forces. For the other university staffers it was not so easy. Regulations prevented the navy giving Professor Room a rank of acceptable status to the university, namely colonel. After protracted negotiation, Room retained his academic title and was kept on his professorial salary; he moved to Melbourne in August. A fierce bushfire shortly before had cracked windows in the Rooms' St Ives home, so his wife and their baby soon joined him. Dickie Lyons moved south that month too, also remaining a civilian. For Dale Trendall, who was new at the university, the transfer process was more protracted.

Two weeks after arriving in Melbourne, Room and Jamieson were sent on a ten-week study tour to 'pick up tips', as Nave put it, from two of the region's code-breaking bodies. Wearing civilian clothes and travelling as 'couriers', the pair left on a Qantas Empire Airways flying boat for the three-day flight to Singapore via Brisbane, Townsville, Darwin, Surabaya and Batavia (Jakarta). They spent six weeks at Nave's old stamping ground, the Far East Combined Bureau. Harry Shaw was still there, and he ensured the visitors were brought up to date with British cryptographic achievements, putting them to work on Japanese diplomatic codes and allowing them to observe FECB decryption of naval messages.

The British disdain for the Australian unit seemed to have mellowed. 'If there was a time when they thought Nave was wasting his time,' Jamieson would later comment, 'that had now passed. They now thought every Allied sigint [signals intelligence] unit was valuable.'

On the way back, Room and Jamieson stopped off at Batavia and spent three weeks in Bandung, central Java, with Dutch cryptanalysts at *Kamer* 14, who had made progress with Japanese diplomatic and naval codes—including JN-25—independently of the British. The British and the Dutch were routinely exchanging their cipher knowledge, and Nave wanted SIB to be in that loop.

SPECIAL INTELLIGENCE BUREAU

'They showed me a lot of stuff I didn't know existed,' Jamieson reported on his return. 'And I brought a lot of stuff back.'

The trip had tested his relationship with Room. The professor was from an academic background that prized close analysis and rigorous testing of theories, whereas Jamieson was by nature pragmatic and instinctive. On their return, Jamieson commented privately that he had found Room 'heavy going' in Singapore.

— ● —

Thanks in large part to the timely return of Eric Nave, the navy had led a rebirth of signals intelligence in Australia in the lead-up to war with Japan. Now, with the country actually at war in Europe and the Japanese menace undiminished, the other services began to take signals intelligence seriously. Everyone had a go. The army, the air force, and Cocky Long with a multi-service bureau—all were developing their sigint resources in anticipation of conflict in the region.

When Australia declared war on Germany, the army had begun building a capacity in radio interception and traffic analysis. Less glamorous than cryptanalysis (code breaking), these could provide insights into enemy intentions through the study of communications patterns, even when the messages were encrypted and unable to be read. A high level of traffic might mean a major operation was being planned and discussed; frequent communication to specific stations from a central station might reveal the chain of command. Sigint is a deductive art as much as a science.

The Australian Army set up No. 1 Special Wireless Section (SWS) under Captain Jack Ryan, a burly former chief engineer with radio station 3AW in Melbourne. The section started training at Seymour, in rural Victoria, in June 1940. Six months later, a unit of two officers and 87 men, renamed No. 4 SWS, sailed for Cairo, in Egypt, where they continued their training at an offshoot of the British cipher organisation at Bletchley Park.

The Australian unit was deployed to Greece at the end of March 1941 and operated alongside the British Army in the foothills of Mount Olympus. Using British-made Kingsley receivers mounted on light trucks, they learned about radio operations on the battlefield, their intelligence-gathering unearthing details of the German command structure and troop movements. German air-to-ground traffic, encrypted in three-letter ciphers, was intercepted and decoded using British codebooks and their own translators. The Australians were learning fast and well in the most practical of schools, constantly on the move. The unit had no intelligence personnel, but Jack Ryan told his team an officer was due to join them. He repeated this news every day or so, but the new man failed to appear. 'Mr Sandford' grew into a myth.

Late in April, the Australian radio crew evacuated along with British troops to Crete, which the Germans invaded three weeks later. On 8 May, during the beleaguered defence of the island, a stranger walked into the Suda Bay camp like a gunslinger come to town in a Western. Mr Sandford had finally arrived.

A lanky extrovert, 25-year-old Lieutenant A.W. Sandford was posted to No. 4 SWS as its intelligence officer. He was different. From the Adelaide establishment, he had studied law and languages at Oxford, where he also edited *Oxford Poetry*. 'Mic' Sandford was the son of a wealthy engineer, Sir Wallace Sandford, who had built his own father's business into a large and thriving enterprise. Both father and grandfather had been conservative members of the South Australian parliament; Sir Wallace had been hugely impressed by Joseph Goebbels, whom he saw at a 1937 conference in Berlin. Young Alastair didn't go into the family business. Instead, he was starting a career in law when war broke out. The charismatic newcomer would develop over the next few years into a significant and intriguing figure in Australian intelligence.

A cosmopolitan raconteur, at ease with everyone with whom he came in contact, Sandford was a refreshing breeze blowing through the dismal reality of life in a combat zone. At a time when few went to university, he stood out in the crowd, but that was only part of his story. He'd enlisted only three months before and was already the liaison between Bletchley Park and the Allied commander in Crete, after attending a GCCS crash course near Cairo. Sandford's analytical skills and single-minded application to tasks made him a larger-than-life figure to the young men of Special Wireless Section. With his endless fund of stories and fanciful exaggerations, he had the gift of making the lowliest soldier feel he mattered.

Working 24 hours a day in a 'dugout' under frequent air attack, Ryan's men provided tactical intelligence to the New Zealand General Bernard Freyberg. Sandford received coded signals from London and took them to Freyberg along with the lower-grade ciphers intercepted by the Australian unit, waiting until all had been read and destroyed. The general had wanted to reposition his forces on the strength of radio intelligence, or Ultra, provided by Bletchley Park, but the Allied commander-in-chief, General Archibald Wavell, refused permission. 'The authorities in London would rather lose Crete than lose Ultra,' said Wavell. Such was the importance of keeping the enemy unaware that its code had been penetrated.

Late in May, with the nearby airfield captured and German paratroops landing, No. 4 SWS was ordered to withdraw from Crete. The men trekked 70 kilometres over the mountains to Sphakia on the island's south coast, the Greek-speaking Sandford and a Corporal Ballard at the front asking for directions and food. They were given goat's milk, oranges and spring onions. At food dumps, troops punctured tins of golden syrup with their bayonets and drank from the cans. Embarking at 3 a.m. on the commando ship *Glengyle*, they arrived at Alexandria the next morning, having survived repeated bombing attacks.

By the end of May, Crete had been evacuated and the island was under German control. The Australian radio unit was moved to Palestine, where it supplied intelligence on the order of battle and tactics of Vichy French forces in Syria until an armistice was signed in July. Australian Army divisions then moved into Syria and Lebanon. 4SWS relocated to a large house at Souk el-Gharb in the hills above Beirut, and Mic Sandford was detached for radio intelligence with a British unit in the Western Desert.

Other trained army personnel remained in Australia and operated the radio intercept station among the apple and pear trees of Park Orchards in outer Melbourne, picking up Japanese consular transmissions into and out of Australia. After the absorption of the army's informal code-breaking group into Nave's unit at Victoria Barracks, Japanese intercepts were routinely delivered in sealed bags to the Special Intelligence Bureau.

In mid-1941, the Royal Australian Air Force (RAAF) ran a course in *kana* Morse and Japanese interception for air force and army radio operators who were already proficient in international Morse. The course took place in Victoria Barracks, and some of the classes were taught by Eric Nave.

Within a few weeks, six newly trained intercept operators, designated No. 1 Wireless Unit RAAF, left Melbourne by train with a letter of introduction to the commanding officer of the RAAF base at Darwin. Led by Corporal Thomas 'Snow' Bradshaw, an inter-service boxing champion, they were to set up a station at the base. Taking a Kingsley AR7 receiver and a cipher machine, they made the eleven-day journey to Darwin by passenger train, cattle train and army truck, trying to keep their precious equipment under control as they lurched over the last 500 kilometres in 'Leaping Lena', a wood-burning vehicle with unequal-sized wheels. At the air base, they presented themselves to Group Captain Scherger, were given accommodation and a workplace on the upper floor of an old building alongside base headquarters, and were thereafter ignored.

The Pacific War still lay in the future, but working four-hour shifts around the clock, they intercepted naval messages from Tokyo and Japanese bases on Truk, Saipan and Palau, in the Mandated Territories. Disguised with a substitution cipher so the base's operators could not tell it was intercepted Japanese traffic, the raw copy was sent through the RAAF wireless network to Nave's bureau. The newcomers were regarded as a nuisance by the airbase operators because they often overloaded network capacity, but standing orders were that their operation should not be obstructed.

Snow Bradshaw's team had difficulties in addition to the cold shoulder of base personnel. The amount of traffic they could usefully intercept increased dramatically. A second AR7 was scrounged to ensure that two operators were always listening as well as encoding intercepts to send to Melbourne. The six men started to succumb to heat and stress. Tempers flared, and one operator tried to take the head off another with his tin helmet. Sent south for 'medical reasons', he never returned. Another man left after his health collapsed in Darwin's steamy climate. The absent operators weren't replaced, and the four remaining signalmen pressed on, intercepting Japanese traffic under great strain until war finally broke out.

Cocky Long also had an eye for a trend. As Director of Naval Intelligence and newly promoted to commander, he'd proposed back in March 1940 that a national intelligence organisation be set up by the three military services to liaise with Allied security bodies and keep a list of people who were a security risk. The idea was supported in principle, but not necessarily with any great commitment, by the three chiefs of staff. By May, Prime Minister Menzies was recommending it to Cabinet.

The three service directors of intelligence met to draw up broad parameters for the organisation but made little progress. Nonetheless, by the end of 1940 the Combined Operational Intelligence Centre (COIC) had been established, with Commander Long as its director. Situated in M Block of Victoria Barracks, next to the Central War

Room, it had all the trappings of a high-security bureau—the only door to the unit was locked, and messages had to be passed through a hatch—but it played no part in operational decisions.

COIC instead became the plaything of its head. Long had access to intelligence as it came into Australia and issued situation reports, but politicians and the three service chiefs of staff were told only what he thought they should know. COIC was staffed largely by navy personnel, with little air force input and none by the army. Each of the services was reluctant to give material to, or trust intelligence from, the others.

Shunted to him by Long, responsibility for the Special Intelligence Bureau continued with Jack Newman. Working on naval as well as diplomatic codes with growing expertise, Nave and his colleagues had to switch between naval codes in *kana* Morse and diplomatic messages using Roman letters, or *romaji*, in International Morse. When the new consular code J-18 was introduced in March 1941, it took over a month to break, but J-19, introduced in August and used by Japan for the Winds and Haruna messages shortly before Pearl Harbor, was broken relatively quickly. The unit managed to break the JN-20 naval code, used for stores, personnel and shipping movements, and later used by Japan's Fourth and Eighth Fleets. SIB moved on to three operational codes for short-term tactical information. One, JN-4, would be used by Japanese submarines in the coming war.

The Australians exchanged naval cipher results with FECB in Singapore which, from May 1941, exchanged intelligence with the US Navy's cryptography units in Washington, Honolulu and Manila. FECB was also sharing more sophisticated codes with SIB as British respect for Australian skills in the area grew. Nave took up an FECB suggestion to pass SIB's diplomatic intercepts to the Dutch at *Kamer* 14 in central Java, and received copies of their Mandated Territories traffic in return. It was an active and productive time for the bureau.

SPECIAL INTELLIGENCE BUREAU

Commanders Long and Newman, respectively Director of Naval Intelligence and Director of Signals and Communications, had been keeping each other mutually informed and seemed to have a good, if somewhat impersonal, working relationship. However, wherever it is pursued, signals intelligence tends to create friction over which umbrella it should come under: communications or intelligence. Communications people usually maintain that they should be in charge because they gather the raw data, while intelligence people merely process it. Australia was not spared this turf war. Cocky Long possessed all the political and personal skills the brooding and gentle Jack Newman lacked, but Newman felt he was carrying the bulk of responsibility for SIB while Long simply used its results to feed his Combined Operational Intelligence Centre and curry favour with the people he needed to impress.

From his time at the combined bureau in Singapore, FECB, Eric Nave was a great believer in sharing information with the various Allied bodies involved in intelligence gathering, and between the army, navy and air force at home. Long's COIC had been set up with that intention, so Nave had no qualms about passing material to Long. He didn't have a view of the effectiveness of Long's organisation, but Newman did—and he suggested to Nave that the Director of Naval Intelligence be left out of the information loop. Nave wouldn't comply. From then on, tension ate into their relationship like a tumour.

However, in December 1941 the Special Intelligence Bureau was bubbling with confidence. It was penetrating Japanese codes; it was building respect. A second war was looming, closer to home, and SIB expected to have an important role to play in it. With the Winds message intercepted and decrypted at SIB and elsewhere, there was excitement in the unit as its members looked for the 'execute' message that was bound to follow. Park Orchards was put on full alert with Japanese-fluent operators. Jim Jamieson was given radio receivers to take home so he could extend the watch.

The Winds message might have indicated imminent war with Japan, but it gave no clue to where the first blow might be struck, and the intercepted messages that provided that information were busy being ignored elsewhere. The answer came soon enough. On 7 December, as Zeros swarmed across Pearl Harbor, daily life in the backwater of Australia changed irreversibly.

At first, the idea of attacking such a powerful nation as the United States seemed almost comically ill-advised, but as the reality became clear, an apprehension close to panic swept the Australian populace. At Victoria Barracks in Melbourne, far from any theatre of war, workers immersed in clandestine military decryption suddenly found themselves surrounded by a nation in fear. Soon the Japanese army had landed virtually unopposed in Malaya and Thailand, Singapore had been bombed, and two British capital warships, a battleship and a battlecruiser, had been sunk by Japanese naval bombers. The Empire of the Rising Sun seemed unstoppable.

Notwithstanding Melbourne's remoteness from the new enemy's bases, air-raid precautions were set up. The roof of G Block in Victoria Barracks was removed and an anti-aircraft gun installed. Slit trenches were dug in nearby Kings Domain for evacuating staff. Lift attendants were given their instructions: take staff to the ground floor, return the lifts to the top floor and immobilise them; exit via the stairway. Blackouts were enforceable in industrial and built-up areas, and blackout practice was begun. Retail shops had to be closed and in darkness by 6 p.m., with no late-night shopping and no illuminated signs or floodlighting. Parks were ploughed to prevent enemy planes from landing. Street signs were taken down so the Japanese wouldn't be able to find their way around if they did manage to land.

With Malaya falling to the Japanese onslaught, Allied forces started looking to Australia as the place from which to launch a counteroffensive. Knowing Jack Newman from his visits to

SPECIAL INTELLIGENCE BUREAU

Singapore, the Chief of Staff at Britain's Far East Combined Bureau asked if the Australian Navy would be able to accommodate FECB's cryptography and traffic analysis sections. Without consulting either Long or Nave, Newman advised that the facilities the British would require weren't available. They withdrew their experienced sigint team to Colombo instead.

Nave was appalled by Newman's response and by his failure to consult others. If facilities are needed you find them, was Nave's philosophy. He would have welcomed the skills and experience of the FECB operators, many of whom he knew and had worked with in the past. He still frequently exchanged material with them, and that was where Newman's problem lay.

When Captain Wylie, the outgoing chief of FECB, visited Australia in 1941, he had declared that he should be in charge of all British intelligence in the Pacific, including the Australian naval unit. Wylie was long gone now, but Newman was not prepared to risk the dismissive English arriving and taking command, either directly or in cahoots with Nave. To Newman, Nave was a Royal Navy officer on loan to Australia, a supercilious Pommie despite his Adelaide origins. Ironically, other interlopers would soon do just what Newman feared the English might do.

The Special Intelligence Bureau was expanding. Despite Newman's unwelcoming attitude, some English operatives managed to find their way there, one way or another. Arthur Cooper, a brilliant but eccentric young linguist who had been with FECB since 1938, reached Java at the beginning of February, joining colleagues evacuated earlier from Singapore. In the scramble from the Japanese assault on Java, he reached Australia by steamer on 27 February. Also on board were two Royal Navy wives who, like Cooper, were put on the SIB payroll. Everywhere Arthur Cooper went, a long tail hung down from under his jacket. Nestled inside the jacket was a pet gibbon he called Tertius.

The New Zealander Dale Trendall, the fourth of the Sydney academics recruited by Nave, got to Melbourne in January. He'd only been in Sydney a short time, and the university had been slow to release him, insisting that the military maintain his professorial salary. Trendall led a group working on Japanese diplomatic traffic that included Cooper and a former British consul in Harbin, Manchuria.

Henry Archer, proficient in both written and spoken Japanese, had been offered a position in SIB by national intelligence director Long back in May, subject to UK Foreign Office agreement. Tall and gaunt, Archer had been slated for the post of consul-general in Mukden, Manchuria, then told the transfer was postponed indefinitely. If the expected war with Japan broke out, the British Consular Service didn't want Japanese-speaking experts interned. A disappointed Archer belatedly accepted Long's offer. By the time he reached Melbourne, Britain was at war with Japan.

Another linguist from the British Consular Service, Hubert Graves, joined the Melbourne unit a month later. A decorated veteran of the First World War, he thought all young men should be at the front, a view he freely shared with others—especially young men.

Nave's Special Intelligence Bureau and its associated radio stations were building expertise. Intercepted intelligence, traffic analysis and direction-finding antennas were keeping track of enemy aircraft carriers, air squadrons and naval units as they moved untroubled around the western Pacific. The cryptographers and analysts knew as much as anyone else in the military machine of what the Japanese were doing and where they were, but at that time signals intelligence received little attention from military brass. They thought aerial reconnaissance was the best way of finding out what the enemy was up to. Although most patrol planes in the Asia-Pacific region had been destroyed in air raids, and radio intercepts were still in operation, the latter played only a minor part in Allied military thinking. As in the lead-up to Pearl Harbor, little importance was attached to material gathered by the eavesdroppers. It would take a breakthrough event to change that, and until it happened, signals intelligence was considered an indulgence in the harsh reality of a war that was going badly for the Allies.

In early February 1942, Australia's Chief of Naval Staff (CNS) was advised on the basis of traffic analysis that the Japanese were mobilising major naval forces at Palau and Truk, and air and submarine forces in the Marshall Islands. All were in Japan's Mandated Territories. Intelligence predicted a probable major attack on Java and the regions to the east and west of it, with a possible view to cutting off Allied reinforcements coming through Torres Strait. The advice included the suggestion that the Commander-in-Chief of the Pacific Fleet be notified of these insights, but a handwritten note by CNS at the foot of the report dismissed the evidence as inconclusive and noted that the army's Chief of General Staff agreed. The advice wasn't passed on.

Four days later, the Japanese captured New Britain, to the north of New Guinea, and bombed Samarai, on New Guinea's eastern tip. On 14 February, they invaded Sumatra, the island west of Java. The Japanese juggernaut was moving south in Australia's direction and its work was by no means finished.

Reduced by illness to four men, with Corporal Snow Bradshaw the most senior, the RAAF radio intercept unit in Darwin had been trying to cope with the volume of signals it was picking up. Early on the morning of 19 February, the shift on duty detected abnormal enemy traffic between aircraft and possible aircraft carriers in the southern Celebes Sea. The indication that an operation was imminent was passed to the communications officer in the next building at the air base. As the wireless unit's activities were secret and no one at the base knew they were intercepting Japanese signals, base personnel had no idea what had prompted the warning. The unit had been set up to eavesdrop on Japan's strategic planning; its integration into the military structure wasn't designed to deal with more urgent intelligence. The base commander's office thanked No. 1 Wireless Unit for the early warning and ignored it.

Shortly before 10 a.m., aircraft transmissions were increasing in signal strength, indicating that planes were heading towards the base. Radar could not confirm this because the apparatus sent to Darwin hadn't yet been installed. Within a few minutes, though, the noise of approaching planes was unmistakable, and 188 aircraft—Zero fighters from four Japanese carriers, along with dive bombers and torpedo bombers—arrived over Darwin's port.

From the upper-floor balcony of their building at the air base, 13 kilometres from the city, Bradshaw and two other operators on duty could see aircraft diving through clouds of inky billowing smoke, attacking naval and civil shipping, harbour facilities, army barracks and an oil store. The radio men weren't observers for long. With a roar, the base came under attack, and they scuttled out of the building and across to the shelter of trenches. Aircraft zipped in all directions near ground level. Pandemonium followed: the scream of fighters and their spitting guns, the rattle of defensive machine-gun fire, and bomb explosions hurling debris through the air. Then, as suddenly as it started, the attack was over, the planes gone. In the eerie silence, there was only the crackle of hangars burning. The headquarters and wireless unit buildings were undamaged.

About midday, there was a distant growling drone and fifty-four land-based bombers roared into view, flying high above the range of anti-aircraft guns that were hampered by defective fuses. Coming from the north, the Japanese planes separated into two groups, released bombs across the whole base area, then turned and came back for a second bombing run. By the time they disappeared into the northern sky, the stores building, barracks area, hospital and mess halls had been hit. In the two attacks on Darwin that morning, eight ships were sunk and twenty-three aircraft destroyed. Deaths were officially placed at 243, but the true figure was probably nearer to 400.

The wireless unit's Snow Bradshaw and Taff Davis were in a trench, partially buried under the rubble thrown up by a near miss. With the planes gone, they were helped out and dusted off. Looking for their two colleagues, they were told the commanding officer had left in his Wirraway trainer plane. The rumour mill, fed by shock and disorientation, had started to grind. In fact, when the raid started the commander was being driven into town to meet with Australian Air Marshal Richard Williams, who was in transit from London.

Bradshaw found his missing men, but their barracks had been destroyed and no one seemed to be in charge. The air-base executive officer drove around in a staff car advising all to evacuate the base. In the confusion, word was going around that he was saying to 'get as far south as possible', but it was later claimed that his order was to regroup off base.

In any case, the road south was choked with vehicles and with people on foot carrying whatever they could manage. The four radio operators decided to stay at the base, living in their work building, which had only minor damage. Meals were improvised at the airmen's mess, and a guard system was organised to keep looters away from the base. When partial power was restored the next morning, the four were able to resume work, but their means of reporting to head office had been severely disrupted.

A couple of weeks later, Melbourne ordered Corporal Bradshaw's evacuation to Wyndham, at the northern end of Western Australia, and the other three to Broome and Groote Eylandt. Landing at Wyndham, Bradshaw's De Havilland Dragon was attacked by Zeros and riddled with bullets. Passengers and crew abandoned the burning plane, throwing their gear out and jumping after it with the aircraft rolling at about 60 kph. They ran into nearby scrub while the plane trundled down the runway, stopping at the end and eventually burning itself out.

— ● —

The war might have found its way to the RAAF radio intercept team, but its counterpart in the army had travelled around the world to get to its war. Trained in Cairo, then driven out of Greece and Crete by the German advance, No. 4 Special Wireless Section was in Lebanon when the Pacific War broke out. With the likelihood of the unit being recalled to Australia, in early 1942 Jack Ryan organised training in *kana* for his Morse operators, using copies of the code given to him by British signals intelligence in Palestine. They were joined in January by Mic Sandford. Newly promoted to captain, he was back from his mysterious Western Desert assignment with the British radio unit and full of anecdotes of his adventures there. On 4 February, the men of No. 4 SWS embarked at Suez for the journey back to Australia, arriving in Adelaide in mid-March.

In Southeast Asia, the Allies were everywhere in retreat. The Australian naval attaché in Washington cabled the RAN's Chief of Naval Staff in mid-February that the US Navy was evacuating its signals intelligence station from Corregidor in the Philippines. He suggested the Naval Board 'should undertake an investigation of where and how these key personnel might be advantageously employed'. He knew they were 'key' because the Americans had told him they were.

Jack Newman was not consulted this time—the transfer was engineered through diplomatic channels—so he wasn't able to resist the incursion on his turf, if indeed he saw it that way. This was a small foretaste of a phenomenon that would sweep through Australian life, changing its fabric even more dramatically than the fear of war on its doorstep. The Americans were coming!

Chapter 4

The road to Corregidor

A year before the United States entered the war, its ability to decode Japanese military communications lagged significantly behind Britain's. It might have built a facsimile of the Purple cipher machine, but that was for decrypting diplomatic messages, not military ones. Scant progress had been made with the main Japanese naval code, JN-25, until Britain's FECB began exchanging codes with the US Navy in May 1941. Like its British counterpart, American signals intelligence had started promisingly enough under the impetus of the First World War, but had squandered its opportunities in ill-chosen priorities, personal vanities and struggles for control.

American sigint was pioneered by Herbert Yardley, a State Department code clerk commissioned during the war as a cryptologic officer with the US Army. A garrulous poker player, he spent his early years learning the mathematical and psychological subtleties of the game and in 1919 set up a peacetime code-breaking unit, the Cipher Bureau, with State Department and Army funding. Yardley was a born salesman, boastful with a taste for the dramatic, who referred to his bureau as the Black Chamber. The Western Union telegraph company was induced to supply it with copies of international cables in breach of US communications law, but by 1924, in the warm glow of apparent world peace, the bureau's budget had been slashed, its staff halved, and its office space shrunk.

Yardley tried to reverse the Black Chamber's fortunes by sending the new Secretary of State, Henry Stimson, copies of decrypted Japanese messages to show the quality of its work. The ploy backfired. Declaring that 'gentlemen do not read each other's mail', the patrician Stimson instructed the State Department to withdraw its funds. The bureau was disbanded in 1929.

In 1931, the unemployed Yardley published a book, *The American Black Chamber*, revealing the extent of American cryptanalysis in the Twenties. It told how Japanese codes had been broken, providing advance knowledge to the US delegation of Japan's intentions at the 1921 Washington Naval Conference. This created a sensation, not least with the Japanese, who began an immediate search for new and better ways to protect their communications. Yardley made good money from his book, but little else. Blacklisted, he never worked again in the United States.

With the closure of the Black Chamber, the US Army made a fresh start with cryptography. The Signal Intelligence Service was set up in 1930 under William Friedman, the son of an interpreter in Imperial Russia's postal service. The family had come to the United States to escape the anti-Semitism that pervaded Tsarist Russia. With a degree in genetics from Cornell University, Friedman had become interested in codes and ciphers while working at Riverbank Laboratories, near Chicago. Like Herbert Yardley, he had been a cryptologic officer in the First World War.

The prime mission of SIS was to create codes and ciphers for the US Army, but the Washington agency also worked on solving foreign codes, not for intelligence but to stay abreast of new developments. When SIS was authorised to hire civilians, Friedman selected three mathematics teachers. One of them was Abraham Sinkov from New York City, like Friedman the son of Russian immigrants. Growing up in Brooklyn, Sinkov graduated in mathematics from the City College of New York. After taking a civil service exam, he received a mysterious letter from Washington asking about his knowledge of foreign languages. He knew enough French to be offered a position as junior cryptanalyst at SIS.

With the other two recruits, Sinkov was instructed in Friedman's mathematical and scientific approach to cryptography as well as undergoing Army training. By 1933, having completed a doctorate in mathematics at George Washington University, Abe Sinkov was decoding Japanese diplomatic traffic in cahoots with a Japanese linguist. Academic in manner and style, he wasn't really a military man, but he was going to be useful to the military even if his work had been on diplomatic codes.

The US Navy had developed a small code-breaking group even earlier than the Army, beginning a long rivalry between the two American services that was punctuated only occasionally by individuals who understood the value of shared knowledge. During the First World War, the US Navy had been passed German naval messages decrypted by the British Admiralty, but it was a brazen criminal act in 1921 that got its pursuit of signals intelligence under way.

In the dead of night, shadowy figures slipped into Japan's New York consulate and picked the lock of its security cabinet. In it, they found a copy of a three-*kana* naval code. The intruders were from the Office of Naval Intelligence, the FBI and the New York Police Department, and the Japanese never knew their consulate had been burgled. Over the next few days, the pages of the codebook the Americans would dub the Red Book were photographed. The book was then put back in the safe undetected.

A year later, an eccentric naval officer was transferred from command of a minesweeper off China to head a code and cipher section being set up to exploit the stolen codebook. Thirty-four years old, Lieutenant Laurance Safford had graduated in 1916 from the US Naval Academy in Annapolis, Maryland, but he'd been a square peg in the navy's round hole with his constantly crumpled uniform and his love of chess, mathematics and mechanical coding machines. He was an oddball whose appointment probably solved two problems for the navy.

Designated OP-20-G—for Naval Operations, 20th Division (Communications Security), G section (Code and Signals)—the fledgling unit was lodged on the top floor of the Navy Department Building on Washington's National Mall. Although this was only a short walk from where the Army would locate SIS, there was never any suggestion that the two units should work together towards a common goal.

By the end of Safford's first year, Navy intercept stations had been set up around the Pacific—at Shanghai, in the Philippines and on Guam—and OP-20-G was breaking its first Japanese naval codes. Training was conducted on the roof of the concrete Navy Building, eight potential radio interceptors climbing a ladder each morning to get to class in a concrete blockhouse intended originally as elevator housing. After learning to copy *kana* characters in longhand, they copied the code on RIP-5 typewriters—Underwood machines with extra keys for *kana* characters. Students practised keypunching cards and spent time at the nearby intercept station at Cheltenham. Styling themselves the 'On-the-Roof Gang', the new elite of intelligence did their cryptographic training in the form of a series of practical exercises. There was no theory backing it up.

Navy's OP-20-G was working on Japanese naval codes at the same time as Eric Nave was working on them in Hong Kong and then London, and some six years before the US Army set up the SIS in 1930. By then, Japanese diplomatic traffic had greatly increased. To avoid duplication, and perhaps to head off simmering inter-service rivalry, the decryption workload was shared. Diplomatic traffic intercepted on odd-numbered days would go to the Navy, and on even-numbered days to the Army. Results were exchanged, and reported to the White House and the State Department by the Navy in odd months and by the Army in even months.

Far more Japanese naval traffic was available for interception than army traffic, so the SIS was left with the lion's share of breaking the diplomatic codes, by this stage mostly encrypted by machine, not manually using codebooks. Late in 1938, decoded messages revealed travel arrangements for a communications engineer to install Type B cipher machines in Japan's diplomatic missions. By February, the old encryption machine was replaced with the new *97-shiki obun inji-ki* (System 97 Printing Machine for European Characters). The Americans called it Purple.

SIS started intercepting Purple messages between Tokyo and Berlin. For a while after the machine's introduction, the Japanese sometimes sent messages in both old and new codes so that overseas missions waiting for their Purple machine could still read the message. It was a grave error. The Americans had decrypted the old code and were able to compare that version of the message with the version sent in Purple, giving them a head start on cracking the new code. Since the cipher keys to the machines were regularly replaced, they still had to keep breaking them. However, by mid-1940, about 25 per cent of Purple was solved.

The Navy's OP-20-G, meanwhile, had been attacking Japan's new naval codes, introduced after an Imperial Japanese Navy commander in China warned that the existing codes no longer appeared to be secure. They were replaced in 1939 with two new systems: the Flag Officers' Code, and JN-25, a five-digit double-enciphered code that would come to be used in some 70 per cent of naval communications. OP-20-G assigned its most experienced code breakers, as well as its branch in Hawaii, to the Flag Officers' Code, but that code was seldom used. With only a small volume of traffic to work on, the pursuit proved fruitless. The code was never broken.

At first the Americans had only marginal success with JN-25, a numerical system radically different from its predecessor. They were unaware that British code breakers were making substantial progress with it. Washington had assigned its younger team to work on JN-25, along with its Manila agency, but in December the system was replaced with a variant, JN-25B, and the process of code penetration had to start all over again. The Americans hadn't made sufficient progress with the initial version to discover, as the British did, that with JN-25B the Japanese had changed the codebook but had not brought in new additive tables.

Meanwhile, the SIS had pressed on with the diplomatic code, and by October 1940 William Friedman was reporting that Purple was broken—indeed, his team had built a facsimile Purple machine. A new SIS analyst had a hunch the Purple machine might use rotary selectors, common in automatic telephone exchanges. With switches scrounged from Western Union, he constructed a machine that followed Purple's encryption rules. It sent out a shower of sparks as its selectors turned, but it worked, enabling more rapid decoding and easier identification of new cipher keys. The Navy's Safford and the Army's Friedman had been prepared to ignore interservice rivalry, allowing the Army analyst to build this Purple replica in the Naval Gun Factory. Additional Purple machines were made available to both Army and Navy. One was given to the naval unit in the Philippines, but for some reason not to the one in Hawaii.

In May 1941, the Japanese ambassador in Berlin was told that Germany's agents in the US believed the Americans were reading Japan's diplomatic codes. Tokyo sent a Purple-coded message to its embassy in Washington: 'ACCORDING TO A FAIRLY RELIABLE SOURCE IT APPEARS ALMOST CERTAIN THE U.S. GOVERNMENT IS READING YOUR CODE MESSAGES. PLEASE LET ME KNOW WHETHER YOU HAVE ANY SUSPICION OF THE ABOVE.' Ambassador Nomura in Washington investigated and told Tokyo two weeks later that it appeared some Japanese codes were being read in the US, but no action was taken in response.

THE ROAD TO CORREGIDOR

The Japanese too were penetrating codes. In August of that year Joseph Grew, the US Ambassador in Tokyo, was secretly given information by a pro-American insider of Japan's Foreign Ministry. The countries weren't then at war, but with conflict seeming inevitable, individual Japanese had differing positions on the US as an enemy. Grew's informant asked him to send the information to Washington in a particular State Department code. Asked why, the man explained that since all America's other diplomatic codes had been broken, his own safety would be at risk if they were used to transmit the message.

Intelligence from decoded intercepts could be crucial to military planning, and it was crucial to keep the enemy from finding out how far its codes had been penetrated. Operations based on decrypts always needed a 'cover story', a plausible other source, to conceal the actual source of the intelligence. Indeed, sometimes intelligence gathered was not acted on to avoid arousing suspicion about how that knowledge had been gained.

— • —

Throughout the 1930s, OP-20-G stuck to naval codes and SIS worked mostly on diplomatic codes. But changes were afoot in America's burgeoning signals intelligence world. Expansionist Japan had become the main interest, with new US listening stations located nearby in Hawaii and the Philippines. Japan's military was devising more sophisticated and secure code systems, requiring more effort and ingenuity to penetrate. Widening the interception net was one response. Mechanisation of code sorting was another.

In 1934, William Friedman wrote to his superior in Signal Corps, Major Spencer Akin, requesting four IBM tabulators, then known as Hollerith machines after their inventor. With an IBM engineer, Friedman had devised a system that could sort code groups five times faster than it could be done by hand. The request went up the chain of command and, six weeks later, a reply came back: there were no funds available. Shortly after that, Friedman came across Hollerith machines sitting unused in the Army Quartermaster-General's office. They had been leased from IBM to help with bookkeeping, but a new commander wanted nothing to do with them. Friedman was able to put them to good use.

The tabulators could sort large stacks of data on punched cards into designated categories or into numerical or alphabetical order, a method known as 'brute force'. They could then determine the frequencies of individual characters and find repeated strings of cipher text. The same cipher group in two messages, especially in similar locations, suggested that the messages had been enciphered with the same string of additives. The IBM lease was renewed on condition that users would not touch the inner wiring, but the SIS operators would take off the cover plate and make adjustments with screwdriver and soldering iron when the IBM man wasn't in the machine room.

One of the US Navy's more experienced code breakers was transferred to naval headquarters at Pearl Harbor in 1936. Tom Dyer had developed considerable expertise on IBM tabulators and secretly took one with him to set up a one-man sigint unit called Station Hypo. The name came from the prewar navy phonetic alphabet's 'H', and here stood for He'eia, the area out from Honolulu where the intercept facility was located. Working on Japan's then-current naval code in his spare time, Dyer was able to read over 50 per cent of it by 1940, but by then the Japanese had replaced it with JN-25.

By the middle of 1941, the Pacific Fleet had moved from San Diego to Pearl Harbor and Station Hypo was growing. Safford's protégé, Commander Joe Rochefort, was sent as station head, with Lieutenant Dyer as his deputy. A few months before, Lieutenant-Commander Ed Layton had joined Admiral Kimmel's staff as fleet intelligence officer. He and Rochefort had studied Japanese language and culture in Japan at the same time a decade earlier. Their friendship of the time was resumed at Pearl Harbor. A tall streak of caustic humour, Rochefort took charge of about forty code breakers and analysts who, later in the year, moved into a windowless basement dubbed the Dungeon. Washington directed Hypo to concentrate on the seldom-used Flag Officers' Code. By the fateful day of 7 December, it had made no progress with it.

The bombardment of Pearl Harbor was directed almost entirely at warships and aircraft, with buildings and oil tanks largely left unscathed. That was cold comfort for Rochefort, for whom the attack was profoundly humiliating. Sickened by his bureau's inability to provide any warning of the air strikes, he was determined to redress the failure. On 10 December, Station Hypo was ordered by OP-20-G to forget the Flag Officers' Code and join the effort to crack JN-25B, along with Washington and Station Cast in Manila. Cast was already exchanging JN-25B code values with the British in Singapore as they were solved, and the Manila unit discovered that the change made to JN-25 before Pearl Harbor was a change of additive tables only, not of the underlying code. Within a few weeks, more of the code was being exposed.

Hypo's office was sealed by a single steel door at each end. The world outside those doors was of little concern to the occupants except as a source of intercepts, which arrived by motorcycle or jeep from He'eia, 50 kilometres away. The Dungeon's occupants worked like demons at desks spread around the office's open space. Previous intercepts were stacked on the concrete floor in piles, neither filed nor destroyed.

The basement was kept cold to protect the tabulators from tropical heat. For a few months, the workers suffered recurring colds and sniffles until the air-conditioning was checked and found to have been recycling the same air all that time. All were taking NoDoz caffeine pills, each about as potent as two cups of coffee. Dyer had a bucket of them on his desk from which he would periodically take a couple before ploughing on with his work. Rochefort rarely left the office, sleeping and eating there. During the day, he wore slippers and a maroon corduroy smoking jacket over his uniform, claiming his pipe and tobacco pouch could be kept in the jacket pockets. His uniform didn't provide that convenience. The slippers were because his shoes hurt from constant pacing on the hard floor.

The art of cryptography tends to attract singular personalities, and Hypo certainly had its share. Having survived December's bombardment, they had experienced the horror of battle, but the war would not touch them so closely again. For their compatriots in the Philippines, the reverse was true. As the marauding Japanese drew inexorably nearer, it was only a matter of time before the Manila code breakers, previously safe in their hideout, would feel the full force of war.

— • —

Initially, American intercept operations in the Asia-Pacific had been piecemeal, carried out on ships by self-trained *kana* operators. Shore-based intercept stations were set up at the Shanghai consulate in 1924. When, six years later, on Guam, signals traffic during a Japanese naval exercise off Korea revealed a trial of landing operations for a coming offensive in Manchuria, a few in the American military began to see potential in cryptanalysis. The US Navy considered expanding its code-breaking operations to Hawaii and the Far East, reflecting a shift in the focus of intelligence work from estimating the enemy's capacity (by espionage) to estimating its intent (by breaking into its coded communications)—in other words, from what the enemy could do to what it actually would do.

The commander of the Asiatic Fleet was a sigint enthusiast and requested an intercept station with decryption capacity in the vicinity of Manila. Designated Station Cast ('C' in the military phonetic alphabet, denoting the third station after Shanghai and Guam), it was set up at the US naval base at Olongapo on Subic Bay, north of Manila, but the inadequacies of the site rapidly became apparent. The station's location wasn't very secure, and it was plagued with noise interference.

Approval for the Navy to transfer its station to Corregidor, an island fortress at the mouth of Manila Bay, drew vehement opposition from the island's Army commander, who thought the higher Navy pay scale would create morale problems for his men. Station Cast moved instead to the navy yard at Cavite, on the southern side of Manila, but the machinery there ensured that the problems of signal interference continued. Only on Sundays was wireless reception clear. When the Army commander was eventually overruled, two years of defence fund wrangling followed. Meanwhile, a tunnel was blasted by Filipino convicts into the rock at Monkey Point, on Corregidor Island. The underground facility was completed late in 1940.

The Cast crew of eight officers and sixty enlisted men moved across the bay from Cavite, bringing with them radio gear, *kana* typewriters and IBM tabulators, sorters and key punches. About 40 metres long, with a side branch halfway down, their buff-painted, air-conditioned tunnel housed the intercept section at the far end, with radio receivers mounted along the walls. The crypto team was tucked away in the side tunnel. A Marine stood guard day and night at the tunnel's double iron gate. Outside on the ridge were barracks and officers' quarters on one side, two handball courts on a flat area in front, and a direction-finding antenna on the other side. A short walk from the tunnel entrance, the rockface fell sheer to the cove below.

Among those moving to the new facility was the recently appointed station head, 32-year-old Lieutenant Rudolph Fabian. A determined individual of modest origins, Fabian was born in a wooden house near Butte, Montana, among the trees of the Basin

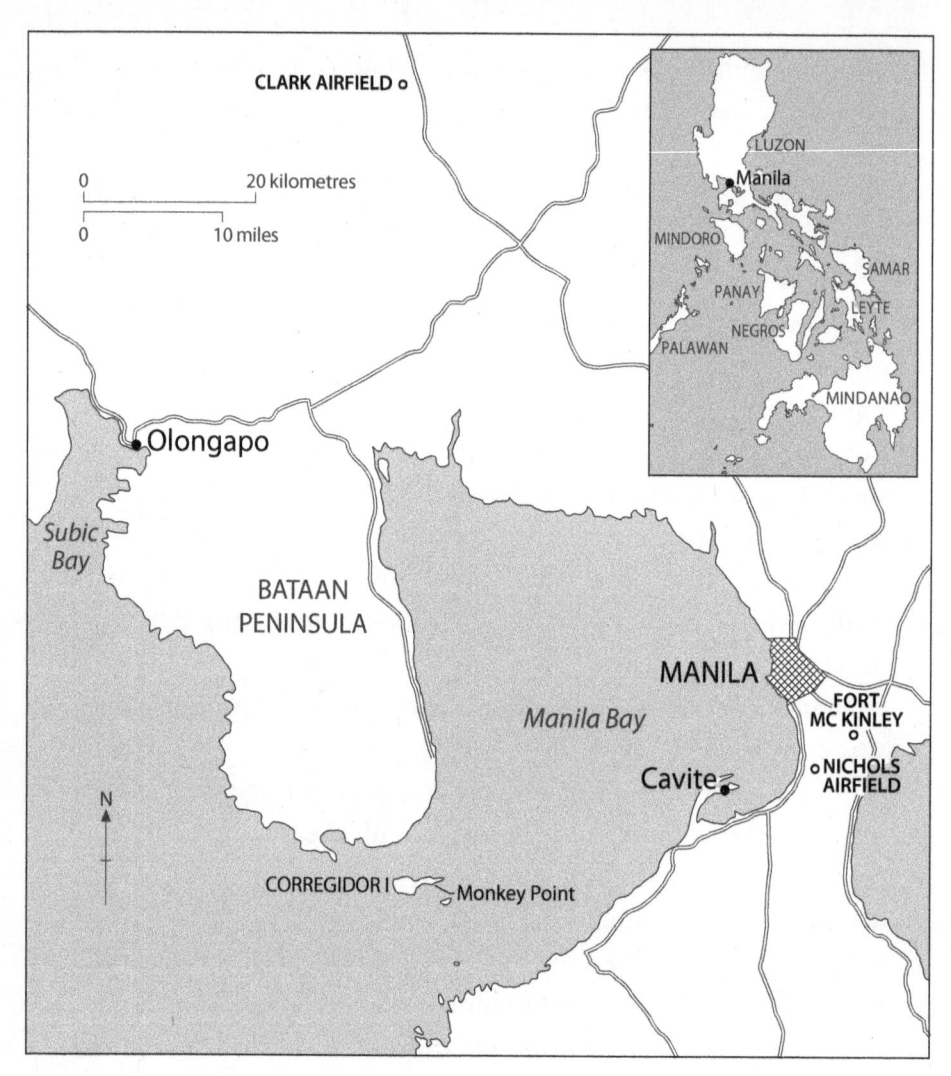

Map 1: Manila Bay

Creek reservoir where his father was caretaker. The family moved into Butte, a copper boomtown at its height, when he was eight and his father became a county commissioner.

As a young man, Rudolph followed his older brother into the Naval Academy at Annapolis, immersing himself in tradition by joining the bugle corps and the annual ring dance. After graduating and spending seven years at sea as a gunnery officer, he was overlooked for graduate training in ordnance, but a letter from Commander Safford of OP-20-G asked for a hold on Fabian's rejection so he could consider an unspecified offer.

It's hard to see what potential Safford saw in Fabian or even how he became aware of him. Perhaps the gunnery officer had previously approached Safford, who liked to gather acolytes. For whatever reason, Rudy Fabian was invited to join OP-20-G and, following the bureau's radio communications training, spent a year in its Washington office before being sent to Manila. With limited signals experience and virtually no knowledge of cryptanalysis, he didn't differ greatly from his predecessors. His was principally an administrative position in a bureau that was struggling to carve out a role for itself.

The team Fabian took over was young and enthusiastic but quite inexperienced. With Washington's more experienced code breakers unable to penetrate JN-25, it's not surprising that Cast too got nowhere. Worse, at the end of 1940 the Japanese replaced JN-25 and the code breakers had to start all over again. Unlike their British counterparts, they hadn't recovered enough of the unchanged additives to be able to work backwards from them. Cast's IBM machines could sort rapidly through large quantities of intercepted material in search of general patterns. But how to recover cipher and code from those patterns eluded the young team.

The agency's recruitment was haphazard and sometimes arbitrary. Robert Dowd had been typing logs on a destroyer when he was interviewed by the Asiatic Fleet's intelligence officer, Commander Redfield Mason, looking for new yeomen (naval clerks) for Cast. Dowd was hired after being asked little more than if he smoked or drank. On arrival, he was told by Fabian to break enemy ciphers by trying his hand on the unbroken JN-25B. Unsurprisingly, the task was beyond Dowd too, and he was moved instead to machine operation.

Within three months of Fabian's arrival, two linguists joined the unit, both lieutenant-commanders who outranked the station head: Gill Richardson, transferred from the Asiatic Fleet where he was intelligence officer under Admiral Thomas Hart, and Spencer 'Swede' Carlson, from the disbanded Shanghai station. They had no interest in administration, which they happily left to their station chief. Fabian was sufficiently deferential for the rank anomaly not to become an issue, but with no significant penetration of Japanese codes, Fabian's position might have been tenuous anyway if not for the British—towards whom he showed disdain, not deference.

— • —

In January 1941 a four-man delegation from Washington, two each from Navy's OP-20-G and Army's SIS, had visited Britain's Bletchley Park. Abe Sinkov was one of the Army team, but for him the visit was mostly six weeks of polite goodwill. The Americans were given a preliminary briefing on the German Enigma code, of which the British had previously kept their knowledge a secret, but they were not shown its decryption in operation. Their main interest was in Japanese codes, but these were pursued by the British at Singapore, not at Bletchley Park.

In the aftermath of the Bletchley visit, however, the Americans got the connection they needed. Nave's friend from Singapore, Malcolm 'Bouncer' Burnett, went to Corregidor and shared with Cast some of the work the Far East Combined Bureau was doing. It was a cautious exchange. Burnett didn't let on that his unit had penetrated JN-25; nor did the Americans reveal they were working on it. Shortly after, however, a Cast analyst went to Singapore and returned with some keys to the latest code, JN-25B.

FECB gave Cast the codebook for JN-25B to the extent that it was known, but by then the Japanese had introduced new additive tables. By April, about one-third of these tables had been recovered, although that was insufficient to read messages. Hard copies of any known values were sent in a metal strongbox built into the hull of a Pan American Clipper flying twice weekly between Singapore and Manila. In return, the Americans sent intercepts and the recoveries they had made using their IBM tabulators. Corregidor picked up more traffic than Singapore, but its penetration of the JN-25B code was slow.

Earlier in the year, Cast had been provided with a Purple machine, with keys sent daily in the Navy's high-security COPEK channel. This machine was routinely used to decode Japanese embassy messages for an Army unit that had been set up in Manila, as well as for Navy analysis. However, the Japanese military didn't trust its diplomats and little of military significance was passing through Japan's diplomatic channels.

In the late 1930s, the US Army had set up a small radio intercept group outside Fort McKinley, in Manila's suburbs. Headed by Major Joe Sherr, Station 6 picked up diplomatic traffic and signals between naval aircraft and their bases in Formosa and Japan. As it had no cryptanalysis capacity, intercepts were recoded and sent to Washington for analysis, but by 1941 diplomatic intercepts could be decrypted locally by Station Cast, using its Purple machine. This allowed Station 6 to produce its own intelligence estimates.

Army intercepts were taken daily in a sealed bag to Manila's dock. Handed to the captain of a harbour vessel, they were delivered to a Cast man waiting on the dock at Corregidor. Decoded, translated and typed in English, they were returned the following day to a Station 6 messenger waiting at the dock in Manila. The decrypts would be arranged in a folder with related earlier messages attached and hand-delivered later that day to General Douglas MacArthur's chief of staff, General Richard Sutherland. He would decide whether the Far East Army Commander needed to be advised of the contents. In all, it took at least three days for an intercept to get to MacArthur, and longer when Sundays or holidays intervened, as the US Navy usually took those days off.

A lengthy delay in intelligence reaching a military commander was unhelpful at this stage. In a war, it would be disastrous. (At this point, though, the content was not significant. These were Purple decrypts, diplomatic messages of limited military value.) The air-base intercepts were not much better. By the time they were decoded in Washington, the Japanese aircraft had long gone. Station 6 was learning, but mostly what it learned was that some intercepts were barely worth the effort.

By September, Fabian's one-year posting in Manila had come to an end and the new bureau head arrived. A heavily built West Virginian who had studied Latin at Ohio University for two years, Lieutenant John Lietwiler had switched to the Naval Academy in Annapolis. No athlete, he was told by the academy's fencing coach that he was 'too short for sabre, to slow for épée and too clumsy for foil'. He didn't dislike sport, but he preferred chess, crossword puzzles and music—classical music, light opera and popular songs. Lietwiler loved playing violin and brought his instrument with him to the Philippines. Before taking up the post, he had cryptography training in Washington under the US Navy's most experienced and skilled code breaker, Aggie Driscoll. The men at Cast soon gave Lietwiler the nickname 'Honest John'. A straight shooter who would help sort out problems as they arose, he was without pretence and far more hands-on than his almost invisible predecessor. Fabian had dealt effectively with the hierarchy, quite prepared to be irritating to get what Cast needed. It remained to be seen how well the new chief could extract favours from his superiors.

Fabian's departure was meanwhile delayed pending word from Washington of his expected transfer to a sea posting. That would put him in a position to press for promotion to lieutenant-commander, but his career ambitions were not high on the US Navy's list of priorities. Uncertain if America would join the two-year-old war in Europe, and aware of the possibility of conflict with Japan, the American military was hampered by its own unpreparedness.

Fabian had a particular fetish about security. This sometimes seemed obsessive, but it wasn't always unjustified. A diplomatic translation Cast had carried out for Station 6 was overheard being discussed by Army personnel on a Manila golf course the following Sunday. Hanging around like an unwanted guest, Fabian made plain that he thought this indiscretion put Cast's work at serious risk. If overheard by the wrong person, such chatter could indicate to Japan that its Purple code had been broken.

The Japanese navy wouldn't be concluding its code had been broken, however. When the additive table for JN-25 was replaced again in August, there was a hiatus in reading intercepted messages, but Cast's IBM machines sped up the process. Much of Cast's military intelligence for the time being was coming through traffic analysis, which strongly suggested that Japan was preparing for war. If war was indeed inevitable, analysts concluded, it would break out in Southeast Asia.

Chapter 5

Scramble to safety

Five hours after Manila radio had announced the Pearl Harbor attack, General Sutherland was hand-delivered a Japanese message, decrypted by Cast, announcing the end of diplomatic negotiations with the US. Four hours later, radar operators in the Philippines detected aircraft over the China Sea heading towards Luzon, the main island of the Philippines. Planes took off from Clark Field, north of Manila, to investigate, saw nothing and returned in the belief that Japan did not have the capacity to mount a war on two fronts. An hour after the radar had seen them, the Japanese planes attacked Clark Airfield, destroying half its bombers and a third of its fighters on the ground.

Nichols Airfield, near Station 6, was bombed during the night by a small formation of seven planes. Having switched its focus from diplomatic traffic to air–ground communication, Station 6 tuned its radio receivers next afternoon to a network of enemy stations transmitting in plain *kana*. Numbers were being sent at short intervals, decreasing to 180. It made no sense until it dawned on the operators that these were compass bearings and that some of the 'stations' were actually planes moving towards the Philippines from Formosa. Lieutenant Howard Brown, the senior operator, rang his chief, Colonel Joe Sherr, and asked for instructions. Told to notify the civilian volunteers manning the Aircraft Warning Service (AWS), Brown did so and received an offhand 'That's very interesting.'

The following day, 10 December, the Japanese radio network became active again and Brown once more called AWS. 'The enemy network is buzzing,' he warned. 'There are maybe a hundred heavies [heavy bombers] in the air and heading our way.' He was thanked for the information.

Brown rang AWS once more an hour or so later and said in his characteristic forthright manner, 'You should start blowing your whistles now. The Japs will be around in fifteen minutes.'

'I'm sorry,' was the response, 'but none of our observers have spotted any planes. We don't think we should sound the alert yet.'

The air-raid siren blared shortly after, almost at the same time as fifty-four fighters and bombers roared over Nichols Airfield and Cavite Navy Yard in three V formations. A dogfight could be seen below the lead formation. Someone yelled, 'Look at those leaflets come down,' but they were bombs. With no formal shelters, everyone had to crouch under the nearest cover. Bombs crisscrossed the navy yard and small fires broke out across the base. Marines opened fire from a ground battery but found the enemy's planes were flying above their guns' range. American fighters that had scrambled from Nichols were routed.

The yard burned out of control after the raiders left, with firefighters trying desperately to keep the flames away from ammunition stores. Cavite's power plant, industrial facilities and supply depots had been completely destroyed and about 1000 people killed. As night fell, all personnel at the naval base were evacuated to Manila.

Five days later, the Station 6 operator called AWS and said Japanese planes were coming from the east side of Luzon, giving an estimated bearing and arrival time. The attack formation arrived as predicted, but there was no ground alert. Lieutenant Brown rang AWS and asked why it hadn't acted on his warning. He was told the planes had come in over a radar blind spot and had been missed.

Howard Brown was not a man to take a backward step. He complained to Station 6's commander, Colonel Akin, and must have convinced him valuable intelligence had been wasted. The next morning, three air force lieutenants reported to the station for liaison and plotting duties, but by then air resistance was barely possible. Only thirty American fighters were left in the Philippines. It was decided to conserve these and use them for reconnaissance only. Without air cover, Admiral Hart was not prepared to keep the Asiatic Fleet in the vicinity and withdrew it to Java.

On Corregidor, cryptographer Vince Chamberlin was shaken awake in the middle of the night of 8 December by a Marine telling him, 'Lieutenant Fabian says the Japanese have bombed Pearl Harbor. Everyone is to report to the tunnel in case they bomb us.'

Bombings were to become a way of life for Cast personnel. Two days later, they stood on the rocky cliff near the tunnel entrance watching Japanese bombers attack Cavite across the bay. The enemy strike went unchallenged thanks to Howard Brown's warning falling on deaf ears. Explosions could be heard, and the distant shore erupted in black smoke. Personnel from the naval radio centre at Cavite were brought to Corregidor on the ferry that did the regular bay run. Battered and bruised, carrying little but the clothes they were wearing, they were to man emergency communications in the Army's tunnel system at Malinta, west of the Cast tunnel.

As the ferry docked, Fabian came on board and called out, 'Is there an Ensign Cook on board?'

One of the few passengers in a clean navy uniform stepped forward. On night shift, he'd been sleeping off site when the base was bombed.

'I'm Lieutenant Fabian. Get your gear and follow me,' Cook was told.

He was one of the few new arrivals with any gear to collect. He assumed he was being taken to the place the District Communications Office had assigned him to, but found himself instead at the smaller Cast tunnel. When he questioned this, Fabian said it had been arranged with the Communications Office.

There was a history behind this incident. Ralph Cook had been a field engineer with IBM in Manila when he was called up and posted to the Communications Office to set up a machine repair unit. Lieutenant Lietwiler visited Cavite in October and showed considerable interest in his background and expertise. Two weeks later, a request came through Admiral Hart's headquarters for the ensign to be released for duty at Cast. Cook's boss, Lieutenant-Commander Fort Callahan, vehemently opposed the move and successfully blocked it. Lietwiler simply bided his time. With the evacuation from Cavite, his opportunity came.

Since hostilities began, Lietwiler and Fabian had been operating a 'buddy' system, jointly guiding the bureau through the new experience of war. Taken to meet Lietwiler, Cook recognised him from the October meeting. He was instructed to use his familiarity with IBM machines to support Cast's operation, but first to acquaint himself with the unit's cryptanalysis and traffic analysis methods. Whether he recognised there was skulduggery in his diversion to Cast isn't certain, but he went about his new tasks methodically, examining the station's equipment and taking a boat trip to obtain parts, cards and materials from the IBM office, which was still operating in Manila.

Fort Callahan had meanwhile been pressing for work space for his communications section in the Cast tunnel rather than in the main tunnel at Malinta. In his proposal, his team's coding machine would be situated in Cast's code room, at the end of the side tunnel. To Fabian, the idea of three radio officers wandering freely through the Cast office area and mixing with cryptanalysts, linguists, Lietwiler and himself, posed unacceptable security risks. Callahan, higher ranked and still smarting from the attempt to poach Ralph Cook, brushed Fabian's objections aside. The pugnacious Southerner was not going to be dictated to by a pretentious Midwesterner. The district commander, Rear-Admiral Francis Rockwell, was no more sympathetic. He regarded Cast's importance as overblown, and said the unit couldn't do much good now that war had begun. Lietwiler was told his complaints about Navy security were 'childish'.

In the midst of this contretemps, Ralph Cook went to the Malinta tunnels to pick up some materials and came face to face with his former chief. Fort Callahan exploded. 'Where the hell have you been? I reported you missing.'

Cook explained that he'd been collared by Fabian and taken to Monkey Point. 'He said he'd cleared it with DCO.'

'He can't do that,' gasped a furious Callahan. 'I need you here.'

The tug-of-war between Callahan and Fabian had escalated, but the protagonists had nowhere to take their fight. After a bit more push and shove, a compromise was reached. Ensign Cook would alternate watches between communications and signals intelligence. Callahan's team would operate its code board in the Cast code room, but when he proposed assigning Lietwiler's juniors to his code board, Rockwell told him to leave things be. In any case, with the Asiatic Fleet gone and messages between General MacArthur in Manila and Admiral Hart in Java handled by army communications, naval communications had very little to do.

Working on the new version of JN-25B that had been introduced just before Pearl Harbor, Cast made a startling discovery. Twelve hours after the attack, a naval signal was intercepted in which the operator had forgotten to use additives. To their astonishment, the Americans recognised some of the code values from JN-25B and realised that the Japanese had changed the additive

Intercept room at Park Orchards, Melbourne, where Japan's Winds and Haruna messages were picked up.

Victoria Barracks, Melbourne—the initial location of Nave's Special Intelligence Bureau.

Lieutenant Eric Nave, 1925    Commander Eric Nave, 1943

Rudolph Fabian (left) in the yearbook of the US Naval Academy, Annapolis, 1931, and Lieutenant John Lietwiler, 1944 (right), chiefs of Station Cast in Manila who subsequently headed up FRUMEL in Melbourne.

Cavite naval yard, Manila Bay, which was destroyed by a Japanese air attack two days after the attack on Pearl Harbor.

American soldiers working in the US Army's Malinta Tunnel on Corregidor island in Manila Bay. Station Cast's tunnel at Monkey Point was a similar workplace.

Monterey apartments in Melbourne's Albert Park, home of the joint Australian and US code-breaking facilities that became FRUMEL.

The file room at FRUMEL.

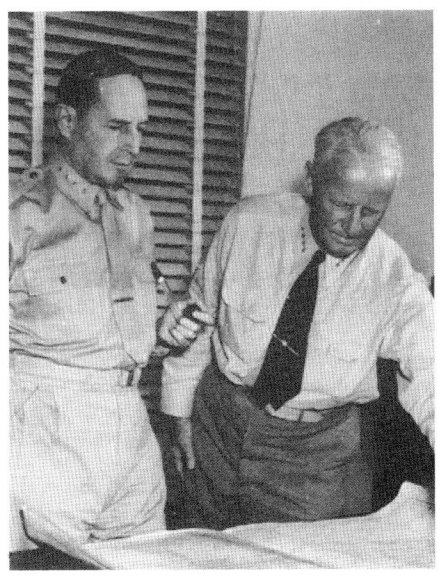

General Douglas MacArthur and Admiral Chester Nimitz

Admiral Isoroku Yamamoto

Joe Rochefort (left), chief of Station Hypo, Hawaii, and his friend and collaborator, Ed Layton (right), Admiral Nimitz's intelligence officer.

USS *Lexington*, after an explosion following bombing by Japanese carrier-borne aircraft in the Battle of the Coral Sea, 1942.

Admiral Yamamoto addresses his troops in Rabaul shortly before his fatal inspection tour of front-line forces around Bougainville.

Pilots who returned from the mission that shot down Yamamoto's plane: Tom Lanphier, Besby Holmes and Rex Barber.

Cranleigh, in Melbourne's well-to-do South Yarra—the initial premises of Central Bureau.

Partners in intelligence coordination: Lieutenant A.W. 'Mic' Sandford in 1941 (left), and Lieutenant-Colonel Robert Little (right).

Nyrambla, at 21 Henry Street, the suburban Brisbane headquarters of Central Bureau.

The No. 1 Wireless Unit blockhouse at Stuart Creek, near Townsville. Only the water tank and steps on the left are real; the rest is painted concrete.

SCRAMBLE TO SAFETY

tables but were still using the JN-25B codebook, for which the British had been supplying values piecemeal. With only a small fraction of the code solved, readings were still very fragmentary. Station Cast's operators had little code-breaking experience, but they now had the well-trained Lietwiler to assist them. They were still exchanging code values with Washington and finding some were incorrect, but the regular exchanges with the British had ceased when FECB pulled out of Singapore. By far the most useful intelligence gained by the Americans was still coming from traffic analysis, particularly notice of impending bombing raids.

Corregidor was bombed repeatedly from the air. The Japanese had landed in the north of Luzon the day Cavite was bombed, and at Legaspi in the south two days later, pushing towards Manila from opposite directions. As they advanced, they built airfields from which to launch further bombing raids. In successive raids on Corregidor, a bomb pierced the roof and two floors of living quarters and buried itself unexploded in the earth beneath, and a second bomb burned another block of quarters to the ground. Bombs shook the tunnel's reinforced-concrete wall but did no physical damage to it.

The air raids were frequent, generally daily, and sirens would sound when the enemy planes were approaching. All those not already in the tunnel had to get to it swiftly or shelter in a slit trench. One of the Cast crew had brought a puppy back from Manila. Blackie would run to the tunnel as soon as he heard sirens and saw the men running. When Japanese bombers left from nearby airfields, he could hear them on the runway or taking off. Even if he was asleep his ears would prick up, and he would stand, listen with tail extended and one paw off the ground, then run to the tunnel. The men learned to follow the dog and would often be near the tunnel by the time the sirens started wailing.

Before long, so many of the quarters were damaged and the raids were so frequent that all the men brought down their bed gear and slept in or near the crowded tunnel. Ovens were moved from mess halls to the tunnel forecourt so diners could take shelter when raids came at meal times. An emergency generator provided power when the lines weren't working, and water had to be brought by tanker from another part of the island. The men bathed and laundered in the cove below the tunnel entrance, using a little fresh water to rinse out the salt.

The main Japanese assault on the Philippines began early on 22 December. Troops landed at three points in Lingayen Gulf and pushed south. MacArthur used tactical stands to delay the enemy advance while his troops withdrew to the Bataan Peninsula, opposite Corregidor. On the nights of 24 and 25 December, MacArthur's headquarters and the Philippines government, including President Manuel Quezon, were moved onto Corregidor.

Station 6 was also relocated to the island, where it was proposed that it too could operate out of the Monkey Point tunnel. Fabian, still finding Callahan's team an irritation, argued that the tunnel was already overcrowded with Navy radio men and Cast's overnight campers. He agreed that if Station 6 set up in the Army tunnel at Malinta, Cast would lay a phone line between the tunnels and provide bearings of bomber groups. The Cast men translated captured diaries for Station 6, while expressing the view that these were valueless—but then everyone else's work was valueless, according to Cast's leaders.

Food was in short supply on Corregidor, not least because MacArthur had refused to stockpile food and ammunition there. He would confront the Japanese on the beaches, he said. Supplies were now being rapidly consumed by thousands of American and Philippine troops. By the end of December, Cast rations were cut to two meals a day: breakfast of spaghetti (with or without tomato sauce), bread and coffee; lunch of rice (with or without tomato sauce), bread and coffee. Sometimes the cook reversed the two meals for variety.

SCRAMBLE TO SAFETY

The cook had previously run a restaurant of some sort in Shanghai. He often added ground meat—mule or carabao (water buffalo)—to the spaghetti or rice, and occasionally provided an additional snack of canned tomatoes or ice cream mix, obtained from who knew where. The men dined outside the tunnel at mess tables under a camouflage screen, all the time watching out for air raids and, when the Japanese got closer, artillery fire.

By the time the new year of 1942 rolled in, the Japanese held all of Luzon except the Bataan peninsula, on the western side of Manila Bay, and Corregidor island, off Bataan's southern tip. Entering the city of Manila on 2 January, General Masaharu Homma's forces set up artillery positions at Batangas, south of the bay, and began regularly shelling Corregidor. Unlike with the air raids, no forewarning of these attacks was available, either by radar or from radio intercepts. In fixed positions facing out to sea, like Britain's guns at Singapore, the big guns on Corregidor were unable to respond. The US Army eventually brought a 12-inch mortar around for fairly inaccurate retaliatory fire on Batangas, using an unarmed Piper Cub as spotter.

As the enemy got nearer, the Navy's leadership began to worry about the potential capture of sigint personnel on Corregidor, and the risk that they might be tortured into revealing the extent to which the Allies had penetrated Japanese codes. Admiral Ernest J. King, Commander-in-Chief of the US Fleet, ordered Cast personnel to be evacuated 'by any means of transportation . . . to preserve [the unit's] continuity'. With the Asiatic Fleet in the Dutch East Indies, a nucleus group and equipment would move to Java and set up with *Kamer* 14, the Dutch sigint group there.

Lietwiler and Fabian discussed the most practical way of carrying out the transfer, dividing personnel into four roughly equal groups. Each could function independently as an intercept and processing unit, and so continue to monitor radio traffic while the other groups were evacuated. The first group to go would be made up of seventeen men, led by Fabian and the two higher-ranked linguists, Richardson and Carlson. There was no reason for Fabian to remain in the Philippines. He wasn't formally part of Cast any more, merely helping out in the emergency.

On the evening of 4 February, the submarine USS *Seadragon* docked at Corregidor and started stowing equipment that had been brought in the afternoon by tractor from Monkey Point. The wharf buzzed with urgency. Six radio receivers and nine *kana* typewriters were manhandled down the sub's narrow hatch, along with two tons of submarine spare parts and twenty-three torpedoes. A torpedo chute had to be opened to get the tripod of Cast's portable direction finder into the hold.

The seventeen men in the first group were given five minutes to leave with only the clothes they had on. Their workmates wouldn't discover they'd gone until morning. Three American officers were added to Fabian's party, and the sub's interior was crammed with people constantly manoeuvring around the boxes of gear stowed on the walkway floors. With equipment and passengers all on board before first light, Lieutenant-Commander William 'Pete' Ferrall slid *Seadragon* to the bottom of Manila Bay, waited silent and motionless through the hours of daylight, and finally slipped out on the night of 5 February.

It took a submerged week to reach Surabaya, at the eastern end of Java. With only one evaporator supplying drinking water and passengers sleeping in passageways, the journey was uncomfortable but uneventful. As he disembarked, Fabian saw *Seadragon* in daylight for the first time, noting makeshift repairs of damage from the Cavite bombing and Zero gunfire dents in the outer hull. Just as well he hadn't seen them earlier, he thought.

From Surabaya, the advance party backtracked by train across Java to Bandung, in the western highlands. Contact was made with *Kamer* 14. A combined headquarters for Allied army, naval and air forces had been set up just north of Bandung. Commander

Redfield Mason worked there as intelligence officer to Admiral Hart of the US Asiatic Fleet. Balding and cherubic, 'Rosey' Mason's appearance belied his nature. From an impoverished background, he was driven and abrasive, using fear to keep people under control. He had involved himself from time to time in Cast's affairs with recruiting and the like, but if Rudy Fabian had resented his interference, he'd kept it to himself.

The unhurried prewar routine of Corregidor had been upended by regular air attacks and the threat of capture and torture. Now, after the turmoil of evacuation and relocation, Fabian was determined to find some equilibrium for his team and get back to work. Cast's radio receivers had been brought on the submarine, and the Dutch began installing them in the Navy Department basement in Bandung, rigging an antenna on the roof. Fabian felt obliged to express some concern to his hosts at the leisurely pace of their work.

With new office space in converted stables, the Cast crew was determined to show what an efficient, highly secure operation looked like. *Kamer* 14 had been penetrating Japanese codes for years, and the Dutch seconded to help Fabian's men were technically skilled. However, they had a different attitude to security. The family of one *Kamer* 14 intercept operator stood around while he copied out Japanese messages, his father watching over his shoulder while others made up message blanks. Fabian bit his tongue: he was, after all, relying on the Dutch for assistance. But he kept them and Indonesians away from American encryption materials.

The lull in Bandung didn't last long. A week after the Americans arrived, and while they were still setting up, a Japanese assault force landed on Java's north coast. Any doubt that the enemy was on their doorstep was dispelled when Zeros strafed Bandung. The Navy Department building wasn't spared, and the men's equilibrium melted away overnight. The Dutch were unlikely to hold off the invasion for long. Fabian was called to a meeting at combined headquarters.

'If I ordered you to leave Bandung, how soon could you be under way?' Mason asked.

'Well, I think about four hours.'

'OK. Get hold of transportation and be in Tjilatjap by morning . . . sunrise.' A ship would take them from the southern Java port to Australia.

Seized with urgency, the party of seventeen set about packing equipment and belongings into boxes and stowing them in commandeered transport. They took off at 6.30 in the evening in a convoy of bus, truck and two cars that drove through the night and over the mountains at breakneck speed. When they were stopped at a Dutch road block and asked to show identification, an Indonesian driver disappeared into the dark and had to be replaced. There was little conversation. Few knew the final destination, only what they were leaving.

When they reached Tjilatjap in weak pre-dawn light, the port was under air attack. They sat on the outskirts until the Zeros left, then Fabian reported to the local American commander.

'*Snapper* is coming for you tonight,' said Admiral Glassford. 'The ship that was supposed to come was sunk, so you'll have to wait a day.'

He called the submarine in and handed Fabian a roll of American money.

'There's a thousand dollars here. When you get to your destination on this sub, take the first train down to Melbourne or down to Fremantle and report there.'

Snapper was instructed to offload its passengers at Exmouth Gulf, a patrol base in north-western Australia that serviced Catalina flying boats. The sigint team was hustled on board, feeling like European refugees they had seen in newsreels, but it was a relief to be away from the Japanese advance, if only for now.

SCRAMBLE TO SAFETY

The group disembarked at Exmouth via a refuelling tender and a runabout, wading the last couple of metres with their gear onto a deserted beach. Taking stock of their situation on dry land, they were dismayed by what they saw. A high, rocky ridge rose behind the beach. Through binoculars, they saw a line of mangroves separating the bay from saltbush, spinifex and claypans. There were hundreds of kangaroos and thousands of buzzing flies, but no sign of human life except on the tender. The landscape was barren and desolate, the dry heat about the century mark.

This was not the destination they had imagined. Clearly, someone had assumed the presence of a base would mean there were support facilities and roads going somewhere. But there was no more to this base than the anchored tender, which had been refuelling a single Catalina when *Snapper* arrived.

Officially, the linguist Carlson was in charge. As a lieutenant-commander, he was the senior officer in the group, but Lieutenant Fabian was left to continue his administrative role. With two others, he ventured cautiously down a rough vehicular track running back from the beach and came across a dilapidated homestead. The sole inhabitant—gnarled, bearded, of indeterminate age—could barely be understood by the Americans and offered little information save the fact that his nearest neighbour was a lighthouse keeper 'twenty mile' to the north. The tender and its Catalinas seemed to have escaped his notice.

The trio returned to their compatriots sitting alongside the emerald water. Some had grabbed the opportunity to swim, their voices bouncing off the still surface. A frustrated Fabian waved and shouted at the tender some distance across the bay. Finally its runabout could be heard putt-putting from that direction. Fabian went back with it and sought out the leader of the tender's crew.

'How can we get to Perth from here?' asked the American.

'You can't, mate.'

'There's no transport? Trucks or buses?'

'Nope.'

The tender had radio contact with Perth, from where a ship was promised to pick up the stranded Americans 'in a day or two'. After two days of waiting in temperatures of 25 degrees Centigrade and more, the evacuees embarked on the submarine tender USS *Holland* for Perth's port of Fremantle. From there, they were transported by train across the flat and treeless Nullarbor Plain, arriving finally at Melbourne's Spencer Street Railway Station on 3 March. It was two days short of a month since their departure from Corregidor, but at least Melbourne had some of the characteristics of home—at first sight, anyway.

— ● —

In the Philippines, the Japanese were already driving Allied defenders down the Bataan Peninsula when the first Cast evacuees left. Those still on Corregidor began to worry that an invasion force might land there before they could get away. Lietwiler set up a roster for beach defence, organising his men into battle stations to meet the invaders, but these were men trained in radio, not warfare. They would be ineffectual against a well-drilled enemy.

The whole island was on edge, any move around it challenged by a Marine or a Philippine Scout. In this atmosphere of dread, two of the traffic analysts took a midnight walk to unfog their brains and returned to find that John Lietwiler and his offsider, Rufus Taylor, had cleared their desks and were carefully stripping their Colt .45s.

Duane Whitlock, one of the analysts, joked, 'You expecting a Jap invasion tonight?'

Taylor looked him square in the eye. 'No. This is for you boys,' he said. 'John and I have discussed it, and we decided not to let a damn one of you fellows fall into their hands. When the time comes, we'll shoot every one of you and then kill ourselves.'

Although the operators remaining on Corregidor went through

the motions of work, there was actually little to contribute and no one of significance to advise since the Asiatic Fleet had moved to Java. The same applied to the radio men sharing Cast's tunnel, whose attitude was not helpful to Honest John's goal of maintaining discipline in his unit. He objected to Callahan, a Southerner from Georgia, drinking in the code room and telling his men anything of interest he'd found in the secret despatch file, but as a lieutenant, Lietwiler was powerless to bring the recalcitrant lieutenant-commander into line.

Even more annoying, Callahan's deputy, Lieutenant-Commander Melvyn McCoy, had run a power line up to an icebox and a light in the quarters left empty after Gill Richardson's evacuation. Lanky and lean-faced, with coal-black hair and an Errol Flynn moustache, McCoy had moved his own beds in and got his senior officer to instruct former occupants to shower elsewhere so as to not disturb any female 'guests', of whom there was a plentiful supply after both MacArthur's headquarters and the Philippine government moved to Corregidor. McCoy was in his mid-thirties and married, but this was a different world. The two radio officers called the quarters the 'passion parlour'.

Lietwiler complained futilely to Admiral Rockwell, who had already indicated that he thought Cast exaggerated its own value. Indeed, he had visited its workplace before Fabian left and told him, loudly enough for the whole office to hear, to fold up the unit's operation because it wasn't any use. Fabian, furious at the effect of this publicly proclaimed opinion on the team's morale, argued the point and eventually got agreement to continue a reduced operation, provided the men started destroying files and other secret material.

Throughout February, every classified sheet and used carbon paper was burnt, keeping only material needed for current intercept work. Cast's Purple machine, intended to go with the first evacuation but left behind in the rush, was pounded into little pieces, taken out to a deep part of Manila Bay and dumped. By the end of the month, however, setbacks had forced the invaders to reorganise their offensive strategy. Japan's High Command had miscalculated by moving to Java the division that had rolled through Luzon and replacing it with a less capable force intended for garrison duty. General MacArthur took advantage of the temporary easing of hostilities. On the night of 12 March, he left Corregidor by sea, along with his wife, son and Cantonese *amah* (nurse), and Generals Richard Sutherland and Charles Willoughby.

Told that a Navy submarine couldn't reach Corregidor before 15 March, Admiral Rockwell allocated four PT boats to the withdrawal—and promptly joined it. Altogether, twenty people left with MacArthur that night, including the general's PR officer and the leaders of Station 6, General Spencer Akin (as he now was) and Colonel Joe Sherr. The patrol boats took their VIP cargo to the southern Philippines island of Mindanao, where they were transferred to a muddy plantation airfield at Del Monte and flown by B-17 to Darwin, arriving on 17 March 1942.

The MacArthur party flew by domestic DC-3 to Alice Springs, then took a train to Melbourne. Stopping briefly at Terowie, north of Adelaide, the general was greeted by a cheering crowd. He stepped out on the platform and made a short speech.

'I came through and I shall return,' he assured them, claiming to have broken through Japanese lines and, on President Roosevelt's order, left Corregidor to organise a counteroffensive against Japan. It was the beginning of the Australian public's adulation of MacArthur, a feeling many who served under him did not share.

At the beginning of March, Admiral Ernest J. King had ordered evacuation of all remaining Cast personnel 'as soon as possible' and 'by any means of transportation'. The submarine *Swordfish* was despatched, redirected through MacArthur's intervention to pick up US High Commissioner Sayre's party of four, then reassigned to take President Quezon and his party south to Panay first. On its

SCRAMBLE TO SAFETY

return, the High Commissioner's party had grown to eleven and the Army had added more. There was no room for Cast.

Meanwhile another submarine, ordered to Corregidor to evacuate MacArthur, arrived on 15 March to find the general already gone. Captain Kenneth Hoeffel, the senior ranking Navy officer after Admiral Rockwell's departure, proposed that *Permit* take Cast personnel instead, and the pandemonium of conflicting instructions continued.

Lietwiler told eighteen of his men to pack a small bag each and be ready to leave. They were taken at dusk by truck to South Dock, then by Navy tug to Mariveles, on Bataan. *Permit* had already left. Making their way back to Corregidor, they came across the sub surfaced in a channel between minefields, waiting for the mines to be cleared. When they finally boarded it, they understood why they'd been told to leave their bags behind on the tug: the sub was already half full of evacuees it had picked up from a marooned PT boat earlier in the day.

The PT's skipper had been landed at Corregidor to join his commander, who was already heading for Australia with MacArthur. Instructions for the PT crew to join the naval remnant on Bataan were ignored by the captain of *Permit*, Lieutenant Wreford Chapple. An ex-boxer and old Philippines hand, he decided the crew should be evacuated as well. Their skipper got wind of this and complained to the naval commander on Corregidor, Captain Hoeffel, who ordered *Permit* back to unload its unauthorised passengers.

With space created on the submarine, Hoeffel asked its skipper, Wreford 'Moon' Chapple—nicknamed after Moon Mullins, a newspaper comic strip character he'd played in Naval College skits—if he could fit more people in. When the burly Chapple reluctantly agreed, Hoeffel rang Lietwiler and asked if he could get another party ready within minutes. It was just before 2 a.m. Within an hour, *Permit*, which had a normal complement of fifty, left with 111 men on board, thirty-six of them from Station Cast.

Instead of going out into the open waters of the South China Sea, Chapple plotted a more direct course through the Philippine Islands to the Sulu Sea in the south. The Cast traffic analysts on board realised from intercepts decoded earlier that day that it was heading to where a division of Japanese destroyers was waiting to pick off blockade runners. The analysts huddled in discussion: should they advise the skipper of the danger that lay ahead? They were in an ethical dilemma that would not be an issue for most, but intelligence security had been drummed into these men. The problem, as they saw it, was that they didn't have authority to pass radio intelligence to someone not authorised to receive it. Even though they too were heading into the danger zone, they kept their silence.

The next night, Chapple surfaced his vessel and found three enemy destroyers on his stern. The robust Midwesterner was a hellraiser on land and not much different at sea. *Permit* fired two torpedoes that missed, and dived amid a volley of depth charges. Those exploding near the submarine rang on the hull like sledgehammers against a boiler, and the vessel shuddered. The cooling system was switched off—its sound would help locate them—and the overcrowded interior was stifling. Oxygen had to be bled sparingly from storage tanks to keep crew and passengers from suffocating. For the Cast men, this was alarming. The crew had tasks to keep them focused, but discomfort and fear ate at the passengers, who huddled powerless in torpedo rooms and passageways.

Now and then in the tense silence, pings from enemy sonar could be heard. Knowing the sub would soon be located, Chapple moved *Permit* each time to a new position on the sea bottom and shut down the engines again. There was an acrid smell of sweat. As the hours passed, with the vessel motionless in the depths, the destroyers renewed their assault with strings of charges. Bunks were shaken loose from the bulkheads, light bulbs fell out of their sockets, and those on board breathed uneasily, but *Permit* suffered only minor outer damage as it remained submerged for over twenty-two hours under repeated blind attacks.

Confident he had eluded the patrolling enemy, Chapple eventually surfaced, and the hatches were thrown open to the cool night air. With the interior refreshed, he slipped away under cover of darkness, running on the surface under diesel by night and underwater on battery power by day.

After several days in tropical waters with damaged air conditioning, the sub sighted a Japanese merchantman somewhere between Borneo and Ambon. Chapple chased it all afternoon without making up any ground. Finally, as night moved in, he fired two torpedoes at the ship, which was still a few kilometres away. Immediately, the veteran skipper screamed, 'Crash dive! Crash dive!'

The submarine pitched downwards, and all on board heard the whirr of torpedo screws passing above. One of *Permit*'s torpedoes had malfunctioned, turning back on its path.

This wasn't the end of the excitement on this voyage. The American sub was attacked by an Allied patrol bomber off the Western Australian coast, but got away unscathed and finally docked at Fremantle on 7 April, twenty-three days after the Cast evacuees had boarded at Corregidor. Put on a troop train, they reached Melbourne twelve days later.

While three-quarters of Cast had by now been withdrawn from Corregidor, the Army's Station 6 was still there *in toto*, apart from its two senior officers. General Jonathan Wainwright, who had been left in command of Allied forces after MacArthur's departure, was instructed to send Lieutenant Howard Brown and ten of his enlisted men from Corregidor to Australia. They were to be transferred to Del Monte, MacArthur's stopover on the Mindanao north coast, to set up an intercept station and wait for further orders.

Flown by B-17 to Del Monte on 28 March, the Army team set up an improvised intercept unit between the airfield and a pineapple plantation, with four scrounged radio receivers, a diesel generator, and wiring cut out of an old B-17 on the ground nearby. They monitored Japanese air movements, providing air-raid warnings and hunches about coming attacks that were mostly ignored.

On 12 April, the order came to leave for Australia. Before dawn two days later, they were called to Del Monte field and told to board a B-17 with Japanese bomber damage that had received only stopgap repairs. The pilot was already on edge. Told of enemy fighters patrolling south of Mindanao, he took off without warning, leaving six of Brown's team behind. It was not to be an easy flight.

With reduced plane performance and two full fuel tanks in the bomb bays, the pilot flew wide around Mindanao. After 45 minutes, an engine started spitting oil and was shut down. Fuel was pumped into the wing tanks until the plane was flying level again. Later, another engine began throwing oil and its power was reduced while the other two engines were stepped up. The B-17 limped into Darwin on three engines but landed safely. Brown and the other four evacuees were flown to Melbourne via Brisbane.

The six radio men left behind were not so lucky. Unable to get out before the Japanese landed on Mindanao, they linked up with Philippine guerrilla forces before buying a fishing catamaran to sail for Australia. A storm off New Guinea blew them onto an island, where they were picked up by the Japanese navy. They spent the rest of the war in a POW camp.

Back on Corregidor, the last twenty-two Cast members were still waiting to be taken off the island, which was now being bombed around the clock and under artillery fire from Batangas and Cavite on the mainland. It was little consolation that the depleted numbers meant everyone could now sleep in the tunnel.

Intercept work was limited. Cast had only one cipher, much of it unrecovered, and only fragments of messages could be obtained. However, traffic analysis indicated that the Japanese were readying an invasion convoy. With a priority request to Washington for decoding assistance rejected, Lietwiler took on the role of cryptanalyst himself and gleaned from the fragments that a Japanese fleet with six aircraft carriers was heading for the Indian Ocean from the Celebes. He advised the British commander, General Wavell, who passed it on to Admiral James Somerville, commander of the British Eastern Fleet. At that time, Britain was trying to reestablish itself in the Indian Ocean to protect shipping and supply the ground war in Burma. Cast's intercept prompted the admiral to withdraw most of his fleet to the Maldive Islands, where the Japanese were unaware Britain had a base. Although the Japanese attack fleet played havoc with the shipping it encountered, the British Eastern Fleet was able to fall back to East Africa and live to fight another day.

In preparation for the third and final Cast evacuation, Lietwiler detailed men to encipher a month's supply of dummy messages and give them to the radio chief to send out each day (the feud with Fort Callahan had by now abated). Ralph Cook, the former IBM engineer, was instructed to disassemble Cast's tabulators, crate the parts in boxes small enough to go down a submarine hatch, and stack them in readiness at the tunnel entrance. It took two weeks to complete the task with coded wiring and mixed parts in the crates. If the boxes fell into enemy hands, without Cook's coding and instruction manuals the Japanese would have difficulty reassembling the machines.

Seadragon, the submarine that had carried out the first evacuation, had been patrolling off Indochina when it was ordered to Cebu to pick up food supplies for Corregidor, mostly sacks of flour and rice. Arriving on 8 April, with nearby Bataan critically close to falling to the Japanese, the sub was transferring provisions to a tender when Captain Hoeffel ordered it to cease unloading and take on board the remaining Cast personnel. Only about a quarter of the supplies had been offloaded.

At 7.30 p.m, the code-room phone rang in the tunnel. The duty operator called out, 'Lieutenant. It's for you. District Commander.'

Those sitting nearby could hear one side of the conversation as Honest John repeated snatches of his instructions: 'Only the clothes on their backs . . . ready to leave in five minutes . . . make that fifteen . . . not possible . . . a truck coming.'

Lietwiler hung up and announced they were to leave in fifteen minutes. No baggage.

No one needed to be told twice. Vince Chamberlin changed into clean khakis and two shirts, one on top of the other, filled his pockets with tooth brush and paste, and put on two caps. Then he rang his mate, Sid Burnett, out on the direction-finder site and told him to come as fast as he could. Burnett raced down from the ridge with tin hat, Enfield rifle and an ammunition belt with bayonet and scabbard attached. He'd thrown them away by the time he got to the tunnel, out of breath.

Ralph Cook, lying on a bunk near the code room, wasn't formally part of Cast, just poached as a part-timer. Unsure if he was part of the evacuation—it hadn't been discussed—he hesitated. Lietwiler looked at him, paused and said, 'Dammit, Cook. If you're coming with us, get your clothes on.'

The ensign dressed, put some spare socks in his back pockets, grabbed a .45 pistol, a razor and a toothbrush, and raced out to a stake-sided truck, already idling and ready to move off. Burnett was the last on, pulled over the back of the truck's tailgate.

Lietwiler had to leave behind his beloved violin, along with his dress uniform and sword. Boarding at sea in the dark meant they could not load the crates of IBM parts. Lietwiler had given Callahan last-minute instructions regarding the dummy signals and the disposal of IBM crates. For all their shenanigans, Fort Callahan and Melvyn McCoy were staying on Corregidor to the bitter end.

At North Dock, the evacuation party boarded a Navy motorboat. As they headed into the inky night, Cabcaban Bay on

SCRAMBLE TO SAFETY

Bataan lit up with an explosion of stored aviation gas, bombs and ammunition. Nerves were already on edge when a line of tracer fire crossed the motorboat bow as it passed a minesweeper. The launch's coxswain hollered the minesweeper captain's name, identifying himself and explaining his presence with all the economy and urgency he could muster.

'I'm stopping everything going through tonight,' a voice called back. 'You can go ahead.'

The launch moved cautiously along the Bataan shoreline without spotting the sub. A crackle of small-arms fire seemed ominously near, with continual pinpricks of light. Flashes of brightness swept from thundering explosions. A voice on a passing boat said a sub was unloading out in the minefield, with a 'sweeper for protection. Motoring to the minefield, they passed under a bower of artillery fire from the guns and mortars of Corregidor. Shooting at Bataan over the narrow passage of water, they were desperately trying to halt the inevitable.

The coxswain found *Seadragon* tied to a tender, dropping off sacks with its lights shaded. Pulling alongside, the residue of Cast crossed the tender's deck to the submarine. As they boarded, a Japanese seaplane dropped a flare, briefly illuminating the bay, but there was no follow-up. As soon as the arrivals were clear of the conning tower, Commander Ferrall shouted, 'Let's get the hell out of here!'

Offloading stopped abruptly, ties were slipped and *Seadragon* headed out to sea. Forty minutes later, Bataan surrendered. Hundreds of troops and nurses were left to escape across the channel to Corregidor using boats, planks or anything else they could find that floated.

Instructed by Hoeffel to come back in two days and complete unloading, skipper Ferrall headed north, waited and returned in the late afternoon of 10 April. Two Japanese destroyers were sitting at the entrance to Manila Bay. *Seadragon* fired four torpedoes, all of which missed their targets, and the sub dived to avoid the retaliatory depth charges. All controls were operated by hand to avoid making detectable sounds; when the air became foul, white crystals were laid out on a sheet to absorb expelled carbon dioxide.

After hiding on the bottom until the early morning, the sub was raised to periscope level and found the warships had moved away. Told by radio from Corregidor not to enter the harbour but go back to Cebu and unload there, Ferrall made a dash for safety. On the way, a further instruction was received that Cebu had been overrun by the enemy. *Seadragon* was to go on to Fremantle.

Moving through the Macassar Strait at night, the vessel hit floating telegraph poles—flotsam from a Japanese merchantman torpedoed by the Allies—but the drama didn't end there. Running on the surface half awash, ready to dive if enemy air patrols came by, south of Borneo they encountered rough water with waves breaking over the conning tower. The hatch had been opened to let in air and rest the main air vent pumps. When a wave hit the conning tower and flipped the hatch shut, diesel engines started pumping air rapidly out of the vessel. Two of the biggest men on board were ordered to force the hatch open while the air ballast was vented. After a struggle they succeeded, and *Seadragon* was prevented from sinking slowly to the sea bottom.

They reached Fremantle on 26 April and were transferred to the destroyer USS *Barker*, which pushed through rough weather in the Great Australian Bight. The last of the Cast crew arrived at Melbourne on 6 May, a day after General Wainwright surrendered Corregidor to a Japanese assault force. Captain Hoeffel cabled from the island, 'ALL PUBLICATIONS AND MACHINES DESTROYED'. Two minutes later, the radio chief followed with, 'GOING OFF AIR GOOD LUCK AND GOODBYE CALLAHAN AND MCCOY.' All three men were taken prisoner by the Japanese. A year later, Melvyn McCoy escaped with nine others from a Mindanao POW camp, joined with Philippine guerrillas, and was taken by submarine to Australia.

The only member of Station Cast's personnel who was not evacuated was the cook, Arthur Thompson. He was deemed safe because he had no knowledge of Cast's code-breaking activities. Captured by the Japanese, he survived the war in a POW camp in Mongolia and commented later that he had found that there was a Japanese spy on Corregidor before the war. The Japanese had arrived on the island with names and pictures of Cast personnel, he said. They were not pleased to find that all had gone.

— ● —

Lieutenant-Commander Redfield 'Rosey' Mason, Admiral Hart's intelligence officer with the Asiatic Fleet, had flown from Java to Melbourne after passing Hart's instruction to Fabian to evacuate to Australia. Vice-Admiral Herbert Leary, the region's US Navy commander, assumed he was the officer in charge of the Corregidor unit and detailed him to arrange with the Australians for the unit to operate out of Melbourne. Mason met with Jack Newman and Eric Nave, who—thinking Fabian was still in charge of Cast—assumed that he must be head of OP-20-G in Washington.

It was decided that the American cryptanalysts would set up under the same roof as Nave's SIB, an arrangement similar to the one planned with the Dutch in Bandung. The two groups would operate independently, each reporting to its own navy, but would assist each other where possible and when this would benefit the Allied cause. In practice, the Australians would provide support to the Americans where required, but receive little in return.

It soon became clear that the expanded unit would need more than the available space in Victoria Barracks. The RAN group had taken on British escapees from Singapore and China, and the Cast detachment had absorbed a group of nine from OP-20-G. En route to Corregidor when war broke out, they had been stranded for some time in Darwin and only recently brought to Melbourne.

Rosey Mason had either been formally put in command of Cast or assumed command while Rudy Fabian was busy bringing the unit's records up to date, developing books of known code values and making arrangements with Jack Newman for supplies and services in Australia. The abrasive Mason was much like the Australian Cocky Long, running hither and thither, setting things up, giving advice, taking charge, without necessarily having much of an overall plan. Fabian was also abrasive, but unlike Mason (and Long) he stuck to the task, a natural administrator. Fabian and Mason were bound to tread on each other's toes before too long, and someone or something would have to give. It was symptomatic. Jockeying for prime position had become endemic in the relocated American command.

General MacArthur had arrived at Melbourne's Spencer Street Railway Station on 21 March and immediately installed himself and his family in the best suite in the Menzies Hotel. He told the Australian press the aircraft bringing him to Australia had been closely pursued by Japanese fighters, but that was untrue. A few days after he arrived, the Trustees Executive and Agency Company building in Collins Street was requisitioned as general headquarters of the Southwest Pacific Area (SWPA) command. From here, MacArthur would plan and direct a counteroffensive against the Japanese that was to culminate in the general's promised return to the Philippines.

In January, the US Army had installed a local headquarters at MacRobertson Girls High School in Albert Park, but it was deemed unsuitable for MacArthur's needs and was used instead for administration and supplies, along with the old wooden Repatriation Building on St Kilda Road. The intelligence group—Willoughby, Akin and Sherr—was accommodated in the school's chemistry lab.

SCRAMBLE TO SAFETY

The US Army in Melbourne was divided into factions based on where personnel had been before Melbourne. Each group tended to see the others as rivals or interlopers. MacArthur gathered around himself his cronies from the Philippines, who became known as the Bataan Gang. The exception was the Australian General Thomas Blamey, who had been recalled from the Middle East to take command of the Australian Military Forces. Most of MacArthur's senior officers were billeted at the Menzies Hotel and stayed aloof from the others when off duty. A large round table was set aside by the hotel for US personnel, but on the second day a sign appeared: 'This table reserved for members of General MacArthur's party.' MacArthur, however, ate in his suite alone or with his family.

With a workspace shortage expected in Victoria Barracks from further Cast evacuations, Long and Nave scouted about for alternative premises. They found a suitable building on Queens Road in Albert Park, on the fringe of the city centre. Monterey, a three-storey block of thirty-two single-bedroom apartments, was newly built and still unoccupied. No one had to be moved out for the new occupants to move in.

Three groups, located on different floors of the Monterey building, would work independently but in liaison. Jack Newman's Australian radio intercept group was put on the ground floor. The middle floor housed the former Cast unit, although only the first of the three evacuation parties had reached Melbourne at this stage. On the top floor was Nave's Special Intelligence Bureau, with its mix of naval and civilian recruits, to which had been added a handful of British escapees from Singapore and China. A new intercept station would be erected on six acres of requisitioned market gardens in Moorabbin, an outer southern suburb. It would be operated jointly by the US Navy and the RAN. Each country retained administrative autonomy, however, as it was assumed the arrangement would eventually end and the two naval groups would go in separate directions.

In the meantime, a way would have to be found to coordinate the mix of eccentrics, dogged processors, security obsessives and lone-wolf operators and shape this unnamed and ad-hoc sigint group into a powerful weapon in a war that was running badly against the Allies. The new organisation would eventually be given the innocuous title of Fleet Radio Unit Melbourne (FRUMEL). With all significant Japanese communication now on military, not diplomatic channels, the Pacific allies had much catching up to do. The lack of success on the battlefield was a source of anxiety for the Australian public. The barbarians were not yet at the gate, but they were certainly heading towards it. The ability of FRUMEL to get on top of its game would be an important factor in keeping them away.

Chapter 6

The turning of the tide

Rudy Fabian's world was the US Navy, and its enemies were his enemies. However, his biggest enemy wasn't the Japanese. The war against Japan was the focus of his professional life, but he didn't take it personally. His most despised foes were members of the US Army, who in his view were inept at everything they did.

Fabian disliked the British only a little less. To him, they always seemed to have a sneering contempt for Americans. The Australians who now surrounded him were basically a lower form of British, there to provide for America's needs while it regrouped for the counteroffensive. There was no question of giving anything to Australia in return. The US would be saving Australia—and the world—from the Japanese. That should be more than enough.

At the end of March 1942, the first code-breaker group from Corregidor began setting up shop as FRUMEL in Melbourne's Monterey building in readiness for the arrival of the rest of the Cast team from the Philippines. High cyclone fencing topped with barbed wire had been erected around the apartment block. New doors were cut in the walls between apartments, creating a rabbit warren of interconnecting offices. The US Navy placed armed petty officers on perimeter entrances and issued security passes to control movement between different parts of the building. Nothing on its exterior gave notice of its function.

Sandwiched between two floors of Australians, FRUMEL occupied apartments in the middle of the building, one of them reserved for IBM tabulators and other machinery on order from the US. For the time being, basic equipment and supplies would have to be found in Australia, but getting hold of the little that was available required a deal of wrangling and cutting through red tape. 'Daily I make a pest out of myself by practically making demands,' Fabian wrote to Washington. 'There is just one speed here—very slow.'

The 'locals', as he called them, did everything wrong. They were unpunctual and unreliable. The construction work took too long. They took too many days off and had no idea of the value of systems and protocols. He'd had similar problems with the Dutch at Bandung, but they were Europeans, so they merited at least some politeness. Fabian had forgotten that the US Navy hadn't worked on Sundays until the war started. Nor did it occur to him that the Australians might be less inclined to cooperate the more he let them know what he thought of them.

He soon found an attack dog to help him sort out these intransigent natives. Vice-Admiral Herbert Leary had been appointed commander of the ANZAC Fleet, a mix of Australian, New Zealand and American warships operating in the seas around north-eastern Australia. Tall, erect and ruddy-faced, Leary had a reputation as a disciplinarian and was widely disliked for his truculence and his grating voice. At Fabian's behest, he 'blasted' the locals to speed up preparation of Monterey for its new occupants. Restrictions were imposed on the circulation of documents to 'get the locals to understand the meaning of security'.

From the outset, Fabian provided daily briefings to Leary and senior US Navy officers in the ANZAC Fleet. He also briefed MacArthur separately, but MacArthur seldom used the information provided. Nor did he pass it on to the naval task forces under his command or allow Fabian to communicate directly with their commanders.

MacArthur had every reason to have doubts about FRUMEL. In the latter part of March, when Rosey Mason—thanks to Leary's confusion about his role in Cast—was in charge of the Melbourne station with Fabian working under him, the linguist Mason wrote a note cautioning that FRUMEL should not rely on traffic analysis without backup of decryption, because data could be misinterpreted or falsified by the enemy. Fabian added his own note that this wasn't an issue in the unit. An addressee on both notes, MacArthur might well have wondered whether FRUMEL knew what it was doing.

The impression may have lingered even after Mason returned to Washington in April and Fabian and the Australian Jack Newman took nominal joint control of operations in Monterey. In a loose and undefined relationship, each country retained its autonomy and answered to its own navy. Fabian and Newman decided which groups would be responsible for which areas of sigint operation, which in practice meant that Fabian would decide and Newman would agree. Newman was perceived as rigid and British, but he was malleable, unlike the remote and suspicious Eric Nave.

The principal naval code-breaking challenge, JN-25B, was reserved for FRUMEL. Other codes were left to the Australians and the English working in Nave's Special Intelligence Bureau. Having taken the glamour code for his team, Fabian had little knowledge of or interest in what the people upstairs in SIB were doing, and always assumed it was minor and largely irrelevant. In fact, SIB was continuing to work on Mandated Territories traffic, tracking the shipping of Japanese troops and supplies, and on enemy submarine communications in the JN-4 code.

In addition to the Englishmen who had joined Nave's unit— Cooper, Archer, Graves, and the linguist Alan Merry, who'd arrived from FECB in December—more Australian linguists were recruited for training in cryptography. Nineteen-year-old Ronald Bond arrived at Spencer Street railway station in February and was met by the former academic Dale Trendall. An honours graduate in Greek and Latin from Trendall's department at the University of Sydney, Bond had written to his former professor begging him 'to extricate me from my pit of misery', an army camp in Sydney. Bond's Classics master at high school had been Ath Treweek. Nave arranged for the newcomer to be promoted to corporal so he could afford to live in the same boarding house on St Kilda Road as Trendall.

When SIB moved to Monterey, Trendall and Bond worked in what had been the bedroom of a top-floor apartment, and Archer and Graves, with two female clerical assistants, moved into the intended living room. While Nave, Jamieson, Treweek and the two mathematicians worked on naval codes, this group decoded intercepts in Fuji, a high-grade diplomatic cipher, and forwarded Purple intercepts to Bletchley Park.

Nine years older than Fabian, Commander Nave—still in the Royal Navy—was higher ranked than the American and had far more technical expertise in code breaking. However, Fabian was an able service administrator, well regarded by his superiors. He was often tactless, but that didn't matter much in the military. One of his men described Fabian as a 'tough cookie', though 'not too bad once you understood him'. Forceful and tenacious, he didn't mind how many noses had to be put out of joint to get things done. His superiors, and particularly Leary, welcomed that.

No doubt Nave entertained thoughts of heading the joint agency, but Fabian was a dominant personality and his people clearly called the shots. There is no evidence that he made any effort to accommodate Nave's aspirations or his pride. Instead, he treated him as a slow-witted local, periodically in need of counselling.

THE TURNING OF THE TIDE

The men who worked in the ordinary-looking apartment block at Albert Park were a kind of secret society. They had undertaken never to reveal the nature of their activities to anyone, not even their spouses. Nave, Helena and their two small children shared a house in genteel Hawthorn with Eric's brother, Lionel. Treweek and his wife rented a flat in Jolimont, near the cricket ground on the fringe of Melbourne's downtown. Trendall and Bond were a short walk from work in their St Kilda Road boarding house. Work was left undiscussed at home or dismissed to family and friends as routine clerical toil. It was easier for the Americans, who were at least far from their families. They rented houses in small groups or boarded with local families, giving vague answers to any questions about their military roles.

— • —

Coming to their shadowy world each day by tram or on foot, the Monterey crew passed through a city tense with expectation of a Japanese air attack. People crowded around radio stores to hear news broadcasts, which were always preceded by the martial music of 'The British Grenadiers'. Children wore ID discs and carried air-raid bags with cotton wool for their ears and a barley sugar to suck on in case bombs ever exploded near them. Clothes were made from recycled materials—blankets, hessian and used parachute silk—and young women drew 'seams' down their legs with eyebrow pencil so it would look as if they were wearing stockings.

As the number of American uniforms appearing on the streets of Melbourne grew, a sense of hope crept in. By the beginning of April, Australian soldiers were returning from the Middle East, arriving in the city by train and heading north to the military camp at Seymour. The public mood became more optimistic; the hysteria diminished. The Japanese advance continued, but it had slowed. Perhaps it could be halted if the Allies could find some way of gaining the ascendancy.

The army's facility at Park Orchards continued to deliver intercepts to Nave's SIB, but they were mostly consular messages whose usefulness was diminishing. FRUMEL was interested only in naval messages, to receive which a new array of antennas had been built at Moorabbin, in Melbourne's south-east. Eight high wooden masts strung with wires were erected behind barbed-wire fencing on six acres of requisitioned market gardens. Two houses had been taken over: a weatherboard cottage with a wrap-around verandah, and a small brick home. With neither electricity nor sewerage, improvised services were provided. Several large huts were hastily erected for accommodation and administration, but their unlined walls and ceilings offered little protection against the coming winter or the heat of summer.

The first personnel to arrive were five young women from the WRANS (Women's Royal Australian Naval Service) and the early group of US Navy radio operators evacuated from Corregidor. Deeply tanned by the Philippine sun, the uniformed Americans looked out of place in the semi-rural locality. Though open and friendly, they were evasive about the nature of their work. The WRANS, on the other hand, were conspicuously un-exotic. Known as 'Jack Newman's girls', many had been drafted from country towns and parachuted into the role with a quick course at Victoria Barracks in *kana* Morse. The gentlemanly Director of Naval Communications took a paternal interest in these young trainees' welfare as they grappled with unfamiliar tasks.

A cool reception greeted the five girls sent to Moorabbin. The Americans, all men, had expected to be joined by Australian men, and at first the atmosphere at the radio facility was strained. The WRANS took down intercepts by hand in International Morse—*kana* Morse had single- or double-character equivalents in International Morse—and later transcribed them into *kana*. To the American telegraphists, who typed intercepts directly on their *kana* typewriters, they were like bumpkins from the backblocks.

But as time went on, they warmed to the Australian women and their lack of sophistication. Getting hold of more *kana* typewriters, they showed them the US Navy method—with Jack Newman's strong support. The RAN had ordered the WRANS to pay for all meals taken in the mess with their sustenance allowance. When the Americans learned of this, they split their own sustenance allowance of eighteen shillings with the Australians.

Working conditions required other adjustments to cultural differences. Unused to central heating, the Australians wanted the windows in work areas left open, but the Americans, unlike the locals, were catching sniffles and colds. As there were more of them, the decision was eventually made to keep windows closed. In the rush to set up the Moorabbin station, living space had been neglected. Newman complained to the military assets people about the lack of privacy in the requisitioned cottage. 'At present no doors are fitted on to their building, and the Wrans ratings are exposed to the gaze of passers-by,' he wrote. 'There is no form of curtaining to restrain public curiosity except blackout curtains.'

Despite the primitive conditions and the need for adjustment to different expectations, Moorabbin's intercepts of Japanese naval traffic were productive. Success had spread the Imperial Japanese Navy far across the Pacific. Powerful transmitters were needed to communicate with ships over such a wide area, and their signals could be picked up as far away as Melbourne. Despatch riders spluttered out of Moorabbin on motorbikes every two hours, day and night, carrying sealed messages to Monterey for FRUMEL to decode and translate. The success of that phase of the intercept process would depend on the penetration of Japanese naval codes, in particular the current version of JN-25.

— • —

While Station Cast was carrying out its staged withdrawal from Corregidor, a palace revolution was taking place at head office in Washington. The failure to anticipate Pearl Harbor and a lack of coordination between Naval Communications and Naval Intelligence had created acrimony and recrimination between the two sections. The best way to deflect responsibility is to find someone else to shoulder the blame, and Laurance Safford was that someone. As head of OP-20-G, the Navy's Codes and Signals section in Washington, he was in favour of decentralising its function, giving the outposts—and his acolytes, Rochefort and Fabian—greater autonomy. One of Safford's deputies, Jack Redman, believed Washington should have stronger control. He was echoed by Joe Wenger, another OP-20-G senior officer. Wenger's view was that Hypo and Cast should do only the more immediate combat intelligence while Washington concentrated on research (that is, code breaking), analysis and tactical projections.

Safford might have been the chief of OP-20-G, but Redman had influence where it mattered. His brother was Rear-Admiral Joseph Redman, who was about to be promoted to Director of Naval Communications, the office to which Safford reported. The pugnacious Redman brothers hunted as a tag team. Joe Redman proposed a restructure of OP-20-G and Admiral King, commander-in-chief of the US Fleet, approved. Jack Redman became head of radio combat intelligence and Wenger was put in charge of cryptanalysis (decoding and translation). Safford was sidelined as head of administrative support and research. There was nothing he could do about it: in the shadow world, there are no courts of appeal. Redman and Wenger would control the outposts, while Safford and his skilled code breakers would generate the raw material.

So focused was Joe Rochefort on atoning for the shame of Pearl Harbor that he didn't recognise he was on a collision course with the Redman brothers. Rudy Fabian, on the other hand, was too far away to be watched closely. FRUMEL was not told of the changes in Washington. As late as May 1942, three months later, both Lietwiler and Fabian were writing letters to Safford congratulating him on his continuing leadership of OP-20-G. Fabian accepted technical guidance and support from Washington when it came, while he set up in Melbourne and continued to service his fleet commander, Admiral Leary. Since his team had only limited expertise, and he did not want to bring Nave, the most experienced code breaker in the building, into the spotlight, Fabian depended on OP-20-G for new code values.

Under Redman, American signals intelligence operated more efficiently, but the changes disrupted existing working relationships, too often the creative lifeblood of code breaking. Differences in intelligence analysis and forecasts became increasingly apparent as the different sigint units began to be competitive about the intelligence they gathered rather than try to find common ground in their estimates.

— ● —

The breaking of Japan's naval codes and decryption of its radio messages was an arcane but tedious process requiring great patience. Military messages were encrypted by codebook, not by the cipher machine used for diplomatic messages. Most naval operational messages were encoded from the JN-25 book, with five-digit numbers substituting for various Japanese characters, words and phrases. The coded message was then re-encrypted by adding random five-digit numbers from a second book to each number in the message using 'false' (non-carrying) arithmetic. The resulting series of five-digit numbers was the transmitted message. At the receiving end, additive tables would show which numbers to subtract to reveal the underlying coded message, and the codebook would enable it to be deciphered. Without either aid, the Allied cryptographers had to break two codes: first the additive cipher, then the message code itself.

CODE BREAKERS

A code breaker looks for patterns in coded messages. The more intercepts are available in a given code, the better the chance of finding patterns. With mechanised tabulators rapidly churning through large numbers of options, the ability to discover patterns increased significantly. Japan's military messages were often in a particular format, and this would help the code breakers infer words. Further help came from occasional Japanese carelessness. In the rush of military action, or when new codebooks were still being sent to the widely dispersed Japanese navy, a message might be sent in both old and new code. Or a transmitter—frustrated at being told a message was unclear or incomplete—might re-send a section of a message in plain text. When some words in a message were known, it became possible to make shrewd guesses at the unknown words. From this long and patient process, the values of a particular code were accumulated.

At the time the first Cast evacuees reached Melbourne, the Allies were making slow progress penetrating JN-25B. Some 60 per cent of Japanese naval traffic was being intercepted, though only about 40 per cent could be analysed because of limited time and staff. Only 10 to 15 per cent of the code groups in any message could be read, but those fragments, in conjunction with the patterns revealed by traffic analysis, provided snippets of intelligence at least.

One actual decrypt ran: 'KAGA AND (blank) (blank) LESS (blank) AND (blank) WILL DEPART BUNGO CHANNEL (blank) MAY 4TH AND ARRIVE (blank) (blank).' This might not tell the analysts everything, but when the source and intended recipient were known, it gave some clues as well as the broad context of the message. The code breakers would spot associations and make guesses. They knew that *Kaga* was a Japanese aircraft carrier and where Bungo Channel was. Tacking these snippets together like pieces in a jigsaw puzzle, they built up a picture of the enemy's intention, incomplete, but good enough to indicate what might be coming.

THE TURNING OF THE TIDE

Particularly with the JN-25 codes, messages would often mention locations and operations for which the five-digit code groups were already known before their meaning was known with any certainty. The Americans gave these names two-letter labels, generally derived from the suspected meaning, until the meaning was confirmed. The two-letter label would often continue to be used as decode shorthand. In February 1942, for example, some intercepts referred to a planned action involving a location the decrypters inferred was Port Moresby. They tentatively called the action MO Operation, but they uncovered little about it. As it happened, Japan's intended amphibious attack on Port Moresby was postponed after *Kaga* was torpedoed.

A Japanese despatch late in March referred to fighters from Rabaul supporting the main task force in a campaign the cryptanalysts called RZP—but where was RZP? At the same time, the army's wireless station in Darwin picked up naval air-control traffic from Timor, the staging base for the previous month's air attacks on Darwin. It showed increased movement to airfields in Rabaul and the recently occupied Salamaua and Lae in New Guinea. This could indicate preparation for a major offensive somewhere in the vicinity. There were reasons to suspect RZP might refer to the seas around eastern New Guinea, the Solomon Sea and the Coral Sea to its south.

By early April 1942, Rudy Fabian's first group was operating in Melbourne, although it had no experienced code breakers. He would call on Australian analysts and linguists from time to time, but only if they were uniformed members of the military. He never consulted civilians or the British escapees from Singapore, or Eric Nave, except in the rare instance that an instruction from above required it. The Americans in Melbourne had reserved JN-25B for themselves, but—as in the Philippines—they relied on input from elsewhere.

Two factors were crucial to the further penetration of the code by teams in Hawaii and Washington. The increased volume of radio traffic as the Japanese prepared for their coming offensive provided these units with more intercepts to sift through and better opportunities to discern patterns. As well, the planned 1 April replacement of JN-25B was postponed until 1 May because the Japanese navy was so widely dispersed it had difficulty getting new codebooks to all locations. The Allies were able to add to their store of JN-25B values instead of starting again with a new JN-25C.

— • —

Some of Nave's team members were drifting into FRUMEL's orbit. Jim Jamieson was one, a navy man not enamoured of the academics and civilians who made up much of Nave's team. Ath Treweek, whose precise personality masked high self-esteem, found Nave rather stuffy and old-school. Sensing a shift in power at Monterey with the arrival of Fabian and his American team, Treweek redefined himself. No longer an academic but now a military man, he attached himself to the Americans while still nominally part of Nave's unit.

During April 1942, clues about the coming RZP offensive accumulated in dribs and drabs. On 3 April, Joe Rochefort's Hypo team in Hawaii declared that reinforced air units in the Solomon Islands were among 'numerous indications which point to [an] impending offensive from Rabaul base'. A few days later, the US Navy's OP-20-G in Washington advised Admiral King that Japanese air-search patterns indicated a strong interest in the Coral Sea. The two units were competing for the attention of the Navy's senior planners. At the same time, the carrier *Kaga*, undergoing repairs at Sasebo naval base near Nagasaki, was transferred to Vice-Admiral Shigeyoshi Inouye's South Seas Force and became an addressee in messages between it and the Japanese Combined Fleet. A decrypted intercept on 9 April was reconstructed in Melbourne as a request for a 'REPORT ON PROGRESS OF REPAIRS TO KAGA; AS SHE IS SCHEDULED TO PARTICIPATE IN RZP CAMPAIGN, WE DESIRE REPAIRS BE COMPLETED AS SOON AS POSSIBLE.'

By 10 April, Admiral Chuichi Nagumo's fast carrier strike force had turned for home after its successful Indian Ocean raid. Although John Lietwiler's Corregidor decrypt had enabled the British commander there to withdraw his Far Eastern Fleet out of harm's way, the raid had accounted for over thirty British ships, including the carrier *Hermes*. The naval base at Colombo had been devastated. The attention of Japan's strategic planners was already deep into the next phase of their Pacific campaign, generating considerable radio traffic out of Rabaul in particular. The capture of Port Moresby would prevent the use of the town as a forward base for any counter-offensive by MacArthur. Moresby and Rabaul could also become support bases for the Japanese seizure of New Caledonia, Fiji and Samoa, cutting supply lines between Australia and the United States. This would seal Japan's substantial gains and could put the US in a position where a negotiated settlement was its best option.

The increased transmission affected Moorabbin, the naval intercept station closest to Japan now that Corregidor and Hong Kong were out of action. Transcribed messages were being rushed into the city by motorcycle every couple of hours, and with JN-25B values supplied from Honolulu and Washington, FRUMEL was able to piece together partial decrypts. The team's achievements in the Philippines had been modest at best, and they were only just getting up to speed, but the smell of opportunity enthused the small group. With skilled linguists in the building, smart guesswork sometimes exposed new code values. When the second Cast group arrived on 19 April, they would have greater capacity to sift through the material that was pouring in.

In the middle of that month, an intercepted order from Rear-Admiral Chuichi Hara instructed the 5th Carrier Division's two aircraft carriers, *Shokaku* and *Zuikaku*, which were leaving the Indian Ocean, to divert to Truk in the Mandated Territories by the 25th instead of returning to Japan. The order was also picked up by the British in Colombo, with the additional intelligence that these carriers were to lead the MO Operation strike force. MO Operation, suspected of targeting Port Moresby in some way, was back on the agenda.

On 17 April, Naval Commander-in Chief King gave Admiral Chester Nimitz, based at Pearl Harbor, command of the Coral Sea area. Nimitz examined his options, rejecting FRUMEL's view that the Japanese might move on MO Operation as soon as 21 April. He doubted the enemy could assemble a strike force before the beginning of May, following the Indian Ocean raid.

The admiral's daily intelligence briefings by his intelligence officer, Ed Layton, included analysis provided by Layton's close friend, Joe Rochefort. Nimitz saw Layton, who had studied in Japan, as a source of insights into Japanese thinking. Layton talked to Rochefort over a secure telephone several times a day in preparation for briefing the admiral every morning at 7.55. Along with Hypo reports and assessments, Rochefort supplied material from other sources, particularly FRUMEL, without attribution. His argument would be that it was irrelevant to Nimitz where the intelligence had originated, only that he got it. A sign above Rochefort's desk proclaimed: 'We can accomplish anything provided no one cares who gets the credit.'

On 18 April, Colonel Jimmy Doolittle led an audacious air raid on Tokyo from two aircraft carriers. Although it caused little damage, the unexpected penetration of Japanese air space threw the high command off balance, and their alarm showed up in increased radio traffic. A new target code appeared in the messages, inferred as meaning Tulagi in the Solomon Islands, where a seaplane base might be under consideration. With the carriers *Hornet* and *Enterprise* occupied with Doolittle in the north

THE TURNING OF THE TIDE

Pacific, Nimitz ordered *Yorktown*, already in the south Pacific for carrier-borne air raids on Lae and Salamaua, and *Lexington*, which was refitting in Pearl Harbor, to get to the Coral Sea by the beginning of May, ready for battle. *Hornet* and *Enterprise* were to replenish in Hawaii and join them two weeks later. On his flagship, *Yorktown*, Admiral Frank Fletcher would be in command of the Allies' spoiling action.

Over the next fortnight, intelligence from radio intercepts built up a piecemeal picture of the planned offensive. On 23 April, Admiral Inouye issued South Seas Force Order No. 13. It was probably delivered by plane from Truk rather than by radio, but elements of it were extracted from decrypts over the following days. Three carriers—*Zuikaku*, *Shokaku* and the incorrectly identified *Ryukaku* (it was actually the light carrier *Shoho*)—and twenty-four escorting warships were to form a strike force. The carriers would provide cover of 127 aircraft for the invasion fleet's transport ships. *Kaga* was apparently still not seaworthy. Occupation forces were identified as RZP and RXB, thought to refer to Port Moresby and Tulagi. FRUMEL deciphered the attack date as 2 May; Hypo thought it was 10 May. In any case, the operation appeared to involve two assault landings.

Activity in support of the offensive had been detected, the Rabaul-based *Kasuga* returning on the 23rd to offload planes and supplies. Air attacks would be key to the operation, and not just on the prime targets. An army intercept indicated that the Japanese would step up their intermittent air raids on northern Australia from 24 April, probably to draw Allied defences away from the Coral Sea area. MacArthur's team in Melbourne saw a possibility of carrier-launched raids on Cape York, Townsville and perhaps even Brisbane. This was confirmed a few days later in an intercepted order to 'RESTRICT THE ENEMY FLEET'S MOVEMENTS [by attacking] VARIOUS AREAS ALONG THE NORTH COAST OF AUSTRALIA'. Washington decrypted a request for a thousand copies of a map of northern Australia. Did the enemy intend to push on from New Guinea?

On Monterey's middle floor, FRUMEL bristled with newfound purpose. Intercepts streaming in from Moorabbin showed a concentration of air attack forces in Rabaul. A 27 April signal used Truk radio rather than shipboard transmitters to conceal that the three Japanese aircraft carriers were in Truk. The Japanese sent other dummy traffic from the Mandated Territories, but the analysts in Melbourne recognised the call signs as fakes. Treweek and Jamieson, familiar with the traffic from those islands, became part of the cat-and-mouse game in keeping track of the enemy while the rest of SIB was isolated in its top-storey accommodation. Deliberately or not, the Australians were separating into two camps. Nave was conscious of the split but unable to prevent it. In charge of the female operators at Moorabbin and patronised by Fabian, Jack Newman joined with the Americans in their excitement. He was still resentful that Nave hadn't sided with him against Cocky Long a year before.

— • —

Sometimes there were red herrings . . . or there appeared to be. Both Melbourne and Washington picked up references to another operation, seemingly on the Aleutian Islands in the far north Pacific, but Joe Rochefort dismissed their conclusions as a misreading of the MO Operation code. Two days later, Hypo intercepted a despatch notice for maps of the Aleutians, but no connection was made with the disregarded operation code. Rochefort didn't need to make it; he had triumphed in his battle with OP-20-G for the spotlight. Washington had reluctantly backed away from disputing Hypo's forecasts, and accepted its estimate of the timing and objective of the coming assault. As it would turn out, MO Operation was only a curtain-raiser for Japan's Pacific strategy. Admiral Yamamoto had a bolder move in mind, and the Aleutians were part of it.

THE TURNING OF THE TIDE

The end of the month approached, and the Japanese changed their call signs and location designation codes. This was usually an indication of an imminent attack, but FRUMEL intercepted a message with old and new designation codes, enabling the new designators to be matched to already-known locations. An even better break for the Allies was Hypo's interception of coded advice that the introduction of a new version of JN-25 had again been postponed, this time to 27 May.

Unknown to the Japanese, the dice were rolling in favour of the Allies. An invasion force of 400 troops set out from Rabaul for Tulagi in the Solomon Islands on 30 April, in the opening move of the offensive. The light carrier *Shoho*, coming southward from Truk, would provide air cover. MO Operation was under way, its invasion fleets travelling under radio silence. A seaplane base in Tulagi would provide support for the assault on Port Moresby, the second phase and prime objective of this offensive.

Traffic analysts, shuttled between Moorabbin and Monterey, noticed a sudden drop in radio activity out of Rabaul and Truk.

'Looks like the wagons are rolling,' commented one, on returning to the city.

The FRUMEL crew kept a watchful eye on events as they unfolded. With Japan's warships silent, much relied on the ability of the analysts to draw astute inferences. Scraps of communication from patrol aircraft and the like, decrypted on the top floor, indicated the movement of the radio black hole. Would that course reflect the picture they had constructed over the preceding month?

Officially, no one in the military was to reveal any more about their own or the enemy's activities than was necessary for personnel to carry out allotted functions. The intercept operators at Moorabbin never knew what their messages said or how they were assessed, but the analysts and translators at Monterey could extract more intelligence from material that came to them if they swapped notes. Each built a general understanding of MO Operation's aims and planned deployment. Having produced little of value in the Philippines, they waited in trepidation to see how their picture of MO would compare with the reality. They may not have known where Nimitz would put his ships in response—he had no need to share that information with them—but they thought they knew what the Japanese would do. They could then make educated guesses at the Allied commander's likely moves.

The locals working alongside them—uniformed cryptographers and Newman's girls—were drawn into the tension. Despite security restrictions on movement in the building, and despite Fabian's disdain for them, the Australians at Monterey inevitably crossed paths with many of the Americans there. Eric Nave, however, wasn't part of that infiltration. He moved further to the side, partly as a result of the polarised command structure and partly of his own accord. He began looking elsewhere for people who might make use of his experience, but that search went unnoticed by Monterey's workers. Focused on what was coming through the airwaves, they had little time to register the standoff between Nave and his American counterpart.

Intelligence reports would have persuaded the Japanese to expect little resistance on Tulagi, a small island on the northern side of Guadalcanal. Its European civilian residents had been evacuated to Australia in February, leaving some fifty Australians on the island, commandos and RAAF men servicing four Catalina flying boats. Tulagi had been bombed daily from Rabaul since 25 April. On 1 May, one of the Catalinas was destroyed. The invaders probably knew the Australians left in their remaining three seaplanes the next day, but it wouldn't have mattered anyway. Three patrol planes weren't much threat to the might of the Imperial Japanese Navy.

Zuikaku and *Shokaku* departed from Truk the day after *Shoho*, moving around the Solomons to head south into the Coral Sea. Not expected to be needed to support the Tulagi landing force, they were to meet the Port Moresby invasion force of eleven transport ships carrying 5000 soldiers. This armada would leave Rabaul on 4 May for the 1500-kilometre journey with an escort of cruiser and six destroyers. The fleet would head straight across the Solomon Sea to the Coral Sea, where air cover would be provided by the two carriers coming from Truk.

Little opposition was expected until they approached Port Moresby. Neither five seaplanes patrolling from Rabaul nor two submarines reconnoitring the nearby ocean had spotted any Allied warships in the vicinity. The Japanese knew from their intercepts that three of the US carriers were in the central Pacific. Although they didn't know where the fourth carrier was, there was nothing to suggest it was anywhere nearby. No American carrier response was expected until the operation was well under way.

The American carrier *Yorktown* was in fact already in the area, but on 20 April had put in to Tonga, beyond the range of Japan's land-based bombers, for maintenance and provisioning. A week later, it departed to rendezvous with *Lexington* in the Coral Sea, meeting it north of New Caledonia on the morning of 1 May. While *Lexington* spent the next three days refuelling, *Yorktown* headed north towards Guadalcanal. MacArthur's headquarters had notified Fletcher that air patrols from New Guinea had sighted the Tulagi invasion force approaching the southern Solomons. The admiral decided the time had come to show his hand.

Moorabbin, meanwhile, was picking up signals in the naval air–ground code. The strike force carriers, tasked with delivering nine Zeros to reinforce the Rabaul base on the way to the Coral Sea, had struck bad weather. After two unsuccessful attempts at delivery, the fighters were forced to return to their carriers, one plane being ditched in the ocean so the fleet could keep to MO Operation's schedule. Monterey's analysts were able to track the passage of *Zuikaku* and *Shokaku* and, encouragingly, it confirmed their earlier estimates.

On 3 May, Japanese naval troops invaded the undefended island of Tulagi and began building a seaplane base there. With radio silence concealing the landings from Allied eavesdroppers, the aircraft from *Shoho* covering the landing saw no action. The island captured, *Shoho* refuelled and moved across the Coral Sea to support the assault on Port Moresby. Submarines set up a patrol line to detect Allied naval forces approaching from the east, little knowing that American warships were already in the Coral Sea.

The Japanese were confident that a major operation was progressing undetected and as planned, but their complacency was soon to be shattered. The next morning, from the other side of Guadalcanal, *Yorktown* launched three strikes on Tulagi with forty dive-bombers and fighters. Three mine-sweepers were sunk, and the destroyer *Kikuzuki* was so badly damaged it had to be beached and abandoned.

Moorabbin intercepted a stunned signal to Admiral Takeo Takagi, uncertain which direction the carrier-launched raid had come from. Word of the decoded message reverberated around Monterey. This was the sort of advantage sigint had been trying to provide for commanders. Finally it was having some success. Predictions of the Tulagi invasion based on radio intelligence had proved accurate, and evidently the American air response had been built on them.

The signal was also received by Admiral Inouye, who was commanding the South Seas Force from the cruiser *Kashima*. Having lost his supposed advantage of surprise, he was forced to improvise a reconfigured tactical plan for the operation's second phase. But because his submarine screen had sighted no ships, he incorrectly assumed there was only one US carrier in the vicinity and that it was out in the central Pacific.

The main Japanese strike force, refuelling 600 kilometres north of Guadalcanal, immediately launched an air search in that direction. *Yorktown* had withdrawn to the south for a prearranged rendezvous with the *Lexington* task force and a joint Australian–American warship force under the Australian Rear-Admiral John Crace. Patrolling too far east, the searchers found no sign of the Allied force, and returned at nightfall empty-handed and mystified.

The failure of the search prompted Admiral Inouye to rethink his assumption. Perhaps US carriers were already in the Coral Sea. A signal from Inouye to Admiral Takagi on the strike force, intercepted and decoded in Melbourne, ordered patrols of that stretch of ocean. If the Allies already knew of the Japanese offensive, there was less need for radio silence and a greater need to coordinate logistics.

Another decrypt reported—incorrectly, as it turned out—that the Moresby invasion fleet was in the Coral Sea and would be joined the next day by the Tulagi Force, which had finished its airbase-building task. At about the same time, MacArthur was advising Fletcher and Nimitz that patrol planes had seen a carrier and escorts in the western Solomon Sea. It was the invasion force, with *Shoho* in support. An attack by three B-17 bombers from Port Moresby made little impact and was driven away. *Yorktown* headed north and in the darkness was briefly only 130 kilometres from *Shoho* before both changed direction, neither aware of the other's proximity.

Takagi's carrier force entered the Coral Sea from the east in the early hours of 6 May. A morning patrol from Tulagi sighted *Yorktown*, but Takagi's fleet was then refuelling at maximum flying range from the American ship. The US task force was under low cloud cover and would be hard to find. Takagi's planes didn't have enough fuel for the luxury of a protracted search. Rather than attack in those circumstances, the Japanese admiral sent his two carriers with two destroyers towards *Yorktown*'s reported position with a view to attacking at first light the next day.

Although the protagonists hadn't commenced battle, Melbourne's cryptographers were elated. The evidence they had

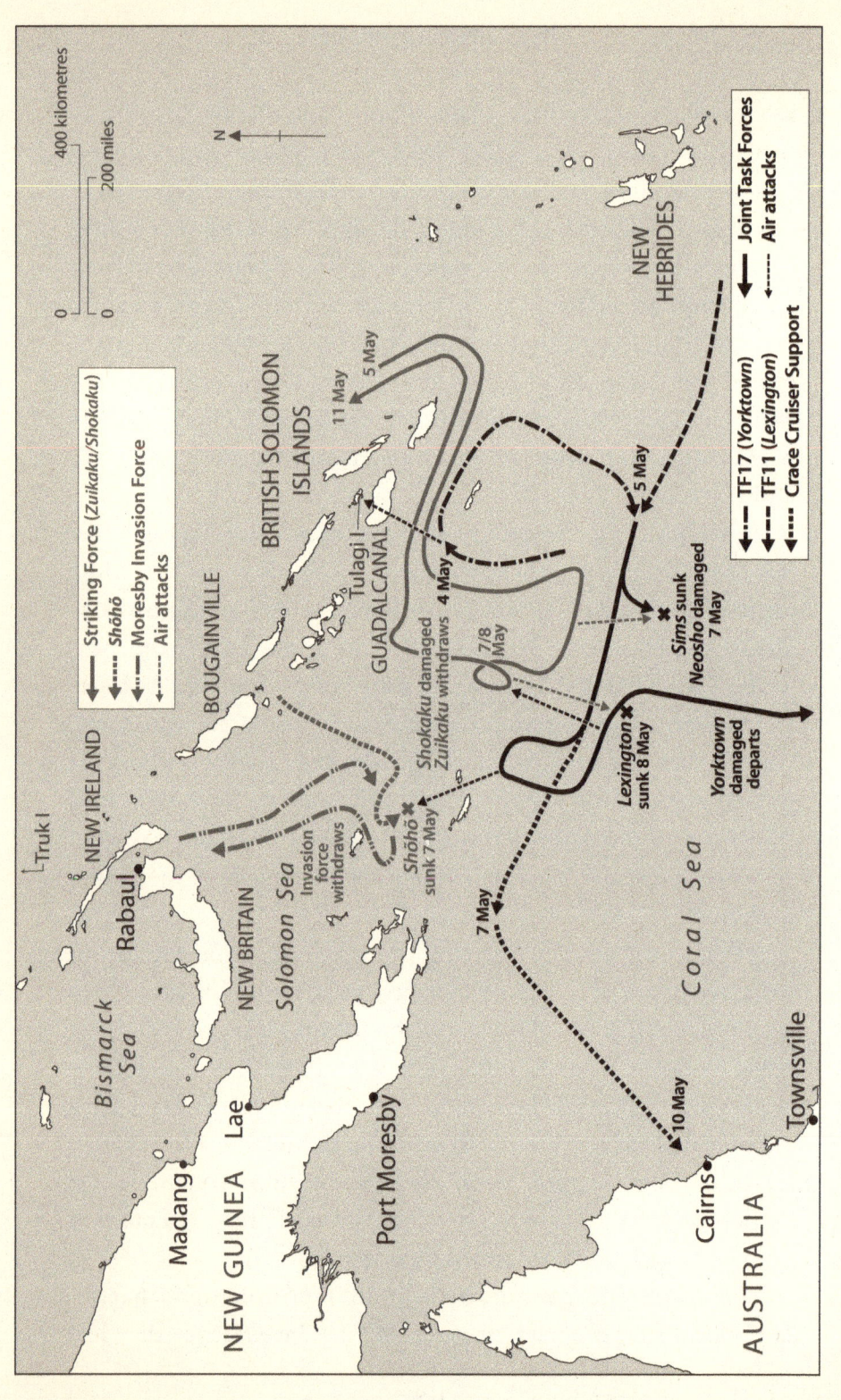

Map 2: The Battle of the Coral Sea, 1942

decoded had come in scattered fragments, but intelligence estimates based on it were proving quite accurate. The Allied naval forces were now strongly placed to disrupt a major enemy operation. There was little the Monterey people could do now—remote monitoring has little to offer in the heat of battle—but collect what information they could and try to deduce the likely outcome.

At first light on 7 May, Admiral Fletcher sent *Yorktown*'s dive bombers out to search for Takagi's carriers, while the Japanese commander, 560 kilometres to the east, sent patrols to scout the area where *Yorktown* had been sighted the day before. At 7.30 a.m., a Japanese pilot reported locating 'one carrier, one cruiser and three destroyers' to the south. An attack was immediately launched from *Shokaku* and *Zuikaku*.

Shortly after, another Japanese scout reported seeing the American carriers to the west. Confused by the conflicting sightings, Takagi continued with the strike under way but moved his fleet nearer to the second reported location. Attack planes reached the first location to find an oiler and a destroyer, but no carrier. The oiler had been misidentified. The two ships were attacked and sunk, but Takagi now realised the American carriers were probably between him and the invasion convoy he was supposed to be protecting. His whole operation was in peril.

American pilots had meanwhile sighted the Japanese invasion force, misidentified it, and then miscoded the report. Believing this was the main Japanese carrier force, Fletcher ordered an air strike. Arriving at the target location through cloud and mist, the American aircraft found the light carrier *Shoho* preparing to launch its own strike force and ill-equipped to defend itself. American bombs and torpedoes tore *Shoho* apart, and it sank in the late morning. The *Lexington* squadron leader radioed, 'Scratch one flat-top.'

The American aircraft returned with the whereabouts of Japan's fleet carriers unknown and the weather deteriorating. Fletcher decided that if the carriers could be located, it would be too late in the day to mount an attack. He preferred to hold off and remain concealed beneath thick cloud cover. After the loss of *Shoho*, Inouye ordered the invasion convoy to withdraw temporarily to the north until the enemy carrier forces could be dealt with.

Both sides spent the afternoon pursuing wrong assumptions from incorrect reconnaissance reports. Japanese planes took off from carriers in squally conditions and found nothing but enemy aircraft. Taken by surprise, they scattered with some losses. Three came across the American carriers after nightfall and, mistaking them for their own, circled to land until anti-aircraft fire drove them away. Takagi had to turn on his warships' searchlights to guide the stragglers back, but he now had some idea where the enemy carriers were located.

As the second day of the Battle of the Coral Sea dawned, the skies were clearing over the American carriers, the low-hanging cloud having moved north over the Japanese force. In the early morning, a patrol spotted the Japanese through a hole in the clouds about the same time as a plane from *Shokaku* found the Americans. Both sides raced to launch their strike aircraft.

Yorktown's dive bombers caused heavy damage to the flight deck of *Shokaku*. Unable to continue functioning, it withdrew from the battlefield while *Zuikaku* remained hidden in a rain squall under low clouds. Japanese torpedo bombers were meanwhile attacking *Lexington*, buckling avgas storage tanks, rupturing a water main and forcing engine boilers to shut down. The *Yorktown* flight deck was penetrated with a semi-armour-piercing bomb, and Japanese torpedoes caused damage below its waterline. By the afternoon, sparks had ignited gasoline fumes on *Lexington* and it was burning out of control. The carrier was abandoned and scuppered before nightfall.

Admiral Fletcher assessed his position that afternoon. Both of his carriers were badly damaged, he had lost many fighters and he could no longer refuel with the early loss of the oiler. Believing both *Shokaku* and *Zuikaku* were still operational, Fletcher withdrew from the battle.

Admiral Takagi told his superior that his pilots reported sinking two American carriers, but aircraft losses meant he now had no air cover for the invasion force. When his patrol planes sighted Admiral Crace's force waiting near New Guinea, Admiral Inouye recalled the invasion convoy to Rabaul, postponing MO Operation to 3 July. The two carriers and their escorts followed, *Zuikaku* heading to Rabaul and *Shokaku* returning to Japan for repairs.

The decoders and analysts at FRUMEL had tried as best they could to follow the two-day battle, but combat generally moves too fast to provide long-distance radio intelligence. Japanese messages were sometimes over-optimistic, and an alternative version was not available to people who didn't know the US Navy's code or have any good reason to break into it. However, when Inouye's recall of the invasion convoy was intercepted and decoded, a collective sigh of relief ran through the building. They knew then that the mighty Japanese navy had failed to meet its objective, and that they had played a part in achieving that.

The Battle of the Coral Sea was famously the first naval battle in history where participating ships never sighted or fired at each other. In the unfamiliarity of combat between carrier-launched aircraft, some wrong judgements were made. Japanese losses were lighter and the only remaining carrier, *Zuikaku*, should have been more than a match for Crace's fleet with no air cover, but thanks partly to excessive Japanese caution, an invasion force had been turned back by the Allies for the first time in this war. It was in the Battle of the Coral Sea that signals intelligence came of age, demonstrating its capacity to predict the enemy's intentions well in advance and with remarkable accuracy.

General MacArthur had been in communication with Admirals Nimitz and Fletcher in the lead-up to and during the Battle of the Coral Sea. Planes under his command had provided reconnaissance, and Crace's warship force had been allocated from Admiral Herbert Leary's command within MacArthur's SWPA. But even though the target for MO Operation was known, MacArthur had done little to strengthen the Port Moresby garrison against a Japanese assault force. Australians believed the Japanese were preparing to invade and occupy their country. Even if MacArthur was not persuaded of that, Port Moresby would serve as a key base in this war for whichever side held it.

On 19 May, FRUMEL's Tom Mackie decrypted a radio message from the Naval Intelligence Division in Tokyo to General Harukichi Hyakutake, whose troops had been in the transport ships on the Coral Sea and were now awaiting further orders in Rabaul. 'ENEMY AIR STRENGTH IN AUSTRALIA AREA AT PRESENT WILL MAKE IT IMPOSSIBLE TO KEEP MORESBY SUPPLIED BY THE SEA ROUTE BETWEEN RABAUL AND MORESBY AFTER THE LATTER IS OCCUPIED,' the decrypted message said. It advised Hyakutake that Japan had abandoned the idea of a sea invasion of Port Moresby and was investigating an overland attack from the northern coast of New Guinea.

A week later, a message from Rabaul reported to Tokyo on conversations with New Guinea people. A road ran from the Mambare River, on the northern coast, inland through the village of Kokoda, over a mountain range of 2300 metres and down along the Laloki River to Moresby, the message said. It wasn't an easy route for an attack force, having been built forty years before to haul ore from the gold mines at Yodda, near Kokoda, but there was no other road across the island.

Forewarned a month in advance of Japan's intention, Australian and American army commanders were remarkably blasé about the threat. A week before a Japanese advance party landed at Gona to start the arduous march along the Kokoda Track, an SWPA military intelligence summary noted advice from MacArthur's GHQ that 'minor forces may attempt to utilize this route for attack on Port Moresby or supply forces who have attacked by sea'. The Japanese were left to take the initiative and were opposed only by militia until they had pushed beyond Kokoda. However, Port Moresby had never been the main objective of Yamamoto's Pacific strategy. Its capture was necessary to secure the Empire's perimeter before he finished what had been intended at Pearl Harbor: the elimination of the US Pacific Fleet as a potent naval force. Once that was achieved, the expanded Japanese Empire could plunder or trade without hindrance to gather the resources it needed from the Asia–Pacific region.

Chapter 7

Midway

Led by Lieutenant John Lietwiler, Station Cast's third and final evacuation party from Corregidor arrived in Melbourne on 6 May, one day before the Battle of the Coral Sea began. It wasn't good timing. The opportunity to participate had gone before the newcomers could get their teeth into decryption work, but Japan's Pacific campaign was far from over. With the positive view of signals intelligence that some higher-ups in the US Navy were starting to take, there would be plenty to do.

A shambling man with a heavy build and an open, country-boy face, 'Honest John' Lietwiler was admired by his men. He stuck up for them when outsiders criticised the unit and, because he did everything by the book, they knew where they stood with him. Rudy Fabian, who had been waiting for reassignment when the Japanese landed in the Philippines and left with the first Cast party, was now entrenched in command of the reconstituted agency in Melbourne, and the US naval command wasn't going to tinker with that. Lietwiler operated as Fabian's deputy in FRUMEL without any apparent resentment. They resumed their working partnership much as it had been on Corregidor, sharing a tiny office in the Monterey building that was never empty. Every hour of the day at least one of them was there, keeping a watchful eye on things.

Fabian was fanatical about security, and he used that obsession against Nave, his more experienced rival for leadership of the joint unit. From the outset, he claimed Nave was handling signals intelligence insecurely. Against his wishes, the Australian sent SIB decrypts—mostly submarine, merchant shipping and navy air communications—to the RAN's Chief of Naval Staff and its Director of Naval Intelligence, Cocky Long. Fabian thought all decrypted material should be sent to Admiral Leary as Commander, Allied Naval Forces, and that Leary should decide whether it should be passed to the Australians whether or not RAN resources had been used to obtain it. Even worse, Nave was willing to work with the Australian Army units pulled back from the Middle East.

Fabian used these security concerns about Nave to justify his reluctance to exchange material with the remnants of FECB (now withdrawn to Kenya), ignoring the fact that FECB had helped Cast in its work on the JN-25 code before the war. The truth was that Fabian was unwilling to exchange material with anyone who had nothing to offer in return. He also believed sigint should be sent solely through the US Navy's encrypted channel, COPEK, which was highly secure but used only by the Navy. In reality, Fabian was driven not only by military interests but by his own ambition and prejudices, and he would use any opportunity to advance or confirm them.

In a front-page story, newspapers across the US on 27 April reported that a major concentration of Japanese naval vessels in the Marshall Islands was 'apparently preparing for a new operation'. The dateline of the story was 'Allied HQ, Australia'. In the lead-up to the Coral Sea encounter, this created a kerfuffle in security-sensitive Washington. General Marshall, the Army Chief of Staff, messaged MacArthur that if the Japanese learned of the story, they would be 'justified in believing their codes broken—which would be disastrous'. He asked MacArthur to bring the matter to the attention of the Australian authorities. MacArthur replied two weeks later that Prime Minister Curtin had agreed to impose general press censorship in Australia, as if the leak could only have come from an Australian source.

On no other grounds than convenience, Fabian got on the bandwagon and let it be known in the world of shadows that he blamed Nave and his sloppy attention to security for the story. Whether Nave had been involved either directly or indirectly, or had simply set a poor example, it didn't matter to Fabian. Nave, already sidelined in the Monterey operation, was privy to little of the intelligence that flowed from JN-25 decrypts on the middle floor, so he was poorly placed to pass it on.

The Associated Press reporter who wrote the story, C. Yates McDaniel, would have had much better sources than the fringe dweller on the top floor. He might have got it directly from MacArthur, an incurable self-publicist, or from Fabian—either directly or through Leary—or from one of MacArthur's staff. In any case, penetration of the enemy's naval code wasn't the only means by which the Allies could have arrived at the information in the AP story. The conclusion could have been drawn purely from traffic analysis, so it didn't necessarily reveal that Japanese codes had been broken.

Holed up in his office, his trim frame tense as he fretted about security, Rudy Fabian spent much of his spare time listening to a radio-phonograph he'd acquired from somewhere, playing classical music and light opera on vinyl 78s. The music-loving Lietwiler had no objection. Fabian was from Butte, Montana, but his family originated in Slovakia and he affected a central-European sensibility and sophistication. Despite his training, he was an administrator with an antenna for political opportunity, not a cryptographer. He left that to the people in his charge.

MIDWAY

As workers in the anonymous, heavily guarded Melbourne building prepared for the expected showdown in the Coral Sea, there were early signs of a further naval operation in the wind. During early May, the sigint units in both Melbourne and Honolulu were reporting that admirals and staff officers of two Japanese carrier divisions had taken part in tabletop war games on Yamamoto's flagship, *Yamato*, moored near Hiroshima. Each of the divisions had two aircraft carriers that were not part of the invasion force for Port Moresby. A few days later, on 9 May, a Moorabbin intercept referred to a new strike force that was to sail on 21 May from Sasebo, near Nagasaki.

Warships unconnected with Moresby Operation were assembling in the Mariana Islands. A decrypted message from *Yamato* ordering speedy delivery of refuelling hose for scheduled operations suggested to analysts that a long-range operation was coming. Increased radio traffic detected through Saipan, in the Marianas, suggested the location would be in the central or north Pacific, since communications for the south Pacific generally came out of Truk. A request from the 4th Air Attack Force, based at Kwajalein, in the Marshall Islands, reinforced that suspicion. The base wanted transmitter crystals for specified radio frequencies to be delivered by the 17th for its aircraft to use in the 'second K campaign'.

The encrypted intercepts in the sealed satchels brought by motorbike from Moorabbin were rammed through the Monterey tabulators. Although these sometimes produced superfluous or incomprehensible messages, the decoders occasionally found a valuable new piece to fit into the intelligence puzzle. Like their colleagues at Hypo and OP-20-G, in early May FRUMEL's analysts were anxiously seeking the target for this major offensive. The coded location, called AF in intercept operators' shorthand until it was identified, kept appearing in decrypts. But where was AF?

This coded location had cropped up in Station Cast's intercepts at Corregidor in the lead-up to a March attack on Pearl Harbor. It was not a designator of Hawaii (whose code was already known) but related somehow to French Frigate Shoals, an uninhabited, crescent-shaped atoll in the north Pacific. It had provided a sheltered anchorage for submarines to refuel Japan's long-range seaplanes for what turned out to be an ineffectual bombing raid, the first K campaign.

Both FRUMEL and Hypo concluded that the AF was Midway Island, the nearest location of any significance to French Frigate Shoals. Midway consisted of two islets in the middle of the north Pacific, protected by a barrier reef. Previously uninhabited and devoid even of palm trees, one of the islets had been set up as a cable and coaling station at the turn of the century and in 1935 was made a stopover for Pan American Clipper flying boats. A hotel and tennis courts had been built near the airstrip and gardens were planted.

Initially, OP-20-G had taken the view that AF wasn't a geographical designator at all, but a transmission mode. Subsequent references to AF made clear that it was a location. The problem was that personnel in Washington, both in OP-20-G and in the Navy's high command, could not reach a consensus on its identity. Some thought it might be Alaska, others the Aleutians or Hawaii or even the west coast of America. What they did agree on was that it wasn't Midway. Commander Jack Redman, the new head of OP-20-G, and Admiral Kelly Turner of the War Plans Division worried that the real objective was in the south-west Pacific. Turner told Nimitz with unshakable conviction that the Japanese would mount an offensive by the end of May on north-eastern Australia, New Caledonia and Fiji.

On the other hand, Ed Layton, Admiral Nimitz's intelligence adviser, was convinced of his friend Joe Rochefort's view—supported by Melbourne—that the prime target was Midway. He in turn convinced his commander, who was already familiar with the island. Although he didn't expect an imminent Japanese attack,

MIDWAY

Nimitz had visited Midway early in May to inspect its patrol plane base after Admiral King expressed concerns about its capability to defend against attack. On his return, he sent the converted rail ferry *Kittyhawk* with additional dive bombers, Wildcat fighters and anti-aircraft guns to bolster the island outpost's defences.

After Coral Sea, Nimitz was prepared to trust Rochefort's judgement over Washington's competing assessment. This put him at odds with his commander, the abrupt and often dismissive King, who accepted the view of his OP-20-G advisers that AF was not Midway. Allied strategic planning was hamstrung by competing analyses, and a circuit-breaker was needed urgently.

Rochefort phoned Layton on 14 May and told him, 'I've got something here so hot it's burning a hole in my desk!'

He had a partial decrypt referring to 'invasion force AF', with an order for air-base equipment to be shipped to Saipan for 'AF ground crews'. This suggested the operation's objective was an island air base—such as Midway. However, at about the same time a FRUMEL decrypt pointed to an enemy naval force operating in the Aleutians. Intercepts in the lead-up to the Coral Sea battle had also seemed to refer to these far north Pacific islands. This interpretation had been pooh-poohed by the supremely self-assured Rochefort. Now they were continuing to surface in Japanese naval radio traffic.

The AF issue was eventually resolved by a suggestion from one of the cryptographers in Hawaii. Why not set up a ruse: report a mishap at Midway's evaporator plant and request an urgent delivery of fresh water, then see how the Japanese radio traffic responded. The plan was approved by Nimitz, and Midway was advised of it by secure underwater cable from Honolulu. On 19 May, the garrison commander reported an explosion in the island's distilling plant using a cipher known to have been captured by the Japanese on Wake Island.

The next day, FRUMEL intercepted a message from Tokyo to Yamamoto advising, 'AF AIR UNIT SENT FOLLOWING RADIO MESSAGE

TO COMMANDANT 14TH NAVAL DISTRICT, AK [Hawaii] OF 20TH. WITH REFERENCE TO THIS UNIT'S REPORT DATED 19TH. AT PRESENT WE HAVE ONLY ENOUGH WATER FOR 2 WEEKS. PLEASE SUPPLY US IMMEDIATELY.'

The ploy had worked, up to a point. It confirmed AF's identity, but it didn't immediately persuade Admiral King that AF was the Japanese offensive's prime target. King signalled to Nimitz that he accepted the enemy was planning an assault on Midway together with a possible feint against the Aleutians, but his strategists were still convinced Midway was a diversion and that the next major Japanese thrust would be on north-eastern Australia or New Caledonia and Fiji. King ordered OP-20-G in Washington to reassess all data accumulated so far and see if they still drew the same conclusion. Meanwhile, he wanted the carriers *Enterprise* and *Hornet* to remain in the south Pacific.

Nimitz instructed Admiral William 'Bull' Halsey on *Enterprise* to allow his carrier force to be spotted by Japanese patrols so he could force King's hand and recall the carriers to Pearl Harbor. The task force was duly seen steaming westward towards the Philippines by a Japanese flying boat from Tulagi. Air–ground messages raising the alarm were intercepted by Hypo. Ordered by Nimitz to return to Pearl Harbor, Halsey turned his vessels around after dusk and arrived in Honolulu on 26 May. They were to replenish there in preparation for meeting the expected Japanese invasion force for Midway, although Nimitz still had little idea how or when this encounter would take place. A day later, the badly damaged *Yorktown* limped in from the Coral Sea. Nimitz disregarded estimates that repairs would take several months. Pearl Harbor Naval Shipyard worked around the clock to have *Yorktown* 'battle ready' in 72 hours.

Service rivals in many ways, Admiral Nimitz and General MacArthur formed an alliance of convenience at this time. Nimitz warned the Melbourne-based army commander that Pearl Harbor had detected that air–ground traffic between the Port Moresby air base and Allied planes was being intercepted and retransmitted to Japan's vessels in the region. The air base changed its codes.

MacArthur proposed radio deception to persuade the Japanese that Halsey's task force was still around the Coral Sea. The seaplane tender *Tangier* and the cruiser *Salt Lake City* began using carrier call signs in radio signals to nearby shore stations, and Japanese traffic analysts duly reported to Yamamoto that the American carriers were still in the south-west Pacific.

Admirals King and Nimitz finally concurred on Japanese intentions in Midway and the Aleutians. Meanwhile, relations between OP-20-G analysts and Admiral Turner deteriorated over minor disagreements to the point that Redman was sanitising his analysts' reports, which disputed Turner's views. Their mutual antagonism escalating, OP-20-G and War Plans busily ignored summaries coming from the two Pacific stations and had little interest or awareness in the decisions made by the two senior naval commanders. On 20 May, the acrimony between Redman and Turner exploded into a confrontation. 'Terrible' Turner, nicknamed for his short temper and reluctance to suffer fools gladly, ordered Redman not to comment on intelligence evaluations and to accept the Turner view as correct.

Hypo had meanwhile generated a partial decrypt of a message from the Japanese navy's 1st Air Fleet: '. . . AS WE PLAN TO MAKE ATTACKS FROM A GENERAL NORTH-WESTERLY DIRECTION FROM N–2 DAYS TO N-DAY INCLUSIVE, PLEASE SEND WEATHER 3 HOURS PRIOR TO TAKE-OFF ON SAID DAY' with an undeciphered map reference '50 MILES NORTH-WEST OF MIDWAY'.

The US Navy's strategists knew this offensive would be targeting Midway and the Aleutians, but they were frustratingly lacking in key details such as dates, participants, and the makeup, deployment and coordination of the component fleets. The search was on in FRUMEL and Hypo to fill the gaps.

Intercepts from Moorabbin were pushed through the Monterey decryption process at a rate of 500 to 1000 a day. Each had its five-digit groups punched into IBM cards. A single message might require 60 cards, a long signal might take 200. The teams, mostly Americans at Monterey and a mix of American men and Australian women at the intercept station, had an easygoing lack of hierarchy. They helped each other when the occasion called for it, with the added support of Honest John Lietwiler's technical experience.

Rudy Fabian would emerge from his room from time to time to encourage his men. Whatever his other shortcomings, he did manage to convey an air of authority and leadership. 'You boys be damned sure you know what you're writing about,' he told the FRUMEL team, 'because they're moving carriers on the basis of what you're saying.' He left Lietwiler to run the show.

Admiral Yamamoto's complex battle plan required coordination of several fleets over a vast expanse of open sea. Japanese intelligence advised him that *Enterprise* and *Hornet* were the only carriers available to the US Pacific Fleet and that they were thought to be still in the Coral Sea. *Yorktown* was believed to have been so badly damaged that it was either out of action or had sunk. Yamamoto had dispersed his forces widely so that their full extent could not be discovered by the Americans until too late, but they were not well placed to come to each other's aid if the going got tough.

Admiral Nagumo's strike force of aircraft carriers would attack Midway along with Admiral Nobutake Kondo's occupation force. The US fleet would rush to the island's defence and, weakened by that encounter, would be subjected to a second attack by Yamamoto's powerful battleship force, lurking further to the west. The plan was for the US fleet to be crushed in a triple pincer with Nagumo's carriers and Kondo's battleships, thus completing the strategy launched six months before at Pearl Harbor. Submarines were to screen the seas between Midway and the Hawaiian Islands to monitor any American ships leaving Pearl Harbor after the Midway attack began, including the two US carriers if they returned to Hawaii. A parallel operation in the western Aleutians the day before the Midway assault was intended as a feint to draw some of the American forces away. This northern force would join the Midway battle after Yamamoto's battleships.

As strike force commander, Nagumo convened a final conference of senior officers of the four main aircraft carriers on his flagship, *Akagi*, still at port near Hiroshima. The conference was scheduled for 26 May, immediately before the fleets' departure for the north Pacific. In preparation, details of the battle plan were sent out to fleet commanders on 20 May in a dozen encrypted messages, each containing a different aspect of the plan.

A young American naval clerk, Yeoman Bill Tremblay, was on duty in Melbourne that night, decrypting JN-25 signals that had been brought in from Moorabbin during the day. There was always an eerie silence when the 'ding' of tram bells ceased for the night, but Tremblay found the quiet solitude easier to work in. The intercepts were the usual mix of clean, unbroken messages and garbled ones in which only sections had been copied down between fadeouts or bursts of interference. The cryptanalysts customarily went through the day's traffic, pulling out the unbroken documents and tossing the garbled reports into an empty cardboard box. It was easier to strip additives off clean reports because they were applied in sequence, just as they appeared in the codebook and not broken by signal dropout. If time permitted, the analyst would go through the garbles, after completing the clean messages.

Ralph Cook, the IBM man from Manila, was called up at 10 p.m. to fix a malfunctioning tabulator. When that was done, he went to the cryptanalysts' area to get a cup of coffee and find an empty desk to sleep at. With no trams so late at night, he couldn't go home.

'How's it going, Bill?' he said to the 21-year-old from Rhode Island, who was the sole analyst still on duty. Sporadic sounds from the watch office indicated someone was still working there.

'Fine. Fine,' said the yeoman. 'Got through this lot quick enough.'

'Anything of interest?'

'Not much. Not that I can see. I'll go onto the garbles soon. See if there's anything there.'

It was getting on for midnight. Cook made a coffee for himself; the guy in the watch office rattled about. Finishing his clear intercepts, Bill Tremblay moved on to the half-filled cardboard box, pulled out a sheet at random and started work on it, stripping off the additives. Although his concentration had been interrupted by the maintenance engineer's arrival, he'd made good progress that night. He doubted much was of great value, but that was the nature of the work. It required patience and application.

As the decoded words emerged from the decryption process, Tremblay stumbled on the word 'attack' and the location they'd called AF until it was identified as Midway. A strange sensation crept through the young decoder. Had he found a significant clue to the coming operation, or was he charging down a blind alley? He settled his anxiety by pouring a cup of coffee before getting back to the intercept.

Cook noticed that Tremblay seemed on edge, lost in thought, sipping at his coffee and pushing sugar crystals around on the kitchen table. At the back of any cryptanalyst's mind is the knowledge that lives could be lost or saved by the accuracy and speed of their decryption. Sometimes that mental pressure could be overwhelming.

'What's happening, buddy?' asked the IBM man. 'Are you onto something?'

'I don't know,' said Tremblay. 'Maybe. I don't know.'

He went back to his garble and carefully decrypted the parts for which he had code values. The result was fragmentary, but the pieces seemed to justify the nervous excitement Tremblay had felt when the first words had emerged. The intercept specified, between the garbles, warship movements to a rendezvous in the north Pacific, the positioning of a Japanese sub patrol off Oahu, and new call signs for some of the vessels that were expected to be part of the Midway Occupation Force.

Tremblay showed his decrypted fragments to the man on duty in the watch office, the linguist Gill Richardson. 'This might be important, sir,' he said.

'Might it?' said the older man. A lieutenant-commander in his mid-thirties, he'd been around long enough not to be rushed by anyone.

While Richardson worked on translating and interpreting the elements they had, Tremblay went back to his cardboard box and looked for further fragments of Nagumo's signals that might be buried with the other garbled intercepts of the day. The nature and range of recipients suggested the coded battle plan had been transmitted more than once through different relay stations, but it turned out to be more complicated than that.

By the time they had sifted more fragments from the box, decrypted and translated them, Tremblay and Richardson had assembled parts of a group of related messages, rather than several versions of the same message, detailing the components of the Midway operation assigned to each of Yamamoto's fleet commanders. There were more prescribed routes, and the timings of coordinated air attacks; arrival of supply and fuel vessels; a reconnaissance or bombing mission, or both, on Oahu; and landings to gain a foothold in the Aleutian Islands. There was a degree of overlap across the differing messages, which the two men were able to dovetail into a composite. It didn't give the complete plan, by any means. There were plenty of gaps, but there was enough to provide some of the detail Nimitz desperately needed to position his own warships and air defences in readiness for the enemy's invasion force.

Richardson sent both the decrypted fragments and the composite attack plan to Hawaii and Washington to see if either of the units there had picked up some of the day's traffic and were able to fill in any of the gaps. The plan assembled by the Melbourne operatives was conspicuously lacking in dates, but there were undecipherable sections that logic suggested contained dates. These appeared to have been pre-encoded before insertion into the JN-25 signal using a different code that they had not detected before.

In Hawaii, Hypo's most experienced cryptanalyst, Wesley 'Ham' Wright, worked with translator Joe Finnegan on filling in the gaps, chasing up garbles in their own collection of intercepts from 20 May. They found a few and identified some locations that had been put in a special code. Crucially, they also tackled the super-enciphered code for key dates. Working overnight on this code within a code, they managed to break into the date cipher and reported the next morning the key date of 4 June (Tokyo time) for the Midway attack, which had been repeated in several of the messages. The landings in the Aleutians were scheduled for 3 June, the day before.

— ● —

Notified by Ed Layton, the fleet intelligence officer, that Hypo had a decrypted intercept with elements of Yamamoto's battle plan for the coming offensive, Admiral Nimitz scheduled a Pacific Fleet staff conference for the next morning, 25 May. Joe Rochefort was invited to brief the meeting. It was the first time the Hypo chief had been invited to a command tactical conference—he usually had to pass Hypo's intelligence through Layton. Final plans for attacking the Japanese operation would be worked through at the meeting.

Knowing this was his opportunity to purge the shame of Pearl Harbor, Rochefort worked with great intensity through the night in the windowless Dungeon, driving his team to check all the material they had accumulated. Deciphered components were confirmed, raw decrypts were retranslated and refined, and a consensus was formed on the intelligence to be drawn from each document. The results of the marathon cross-referencing session were set out in a fresh intercept report, as if a single coded message had just emerged from decryption and translation.

Next morning, Rochefort arrived at the conference dishevelled and half an hour late. In his hands was the report Hypo had compiled from intelligence harvested in Melbourne and Hawaii, although the document didn't identify its sources or acknowledge that it was a composite. Rochefort was tense with pride and fear, but he had committed himself and couldn't retreat—too much was at stake. When he shared the document's contents, the astonishment of the Pacific Fleet strategists was pure joy to Rochefort. Impassive during the Hypo chief's presentation, the snowy-headed Nimitz asked how certain he was of the number of enemy aircraft carriers. If there were more than four, the Pacific Fleet would be at a considerable tactical disadvantage, and worse if *Yorktown* was not repaired in time.

'There will be only four carriers,' said the softly spoken Rochefort. 'I'm sure of it.'

The material in the document seemed almost too good to be true. It provided a far more detailed insight into the enemy's plans than the Allies had enjoyed before the Coral Sea battle. Some officers thought the degree of detail suggested Japanese deception. They questioned why Yamamoto would use his entire available fleet on the Aleutian Islands and Midway. Why send secret information by radio, risking the decoding and exposure of the Japanese battle plan? Nimitz responded that Yamamoto might be short of time and that radio was the only way of getting the details to all who would attend the *Akagi* conference. The Japanese believed their double-encrypted naval code was impregnable. Perhaps Yamamoto wanted to draw out the weaker US fleet and destroy it, speculated the admiral. His comment showed remarkable prescience, although it was only a passing thought.

The intelligence presented didn't reveal that Yamamoto would be at sea on *Yamato* with the main fleet. On 21 May, FRUMEL's traffic analysts had made the station's only serious mistake of the campaign by concluding that the Japanese commander-in-chief would actively direct operations, but from a distance too far back to participate in the attacks. As a result, the movement of the main body of the Japanese fleet to 1200 kilometres west of Midway would go unnoticed.

In Washington, the consensus was still that the Midway operation was a ruse to cover a major raid on Hawaii or the US mainland. The stand-off between War Plans' Admiral Turner and OP-20-G's Jack Redman prevented both groups from paying much attention to the intercepted battle plan. But Nimitz was prepared to gamble on the accuracy of Rochefort's analysis. He rushed his carriers to Midway, leaving Hawaii exposed, although he provided some backup by ordering the carrier *Saratoga* to come from San Diego. *Enterprise* and *Hornet* returned to Pearl Harbor the next day, were replenished and left on 28 May, while the dockyard worked at breakneck speed to prepare *Yorktown* to follow them. It left Pearl Harbor two days later, under radio silence like the other two carriers. Nimitz had built up aircraft numbers on Midway to 110 fighters, bombers and patrol seaplanes, so that the airfield there would provide the Americans with a fourth air platform to match Nagumo's four carriers.

Having already seen the Japanese carriers' air-battle ability in the Coral Sea, King and Nimitz had decided not to confront the Japanese fleet head on but to reduce the enemy by attrition with submarine attacks and air bombing—stealth rather than strength. The Americans had the advantage of surprise, an advantage the enemy imagined itself to have. Nimitz's Operation Plan No. 29-42 placed the US carriers north-east of Midway by 2 June, with submarines standing by to attack the Japanese carriers. Defence and patrol aircraft were to come from Midway and long-range attack planes from Hawaii. American servicemen, unaware of the existence of Station Hypo or even of signals intelligence, assumed the meticulous planning was made possible by spies in Tokyo.

At midnight on 27 May, the Japanese navy finally introduced its twice-postponed new JN-25 code. Both codebook and additive cipher were replaced, and the Allies' ability to read Japan's naval traffic came to an abrupt halt. For future operations, the Allied code breakers would have to start from scratch to penetrate JN-25C. For the coming Midway battle, though, the genie was already out of the bottle.

From Hypo's additional work on the garbled gaps and the date cipher, new values in the discarded JN-25 code had been solved and sent to FRUMEL. Although the Japanese navy was now using the new code, Melbourne cryptanalysts were able to go back over past intercepts and draw further intelligence from them. A 26 May intercept proposed using American civilian engineers captured at Wake Island to rebuild Midway. A message intercepted the next day said heavy bombers were to be deployed on 1 June to Wake, within flying range of Midway. Hypo analysts found in an old message the detail that on 31 May fighter pilots from the carrier *Zuikaku* were to be transferred to the Northern Force's two light aircraft carriers. This meant *Zuikaku* would not participate in the coming operation, confirming Rochefort's assurance to Nimitz.

FRUMEL was not told how Nimitz would deploy his forces because it had no formal need to know. Concerned about the press leak before the Coral Sea battle and convinced by MacArthur that its source was Australian, Nimitz had insisted that neither the British nor FRUMEL should be briefed about the gathering intelligence on the Midway operation. He was unaware of the irony that his own most crucial intelligence had originated from Melbourne.

In the dark since the switch to JN-25C and unbriefed about Allied strategy, the cryptographers at FRUMEL were as ignorant about Allied plans for the coming battle as the world was about FRUMEL's existence and operations. Those on the middle floor at Monterey had to wait until somebody chose to let them know how the battle went or it became public knowledge. Those on the top floor knew even less. Any intelligence Trendall's group picked up from merchant shipping in the Mandated Territories was taken down to the floor below, but in return they were given no insight into the growing expectation of an attack on Midway.

— • —

For all its remarkable achievements, the apartment building in Melbourne was not a happy camp for its Australian occupants. Mutual suspicion had grown between Nave and those who had moved into Fabian's orbit, principally Treweek and Jamieson. Nave was still receiving code values from his friend Malcolm Burnett at FECB, now relocated to Colombo. He kept these locked in his office safe. Increasingly secretive and isolated in his fear that Fabian might take steps to take over his source, Nave was unwilling to share the codes with those in his team whose loyalty was uncertain. Still working from a desk on the same floor, Treweek waited until Nave's day off, opened the safe and copied any code values he thought of use. They weren't for JN-25 because the British were no longer in a position to decrypt such messages, but they were for other codes Nave's group worked on, submarine, merchant shipping and air–ground ciphers.

The gaiety of the younger Nave had gone, replaced by the reserve of a family man, but Treweek was oblivious to the possibility that he might have been a factor in Nave's reluctance to share information. Brought up by a battling widowed mother and educated through scholarships, Treweek was in thrall to Fabian's outa-my-way leadership and Lietwiler's patriotic dedication. He dismissed the two mathematicians in SIB as bumbling academics. Treweek's fellow classicist, the New Zealander Trendall, was not so drawn to the Americans. More circumspect about the process of untangling codes, he found he could see patterns in encoded text under the jumble of characters in diplomatic messages he worked on: 'You get a feeling for it. Your eyes light upon something, and . . . bang.'

— • —

By 1 June, the Japanese invasion force was steaming eastwards through fog, rain and high winds, secure in the belief that the Americans were unaware of its approach. FRUMEL noted the high volume of traffic broadcast to units known to be part of the Midway operation, and the lack of traffic coming back from them. The operation had apparently begun and was under radio silence. Some distance further back, Yamamoto's main body briefly broke radio silence to find a tanker in the dense fog. Increased radio traffic from Hawaii followed, but Yamamoto was not concerned if the enemy now knew of the presence of this part of the fleet, as his plan was to draw out the US carrier fleet anyway.

An urgent message from Tokyo to Yamamoto and Nagumo on 2 June said it was now thought that the Americans were probably aware of the invasion plans and were sending carriers to oppose them. It was a possibility that was growing in Yamamoto's mind anyway, but didn't greatly worry him. It didn't mean the Americans knew details of his battle plan or that the naval code had been broken, only that their planes must have sighted Japanese warships. Yamamoto didn't break radio silence and pass Tokyo's warning on to his strike force commander because he assumed Nagumo had already received it. He was unaware that *Akagi*'s antenna was too weak to pick up long-distance transmissions.

As part of the counterattack, Nimitz had sent Admiral Robert Theobald with a task force to defend the Aleutians from the anticipated assault. The principal target was expected to be the US naval base at Dutch Harbor. Theobald decided the intelligence warnings were the product of enemy deception and positioned his force 1000 kilometres away, near Kodiak Island in Alaska, where he set up a base. On 3 June, aircraft from the light carriers *Ryujo* and *Junyo* conducted a pre-dawn bombing raid in dense fog on Dutch Harbor, causing little damage. Planes from a nearby airfield were unable to locate the Japanese fleet in the bad weather.

The Japanese returned to Dutch Harbor the next day, destroying the base's oil storage tanks and severely damaging the hospital and a barracks ship. This time the land-based pilots located the enemy carriers, but bad weather closed in before they could inflict much damage. Theobald's task force had played no part in the action up to that point.

On 5 June, Theobald sent his force to investigate a report of enemy warships in the Bering Sea to the north of the Aleutians, while Japanese marines occupied the lightly defended west Aleutian island of Kiska, followed the next day by Attu, even further west. Local US Army planes, instructed to attack the occupation fleet, got lost in heavy cloud. No warships were found in the Bering Sea. The Japanese light carriers were by then already a day away, steaming south to join the Midway attack.

While the sideshow on the northern rim of the Pacific was unfolding without much success for the defending forces, the main Japanese invasion fleets closed in on their objective of Midway Island. Thanks to Allied signals intelligence, the Americans—rather than rushing to find out what was happening in the north Pacific—were able to meet them on something approaching equal terms. The outcome of the impending battle would depend not on which side had better tactics but on which side made the fewest mistakes.

On 4 June, before dawn and in poor weather, Nagumo launched an attack by dive bombers and torpedo bombers on Midway Island. The 108 aircraft were half the total available to him and were drawn from all four carriers. As they swooped, a Catalina from

Midway spotted two Japanese carriers with empty decks, indicating that an air strike was under way. Buildings and hangars were damaged and many planes lost, but most of the island's ground defences, its runways and its refuelling capacity were still intact. Half the Japanese planes used in the raid were destroyed or damaged. Meanwhile, bombers from Midway attacked the Japanese carrier fleet but were driven off.

The lead pilot of the initial Japanese attack radioed that a second strike was needed. With the first strike force still in the air, if carriers were occupied with launching a second strike, returning planes would have to be ditched as fuel ran out. The decision to fly the first sortie from all four carriers had become a liability. Nagumo, still unaware that he had any more to deal with than Midway-based defenders, ordered the returning planes to land first. In the meantime, the carrier bombers would replace their torpedoes with bombs for another raid on the island.

Unknown to the strike fleet commander, the US Pacific Fleet was waiting north of Midway Island, with Nimitz coordinating when necessary from Pearl Harbor. Based on sightings by early-morning air patrols, Admiral Frank Fletcher, in command at sea, ordered air attacks from his three carriers shortly after sunrise. Take-offs from *Enterprise* and *Hornet* were rushed and piecemeal. At the same time, shortly before 8 a.m., a Japanese patrol plane sighted a flotilla of ten US ships, although it could see no carrier with them.

Nagumo was blindsided by this report. All his calculations were built on the assumption that he was dealing only with island-based aircraft until US warships could travel the necessary distance to retaliate. It should not have been possible for them to be there in two hours. Forced to improvise in response to the unexpected, he ordered bombs unloaded from carrier planes and torpedoes reloaded.

The American carrier planes had difficulty locating their targets. Some followed a wrong bearing and ran out of fuel. No dive bombers found a target. *Hornet*'s torpedo bombers sighted the Japanese carriers but their fighter escort was running low on fuel and turned back, leaving the bombers to be shot down with no hits on enemy ships. Two minutes later, the *Enterprise* torpedo squadron attacked, scoring no hits and losing all but four of its planes. *Yorktown* torpedo bombers arrived half an hour later with fighter protection, but Zeros swarmed over both, shooting down all but two of the bombers and scattering the fighters with small loss to themselves.

What the Americans did achieve, however, was to distract Nagumo's surprised strike force from its attack and force it to concentrate on defence. By this time, a Japanese patrol had reported a carrier within the US fleet. Clearly, the US aircraft were carrier-based. The fleet they came from supposedly had no prior knowledge of this operation but was now within flying range of the invasion force. It was mid-morning. As Nagumo changed his instructions, leaving bombs and torpedoes stacked in the open and fuel lines running across the flight deck, dive bombers from *Enterprise* and *Yorktown* appeared from the cloud cover over the carriers *Kaga* and *Akagi*. The Zero fighters had become scattered chasing off the earlier attacks, and anti-aircraft gunners on the Japanese warships had paused after repelling the earlier raids. The *Enterprise* group split into two, intending to attack both carriers, but through a miscommunication both groups dived on *Kaga*, which sustained five or more direct hits. Gasoline and munitions exploded in the hangars below the top deck, setting off raging fires and destroying the water mains that might have brought them under control.

Three of the dive bombers, spotting their mistake, pulled out of the *Kaga* attack and turned on *Akagi*, scoring one direct hit. It was a lucky strike for the Americans: their bomb shot through a deck elevator to the upper hangar deck, where it exploded among armed and fuelled aircraft, leaving *Akagi* burning out of control. *Yorktown*'s dive bombers meanwhile attacked a third Japanese carrier, *Soryu*, with three hits inflicting extensive damage. Within a few minutes, the carrier was ablaze. In just seven minutes, Admiral Nagumo had lost three of his four carriers and the Midway battle. Twenty minutes later, he abandoned his flagship for the light cruiser *Nagara*.

Of the Japanese carriers, only *Hiryu* was still operational, and on it, Admiral Tamon Yamaguchi effectively took over the battle, steaming towards Fletcher and *Yorktown*. Yamamoto, on the battleship *Yamato* in the fleet's main body, was too distant to be able to intervene in the short time in which the battle had completely turned around. With no carriers in his group, he ordered *Ryujo* and *Junyo* from the Aleutians to speed south, but they were three days away. Yamamoto had spread his fleets too widely.

Fletcher learned shortly before midday that his fleet had been sighted, but at that stage he didn't have a clear picture of the battle. Thinking two of Nagumo's carriers were lurking to the north, he sent out patrols and fighters while returning aircraft landed. Yamaguchi, on the other hand, had good knowledge from his patrols of where the American ships were located. His dive bombers briefly lost their fighter cover and suffered losses from American planes and anti-aircraft fire, but succeeded with three hits on *Yorktown*. With fires from explosions in the hangar and the ship's boilers badly damaged, the American carrier was temporarily out of action.

By early afternoon two boilers were operating again and the fires had been put out. *Yorktown* was under way, but not for long. At 2.30 p.m. a second strike force from *Hiryu* arrived, this time torpedo bombers. There was a hiatus in *Yorktown*'s defences, and two torpedoes struck its port side. With a list of 25 degrees and on the verge of capsizing, *Yorktown* was abandoned.

The Japanese counterattack was short-lived. At the same time as the second attack took off from *Hiryu*, dive bombers sortied from *Enterprise*. It wasn't until late afternoon, two hours after *Yorktown* had been abandoned, that a scout plane located *Hiryu*. Despite strong Zero cover, five bombs struck the remaining Japanese carrier, leaving it ablaze and unable to launch aircraft. Shortly after 7 p.m., both *Soryu* and *Kaga* sank. *Akagi* lasted until dawn, *Hiryu* until nine o'clock the next morning.

An attempt by Yamamoto to regain some of the initiative with a night attack by his heavy surface ships was thwarted when the American forces withdrew overnight far to the east. When he found the attack was not feasible, the Japanese commander-in-chief abandoned the Midway enterprise and ordered his ships to return home. The Americans chased after the retreating fleet with minor skirmishes but gave up the chase by Wake Island. The crippled *Yorktown* stubbornly stayed afloat, and although a Japanese submarine put two more torpedoes into it during a salvage operation, it didn't finally capsize until the morning of 7 June, the third day after the main battle.

The Battle of Midway was a decisive tactical and strategic victory for the Americans. Japan lost four front-line fleet carriers and 250 aircraft, with over 3000 killed. The Americans lost one carrier and 144 aircraft, with over 360 dead. Both sides lost just over 100 aircrew, but the Japanese dead included hundreds of skilled and experienced ground crewmen. The Imperial Japanese Navy had set out to destroy the remnants of the US Pacific Fleet, but had emerged from the battle as the underdog.

— ● —

The code breakers in FRUMEL were left in the dark about how useful their intercepts and decrypts were in staving off the Japanese invasion of Midway Island. They knew the attack was coming, but didn't necessarily know when it was planned to start, as that date had been decrypted by Hypo in Hawaii. They didn't know what Hypo had added to the partial decrypt FRUMEL had sent to Hawaii and Washington or how Hypo had presented the resulting messages— nor, indeed, how Admiral Nimitz had responded to the signals intelligence presented to him. This sort of information was passed

MIDWAY

only to those designated with a 'need to know'. The FRUMEL operators didn't have a need to know, only a desire to know.

They would find out the details of the battle when an internal security report was circulated from Washington; from their subsequent intercepts—although until the new version of JN-25 was penetrated, traffic analysis was all they had to go on; or from local newspapers. Apart from a few whispers floating through the building, their first indication that the confrontation had begun was in the Melbourne newspaper *The Age*, on 5 June, a Friday. The headlines referred to the sinking of Japanese supply and transport ships and the recent Japanese mini-submarine raid on Sydney Harbour. A small item, 'JAPAN'S THREAT TO AMERICA: RAIDS ON ALASKA', reported raids the day before on Dutch Harbor in the Aleutians with 'no serious damage'.

FRUMEL intercepts the next day revealed contact between Japan's Midway force and *Ryujo* in the northern fleet near the Aleutians, with some indication that the two light carriers were coming south. Strangely, there was no traffic from the Midway carrier divisions. The 1st Air Fleet chief of staff had moved to *Nagara*, however, suggesting that the carrier *Akagi* was either sunk or out of action. *The Age* that day shed some light on what was happening. It wasn't yet making headlines, but in a story low on page 1 Nimitz announced damage to a Japanese battleship and carrier after a heavy attack on Midway Island. Radio signals from Yamamoto, analysed at Monterey later that day, suggested *Akagi* was badly damaged and was with a destroyer escort.

A picture was emerging for the team in Melbourne of a battle in which the enemy had some initial setbacks, but with no newspaper on Sunday and no new clues in the traffic, all were on tenterhooks wondering what the outcome would be. The next day they found out.

'SMASHING BLOWS ON JAPANESE FLEET' screamed a banner on the front page of Monday's *Age*. 'CARRIERS SUNK; HEAVY SHIPS

DAMAGED: GREAT BATTLE IN PROGRESS.' The story, datelined Washington, 7 June, reported that heavy losses had been inflicted on the Japanese naval force in the Midway area 'in the greatest air and sea battle fought in this war'. Nimitz was calling it 'a momentous victory in the making'.

The article cautiously claimed that two or possibly three carriers had been destroyed with all planes, and one or two more had been damaged. It did not say how many carriers were in the attack force, but the FRUMEL workers knew there were four. That sounded like a resounding victory, measured against the single US carrier hit. The massive Japanese attack on Midway had been 'surprised and smashed by American forces', but the article offered no explanation of how it had been possible to mount that surprise. As well, the day's traffic through Moorabbin indicated that the Midway Occupation Force was returning to Saipan. This information was not made available to newspapers.

It was in the nature of their secret work—and their distance from Hawaii and Washington—that naval sigint personnel in Melbourne had to wait for a local newspaper to let them know the outcome of their efforts. Most of the Australians upstairs at Monterey did not even know what those efforts had involved. At Pearl Harbor, on the other hand, Joe Rochefort was the golden boy. A couple of days after Midway, Nimitz told a debriefing conference of Pacific Fleet command, 'This officer deserves a major share of the credit for the victory at Midway.' Sometimes the messenger isn't shot but is presumed to be the author of the message.

Subsequently, the commander of 14th Naval Division in Hawaii asked Rochefort to compile a list of names for awards to radio intelligence personnel after the Battle of Midway. Rochefort gave the task to a staff member, despite his stated concern that awards given in wartime draw attention to code-breaking success. A list of Hypo veterans and a recommendation of Rochefort for a

Distinguished Service Medal got Nimitz's imprimatur and was forwarded to Admiral King.

Jack Redman had been arguing in Washington that OP-20-G should share credit for the success of the Midway defence, possibly because many of the JN-25 values were solved by his section and perhaps also because he knew the crucial decrypt had come from Melbourne, not Hypo. Without doubt, his prime reason would have been political. The medal for Rochefort was rejected by King, with the explanation that Rochefort had 'merely efficiently used the tools previously prepared for his use'.

No one suggested that a medal might be appropriate for anyone in Melbourne.

— • —

In the aftermath of leadership changes at OP-20-G, Washington was pushing for centralisation of sigint operations. As interception units were loosely organised, the argument ran, unnecessary duplication of effort would be avoided by bringing all relevant intelligence to a central point for analysis. That central point was OP-20-G. Redman advised Naval Operations that the capability of units in combat areas was limited to 'reading enemy messages and performing routine work necessary to keep abreast of minor changes in the cryptographic systems involved'. His brother Joe, the Director of Naval Communications, dismissed Station Hypo as being 'by virtue of seniority, in the hands of an ex-Japanese language student . . . not technically trained in Naval Communications'.

Rochefort was clearly in the Redman brothers' gun sights, but he took no notice. He'd hitched his star to the hero of Midway and by September was telling Washington he was answerable only to Nimitz. For Jack Redman, already furious at having been shown to be wrong on the identity of the AF target, this was too much. On 22 October, Rochefort was summoned to the Navy Department in

Washington for 'temporary additional duty'. Nimitz's protest that he needed Rochefort's 'expert advice' was ignored.

A month later, Nimitz was advised by post that Rochefort's new duty was permanent and that Captain William B. Goggins would take over as head of Station Hypo. In Washington, Rochefort refused to work anywhere in radio intelligence apart from heading the Hawaiian unit. Failing that, he insisted, he should be transferred to combat duty. Offered command of a destroyer, he turned it down because of a family commitment at that time and ended up in command of a San Francisco dry dock. Joe Rochefort never worked in codes again.

Goggins, meanwhile, presided over a Hypo that was being wound back as the US Navy's cryptographic operation was increasingly centralised in Washington. It was a portent of what was eventually to come for the other Pacific decryption station in Australia.

— • —

With a seaplane base already constructed on Tulagi, in the Solomon Islands, a Japanese naval party landed on 4 July on nearby Guadalcanal. Its mission was to build an airfield from which long-range bombers could attack the supply lines between America and Australia. Admiral King proposed a naval and marine counter-offensive against Guadalcanal, but General MacArthur objected to what he saw as a Navy move to control all operations in the Pacific and place the Army under its command. The Joint Chiefs of Staff gave King's proposal the go-ahead anyway.

Under cover of bad weather on the night of 6 August, United States Marines started landing on Guadalcanal and Tulagi with limited resistance. Over the following two days, Rabaul-based Japanese aircraft attacked the amphibious force, causing such damage that some Allied ships were withdrawn from the area. Cruisers and destroyers that stayed behind to protect the still-unloading transports were surprised that night by a fleet from Rabaul. In the ensuing Battle of Savo Island, four Allied ships were sunk and three more damaged. Eleven thousand Marines were left behind on Guadalcanal with minimal equipment and provisions.

Allied code breakers had been struggling with the new version of JN-25, but they were now starting to make progress. The fact that some messages in JN-25C had been enciphered with the previous additive tables opened the door slightly into the new code, though too late to forewarn of the Japanese landing at Guadalcanal. Traffic analysis had detected the presence of a Japanese strike force in the Solomons, but that had little impact on the naval battle that followed.

Then, just as Allied sigint seemed poised to recover the knowledge of enemy codes it had enjoyed before Coral Sea and Midway, it suffered a serious setback. Marines landing on Guadalcanal found a cache of codebooks abandoned by airstrip defenders when they had retreated into the surrounding jungle. These were mostly for minor codes, but they included a codebook for JN-25C. They were sent in triumph to Station Hypo. Basking in the glory of Midway and unaware his days at Hypo were numbered, Rochefort was horrified when he saw the JN-25C book. The Japanese were almost sure to realise that this could have fallen into Allied hands—and he knew just what they would do in response.

A few days later, routinely working through intercepted messages on Monterey's top floor, Eric Nave found one that had been transmitted in JN-20, a general-purpose code that was sometimes used as a backup code for JN-25. The message advised that JN-25C was about to be replaced with a new version. Until codebooks for the new code were distributed, JN-20 should be used for operational messages. On 14 August 1942, the Japanese navy began coding its messages in a new code the Americans dubbed JN-25D. Allied code breakers had to start the long, painful process of decryption all over again.

After the excitement leading into the two key Pacific battles, FRUMEL found itself at a loose end. The neutered Imperial Japanese Navy had withdrawn to lick its wounds, but whatever its strategic planners had in mind as their next move remained unknown to the Allied cryptographers. Rudy Fabian, however, had consolidated his position politically. He had admirers in the US Navy, particularly Admiral Leary, commander of the Allied naval forces in the region. MacArthur's Bataan Gang, the Army officers who actually ran the SWPA, were not so keen on Fabian, but they had moved to Brisbane in July.

When a change came in the hierarchy, it seemed benign enough at first. Leary reported to MacArthur as well as to Admiral King. His reluctance to risk his ships had irritated the general, as had Leary's habit of communicating directly with King rather than through MacArthur. In September, MacArthur replaced Leary with Admiral Arthur Carpender, who since July had been in charge of naval forces, mostly submarines, on the west coast of Australia. Carpender relocated to Brisbane. As JN-25 activity had been minimal during his brief time in Australia, FRUMEL didn't attract much of his attention. Nave's group was still decrypting enemy submarine signals, but Fabian wasn't rushing to let Carpender know that. Far from SWPA's new headquarters, he felt unthreatened and turned his mind to other things.

Eric Nave was still exchanging code values with the remnants of FECB in Kenya and Colombo through his friends Malcolm Burnett and Harry Shaw. He had loaned the two mathematicians in his team, Room and Lyons, to the Americans to work on the new JN-25 additives. Gerry Room had devised a method that could expose the cipher in a few hours. The result had been supplied to Washington, but Nave offered it to Bletchley Park as well.

The Australian felt a responsibility to his intelligence partners, but his move must have infuriated the security-obsessed Fabian. The

American had asked OP-20-G to inform its London counterpart that he refused to allow code values to be handled in the 'practically public [Australian Navy] code room where over 300 civilian clerks are employed'. He claimed Nave handled cryptographic information insecurely and that his use of the phone violated security rules. Fabian had 'bawled the hell out of him', he said, complaining that Nave 'was in the clouds as far as his work was concerned; he just forgot these simple little other rules that governed people'. It is unclear how Fabian could possibly have known what Nave, on a different floor and otherwise ignored by the American, did with his phone or what specific rules he was breaking.

Shortly before this outburst, Fabian, now promoted to lieutenant-commander, had sent a memo to Nave saying: 'In order to be assured of security "purple" it is requested that: (1) Only two smooth copies of translation be made. (2) Purple work sheets be destroyed immediately after translation completed. (3) Translations not be permitted to accumulate for long period—should be destroyed when purpose served. Very respectively [*sic*], R.J. FABIAN.'

This was the sort of instruction that might be given to someone who had just joined the unit. Moreover, Fabian had no formal authority over Nave. But Nave bit his stiff upper Royal Navy lip and replied politely, 'Your memorandum regarding "purple" security has been received and I am in complete agreement with you on the arrangements outlined. They will be carried out.'

The 'request' and the security risks it implied appear faintly contrived, as did a story that did the rounds of the Monterey building at about this time. A WRANS was said to have overheard the conductor on her tram say, as it passed her workplace, 'See that building over there? It's a big spy place. That's where they break all the Japanese codes.'

It's a story that stands out in the sparse archival material on FRUMEL, reflecting either the failure of all Fabian's security efforts or a remarkably well-informed tram conductor. Given that FRUMEL's involvement in the Battle of Midway is still barely known several decades later, it seems implausible, to say the least.

— • —

As American signals intelligence developed and cryptographers needed less help from Britain, the Americans became less obliging and more obstructive. Suspecting their ally was holding out on them, OP-20-G refused to give the code breakers in Kenya secure US cipher machines on the grounds that British security was lax. A delegation from Bletchley Park visited Washington in September to start talks about greater cooperation.

The next month, the two powers came up with the Holden Agreement, principally a framework for sharing intelligence responsibilities in Europe, but with a side plan for the Pacific War whereby the US Navy would take over responsibility for Japanese naval traffic decryption. Britain would also disband the so-called British–Australian naval unit in Melbourne and transfer to FRUMEL any personnel the Americans wanted. This did not include Commander Nave, who was to be 'sent home' to the Royal Navy.

In fact, neither the Admiralty nor the British code-breaking operation centred on Bletchley Park had any authority over Nave's Special Intelligence Bureau, a purely Australian unit with some refugees from FECB and the British consular service. However, the British Eastern Fleet was dependent on US Navy sigint support and would back any proposal that advanced that interest. Weak and under Fabian's thumb, Jack Newman raised no objections, as his intercept WRANS were to be retained in FRUMEL. The RAN agreed to disband SIB and disperse its personnel.

Eric Nave was in a bind. The Admiralty wanted him back in London, even though the British had no interest in Japanese codes, and he could no longer plead ill health. He hadn't had a recurrence of his tropical disease for some time. In any case, London wasn't the tropics. But Nave's family and all his connections were in Australia, and Australia was still under threat of Japanese attack. His skills would be much more useful in Australia than Britain. It was where he felt his duty and his responsibilities lay.

As Nave desperately looked around for something that would keep him in his homeland, a telephone call came out of the blue from a contact in army intelligence.

'Eric', said a voice on the phone late in October 1942, 'Mic Sandford here . . . down from Brisbane for a few days. I've got a proposition we'd like to put to you. When can we get together?'

Chapter 8

Central Bureau

There was little for those on board to do but smoke on deck, gaze at the sea and strike up conversations with whoever was around. Captain Mic Sandford and Captain Jack Ryan's No. 4 Special Wireless Section, returning from Suez in February 1942, had transferred to SS *Orcades* at Colombo. The ship stopped over in Java to take on Allied officers pulling back from the Japanese onslaught, among them Brigadier Colin Simpson, chief signals officer of the Australian Army's I Corps. He started chatting with Sandford and Ryan.

They were an odd trio—Simpson, the Scottish plumber's son who had become a pharmacist through apprenticeship; Sandford, the Oxford-educated scion of the Adelaide establishment; and Ryan, the burly radio engineer. Simpson and Ryan were both veterans of the previous war, whereas Sandford had been catapulted into this one. On the surface there was not much common ground among them, but they found some in their mutual wartime interest. Simpson grew excited about the potential of an expanded signals intelligence role for the Australian Army.

'Why don't you prepare a proposal for me along the lines we're talking?' he said. 'Let's see what you can come up with. Not much else for you to do here.'

Indeed there wasn't. It was not an opportunity to let slip. The two junior officers beavered away, discussing and writing, talking to others on board who were interested in contributing. On 8 March, they presented a report to the brigadier proposing a special wireless group that would focus on intelligence work. A week later, when they disembarked at Adelaide, Simpson took the proposal to his senior commanders. He was the right person for the job, a confidant of General Thomas Blamey, who had been brought into MacArthur's inner circle and was the only officer in it who wasn't part of the Bataan Gang.

Coincidentally, just a week before in Melbourne the Director of Military Intelligence, Colonel Caleb Roberts, had proposed a similar local bureau. To be set up by the Australian Army jointly with the RAAF and the US Army to intercept Japanese army signals, it would have research (code-breaking) and decryption functions, as well as coordinating radio listening units in the field. Roberts tentatively called his proposed organisation Central Bureau. He hoped it would combine the roles of Bletchley Park and its outposts into a single Melbourne agency of thirty personnel.

Roberts's proposal was more detailed and prescient than the paper put together on *Orcades*, but the latter was sufficient to bring Sandford and Ryan into the planning orbit. On 30 March, a meeting of officers from the US Army, the Australian Army and the RAAF confirmed that the centre should be set up in Melbourne and 'maintain close liaison with the existing naval cryptographic bureau'. It recommended that the new bureau's director come from the US Army. The following morning, Sandford met with General Akin, MacArthur's signals chief, at offices set up in the requisitioned MacRobertson Girls High School. Roberts, meanwhile, was advocating that Ryan's section, back in Melbourne, not be sent into the combat zone but remain in Melbourne as the nucleus of the new bureau.

The proposal was approved by the Australian Army, and MacArthur was briefed about it. Already frustrated by the circuitous route intelligence took to reach him through US Navy intransigence, the Southwest Pacific Area commander radioed Washington requesting that trained staff and equipment be sent to Australia. 'The time delay and transmission uncertainties incident to sending interpreted material to Washington and elsewhere,' he told General Marshall, 'dictate that this work be handled locally. Allied forces here are organizing such a bureau.'

On 6 April, a conference at Victoria Barracks to coordinate signals intelligence in Australia was chaired by Brigadier Simpson. Rudy Fabian, Jack Newman and Eric Nave from the naval teams in Monterey were present, as were representatives from the RAAF and the US Army, the latter led by Colonel Joe Sherr, who had headed Station 6 on Corregidor. The conference endorsed the Roberts plan for a US–Australian 'Research and Control Centre' in Melbourne, under one roof and with a projected staff of 100. It was to liaise with Washington, London, India (where the British Army had a sigint station) and FRUMEL.

The proposal was gaining momentum. An executive committee, with Joe Sherr as chair, met the next day to set up a number of subcommittees. Cocky Long was on the executive committee, but Fabian and Nave were not. Newman and Ryan were on a technical subcommittee and were investigating operator training. Flight Lieutenant Roy Booth, the Sydney solicitor who had been at FECB in Singapore when war broke out, was to organise an RAAF wireless unit to operate in the field as soon as possible. Premises for the new bureau, to be no more than 5 kilometres from Victoria Barracks, were to be selected by Sherr and Sandford. It was suggested that half the accommodation and operating costs come from the US Army, with the other half shared between the Australian Army and the RAAF. Mic Sandford was appointed secretary of the executive committee. He was clearly on the rise, impressing senior officers as engaging, intelligent and energetic, just as he had done with young soldiers in Crete.

Cocky Long was on the executive committee but played no active role. He saw himself as an entrepreneur, not a hands-on type. In April 1942, soon after MacArthur coopted the Combined Operational Intelligence Centre (COIC) into SWPA General Headquarters, Long handed it over to an RAAF appointee. He returned to the post of Director of Naval Intelligence but used his connections to ensure that information continued to flow through to him. In an odd twist, the man who took Long's place at COIC was the husband of the woman whose secret love letters had been decrypted by the University of Sydney's code breakers in 1940, but as an RAAF man he had no reason to sift through the army's files.

By the next meeting of the executive committee, a few days later, Roberts's temporary name for the new agency had stuck. It would be called Central Bureau, and Joe Sherr was authorised to request £100,000 to purchase and install the equipment it needed. The US Army's half would be paid by the Australian government and debited to the United States under Reverse Lend Lease, the scheme through which the US supplied military equipment to its allies, including later the Soviet Union. The other half would come from the coffers of the Australian Army and the RAAF. The RAAF was also to set up an intercept station in Townsville, and Sandford was put in charge of safe-keeping and distribution of all captured Japanese documents.

As there was no proposal for the navy to be part of the new bureau, Eric Nave had resumed relocating his team to Monterey. It was too early to determine if he could assist the new agency with its code-breaking needs, although he noted with some unease Fabian's contempt for it from the outset. Fabian had nothing to do with Central Bureau after the initial conference. He claimed after the war that the bureau had wanted FRUMEL to merge with it, and that he had looked into the proposal and rejected it. That is fairly unlikely. Central Bureau was conceived from the outset as a separate body, since at the time the code systems used by the Japanese army and navy seemed too different for a merger to be of much benefit.

At this early stage, much of MacArthur's signals intelligence was coming from FRUMEL, though at first it came indirectly through the US Navy in Washington. The general's intelligence chief, Colonel Charles Willoughby, complained that the high command was getting only a selection of the FRUMEL output and then only when it suited the navy. The navy had reservations about the army's attention to security and supplied it with sigint on a 'need-to-know' basis.

This was unacceptable to MacArthur as Supreme Commander of SWPA. He told Admiral Leary that he wanted to be supplied with all intelligence produced by FRUMEL. This demand was passed on to Fabian, who had little alternative but to cooperate. Nonetheless, he drafted a protocol for Leary to hand to his commander. Its three main requirements were:

1. Fabian or a FRUMEL representative would report to MacArthur's HQ at 2 p.m. each day and was not to be kept waiting in an outer office.
2. No one at GHQ would be permitted to make copies of FRUMEL material.
3. Only MacArthur and his chief of staff, General Richard Sutherland, were to be present at the briefing.

It is not known if Leary handed this presumptuous set of conditions to MacArthur. More likely, he assured Fabian that he had without actually doing so. Either way, MacArthur was briefed daily as the protocol envisaged—without Willoughby's presence. On one occasion, Fabian burned in full view of Willoughby the report he'd just shown MacArthur and Sutherland. Ostensibly this complied with security procedure, but it added Willoughby to the list of people who would not be coming to Fabian's aid if and when he needed it.

CENTRAL BUREAU

Central Bureau was formally activated on 15 April 1942 under the command of General Spencer B. Akin, one of MacArthur's inner circle, thereby ensuring that the agency would be a protected species. Its director was Akin's offsider Joe Sherr. Although a joint facility, it was clearly to be under American control, but it was modelled more on Britain's Bletchley Park than on any American agency. Within a few days, the new organisation started setting up in opulent premises Sandford had located a short distance along the river from Victoria Barracks.

Cranleigh was a large ivy-covered mansion on a half-acre block on Domain Road, in Melbourne's socially desirable suburb of South Yarra. The three-storey brick residence had twenty-eight rooms, including attic rooms under a tiled roof, a ballroom, and a billiards room 'with a floor sufficiently reinforced to carry a number of machines which are being brought out from America'. The building was acquired under National Security (General) Regulations. Its owner, Dorothy Jack, in her thirties and heiress to her father's insurance-brokerage wealth, continued living in one part of the house when Central Bureau moved in, despite the secrecy surrounding its work. This would have horrified Rudy Fabian if he learned of it, confirming his view that the US Army was sloppy with security.

Mic Sandford, still only 25 years old, was put in charge of setting up the new organisation and its day-to-day activities, but with little experience to draw on, Central Bureau had a frustrating start. The radio operators with experience in Crete and the Middle East were finding *kana* signals difficult, and errors were made in the early days. While the US Navy was cock-a-hoop after Coral Sea, Central Bureau couldn't decode the Japanese army's ciphers.

The personnel making up the fledgling agency were an uneven mix. The Australians who had returned from the war with Germany dominated its early work, which consisted mostly of traffic analysis. They could reconstruct enemy radio networks, locate transmitters and identify call signs, but they couldn't read the enciphered texts. Jack Newman passed on any army call signs that his naval interceptors knew about, although by June the US Navy's Admiral Leary had put a stop to that. Members of the WAAAF (Women's Auxiliary Australian Air Force) soon began arriving as teleprinter operators, secretaries and typists. The RAAF trained more *kana* operators at the Melbourne Showground, north of the city, and started a course for thirteen WAAAF radio operators.

The Americans, survivors of Station 6 in the Philippines, contributed very little at first, although their numbers soon expanded. Eighteen men from the US Army's 837th Signal Service Detachment were sent in late April in response to the plea to Washington from MacArthur. Catching a commercial flight to San Francisco, they were flown to Hawaii by an Australian crew in a military plane full of machine guns and aircraft parts. It was so cold the men spent the fifteen-hour flight wrapped in blankets. Hitching the remaining 11,000 kilometres to Sydney on RAAF and USAAF (United States Army Air Force) planes, they arrived to find that MacArthur's HQ was in Melbourne, not Sydney. A long train ride completed the journey.

Also in the mix were British intercept operators and a cryptanalyst who had made their way to Melbourne from Singapore as the invaders closed in. Lieutenant Norman Webb, the only British representative on Central Bureau's executive committee, had been an oil company rep in China and Japan before the war and had lived with a Japanese family. When the war started, he joined the British Army in Hong Kong and moved to Singapore with FECB, escaping to Australia before the island fell to the Japanese in February.

There were few Japanese speakers in the early Bureau, but over time it drew on linguists already in the American intelligence community. Larry Clark had worked on the Purple code before the war, and Hugh Erskine was born and raised in Japan by missionary parents. Clarence Yamagata, a Hawaiian-born Manila lawyer who had acted as legal adviser to the Japanese consulate, offered his services to the US Army when the Japanese attacked the Philippines. He was posted with signals intelligence and left Corregidor airstrip in April in a patched-up trainer aircraft. Transferred to a B-25 bomber at Panay Island, he arrived in Australia after a gruelling seventeen-hour flight. The 39-year-old was assigned to Central Bureau, but surprisingly few *nisei* (second-generation Japanese-Americans) were ever sent to Australia.

By the beginning of May, Central Bureau had sixty-eight staff, all of them living off site in their own homes, in rental accommodation, in camp barracks or boarding in private houses. If they didn't live within walking distance, they took the tram to work. The WAAAF women, mostly from the country, were a separate consideration. Concerns for their moral safety overrode any thoughts of comfort. Segregated initially into a large, grubby building in a former girls' school in Malvern, a few suburbs away, they slept on straw mattresses laid on creaking iron bedsteads. In time, they were moved to several large houses acquired as WAAAF accommodation in Toorak, adjacent to South Yarra and just as affluent.

Some of the Americans clubbed together to rent houses, one group renting a villa in St Kilda, a bayside suburb with a beach, an ice-skating rink and a big theatre. The cottages there were filled in the summertime with vacationers from Victoria's country towns and farms, but they were empty in July when the overseas arrivals were looking for accommodation. As it turned out, the men would be gone before summer returned.

Security was a worry, particularly with staff living in general barracks and the possibility that friendly conversation with fellow soldiers might leak details of their secret work. In a hunt for accommodation to keep Bureau workers behind a wall of secrecy, the two-storey Grosvenor House was found. Around the corner from Cranleigh, it could hold up to 80 men. But when Army Minister Frank Forde learned that it was owned and occupied by a frail retired grazier, his unmarried son and a full-time nurse, he refused to approve its acquisition. Instead, he suggested that the bureau move out of the city or requisition a hotel. It did neither, and shelved the problem for the time being.

Although those at Central Bureau made slow progress, they were full of enthusiasm. Workers would slip out for a meal in the nearby Chinese restaurant, returning to their clandestine office to work into the night. Some played volleyball in their lunch break on the lawn alongside the house or went to the Botanic Gardens for 'a walk and a pie'. Men from one boarding house fed the ducks there with the soggy beetroot sandwiches that their landlady regularly made for them.

The Americans were adjusting to morning and afternoon tea breaks and lunch hours that extended beyond the hour. To the Australians, the newcomers were men who wore tight trousers, never ate mutton unless it was renamed veal, drank endless coffees, and thought the war had started in December 1941. Over time, each group became accustomed to the ways of the other as the Bureau plunged into a seemingly near-impossible task, the decoding of Japanese army ciphers, which were frustratingly more elusive than their naval counterparts.

The paths of Mic Sandford, the bright star of the army agency, and Eric Nave, the pioneer of Australian naval cryptography, had crossed just once, at the signals intelligence conference in April. Jack Newman had commented to Sandford on Nave's ability to train new code breakers, speaking highly of his skills. Aware of Fabian's disdain for Central Bureau, Sandford cautiously asked Nave if he would be prepared to train some of the Bureau's operators who were to be sent to forward intercept stations being set up in Darwin and Townsville. Since his days in British sigint, Nave had seen cryptography as an interservice discipline. He had no hesitation in agreeing.

CENTRAL BUREAU

Nave's small classes in untangling Japanese army and navy air–ground codes were held in an attic room in Cranleigh, with the winter sun slanting through the lead-paned gable windows. Early in the year, the British Army had captured a Japanese army air–ground codebook in India. Similar books had been found by Allied troops in the Philippines before they were forced out. By the time the books reached Central Bureau the codes were no longer in use, but they gave an insight into how Japan's air–ground code systems were constructed. Nave's training built on this. His pupils were soon able to read the three-*kana* code used by enemy pilots to signal to their base, and to reconstruct the codes readily when they were changed. Used by Japanese naval pilots in mid-flight, the signals required speedy encryption and had no added cipher. Intercepted pilot messages seldom had long-term or strategic significance, but their usefulness in front-line locations under threat of air raid could be immediate and crucial.

With Nave providing training and Newman call signs, Central Bureau tried to set up a regular exchange of material with FRUMEL. Backed by Admiral Redman in Washington, Fabian said he wasn't interested. For him, JN-25 was the main game. The US Navy unit, he insisted, was 'concerned solely with information on Japanese naval circuits, whereas Central Bureau was not'.

It was a specious argument, fuelled by Fabian's tribalism. This war was fought across oceans and, since Japanese army units in the field were separated from their bases by large expanses of sea, some of their traffic passed on naval circuits. It was often coded from one system to another, which provided potential cribs. Messages sent in JN-40 (merchant shipping) and JN-11 (auxiliary fleet system) codes, for instance, included some army intelligence, such as troop movements. There was probably material coming into FRUMEL that would be extremely useful to Joe Sherr's people, but this was not an argument Fabian was prepared to hear. In his view, Central Bureau should set up its own interception of the Japanese army circuits.

If the agency was to go it alone, it would need to expand its expertise. In further response to MacArthur's plea to Washington, a second group of army cryptographers arrived at Melbourne in June 1942. In the party was Abe Sinkov, the ex-schoolteacher from Brooklyn who'd been part of the 1941 American delegation to Bletchley Park that had been treated with polite indifference. Recently married to a Washington cryptanalyst, he'd been the second choice, but he was determined to make the most of the opportunity, even if it meant leaving his new wife behind.

Central Bureau was ready to organise itself into service divisions. Major Sinkov took command of its expanding US Army contingent, with Captain Sandford in charge of the Australian Army section and Squadron-Leader Roy Booth the RAAF group. A hard-working, demanding supervisor, the laconic Sinkov was not difficult to work with. Short and bespectacled, more like a professor than a military commander, he let his team know when he was unimpressed with their results, and he showed his appreciation when good work was done.

The Australian contingent at Cranleigh was put to work on air–ground codes. They would be used in the pilots' messages the planned forward intercept stations would be targeting. The Americans attacked the Imperial Japanese Army's low-level three-digit regimental codes, assuming them to be less secure than the four-digit ciphers of divisions and higher command levels. The assumption proved false. Each Japanese regiment had its own code and would only need to signal its constituent units and its parent division. Because the units of any regiment usually operated near each other, their messages could be sent on low-power circuits after contact had been made at higher power. The weak signals made ungarbled interception difficult, and the code breakers couldn't get enough signals in any of the regimental codes to find patterns.

High-command signals were transmitted on stronger power for clear reception over a wider area, or relayed through two or three radio links, some of them naval circuits. They were easier to intercept than the regimental signals, but with too little traffic to process without access to US Navy-controlled intercepts, Central Bureau—indeed Allied cryptographers in general—had been unable to break into the Japanese army's higher-level codes. It needed to make the most of its limited progress to that point and that meant front-line interception, with smaller units spread widely across northern Australia and eventually further to the north, to the edge of the expanded Empire of the Rising Sun.

— • —

The army intercept station at Park Orchards in suburban Melbourne had continued to pick up Japanese diplomatic signals, as it had before Pearl Harbor, but these had become less important since Japan had entered the war. The facility was more useful for intercept operators evacuated from Singapore to provide *kana* training to Jack Ryan's unit back from the Middle East. With a cold, wet Melbourne winter on the way, the men slept under half a dozen blankets in tents surrounded by mud.

The group, grown to over 180, was renamed the Australian Special Wireless Group in May 1942 and moved to a training camp at Bonegilla, near the New South Wales border. Living conditions improved a little, but training became more serious and more military, with route marches, rifle drill and lectures in hygiene and security. If the men thought the increased training rigour would make heroes of them, they were soon disabused of that notion. Recruits were told, 'Not only do you not exist, you never will have existed. You will remain for always unknown and unacknowledged. There will be no awards, no glory. There will be no medals for this unit.'

Jack Ryan, promoted to major, was put in command of the training facility. At the same time, new operators from the Australian Women's Army Service (AWAS) started arriving for a three-month intensive course. If they passed the rigorous test at the end, they would start immediately as intercept operators. From then on, more and more recruits trained at Bonegilla would be women.

An army intercept team went by train and truck to Darwin in June. It initially set up camp at Winnellie, across the dusty Stuart Highway from the city's airfield. The RAAF intercept unit had operated at the airfield until the Japanese bombing raid in February. Sleeping in the open under mosquito nets, No. 51 Wireless Section worked around the clock with two truck-mounted intercept receivers. Bites from green ants and march flies added to the discomfort of heat, swirling dust and blowflies. With the Japanese consolidating their hold on the Dutch East Indies and Timor, and Darwin under daily attack, the unit's task was to locate aircraft activity north of the town. Messages in high-level codes were sent back to Melbourne for code breakers to attempt solving; decryption of air–ground codes and traffic analysis were done by the unit, and they helped pick up Japanese fighter and bomber movements.

The Japanese had taken over commercial telegraph stations in the Dutch East Indies as ship-to-shore stations, but at first they depended on local staff, mostly Eurasians, to operate them. These Morse signallers used plain-language English to message each other, passing snide comments about the Japanese, but switched to code when a Japanese serviceman shared the watch. Later the Japanese used their own call signs, but they were easily tabbed by the intercept unit, as were monthly changes of call sign.

Most of the movements No. 51 Wireless Section tracked were by naval aircraft using the code they'd been trained to decipher. The Australians also took advantage of a common weakness in Japanese encrypted signalling. Japan's empire was spread so widely across the western Pacific and Southeast Asia that changes in their codes were not uniform, the same message sometimes being sent to one station in uncoded *kana* Morse and another in code. After a code change, a receiving station might signal back, 'We haven't changed to the new code yet,' and the message would be repeated in the old code, providing interceptors with another crib for the new code.

After a few weeks at Winnellie, the radio men moved to a new location with improved working and living conditions. At Coomalie Creek, 80 kilometres south of Darwin, they set up camp on a low hill that picked up the breeze. Beneath high gum trees and swaying palms, they built a spacious operations hut from local timber, with a corrugated iron roof, roll-up hessian sides and compacted dirt floor. Alongside it were a large mess and recreation hall and a kitchen. Engineers from the nearby military base at Batchelor sunk a bore to pump water from the creek alongside the camp up to a tank supplying a shower block.

The bush teemed with wallabies, the tents with insects. Trip wires attached to empty jam tins were set up around the camp perimeter to warn of intruders, but only units on night exercises from the military base ever triggered them. Mosquitoes were a constant problem. The men wore long trousers in the evening with shirt sleeves rolled down, and tried to smoke out the insects by lighting fires in kerosene tins filled with wet grass. Violent tropical thunderstorms regularly pounded the site in the late afternoon, with disastrous results for anyone unwise enough to leave his tent open. The men developed a range of itches and rashes, and soon mildew started growing on boots and other leather. With Japanese bombers also pounding the area, slit trenches were dug around the tents to provide rudimentary shelter from the debris of explosions.

The workplace was informal. The men wore only shorts and boots during the day. Little attention was paid to rank, in keeping with the personality of the unit's commander, the cheerful and egalitarian Captain Ralph Thompson. The radio men's principal tasks were to trace aircraft movements, identifying types and numbers, advising of concentrations and locations, and warning of suspected imminent air raids. They detected aircraft being brought up to Timor, then forward to bases in New Britain and New Guinea for raids on Darwin. The Japanese kept their fighters and bombers at rear bases in Singapore and the Philippines, bringing them forward on the afternoon or evening before a planned attack. Detection of these movements by traffic analysis provided one or two days' warning of impending raids.

With the assistance of codebooks retrieved from downed Japanese planes, they decrypted naval air–ground messages sent in three-*kana* and three-digit codes. These intercepts, providing departure places, destinations and times, weather reports, and sightings by the enemy, were sent to Central Bureau by landline from Darwin. Code-group meanings solved in Brisbane were sent daily to field units. Details of convoy positions, submarine sightings and the like were passed from Central Bureau to GHQ and units in the field. Mainline army traffic was also picked up by No. 51 Wireless Section, but none of it could be deciphered.

For all the busyness of work in this remote tropical listening post, the men found it 'flat and boring'. They were 3000 kilometres from the nearest capital city, too far from the sea for swimming, and had no fresh meat, fruit or vegetables. Meals consisted of bully beef, powdered egg, tinned butter they called 'axle grease', baked beans, and dried peas left to expand between layers of wet hessian before cooking. They tried growing fruit and vegetables with mixed results.

Some of the men tamed parrots and white cockatoos, which they chained to tent poles. Pet wallabies and kangaroos hopped about the camp. Evenings might be enlivened with sing-alongs and cards or draughts in the mess. Much of their spare time was spent aimlessly observing nature, particularly the geckos. 'When you've been in Darwin a few months, you find yourself talking to the lizards,' one wit wrote home, 'but after another couple of months, the lizards start answering.'

In August a new unit of fifty men, designated No. 55 Wireless Section, was transferred to equatorial New Guinea on the Dutch trader MV *Maetsuycker*, along with eight vans and trucks. Camping in the open on their first night in Port Moresby, the men endured a raid by three Japanese bombers. The bombs fell wide, but for most of the men it was their first taste of enemy action. With stores and equipment brought ashore on barges, they set up an intercept station at nearby Fairfax Harbour, in a ready-made room with louvred walls for ventilation. A detachment was sent by boat to Wanigela on the north Papuan coast, where two tons of mobile direction-finder equipment was landed by long boat on swampy ground. Any aircraft movement towards New Guinea that was detected by No. 51 Wireless Section was passed on to No. 55 so it could be closely tracked, but as the enemy withdrew along the coast the usefulness of this information receded. The detachment lugged its gear by ship back to Moresby and on to Kerema, further around the Gulf of Papua. As intercept stations spread across Australia's Top End and northern approaches, enemy air activity could be detected on a far greater scale than with just one station operating near Darwin. Apart from the Wanigela station, however, New Guinea's towering Owen Stanley Range was a barrier to intercepting the low-power regimental transmissions. Those codes remained unbroken.

— • —

The RAAF was also venturing north, having trained *kana* operators in classrooms under a stand at the Melbourne Showground. Tasked by Central Bureau's executive committee in April with setting up an intercept station in the north Queensland city of Townsville, Roy Booth commandeered two houses back to back on a high spot in the suburb of Pimlico. Aerials were erected in

June and radio receivers installed. The station was able to locate enemy airfields and intercept early signals from bombers heading towards New Guinea and northern Australia. The unit was designated No. 1 Wireless Unit RAAF, taking over the title of the Darwin unit that had dispersed after the February air raid.

By mid-1942, tensions were building in Townsville, a small city swollen with transients to four or five times its normal population of 25,000. Anti-military feeling, sometimes mutating into anti-Americanism, simmered in the permanent residents, even after air raids in June reminded them how close the war was. Troops ran the town, and its citizens felt pushed around. Civilians stood in queues with ration cards while the US Army baked 5000 loaves a day for its GIs. The Americans were unconcerned what they paid for food, and prices went up. Soldiers fell into two economies. Australian troops lined up at Townsville's wet canteen, exchanging tickets for beer served in old fruit tins. It was a far cry from the sophistication of the American canteens.

The newcomers got drunk and joined queues outside brothels in Ford Street, known colloquially as Broadway. Cash-strapped Australian soldiers were known to stand in brothel queues and sell their place to an American when they were near the door. Demand in Ford Street far exceeded supply, and some prostitutes plied their trade in Townsville's parks.

A team of twelve covert *kana* intercept operators and linguists arrived by train in early June after an arduous journey over two state borders with frequent halts on sidings waiting for southbound trains to pass through. Four of the group were US Army evacuees from Corregidor, among them the quietly unassuming and always smiling ex-lawyer Clarence Yamagata. Three of the Australians had been in Darwin during the Japanese bombing. The unit set up in the Pimlico houses. Some of the messages they intercepted—such as advice of imminent bombing raids—were to be handled locally, but most were sent to Melbourne for processing and action, provided processing was possible and the time for action hadn't passed.

Later in the month, fifty-five US Army personnel were transferred to Townsville to train at No. 1 Wireless Unit with the remnants of Manila's Station 6 under Howard Brown of the US Army. Promoted to captain, Brown was put in command of the expanded unit, a joint US Army–RAAF operation. He had come to Townsville in April, flying from Brisbane over thick cloud with a pilot whose date had stood him up the night before. The pilot asked Townsville for a radio bearing.

'That can't be right,' he muttered crankily to himself. 'We haven't been in the air long enough.'

He flew on for an hour and a half until he found a hole in the clouds, then followed a railway line, but all station names had been taken down to inconvenience any Japanese invasion. He flew north for another hour and landed on an airfield below another break in the clouds. RAAF ground crew came over, and the pilot opened his door.

'Where are we?'

'Cooktown,' said an RAAF man. The name meant nothing to the American, but it clearly wasn't Townsville. That took another day.

'Brownie' to the Aussies in his team, the unit commander expressed his personality freely with his service pistol, taking pot shots through his window at pigeons on a telegraph wire when he had nothing better to do. On one occasion, he fired a round through the ceiling of his living quarters.

He drove around Townsville in a US Army command car, parking it at night in the street. One morning it went missing and off-duty intercept operators were formed into a posse to find it. When it was found abandoned on the outskirts of town, men were staked out across the road with instructions to 'shoot to kill' when the thieves returned. They never did.

Brownie was living his own Wild West movie. For the most part, the Australians enjoyed his antics, but the gung-ho commander of this remote listening post was also useful for his high-level contacts at Central Bureau. He'd been with General Akin and Colonel Sherr in Manila and Corregidor. Those connections opened doors through which necessary items in short supply could come the unit's way.

Work had commenced at the end of May on a purpose-built intercept station at Stuart Creek, 15 kilometres out of Townsville and fairly inaccessible. By mid-July the occupants could move out of their suburban houses in Pimlico to the remote new station, completed ahead of schedule. The operations building was a bomb-proof blockhouse 70 metres square with thick reinforced concrete walls and no windows. Its only entrance was a sliding armour-plated door. To ensure that this anomalous structure in the middle of the scrub did not attract the unwelcome interest of Japanese patrol planes, it was painted on the outside to resemble a Queenslander, the type of wooden house set up on brick buttresses that was widespread in the state. The *trompe l'oeil* paintwork included doors, windows, verandah, railings and trellis. The only features that weren't fake were steps leading up to a false door, and a water tank. Sloped corrugated-iron sheets concealed the flat concrete roof. Rhombic aerials and antennas were hidden among the surrounding eucalypts. A few dilapidated houses nearby were converted into living quarters. From the air, the station would look like a typical Queensland farmhouse set among the gum trees, accessed by a rough dirt road.

The air-conditioned working area was divided into an intercept room, with a dozen or more radio receivers around the walls, and an intelligence section with plotting tables, scramble phones, maps, and a teleprinter connected to Central Bureau in Melbourne. Concrete direction-finder (D/F) stations were built inland at Julia Creek and further north at Tolga, on the Atherton

Tableland. Together with one already operating at Rockhampton, these created a 300-kilometre arc to pinpoint enemy radio sources. Intercepts of air-to-base and air-to-air transmission located aircraft positions at the intersection of their bearings from any two of the D/F stations.

Intercept operators worked eight-hour shifts, with each receiver tuned to a different radio frequency. When a signal came through on the operator's earphones, he would grab a pencil and put his hand up. The shift supervisor—called the 'trick chief' by the Americans and, before long, by everyone—would stand alongside the operator, noting the frequency and taking the completed message to the intelligence room for decryption and translation. With air-to-ground signals, D/F stations were put on alert to fix the plane's position. Translated messages were phoned to fighter control at Townsville air base if urgent, or enciphered and sent by teletype to Central Bureau. If later an uncoded message, 'HE HE HE', was picked up, jubilation would erupt in the intercept room. It was Japanese pilot shorthand for 'I'm being attacked!'

The atmosphere in the operations room was a mix of tense professionalism and informality. To assist decryption, operators rated their intercepts according to reception quality from 1 (not reliable) to 5 (very accurate), but a request by a Japanese operator for a repeat of a message that had been successfully copied by the eavesdroppers drew hoots of derision. The joviality was a means of avoiding the harsh reality of their mission: their successes would save lives, their failures would cost lives. It preyed on most of the men's minds. Some found the responsibility a heavy burden; others managed not to dwell on it.

On 25 July 1942, a week or so after the move to Stuart Creek, two Emily (Kawanishi H8K2) flying-boat bombers left Rabaul harbour heading south. A message back to base, sent in *kana* Morse by the lead plane, was picked up by a No. 1 Wireless Unit operator, who recognised the call sign as Rabaul HQ of the Japanese navy's

14th Air Group. He concluded the planes were on either a reconnaissance or a bombing mission, probably to Port Moresby or to Milne Bay, at the eastern tip of New Guinea. Townsville's Garbutt Air Base was asked to get a bearing on the next radio transmission from the lead plane. Four hours later, it was obvious the aircraft had overshot New Guinea and were heading further south. The signals became louder, and D/F fixed the planes on a line towards Townsville, estimating that they would reach there about 11.30 that night.

The RAAF's Operational Group in Townsville was notified of the suspected threat, but traffic analysis was a new concept for its people and they preferred to rely on their own radar. The two enemy planes were not identified on radar, and they flew over the sleeping city before midnight unopposed, proceeded out to sea and returned about an hour later to drop fifteen bombs. These fell fairly ineffectually around a wharf with three ships tied alongside, but in the aftermath residents of Townsville started urgently digging more slit trenches for shelter.

Two days later, another Emily bomber taking off from Rabaul was intercepted by No. 1 Wireless Unit operators. Townsville defences were alerted with seven hours' warning. This time, when the plane arrived at 2.30 in the morning it was greeted by searchlights and anti-aircraft gunfire. The Japanese dropped eight bombs hurriedly on a ridge they mistook for the air-base runway. Six American Airacobras chased after the intruder, but their inexperienced fighter pilots were as ineffective as the enemy's bombing.

The next day, 28 July, another Kawanishi left Rabaul heading for Townsville and No. 1 Wireless Unit again gave seven hours' notice of its approach. Townsville radar reported after midnight that the plane was thirty minutes away. Searchlights bailed up the intruder. Anti-aircraft fire was held off so two Airacobras, already in the air and waiting, could close in and rake the enemy plane with gunfire. With its rear gunner silenced and a shell appearing to explode inside the tail, the bomber dropped most of its payload in the bay and turned back. Its eighth bomb fell close to the racecourse, shattering windows but doing little other damage.

The fighter pilots reported that they'd downed the plane, and a story of their success appeared in the Melbourne newspaper *The Argus*. In fact, No. 1 Wireless Unit had tracked the wounded plane back to Rabaul and reported this to MacArthur's GHQ in Brisbane, but it was decided not to tell local RAAF, US Air HQ or the press. Tokyo radio, meanwhile, was reporting that three bombing raids had smashed military installations in Townsville. There was a war being fought and there were stories being told, but the two didn't necessarily coincide.

In October, a further twenty-four trained *kana* radio operators arrived and No. 1 Wireless Unit was able to set up a round-the-clock watch of three eight-hour shifts. Japanese operators were quick, sending *kana* Morse at 40 to 50 words a minute, whereas RAAF operators sent at about twenty-five.

Technical aids—two in particular—were introduced to help intercept operators recognise enemy transmitters and operators. Radio fingerprinting identified the transmitting set from the technical characteristics of its signal, exposing a call sign transferred to a new location or a changed call sign of a known transmitter. TINA (named after Serpentina, a flexible carnival curiosity) analysed the waveform display of the signal as an enemy operator tapped out his keystrokes, comparing it with past analyses, so a new call sign could be shown to be a known operator. Radio fingerprinting identified the machine which sent the message, TINA the operator who tapped it out.

Experienced interceptors often found TINA slower than the intuitive system they already used—recognising individual signallers by their 'fist', the characteristic manner in which they used the Morse keys: their speed and pauses, and the length of their taps for a dot or dash. It was rather like recognising pianists by the way they play. As the eavesdroppers didn't know the signallers' names, they gave them nicknames. The advantage of 'fist' was its immediacy. TINA took time to process its information and, in the opinion of many of the intercept operators, was far less reliable.

— • —

Back in July, while Central Bureau was putting in place a divisional structure, its principal client, the Southwest Pacific Area command, concluded that the Japanese advance had been blunted by the failure to land an invasion force at Port Moresby, and General MacArthur decided to move his GHQ nearer the front. On 20 July 1942 it set up in the AMP Society building in the middle of Brisbane. A second US Army headquarters, the US Army Forces in the Far East (USAFFE) under General Richard Sutherland, moved into the Temperance and General Insurance building, a block away. Sutherland headed the general staffs of both headquarters, but since he reported to MacArthur, his office was in the AMP building.

Central Bureau followed MacArthur north. In September, Mic Sandford sent a scout to Brisbane to ensure the agency's accommodation would be suitable. It was his fellow Greek speaker from the march to the Cretan coast a year before. Geoff Ballard arrived in a city transformed into a garrison, with thousands of American and Australian troops in camps dotted around its suburbs. In his first tangible evidence of the nearness of the Pacific war, he saw a group of wounded Japanese POWs captured in New Guinea and brought down in the hospital train from Townsville. He was struck by how short these enemy soldiers were.

At MacArthur's headquarters, Ballard was told a large mansion had been acquired for Central Bureau in Ascot, a quiet residential suburb twenty minutes' drive away. Nyrambla had been built on 15 acres of bushland before the turn of the century for the manager of the Australian Joint Stock Bank. In 1905, much of the bush was cleared and the estate was subdivided into blocks. On little more than an acre and surrounded by newer houses, the original brick building was converted into flats in the late Twenties. By the time it was taken over by Central Bureau, it had become tatty and was rumoured to be operating as a bordello, but many of the features of its grander days were still intact. Red glass panels etched with classical female figures flanked the imposing main entrance, and an elegant cedar staircase rose from a spacious arched hall to six bedrooms and a sitting room upstairs. The large rooms had high, ornately plastered ceilings, red cedar doors and architraves, solid beech floors, and fireplaces with tiled hearths and marble mantelpieces.

An ornamental ironwork railing ran along the open verandahs on the upper floor. At the back were a double garage and a two-storey wing that had been maids' quarters with kitchen and breakfast room. Nyrambla was dusty and gloomy, but it looked acceptable to Ballard as bureau quarters. It was not as much of a step down from the grandeur of Cranleigh as he had expected. With the new premises approved, the building was rapidly fitted out with new electrical wiring, partitions and shelving, blackout shades for night work, and a teleprinter.

Central Bureau's staff began migrating to Brisbane. A group of two dozen Americans arrived first, after a three-day train trip from Melbourne over the different gauges of three states' railways. The first Australians followed in trucks. The bureau's equipment came by rail under armed guard, all of it unloaded and reloaded onto a new train at each state border. In Brisbane, the new arrivals were put in interim accommodation. The Australians were at Ascot Racecourse (now Eagle Farm). The Americans were in a temporary camp at the dusty Doomben Racecourse nearby before being moved to the open balcony of Central Bureau's new premises, which was always referred to as 21 Henry Street, its address in Ascot, rather than Nyrambla.

The mansion accommodation didn't last long. As more personnel arrived, the residents were moved out of Henry Street so additional work spaces could be set up. They were billeted with families, or boarding houses or rented rooms were found for them. Eight Americans rented an empty house in nearby Hamilton, bought a dining-room suite and hired a housekeeper. Their rooms were empty apart from GI stretchers and a few pieces of furniture loaned by nearby residents. Occasionally an obliging neighbour came over and grilled steaks for them.

The outsiders were struck by Brisbane's shanty-town suburbs, which sprawled over its hills alongside a wide river snaking towards Moreton Bay; by the queues of silver trams clanging along Queen Street in peak hours; by the sweet tropical aroma of mango and pawpaw drifting out of fruit shops. It all added to the disconnected feeling of doing work that couldn't be revealed to anyone.

The bureau's Australian workers either remained in military camps or were boarded in private houses. The placements didn't always work out. After numerous complaints about a boarding house known as The Shambles by its residents, the lodgers were moved to tents on Doomben Racecourse. Officers fared better, renting in the vicinity of Ascot. Mic Sandford, now a major, found accommodation in a large and splendid house on Eldermell Terrace, in the adjacent suburb of Hamilton, along with his batman, Private Wainwright, a young soldier with a disconcertingly theatrical manner. They made an odd couple.

— ● —

Back in April 1942, the new code-breaking station had requested IBM equipment from the US to collate and tabulate its intercepted messages. Machine parts were shipped in crates from San Francisco to Sydney, but Central Bureau wasn't notified of their arrival until a few months later, when a clerk found the shipping invoices. An officer sent by Abe Sinkov to investigate found large wooden crates, coated with grime and sea salt, sitting at the end of a Sydney Harbour wharf. They were rail-freighted to Brisbane.

The parts were taken out of their boxes, stripped and cleaned of corrosion. One box had a picture of an assembled machine but no instructions on how to assemble it. Many of the boxes had parts in numbered envelopes, but there was no parts list. As luck would have it, one of the enlisted Americans had trained on IBM equipment and knew what many of the parts were. Trial and error determined what the others were for.

When the tabulators were eventually assembled, they were set up in 21 Henry Street's double garage, by then air-conditioned and insulated. An American, Zac Halpin, was put in charge of the machine section. The early work of the Bureau had been done by hand, but now it had the capacity to sort the content of intercepts much more rapidly. Progress was made with army air–ground codes, drawing on the initial training in Melbourne, although Eric Nave was no longer available to the Bureau. Intercepted weather reports from reconnaissance planes indicated imminent Japanese air raids. Land-based air cover indicated the progress of Japanese convoys and enemy sightings of Allied convoys. These identified immediate threats but gave little insight into longer-term Japanese strategy.

Before Pearl Harbor, the Japanese army had a single system for communication at higher levels, much like the navy's JN-25 code, but as the Japanese Empire spread across the Pacific, new additive tables were introduced for different regions. By May 1942, the main army system had been split into two. A third system was used by the Water Transport section, which was responsible for moving troops and supplies around the Pacific. All three systems had several additive tables for use by divisions in different areas. Indicators of the starting point in additive tables were enciphered in a code that remained impenetrable to the Allies. Without the additives, they couldn't get to the underlying code. By the end of

1942, they had made no progress with any of the army codes used for strategic messaging.

Despite the limited success, Central Bureau expanded, fuelled by high expectations of signals intelligence after the naval successes at Coral Sea and Midway. Luna Park, on the edge of Brisbane, had been hired in September by the US Army as a camp for its Signal Corps, which used the Cloudland Ballroom as barracks. The park became home for additional sigint personnel arriving from America; one of the GIs described it as 'a magnificent, jerry-built, unsuccessful Coney Island'. Other enlisted men moved into tents on Ascot Racecourse, not far from Doomben, while officers continued to rent in the surrounding suburbs. Female staff transferred from Melbourne were accommodated in army barracks at Chermside, 5 kilometres away, or an air force camp built on Victoria Park Golf Course, on the northern rim of the city. By the end of 1942, about 150 personnel were employed in the Henry Street mansion.

The main building was a rather gothic, almost Dickensian workplace. Its spacious but shabby and dimly lit rooms were cluttered with wooden desks, filing cabinets and messy shelves of papers, manuals and books. As the number of workers grew, the desks were moved closer together. Screens started to appear around some of the individual work spaces. Rooms reverberated with the sounds of paper rustling and various clicks, taps and chairs squeaking, but there was an eerie lack of voices. If people wanted to talk, they'd go out onto the front balcony or into the garden or make tea or coffee in a kitchen.

The limited number of translated decrypts and intelligence summaries the Bureau produced went to Abe Sinkov, who decided which should go by courier to General Spencer Akin in the city. Occasionally Sinkov would come to the AMP Building to brief Akin, a gangly technocrat who rarely visited Central Bureau, ostensibly so no one could infer a link between its work and his position as MacArthur's signals chief. Generally the cryptanalysts were not told what use was made of their work. Sinkov was unaware what Akin did with the reports but presumed they were sent to MacArthur and Willoughby. In fact, Akin decided which material should go to Sutherland, who in turn determined what went to MacArthur. Little of it went directly to the German-born Willoughby, who had the accent and mannerisms of a Prussian officer. Instead, intercepts were re-enciphered and radioed to Arlington Hall, on the outskirts of Washington, where a former girls' school had been taken over by the US Army for its Signal Intelligence Service. It was decided there whether any should come back to Willoughby. High-level signals intelligence, code-named Ultra, was assembled into regular summaries.

With his habit of reversing interpretations overnight for no apparent reason, Willoughby was kept on the periphery. The highly competent Sutherland, a foul-tempered egotist, disliked him intensely and at one time would have sacked him if MacArthur hadn't intervened. Promoted to brigadier-general, Willoughby had to make do with delayed signals intelligence selected by Sutherland's office or sent back by Arlington Hall. His unit integrated this with information from other sources—aerial reconnaissance, captured documents, spies, POW interrogations and the like—to produce intelligence summaries, sometimes including analysis that had been overtaken by events. One of MacArthur's generals once wryly commented, 'Willoughby has the best hindsight of any intelligence officer in the army.'

Central Bureau still had little expertise in cryptography. Trained in the less sophisticated air–ground codes, its Australian operators were mostly stationed in field units like Townsville or Darwin. Newly arriving Americans had little experience of Japanese military codes, having worked on European ciphers or the consular Purple code. The Bureau's three commanding officers, Sinkov, Sandford and Booth, worked at coordinating their respective services within the expanding agency, evolving a harmony that had not been evident at FRUMEL. In this, Sandford's drive and energy were key. Gaining a reputation as a problem-solver, he used his charm to deal with both administrative obstacles and hidebound military conservatives.

Sandford built connections to other parts of the intelligence world, not so much to the United States, which he left to Abe Sinkov, but to British intelligence at Bletchley Park and its outpost in India, the Wireless Experimental Centre, and particularly to the Australian Army's Directorate of Military Intelligence, which had remained in Melbourne. In June, Colonel Roberts had been appointed Controller of the Allied Intelligence Bureau, a joint intelligence agency reporting to General Willoughby with a brief that didn't include signals intelligence. Brigadier John Rogers, brought back from the Middle East, was appointed Director of Military Intelligence and Lieutenant-Colonel Robert Little became his assistant director. An alliance developed between the gregarious Sandford and Little, who was gentle and polite. They worked as a team, exchanging information and insights. Little operated mostly from his Melbourne base, while Sandford was often on the move, flying to Darwin or Port Moresby to deal with army field unit problems, or to Melbourne to keep his lines of communication open and stay abreast of developments there.

— ● —

Through 1942, Mic Sandford had kept regular contact with FRUMEL's Jack Newman. The pair dined occasionally with Ath Treweek and his wife at their Jolimont house. When the Holden Agreement was under discussion, Sandford was well placed to know that the Special Intelligence Bureau was to be absorbed into FRUMEL and Eric Nave recalled to the Royal Navy. Nave had phoned Little, seeking a meeting about his unwelcome relocation to London, and this was doubtless passed on to Little's contact in

Brisbane. Keenly aware of the value of Nave's training at Cranleigh earlier in the year, Sandford got on the phone and arranged a meeting.

The two met in late October, and Nave agreed to be loaned to the Australian Army if that could be arranged with the relevant hierarchies. At Sandford's request, Robert Little asked General Ken Smart at the Australian Military Mission in London to seek Admiralty approval of the loan of Nave to Central Bureau, Little passing on Joe Sherr's advice to Sandford that General MacArthur 'desires that steps be taken to obtain Commander Nave's services'. Whether MacArthur actually expressed such a desire is a moot point.

Nearly two months passed without a response to the November request, although assurances came from several quarters that when it did arrive it would be positive. Smart reported on 16 November that he had been given to understand that the Admiralty would approve. Captain Foley of the Australian Navy Board told Little that agreement was anticipated but was delayed because some paperwork—he didn't say whose—had been mislaid. Cocky Long, the constant networker, was also assured by his Royal Navy counterpart that the Australian request would be approved. With the agreement seeming only a formality, Nave moved to Brisbane on 20 December when his leave expired and began working at Central Bureau. Four days later—on Christmas Eve—the Admiralty declared that the recall of Nave to the Royal Navy would stand.

A desperate military went into combat mode. Australia's Chief of Staff, General John Northcott, asked Smart to put the case to the Admiralty for a continued loan as strongly as possible. Nave's service with Central Bureau, Smart was to stress, was 'PROVING OF GREATEST VALUE ON ACCOUNT OF HIS VAST KNOWLEDGE OF CIPHERS AND JAPANESE. IT WOULD BE LITTLE SHORT OF DISASTER IF ADMIRALTY ADHERE TO THEIR DECISION TO RECALL NAVE.'

During the wait for an amended response, the water was muddied when General Sutherland asked that London be advised that GHQ had withdrawn its support for retaining Nave. It's not clear who initiated that—it's not a matter Sutherland would have had a strong view on—but Northcott duly advised London, adding: 'MY REPRESENTATIONS DEFINITELY REMAIN UNCHANGED.' In the end, the interference made no difference. On 20 January, Smart cabled Northcott that the Admiralty had finally agreed that Nave could stay in Australia so long as two British diplomatic translators working in Melbourne were allowed to return home. The fight for the pioneer Australian code breaker had been won.

— • —

Meanwhile in Melbourne, the US Navy's FRUMEL took control of all naval signals interception in Australia, with Australian service personnel from the Special Intelligence Bureau, such as Jim Jamieson of the RAN and Ath Treweek, an army major, absorbed into its structure. SIB's civilian personnel who had worked on diplomatic traffic were transferred from the RAN to the Australian Army in November, moved to Victoria Barracks, and named D Special Section; their remit was to continue intercepting and decoding those signals. The section was to be headed by Dale Trendall, the classics academic Nave had recruited to SIB.

But the navy's preservation of the group and transfer of it intact to the army wasn't an act of generosity or vision. A month before the transfer, with the Holden Agreement negotiations rumbling in the background, the Englishmen Henry Archer and Hubert Graves visited Robert Little. They were not happy that middle-ranking US Navy officers were making decisions about diplomatic intercepts over the heads of British Foreign Office officials and naval intelligence director Rupert Long. Australian intercepts were going through Washington and London before Australians got to see them. The next day, Trendall and Arthur Cooper phoned Little with similar concerns.

Archer hand-wrote long diatribes to Little and memos to the Foreign Office in London explaining why diplomatic intercepts in Australia were so important and should be continued, extolling his and Graves's superior skills, and bemoaning the junior personnel to whom they'd been answerable. The unflappable Little took the missives in his stride. He had his own gripe, anyway. The army had not been treated fairly 'since the advent of U.S.N. Crypto[graphy] Sec[tion] under Lt. Comdr. Fabian', he observed in memo-ese to his director. The army had supplied all diplomatic intercepts, but had been allowed only a précis of the diplomatic intelligence gleaned until recently, when an army representative was allowed to read diplomatic messages supplied by Nave, but only in the presence of a naval officer before being taken away.

Little argued to Rogers that the diplomatic group should not be disbanded but should continue to benefit Australia and its forces, kept within the Australian Army rather than the US-controlled Central Bureau. Chief of General Staff John Northcott wrote to his naval counterpart proposing that Military Intelligence take over SIB's Diplomatic Section, which was then in the process of being severed from FRUMEL.

Settled into Victoria Barracks, the new D Special Section set up a direct line to the army's radio station at Bonegilla. Copies of each night's intercepts were brought down to Melbourne by 'safe hand' despatch rider the next day. Because it was difficult to deliver new codes widely during the war, the Japanese often continued using consular codes longer than was prudent. As a compromise, changes would be introduced to the existing codes, but if the previous system and code were known, it was usually not difficult to work out the changes.

D Section was able to provide useful intelligence on a number of fronts. Intercepted material was passed to Bletchley Park after processing in Melbourne. Messages between Berlin and Tokyo were particularly valuable. Japanese diplomats in Berlin were sending details of German planning to their superiors in Tokyo, but while English intercept stations were having trouble receiving them, Bonegilla was picking them up clearly. Also useful were higher-grade ciphers penetrated by the section, which revealed the reactions of Japan's government to military and political events abroad. In one instance, a Japanese cable from Timor revealed that the enemy was reading Australia's covert operations codes. The existence of D Section was known only to a select few. Intelligence that it circulated was notated simply with 'information available from a secret but entirely trustworthy source'.

Of the Englishmen attached to the Special Intelligence Bureau, Cooper returned to London after it was disbanded, his pet gibbon donated to Melbourne Zoo. Transferred with Trendall to the new sigint group, Archer and Graves remained in Australia for the remainder of the war.

While negotiations over Nave were under way, only the mathematicians Gerry Room and Dickie Lyons remained unaccounted for. Aware of the changes at FRUMEL, Bletchley Park offered the pair positions in Britain, and Nave worked hard at persuading them to accept. Room did so, then changed his mind. When the British offer lapsed, Lyons returned to the University of Sydney to resume his academic career. Room joined Central Bureau.

— ● —

Eric Nave's wife and children had moved with him to Brisbane in December. They lived in a Queenslander with a large yard on Windemere Road, a few blocks south of Henry Street. Nave reported to work at Central Bureau in his naval uniform and continued to dress as a naval officer throughout his time there. He was initially put in charge of air–ground traffic, on which he had worked productively at FRUMEL. Left alone with the task at a desk set up in the wide upstairs corridor, a small lamp relieving the gloom, Nave went through piles of traffic from the field units in northern Australia and New Guinea, and material recovered from downed Japanese naval aircraft. Before long, the naval air–ground code was in his grasp.

Nave provided instruction in *kana* code systems to Australian and American personnel in a training room upstairs at Henry Street that reverberated with a painful memory. In December, US personnel were being shown how to dismantle and reassemble handguns. As the session came to an end, one man accidentally fired his .45 pistol just as a fellow American, John Bartlett, entered the room. Bartlett was hit and seriously wounded; he later died. The shocking accident cast a pall over the organisation that took some time to dissipate.

The gloom of Bartlett's death compounded the cryptanalysts' frustration at making so little headway with the Japanese army's mainline code systems. In nearly a year of operation, the Bureau had penetrated none of the high-level codes. Nor had any other Allied code breakers, but that was cold comfort for a front-line unit. For now it had to satisfy itself with its successes with low-level air–ground traffic under Eric Nave's guidance. Central Bureau had been expanding, gathering expertise and building a viable structure, but so far for very little return. It was all dressed up with nowhere to go. It desperately needed a breakthrough.

Chapter 9

The Water Transport Code broken

Good-looking—handsome, even—and muscular, Joe Richard got into code breaking by chance. Drafted into the army in 1941 and sent to Fort Monmouth, New Jersey, for training as a radio repairman, he ran into an old school buddy who was doing the cryptography course. Code breaking sounded exciting, so Richard talked the authorities into letting him do the cryptanalysis course when he finished the radio one.

The Bundy brothers were on the same course. William would go on to work on the Enigma code in England; McGeorge would become National Security Advisor to two presidents, Kennedy and Johnson. The Bundys progressed so quickly that Richard wondered if someone was giving them the answers. Assigned on graduation to the Washington, DC, office of the Signal Intelligence Service, Richard packaged solved codes by day to send to various agencies and did an evening shift with the traffic analysis unit.

Joe Richard was a self-starter. Routinely copying three-digit code groups from message intercepts onto a form to be punched into IBM cards, he amused himself in his spare time by sifting through the

THE WATER TRANSPORT CODE BROKEN

'TO' and 'FROM' two-digit place-name codes in Japan's message preambles. He concluded the Japanese were using a 10 × 10 square with numbers down the sides and place names in the matrix. The coordinates changed monthly. The Japanese changed that code system about the time the Signal Intelligence Service was moving to new offices and Richard applied for an overseas posting. He was sent to a new facility in Australia called Central Bureau.

Richard travelled to Melbourne in June 1942 with the anti-aircraft gunnery crew on a slow convoy. The job entitled him to three meals a day instead of the two given to soldiers in the hold. A lanky, easy-going, knockabout fellow, he got on well with Australians from the start. Assigned to Cranleigh, as a technician he worked a hand-operated sorting machine designed to find repeated strings of additives in low-level Japanese army messages. The day was spent in teams of three, subtracting additives from three-digit code groups and trying to match positions in messages. Matches were written into grids on large sheets of paper in an attempt to reconstruct additive books. It was a long and tedious process producing random matches, but they made no real inroad into the codes. They could read sender and recipient locations in the message header, like GADARUKANARU (Guadalcanal) and RABARU (Rabaul), but little else.

Life away from the workplace was more stimulating for the young technician, who lifted weights to stay in condition and was always ready with a smile and light, humorous conversation. Joe Richard was falling in love with Australia. He was one of a group of Americans who rented a cottage in St Kilda left empty by the departure of summer vacationers. Their sergeant made the rental arrangements and discouraged anyone else from seeing the landlady. Eventually the others discovered the reason. She had an attractive daughter, and the sergeant did not want anyone getting in his way, especially the tall, dark-haired young technician with the easy-going manner.

After a few months in the winter of the southern city, Richard was moved up to Brisbane with the rest of Central Bureau, helping to drive a truck loaded with photographic equipment and filing cabinets full of classified documents. Their concession to security was to take turns sleeping in the truck at night. Once in Brisbane, he resumed his monotonous work on the open verandah of 21 Henry Street, sorting code groups by hand until the tabulating machines were installed in the garage.

An emotional thread ran beneath Joe Richard's affable exterior. John Bartlett, the man shot in the training room, had been a friend of his. Richard took his death very much to heart, and regretted not taking him to hospital when an ambulance was late arriving. Disappointment with himself clouded his sunny demeanour. Brooding about it in the aftermath of Christmas, he needed some distraction.

He said to Abe Sinkov, recently promoted to colonel, 'Boss, I'm getting no sleep stewing over John Bartlett. Is there some task I could do at nights to take my mind off what happened to him?'

Sinkov thought about it. 'What could you do? Any ideas?'

'Sorting codes or something? Maybe the four-digit traffic.'

'Well, you could have a shot at that, I guess,' said his division head. 'See if you can find any patterns. No one else has. Go see Major Webb.'

Richard went to Norman Webb, the British Army escapee from Singapore who managed the files of daily traffic. A grumpy stickler for military procedure, Webb had messages filed by the day, not the site, of interception and agreed without enthusiasm to release one day's worth at a time. As a starter, Richard was given a manila folder of the messages intercepted on 19 December. He leafed through them on a large wooden table in an upstairs room

Under a weak droplight, with blackout curtains drawn, Joe Richard pored over the intercepts almost every night for several weeks, initially sorting them into the Imperial Japanese Army's

THE WATER TRANSPORT CODE BROKEN

three main code systems: the Water Transport Code (*senpaku ango-sho* 2); the Army Air Force General Purpose Code (*koku ango-sho* 3); and the General Administrative Code (*rikugun ango-sho* 4).

On that first night, Richard found seventeen messages between Japanese radio stations in Rangoon and Saigon sent in the General Purpose Code, where the first twenty-one four-digit groups in the text were identical. This left him a long way from breaking into the code, but at least he had his foot in the door. He doggedly pursued this code over the following weeks, deriving short strings of additives and about thirty code values. Then, in March, the Japanese suddenly stopped using the code. When they resumed ten days later, it had changed, but by then Richard was making more progress with another army code.

This was the Water Transport Code, used in controlling merchant ships leased by the Japanese army to deliver troop reinforcements and supplies. Advance notice of these movements would allow MacArthur's strategists to anticipate enemy strengthening of its forward garrisons. Even better, it would enable the Allies to disrupt Japan's supply lines by submarine and air attacks on the delivery ships.

Scrutinising Water Transport traffic, Richard noticed that the third four-digit group transmitted was the same as the last group in each message. Working on successive days' traffic, having started with 19 December, he prowled around the dimly lit table in his well-laundered naval uniform, lifting sheets from the day's master pile, inspecting the first digit in the repeated code group, and slapping the sheet down on one of the ten piles he was assembling. By the third night of sorting, he noticed that the ten piles were not roughly the same size, as they would have been if all the first digits were randomly distributed in the code groups. Instead, four piles—for the digits 0, 1, 4 and 5—grew at about the same rate, but the other piles never had more than one or two sheets and often none. He had found another small crack in the wall.

Richard concluded that the coded messages, like those in the navy's JN-25 codes, were double-enciphered using additive tables. But the indicator of the starting point in the Water Transport additive table was encrypted in a manner he couldn't fathom. Without knowing how the indicator was encoded, cryptanalysts wouldn't know where to start in the additive table to expose the coded message underneath. Suspecting that the repeated code group indicated a starting point in additive tables, he showed the early results to his division chief.

Sinkov had seen a pattern like this before. Some years earlier, he'd been shown an early weakness in the German Enigma code that lay in the indicator of rotor settings for the encryption machine. That weakness had been rectified by the Germans, but not before it was exploited by a Polish code breaker. This looked similar.

'Write them over each other,' he suggested to Richard, 'and differentiate the groups in each column. Then you can compare the differences.'

It was a long and laborious process. As luck would have it, though, Richard was able to tap into the academic expertise of the recent arrival at Central Bureau, Gerry Room. As a mathematician before the war, Room had specialised in the theory of matrices and willingly shared his erudite knowledge. Night after night, the young American applied Room's advice, pursuing other relationships between code groups, looking for further patterns. Resolute determination gave way to anticipation. Joe Richard felt he was getting somewhere with this project. The ready smile returned, but January rolled into February and progress was slow.

Sinkov saw a glimmer of possibility in his technician's labours and looked at bringing additional hunters into the pursuit. The Brisbane agency circulated monthly progress reports to its US Army counterparts at Arlington Hall near Washington, and to the Wireless Experimental Centre outside Delhi, a British Army

THE WATER TRANSPORT CODE BROKEN

outpost of Bletchley Park. Richard's chief used the February 1943 report to notify the other stations of the tentative advances so far made into the Water Transport Code. He also shared his discovery of the non-random digit and some of the working aids that had been developed with Room's guidance.

Later in the month, Sinkov showed Richard a three-page typed letter. 'Here's something that might interest you.'

It was from Delhi, reporting that the analysts there had arrived at the same non-random result with the first digit of Water Transport's repeated group.

A few days later, a message came from the Arlington Hall staff that they were going to test the non-randomness of this message position with an IBM run of their Water Transport traffic. Ten days later, they reported back on the tabulator's analysis, but it wasn't confirmation of the findings of Richard and the Delhi analysts.

'We've got a problem here, Joe,' Sinkov told Richard. 'Arlington Hall have repeated your work with their own traffic and got no non-randoms.'

'But Delhi did,' said Richard.

'Yes, and SIS haven't.'

Mystified, Richard took Arlington Hall's notes on the breakdown of their intercepts up to his work room—actually the daytime workplace of two cryptanalysts, a once-spacious bedroom divided with a plasterboard partition into two offices. There was no question that the US unit's indicator figure was random, but he couldn't find a reason for the different result. It frustrated him. To clear his mind, he put the problem to one side and went back to the General Purpose Code. The system had just come back on air, but he couldn't make anything work with the little he had.

'I'm going backwards on this one,' he was thinking, when a flash of recognition struck him. The code had been changed!

Earlier in this assignment he had noticed that when he pooled Water Transport messages over a period of two months or more, the indicator digit was random. It was only when he narrowed the time period that the randomness disappeared. It seemed that the indicator code was changed with reasonable frequency, maybe monthly. With that in mind, Richard had continued his research within narrow time spans, since a longer period risked straddling a code change. He'd put this to the back of his mind and, since he'd neglected to tell Sinkov about it, the overseas agencies hadn't been warned.

With this thought, Richard looked again at Arlington Hall's report. Sure enough, they had run messages from December 1942 to February 1943 through their machines. During this time, the indicator code would have changed, with the frequencies of the non-random digits cancelling each other out.

Richard told Sinkov of his discovery and admitted he'd overlooked telling him how often the indicator code changed.

'I got in the habit of looking at narrow time spans,' he explained to his chief, 'and had forgotten why.'

'Not very happy with that,' said the colonel, 'but let's get on with it. I'll let Arlington Hall know where they've gone wrong and you can try to nail down the exact dates the codes were changed.'

That evening, Richard set about pinpointing the change dates. He took folders of intercepted Water Transport messages down to Henry Street's double garage. The IBM machines had only recently become operational and were churning away noisily twenty-four hours a day. Richard asked the operators to index cards by date as well as code groups. Messages from around a suspected change date were punched into cards and run through the tabulators.

The Queensland summer still lingered in the late March air and, despite the air-conditioning inside the noisy garage, it was a stifling space to work in. By eleven o'clock, sleep was overtaking Joe Richard. The repetitive process of transferring intercepts to cards was tedious, and he sensed it would take all night to get through his stack of messages.

THE WATER TRANSPORT CODE BROKEN

He had, however, made useful progress that night, spotting another relationship in the four-digit code groups. For any first digit of a given group in the message, the first digit of the next group would be one of only three of the ten digits possible (0 to 9), never any of the other seven. Those three options differed for each of the ten digits that headed the initial group. Richard made a 10 × 3 table of these relationships, put a halt to the tabulator card-sorting for the night, and took his weary brain home to the house nearby where he lodged with another American.

Next morning, 1 April, Richard conferred with Sinkov. The table he'd drawn up the previous night would have gone in the next monthly progress report to other crypto units, but a report had just left by courier that morning. A month was too long to wait. Richard's table was sent to Arlington Hall that day as an encrypted radio signal instead.

When there was no response from Washington, Abe Sinkov set up a meeting to plan the next stage of attack on the code. With the research continuing to look promising, and bearing in mind that at this time none of the major Japanese army code systems had been penetrated by the Allies, he brought extra effort into the task. Three people were asked to join a meeting with Joe Richard, one of them, Major Larry Clark, a senior officer who'd worked on the Purple code before the war. Zac Halpin was also at the meeting to coordinate the project's use of his IBMs.

By this time, Richard had completed the exhaustive process of running Water Transport intercepts collected on successive days through the tabulators. Changes in the indicator cipher were found to occur roughly four weeks apart. With that clarified, all messages from the first period were put onto cards, and by 6 April an index had been compiled for the expanded team to scrutinise. Soon Larry Clark spotted a relationship between the fourth and fifth code groups, then other numerical links to these groups were picked up. The newcomers on the team spent the rest of the morning jotting down these relationships, producing a list of 100 items.

Richard had spent the morning doing his day job on the open verandah. Lately, winds had been blowing classified documents about, and there was a plan afoot to enclose the verandah, but his mind was elsewhere anyway. He came around to the workroom as Clark and his offsider were getting out their packed lunches to take down to the cockroach-infested kitchen in the building's rear wing.

Richard started to copy the lists the others had compiled so he could work on them. Realising he couldn't copy all of them within one lunch hour and wondering what to do about that, it occurred to him that the lists might be condensed into a table similar to the 10×3 table he'd drawn up a few days earlier. Using methods he'd been taught back in his early training and had applied in his spare time in Washington, Richard imported the lists into one 10×10 square.

Larry Clark came back from lunch and saw the matrix Richard had constructed.

'What's this you've got here, Joe?'

'Oh, I've transferred figures from your notes into a square. Seemed more useful than just copying your listings.'

Clark studied the square intently.

'You know,' he said, 'your three columns from the other night should be in here somewhere.'

After a search, they found three columns that contained the digits of Richard's earlier matrix, although—as the men anticipated—the order of the columns had moved around. After supper together at the Ascot military camp, Clark went home and Richard wandered back to Henry Street, determined to recover the column coordinates of the square. These would be the 'true numbers' in the 10×10 array that would specify the number of the additive book used to encipher the coded message, its page number in the book, and the row and column numbers on that page. This would

THE WATER TRANSPORT CODE BROKEN

be the starting point for the string of additives used to double-encipher that particular message. The Japanese transmitters had three additive books to choose from, hence the non-randomness with three digits.

Upstairs in the main building, Richard stood at the work table, now cleared. The intercepts had been returned to the double garage in their manila folders so Norman Webb's workers could re-file them. To the distant clip-clop of racehorses being led down Henry Street back to their stables, Richard leaned over clean sheets of paper, pencil in hand, trying to reconstruct the Water Transport Code indicator's true square.

He tested a range of combinations. Those that worked out he placed on the master diagram. Many of them took him down what proved to be a numerical cul-de-sac. From time to time he sensed he was on the verge of a solution, only to find it slipping away from him. As the night drifted on and he grew drowsy, solutions became increasingly elusive.

The phone on the desk rang, jolting him out of his lethargy.

'Hey buddy,' said the voice of Larry Clark. 'Are you still there? Are you getting anywhere with that square?'

'I was. Now I'm not. I'm getting sleepy and it's goddamn sliding away from me!'

'I'm coming in.'

Having someone to bounce ideas and options off was a shot in the arm for Richard. Together, he and Clark were able to pull together the remaining coordinates. Shortly after midnight, they completed the square for the period before the first Water Transport code change.

They locked up and made their way to their respective homes, sensing they had made a significant breakthrough, but too exhausted for any certainty. They would leave that for the morning.

In the clear light of day, they knew they had made the breakthrough the army code breakers had been pursuing. Abe Sinkov and Gerry Room agreed. But so drained was Richard by the three-month effort that success almost felt like an anticlimax. Sinkov, however, had no doubts. He telegraphed the square to the other two centres that morning.

In the afternoon, a telegram came back from Arlington Hall: 'WE HAVE ALSO DONE THIS.' They sent a square they had drawn up for the period up to the date of the second code change. Washington also told the two stations what their responsibilities would be in the next phase of penetrating the Water Transport Code. Central Bureau was to reconstruct one of the three additive books; Arlington Hall, with more staff, the other two. Recovered codes and additives would be exchanged daily by radio.

Arlington Hall later claimed they hadn't told Sinkov earlier about their reconstruction of the whole square because at that time the Americans were negotiating with the British for assistance in reading the German Enigma code. The Bletchley Park people were concerned about the Americans' sometimes casual approach to security, and Washington hoped to use the Japanese army code as a bargaining tool to get around this.

'How very convenient for them,' Sinkov commented privately. 'Let them claim to be first to the finishing line if that's what they want, but in the scheme of things it's more important that we got to this point than who got there first.'

Two factors undermine Arlington Hall's story. Bletchley Park would have been aware of the progress with the Water Transport Code from Sinkov's reports to its colleagues in India. In any case, an outcome of the 1942 Holden Agreement between the US and Britain—the agreement that proposed to return Nave to the Royal Navy—had been that the British would leave Japanese codes to the Americans. The British had little interest in keys to the Water Transport Code so long as its analysts in Delhi had access to them. Most likely is that the Arlington Hall code breakers piggybacked on the reports coming from Brisbane, building a solution to the

THE WATER TRANSPORT CODE BROKEN

second indicator square while Central Bureau solved the first square.

After reconstructing indicators on all messages up to a 15 May indicator code change, the Solutions section at Central Bureau began stripping additives off Water Transport messages, enabling the code groups underneath to be deciphered. Otto Mahrt, who had spent his first eighteen years in Japan, was the Solutions section's most successful hand at recovering code groups, a gift that relied more on inspiration than skill. Arlington Hall would routinely send lists of possible code group meanings for Central Bureau to test and confirm or reject.

'I'm not sure I benefit by getting all these recoveries from Washington,' Mahrt commented at one stage. 'I think at least one-third of them are wrong, and it takes me three times as long to correct a wrong recovery as it takes for me to make a new recovery, so I would be making just as many recoveries if I didn't get any help from Washington.'

By June 1943, the Allies were routinely reading messages in Water Transport Code. The Japanese often split their messages in two, with the second half transmitted first and vice versa, so decrypters would look for the *dendai* (message number) in the centre of the signal to find where the message actually began. The worker who kept a list of message numbers for the section to access was nicknamed Dendai Dick.

Decryption was still a laborious process. The result, when it finally came, was not always current, but it often revealed advance planning of dates and routes for troop transport and supply ships. A delayed solution could still be applied to good effect. For example, a message was decrypted on 20 August, nine days after it had been intercepted, that a supply convoy was leaving Palau on 26 August to unload at Wewak in New Guinea. It was still timely. On 1 September, five cargo ships and two escorting destroyers were attacked at Wewak by US medium bombers swooping in at masthead height. The breaking of the Water Transport Code, set in train by Joe Richard's gloom over his friend's tragic death, was starting to pay dividends.

— ● —

In January 1943, while Joe Richard was setting out on his journey to break the Water Transport Code, Central Bureau was formally placed under the direct control of General HQ in General MacArthur's SWPA. The commanding officer was the perpetual absentee General Spencer B. Akin, known to many of the Americans as S.O.B. Akin. The young Australian Mic Sandford, still only 26 years old, was the bureau's executive officer, running its day-to-day operation. He was in effect second in command to the American Joe Sherr, whose office was in the city with Akin.

Sandford had been involved in the protracted negotiations with the British Foreign Office and the Admiralty for Eric Nave's transfer from FRUMEL to Central Bureau. The Admiralty didn't finally agree to the transfer until late January, by which time Nave had been working in Brisbane for a month. The effort was already paying off. Sandford, in regular contact by phone and memorandum with Robert Little, the assistant Military Intelligence director, wrote: 'Nave is quite invaluable. We are now reading air operational traffic of the utmost importance.' A new teleprinter line was expected to enable air headquarters to 'receive information simultaneously with the Japanese'.

Sandford, now a lieutenant colonel, went to the signals intelligence centres in Washington and London in March for a series of briefings and negotiations to improve coordination across the centres. After island-hopping by plane across the Pacific to San Francisco, he travelled by train to Washington, where he made connections with the US Army cryptographers at Arlington Hall. In the week he was there, Sandford attended a conference attempting to resolve the impasse between Central Bureau and

THE WATER TRANSPORT CODE BROKEN

FRUMEL. Rudy Fabian was there, parroting his view that Japanese army and naval codes were so different there was no need for joint action. The impasse remained.

After a week of mixed success in Washington, Sandford left for London to talk to the War Office and Bletchley Park, but issues he had raised in the US were re-examined after he'd gone. Sandford had reported that although Central Bureau had made material freely available to FRUMEL, it ceased doing that when FRUMEL declined to reciprocate. Worse, Fabian had withheld valuable information from the Brisbane agency, such as a captured call-sign book that was not solely of interest to the Navy.

These concerns were revived at a Washington meeting of senior Navy and Army sigint officers held—ominously for Fabian—after he had returned to Melbourne. Joe Wenger, of the US Navy's OP-20-G, told the meeting that Fabian had reported in 1942 that Central Bureau had 'grandiose plans but few trained personnel' and, more recently, that the US Army had nothing to offer and employed such poor security as to be a 'menace'. Wenger was careful to neither defend nor decry Fabian's position, but in so doing he left the issue to fester. Like the earlier meeting Sandford had attended, this one resolved nothing, but the temporary victory for Fabian probably sowed the seeds of his eventual demise. The US Navy was rethinking its position as useful material started to come from the cryptographers the British had withdrawn from Singapore to Kenya.

Meanwhile, across the Atlantic, John Tiltman, the elder statesman of British cryptography, had convened a conference at Bletchley Park of senior code breakers working on the Japanese army's high-level codes. Although Sandford was an intelligence man, not a cryptanalyst, he joined the forum. He represented both the Australians and the Americans working at Central Bureau in discussion with representatives from Arlington Hall and the British unit in Delhi, the Wireless Experimental Centre. It was agreed that

Bletchley, through WEC, would focus on army air operational codes, Arlington on high-level codes of ground forces, and Central Bureau on the low-level codes of forward field units and on the Water Transport Code—on which they knew Joe Richard was making promising progress.

At the end of April, Sandford was invited to another meeting in London, chaired by the former Government Code and Cipher School head Alastair Denniston, to discuss liaison between the Australian Army's new D Special Section and Bletchley Park. Melbourne's D Section, headed by Nave's recruit Dale Trendall, was the consular crypto group that FRUMEL had dumped when it absorbed Nave's Special Intelligence Bureau. Sandford outlined the structure and interrelationships of signals intelligence groups in Australia and quoted from Henry Archer's diatribes to Robert Little when the SIB was under attack. Little had passed them to Sandford for that purpose. It was agreed at the meeting that London and Melbourne would exchange intercepts relevant to each other, both as texts and as translations. Sandford would liaise with Bletchley regarding Japanese circuits that the Australian team might focus on. There was particular British interest in Berlin–Tokyo traffic.

Mic Sandford was making his mark on the international stage of Allied signals intelligence and would increasingly become Australia's 'go-to' man at this level. While in London especially, he had been used as a troubleshooter for a number of intelligence and technical issues that had arisen between Britain and Australia, and the Americans there. Returning home via India, Sandford built on the established ties between Central Bureau's Singapore escapee, Norman Webb, and Colonel Patrick Marr-Johnson at the Wireless Experimental Centre in Delhi. Further channels of communication were set up with the British Army's Director of Military Intelligence in India, not always with the endorsement of the Government Code and Cipher School, which preferred that all communication within the British Empire be routed through it. Sandford, in his outgoing 'good-chappie' way, had forged a short-cut around that to speed up the exchange of information.

— • —

In early 1943, Central Bureau was able only to decrypt Japan's air–ground traffic and draw conclusions from traffic analysis—Joe Richard was still working on the Water Transport Code at this time, and other mainline Japanese army codes remained unbroken—but that was sufficient for some telling blows against the enemy, sometimes achieved by trial and error.

The war had reached a temporary stalemate in eastern New Guinea, with the Japanese driven back from Guadalcanal and Kokoda. In a war of attrition, American industrial capacity could replace lost equipment, weaponry, aircraft and ships faster than Japan could. General Hitoshi Imamura, commander of the Japanese Eighth Army in southwest Pacific, resolved to regain the initiative by securing Lae on New Guinea's north coast and attacking Wau, a short distance inland and at the time lightly defended by the Australian Kanga Force.

Intercepts on 2 January by the Australian field unit in Port Moresby suggested an escorted convoy was about to leave Rabaul to reinforce Lae. This intelligence was passed to General George Kenney, MacArthur's air force commander, who ordered USAAF and RAAF planes to find and attack the convoy. Five destroyers and five troop transports, shielded by low clouds and Japanese fighters, were spotted on 6 January and shadowed. Over two days, thirteen missions were sent out, mostly single-plane sorties, in an uncoordinated mix of aircraft. Most reached the target, but their bombing was largely ineffective. An RAAF Catalina sank one transport, which lost 340 troops, and another transport was so badly damaged by American B-25 Mitchells that it was beached at Lae. The convoy reached its destination on 7 January, landing most of its troops but having lost half its supplies to the air attacks.

The Allied code breakers missed a mid-January movement of 10,000 troops from Palau to Wewak. Signals had been sent in the newly introduced JN-25F, with which FRUMEL in Melbourne and Hypo in Hawaii were still struggling. The messages weren't decoded until six days after the Wewak landing.

The Japanese attempt to capture Wau from its Australian defenders was repulsed by a garrison reinforced by air, but there were indications that a new convoy was being prepared to transport more Japanese troops to New Guinea. A floatplane, generally used before a convoy set out, was seen patrolling the waters off New Britain, and Allied reconnaissance over Rabaul found an increased number of vessels in port. The No. 1 Wireless Unit detachment in Port Moresby, armed with Japanese army air codes solved at Central Bureau, was picking up signals traffic into and out of Rabaul. Intelligence from the unit's decrypts, pooled with fragments gleaned by FRUMEL and Hypo, was the basis of advice to MacArthur and Kenney that an escorted convoy of perhaps six transports was likely to take a force of several thousand troops to Lae in early March.

Kenney ordered Port Moresby to move aircraft across to captured airfields around Dobodura, on the north side of the Owen Stanley Range, so towering mountains and bad weather couldn't conspire to block an Allied counterattack from Moresby. RAAF tacticians, seeking something better than the scattergun approach that had been so ineffectual against the earlier Lae landing, experimented with low-level strikes at mast height within a coordinated attack from different altitudes and directions.

Signals traffic picked up by the Port Moresby detachment indicated the convoy was leaving Rabaul before midnight on 27 February, 6900 troops in eight merchant ships escorted by eight destroyers and with about 100 fighters as air cover. Lashed by tropical storms, the convoy pushed its way across the Bismarck Sea, the low cloud hindering Allied patrols trying to locate it.

If not for signals intelligence, the weather would have been perfect cover for the Japanese operation. No routine patrol would be likely to sight it in such conditions. However, decrypted intercepts told the Allies that a large convoy had left Rabaul, that it was headed for Lae and that it was on the Bismarck Sea. The Japanese were out there somewhere, although it wasn't until late afternoon on 1 March that the convoy was located. A B-24 Liberator bomber spotted it through a break in the clouds. B-17 Flying Fortresses sent to the location, however, had still not found the ships when darkness fell and the convoy disappeared under low cloud.

At dawn, six RAAF A-20 Bostons attacked the Japanese fighter base at Lae to forestall its ability to provide air cover, and when another Liberator sighted the convoy in mid-morning, two waves of Flying Fortresses attacked it, sinking one of the merchant ships. Two destroyers picked up survivors—950 of the 1200 soldiers on board—and sped them to Lae ahead of the slower-moving convoy. USAAF bombers attacked the flotilla in the afternoon, inflicting only minor damage.

Bad weather closed in overnight, and by morning the convoy was difficult to locate. About ten o'clock, a formation of B-17s found and bombed it from medium altitude, causing little damage but scattering the convoy formation. Expecting a repeat of January's high-level bombing, the air cover prowled at 7000 feet. Both sides were caught up in dogfights, and Japanese anti-aircraft fire was focused on medium-altitude bombers, allowing RAAF Beaufighters to approach at mast height and create the impression they were making a torpedo attack. The Japanese ships turned to face them so they would present a small target for torpedo fire, but in so doing they provided the ideal orientation for low-level bombing.

Japanese sailors thought the enemy planes would crash into the bridge, but the attackers swooped over the top, bombs exploding behind them down hatches and in engine rooms. Troops rushed to the upper decks, where they were strafed by machine-gun fire, as were sailors in the water.

Three destroyers were fatally damaged in those strikes, one of them colliding with and disabling a troop ship. By evening on the 3rd, all seven transports had been seriously damaged, and most were on fire or sinking. Four of the destroyers picked up what survivors they could, some 2700 of them, and withdrew to Rabaul. About 2890 Japanese soldiers and sailors had been killed in the Battle of the Bismarck Sea, and only 1200 of the original 6900 made it to Lae. Multi-level attack lines and mast-high strikes had been a productive tactic, made more effective with advance intelligence about the enemy operation.

Even without access to mainline Japanese army ciphers and codes, signals intelligence was enabling the Allies to mount constructive responses to enemy attacks that radio field units were able to pick up in the preparation stages. The high-grade army codes, such as Water Transport, would enhance that ability by providing intelligence about troop and supply movement with greater lead time. It was imperative that the Japanese remained unaware of the extent to which the Allied code breakers had penetrated their cipher systems. Reconnaissance patrols were sent out to serve as a plausible source of the Allies' apparent advance knowledge of a coming operation. But one operation in particular involved a target so prized by the Americans that normal prudence was put to one side, and the Allies' cryptographic supremacy nearly came unstuck.

Chapter 10

The admiral's itinerary

The solitary figure of Admiral Yamamoto stood on a grassy rise beside the runway at Rabaul's Lakunai airfield, a short, stocky man resplendent in white uniform. As each Zero roared down the strip and took to the sky, he waved his cap in a circle above his head in a sweeping, theatrical gesture of solidarity with his men. This was his life, and these pilots were his family.

This sortie was of particular importance. It was the opening salvo of Operation I-Go, Yamamoto's bid to stop Allied advances in the Solomon Islands and New Guinea and regain the ascendancy in the Pacific War. Over 200 Japanese fighters and dive bombers rose into the red-tinged dawn from Rabaul, on New Britain, and Ballale (Balalae), in the western Solomon Islands, to mount I-Go's first offensive.

Since Japanese forces had been withdrawn from Guadalcanal in February, three months earlier, the war had entered a temporary stalemate, each side regrouping to assess its position. With the attempt to reinforce the garrison at Lae thwarted in the Battle of the Bismarck Sea, the commander-in-chief decided on a major air offensive against Allied shipping and bases in the south-western Pacific. Three hundred planes were brought from the Truk-based carriers of the Japanese 3rd Air Fleet to add muscle.

The admiral had moved his headquarters forward from Truk, in the northwest Pacific, to the enormous base at Rabaul, with its five airfields, large harbour and 100,000 troops. Flying there on 3 April, he set up an advance command centre in the dingy wooden buildings of the Southeast Area Fleet HQ. He spent the next day, his fifty-ninth birthday, with the fleet's commander, Vice-Admiral Jinichi Kusaka, planning I-Go's strikes. At Lakunai, Yamamoto addressed Zero pilots about to take part in the offensive. It was scheduled to begin the following day with an attack on the Americans at Guadalcanal.

Heavy rainstorms forced postponement of this opening raid on three successive days, but on 7 April Yamamoto was at the runway to wave his warriors off. After three hours of fierce fighting over the Russell Islands and Guadalcanal, the flight leaders returned brimming with excitement and exaggerated reports of enemy ships sunk and planes downed. In fact, Central Bureau's field units in New Guinea had become aware of the impending offensive and many of the US ships and aircraft had been moved out of the way, limiting the attack's effectiveness. Convinced the raid had left Guadalcanal crippled, Yamamoto turned his attention to other Allied-held areas.

Two days later, Emperor Hirohito sent the admiral a telegram congratulating him on the success of the raid on Guadalcanal. Chuffed, Yamamoto decided to make a personal tour of inspection to the forward bases in the western Solomons. He would use the emperor's telegram as a morale booster for the troops there after Japan's disheartening evacuation of Guadalcanal. His staff officer, Captain Yasuji Watanabe, was instructed to compile an itinerary for the tour while Operation I-Go moved on to new targets.

On 11 April, a formation of nearly 300 aircraft mounted an attack on Oro Bay, on the north Papuan coast. Returning pilots reported four Allied ships sunk and twenty-two planes shot down

THE ADMIRAL'S ITINERARY

for the loss of only six of the Japanese raiders. The next day, Port Moresby was the target. The pilots said they had downed twenty-eight planes, sunk a transport and badly damaged the airfield. Finally, on the 14th, it was the turn of Milne Bay, at the eastern tip of New Guinea. Ten transports were reported sunk and forty-four planes downed. So much damage was supposedly inflicted in the four massive raids, for the loss of only forty-two aircraft and their crews, that Yamamoto suspended Operation I-Go while he made his tour of inspection. He knew what he had lost, but he couldn't know that the Allied losses were significantly less than his pilots had claimed. The American count was one destroyer, one tanker, several small boats and twenty-five aircraft.

The day before the Milne Bay raid, the itinerary Watanabe had drawn up was approved by his commander-in-chief. Yamamoto was to leave Rabaul at 6 a.m. (Tokyo time) on 18 April, fly to Ballale, south of Bougainville Island, visit Shortland Island nearby, and fly on to Buin, on Bougainville, returning to Rabaul at 3.40 p.m. the same day. He would travel in a medium attack plane with an escort of six Zero fighters. Japanese military schedules were always expressed in Tokyo time. Local time in Rabaul was two hours ahead of Tokyo.

An encrypted message with the details of the itinerary—destinations, arrival and departure times, and the like—was ordered to be sent to the destinations, but only in the navy code, JN-25. Captain Watanabe suspected the army's codes were not secure. He would take no chances with his commander's safety.

Admiral Yamamoto's day before the tour was spent in conference with his senior officers. It was decided that his Chief of Staff, Vice-Admiral Matome Ugaki, who was in bed that day with fever, would join him on the tour if his health recovered, flying in a second medium bomber.

Over lunch, General Imamura, the Army commander in Rabaul, told of his narrow escape from being shot down over

Bougainville two months before. On his way to Buin, he said, he had been ambushed by American fighters, but his pilot managed to slip under cloud cover in the nick of time. Urged by Imamura to cancel the inspection tour, Yamamoto responded, 'Yes, they're penetrating our front and we must stop them. That's why I'm flying there tomorrow . . . with cover.'

The army man wasn't the only senior officer worried about the safety of the venture. Rear-Admiral Takaji Joshima flew from Bougainville in the afternoon, echoing concerns already expressed by the local navy commander, Vice-Admiral Jisaburo Ozawa, urging it be cancelled. Both were aghast that the itinerary had been sent by radio, even if in code. Neither was certain that the Allies had not managed to penetrate the Japanese navy code.

'I told my staff when I saw that foolish message that this is madness,' said Joshima. 'This is an open invitation to the enemy.'

Yamamoto brushed aside their concerns. 'Is this a conspiracy between you and Imamura?' he joked. 'Even if it is dangerous, I can't turn back now. I've told all these people. They'll be waiting for me.'

Admiral Ugaki was the sole senior staffer who believed the tour would boost front-line morale, and he wasn't present at the discussions. Admiral Kusaka asked Captain Kameto Kuroshima of staff operations to tell the chief of staff that six fighters was not enough protection and let him know Rabaul could provide more, but Kuroshima didn't see Ugaki before the mission left. The message was never delivered.

After dinner that night, Admiral Yamamoto relaxed over a game of *shogi* with Captain Watanabe, then went to bed before midnight. He slept badly.

— ● —

Inside No. 1 Wireless Unit's fake wooden Queenslander just outside Townsville, Keith Falconer was on duty, monitoring

THE ADMIRAL'S ITINERARY

SO-SU-HU (Rabaul) frequencies to Japan's operational bases on the I-KA-MI circuit. Messages, erupting from the background hum in shrill bursts like machine-gun fire, were copied by hand. One signal intercepted by the nineteen-year-old operator came from the commander of the Japanese navy's Southeast Air Fleet to some recipients on the circuit, but Falconer had no idea of its content. He was an interceptor, not a cryptanalyst.

Falconer's hand went up and a figure materialised behind him, but the young operator was too focused on the immediate task to take note of who it was. When the electronic gunfire was over, he waved in the air his pages of *romaji* notations—the Romanised transcripts of Japanese characters that the interceptors used—and they were taken away by the 'trick chief' into the other half of the building, where the intelligence section was housed. Outside, the melodic chirps and whoo-oops of north Queensland's tropical forest creatures came back into earshot as Falconer settled back and waited for the enemy's next communication.

The intercept was identified in the intelligence room as army air–ground code, which circumstances obliged the Japanese to use in communicating with their outlying bases. Captain Watanabe's insistence that only the navy's JN-25 should be used to encrypt Yamamoto's itinerary hadn't got through to someone in Rabaul's signals section. This message was in a relatively simple *kana* substitution code that probably could have been decrypted at Stuart Creek, but base-to-base communications were not that unit's responsibility.

The coded message was sent by teleprinter to Central Bureau in Brisbane, where it was decrypted by William 'Nobby' Clarke, a veteran of Middle East radio interception. Clarke's decoding was incomplete, but sufficient to show that the message might be significant. It looked like an itinerary of some sort, perhaps a tour of inspection by the commander-in-chief of Japan's Combined Fleet. If so, it could bring Admiral Yamamoto closer to the front line than he had ventured before. As Bougainville, in the western Solomons, was in the South Pacific Area, Admiral Nimitz's zone of responsibility, not in General MacArthur's Southwest Pacific Area, the Australian army man sent his decryption and its source, the coded intercept, to the navy cryptography unit, FRUMEL, in Melbourne. Its linguists translated and tidied up the decrypt. The result was extraordinary:

> ON 18 APRIL CINC COMBINED FLEET WILL VISIT RYZ [BALLALE], R___ AND RXP [BUIN] IN ACCORDANCE WITH THE FOLLOWING SCHEDULE:
> 1. DEPART RR [RABAUL] AT 0600 IN A MEDIUM ATTACK PLANE ESCORTED BY 6 FIGHTERS. ARRIVE AT RYZ AT 0800. PROCEED BY SUB-CHASER TO R___ ARRIVING 0840. (___ HAVE SUB-CHASER READY AT #1 BASE) DEPART R___ AT 0945 IN ABOVE SUB-CHASER AND ARRIVE RXZ AT 1030? (___) DEPART RXZ AT 1100? IN MEDIUM ATTACK PLANE AND ARRIVE AT RXF AT 1110. DEPART RXP AT 1400 IN MEDIUM ATTACK PLANE AND ARRIVE RR AT 1530.
> 2. AT EACH OF THE ABOVE PLACES THE COMMANDER IN CHIEF WILL MAKE SHORT TOUR OF INSPECTION AND AT ___ HE WILL VISIT THE SICK AND WOUNDED, BUT CURRENT OPERATIONS SHOULD CONTINUE. EACH FORCE COMMANDER ___ IN CASE OF BAD WEATHER THE TRIP WILL BE POSTPONED ONE DAY.

Two days after he had intercepted the admiral's itinerary, Keith Falconer was driven from Stuart Creek to the base at Townsville, where he was interviewed by the FRUMEL linguist Gill Richardson and another US naval officer. Questioned about the intercept, Falconer consulted his log of the night in question and confirmed that he had given its reception a maximum reliability rating. He was confident his transcript was an accurate rendition of the signal sent, but he wasn't told the contents of the message. There was no need, in the military's view, for him to know.

THE ADMIRAL'S ITINERARY

The decrypted message was sent to the US Navy's signals intelligence units in Hawaii and Washington, where staff went through their JN-25 traffic of 13 April (Rabaul time) looking for comparable signals. A new additive table for JN-25D had been introduced by the Japanese two weeks before and the Americans were only in process of resolving it, but through partial decrypts from listening posts in Oahu and the Aleutians, the Hawaiian agency was able to confirm the itinerary and that it had been sent in the naval code to other recipients.

Meanwhile, FRUMEL had picked up a subsequent message from Rabaul Base Force, probably initiated by General Imamura and referring to 'the special visit of Yamamoto' and precautionary arrangements 'in view of the situation regarding air attacks on the post', including moving the 'post' to a new location. If confirmation of the Yamamoto tour was needed, this provided it, although exactly where or what the 'post' was remained unknown.

At Pearl Harbor, at 8 a.m. on 14 April, Admiral Nimitz was handed a sheet of paper by his fleet intelligence officer, Ed Layton. It was the decrypted Yamamoto itinerary, which had been passed to Layton from Hypo Station, no longer headed by his friend Joe Rochefort. As with the intercept that changed the direction of the Battle of Midway, there was no mention that this one had come from Melbourne. Layton was probably unaware that it had actually originated in Central Bureau from a Townsville intercept. Nimitz ran his fingers—he was missing one after an accident—through his thinning, sun-bleached hair.

'This couldn't be true, could it?' he muttered in amazement. 'It's heaven sent if it is! But what are the risks?'

'I suppose you should consider first what would be gained by killing him,' Layton told his commander. 'He's unique among their people. The younger officers and enlisteds idolise him.'

Nimitz was wary of taking any action that might reveal Allied progress in penetrating Japanese codes.

'What about our code work, our gains there? We might compromise that . . . give it away and pay dearly later.'

'I agree. That's something we should not leave to chance,' said the intelligence officer. 'We'll have a cover story ready.'

Nimitz wrote out a despatch to Admiral Bull Halsey's Noumea headquarters in New Caledonia with details of the Japanese admiral's flight. He authorised preliminary planning for an ambush while presidential approval was sought. Layton asked Captain Ellis Zachariah in Washington naval intelligence to seek Roosevelt's imprimatur for the audacious mission. It would also need the backing of Frank Knox, Secretary of the Navy.

A fit-looking 69-year-old, Knox lived on a US Navy yacht moored on the Potomac River. With the Layton request spread out on the cabin table, Zachariah presented to him the benefits of Yamamoto's death. The word 'assassination' wasn't used. An undecided Navy Secretary rang US Army Air Force chief Hap Arnold, who strongly supported Zachariah. That was good enough for Frank Knox.

Roosevelt's curt response to the request was a simple, 'GET YAMAMOTO!' Neither Knox nor Roosevelt recorded the request or its approval on their office log. If the strike turned out to be a disaster, the paper trail wasn't going to lead to either of them.

Meanwhile, an overnight reply came to Nimitz from Halsey's executive officer in Noumea. His commander was in Australia, he said, but the proposed mission had been examined and was thought to be feasible. Admiral Marc 'Pete' Mitscher, the newly arrived commander of the combined air force in the Solomons, had advised that P-38 Lightnings from Guadalcanal could handle the mission and that preparation was under way. They were awaiting a formal go-ahead from Admiral Nimitz. When that came, they would move onto an operational footing with the mission, designated Operation Vengeance.

THE ADMIRAL'S ITINERARY

Isoroku Yamamoto was a fighter. Without connections to ease his way to the top of the Imperial Japanese Navy, he had to battle there on his own, earning his stripes with unwavering determination and strategic vision. Born Isoroku Takano in north-western Honshu, the son of a village schoolmaster who had been a middle-ranked *samurai*, he learned English from an American missionary and calligraphy from his father. Both would be influential in shaping his distinctive personality. At sixteen, he graduated from the Imperial Japanese Naval Academy and served as an ensign on the cruiser *Nisshin* during the Russo-Japanese War. After losing two fingers in the Battle of Tsushima, the young officer was nicknamed '80 sen' at the *geisha* parlour he frequented: at the time, a *geisha* manicure cost 1 yen (100 sen). By the age of thirty-two, he was a lieutenant-commander and already a rising star.

Following the death of his parents, Takano was adopted into the family of a former *samurai* and took its name, Yamamoto. It was customary in Japan for *samurai* families without sons to adopt suitable young men so their name could be carried on. Social rank and income came with the arrangement.

After two years at Harvard studying the oil industry and US aircraft, Yamamoto was posted as a naval attaché to the Japanese embassy in Washington and made a detailed study of defence industries in the United States. Returning to Japan a year later, he commented: 'The American navy is a social navy of bridge and golf players. A peacetime navy.' That perception would reverberate at Pearl Harbor.

Yamamoto developed an early vision for military aviation, leading the push to build a naval air force in Japan. 'The most important warship of the future,' he told an American reporter, 'will be a ship to carry airplanes.'

In 1934 Yamamoto, by now a rear-admiral, led the Japanese delegation to the London Naval Conference. He was determined to break the 5:5:3 ratio of battleships mandated for the US, Britain and Japan by the 1921 Washington Disarmament Conference. Exuding a warm and friendly manner at the negotiation table, Yamamoto insisted Japan could no longer be bound by those constraints. The conference ended inconclusively after two months of talks, and the treaty collapsed. Yamamoto's delegation returned to Tokyo in triumph, to a street procession of 2000 people and the congratulations of Emperor Hirohito.

In 1937 the Japanese army moved into China, having previously occupied Manchuria. The armed forces had become the powerhouse of Japanese politics and were pressing for Japan to form a military pact with the European belligerents, Germany and Italy. Yamamoto opposed his country's military adventures, believing the army had seriously underestimated America's industrial capacity should it be drawn into a war. His public stand against antagonising the United States, and an apology for the sinking of the US gunboat *Panay* on the Yangtze River, drew the ire of pro-war activists and brought assassination threats. With some young army and naval officers publicly condemning him as working against 'Japan's natural interests', the Navy Minister, a moderate, reassigned Yamamoto to a sea posting to keep him out of harm's way. He was appointed Commander-in-Chief of the Combined Fleet.

Isoroku Yamamoto was promoted to full admiral in 1940 at the ripe age of fifty-six. He kept remarkably fit for his years with regular exercise. Impeccably dressed and always courteous, he was an emotional man with strong likes and dislikes. He was popular with the men and officers of the navy, though not with the pro-war faction of the military, which was tightening its grip on Japan's political machinery. On the other hand, he was an avid gambler, playing *shogi* (a Japanese variant of chess) and *go* (another board game), bridge and poker. A complex and contradictory character, he enjoyed calligraphy, poetry and *geisha* girls. His favourite *geisha* was probably closer to him than his wife, Reiko.

In 1940, when Japan signed the Tripartite Pact with Germany

and Italy, Yamamoto was far from convinced that the Japanese navy was fully prepared for war. 'If I am told to fight regardless of the consequences, I shall run wild for the first six months or a year, but for the second or third years, I have utterly no confidence,' he told the prime minister. 'I hope you will endeavour to avoid a war with America.'

The hawkish army general Hideki Tojo took power in Tokyo a year later. As Yamamoto had publicly opposed his championing of the Japanese invasions of Manchuria and China, Tojo was expected to move the recalcitrant admiral out of the way to some ineffectual posting, in charge of a naval base perhaps. Instead, he left Yamamoto in command of the Combined Fleet. Still extremely popular within the fleet, Yamamoto was respected as the most astute naval strategist of his generation. Tojo decided this was not a boat to rock.

Although Admiral Yamamoto had serious reservations about the army's belligerence, he accepted that war was inevitable. He was the prime instigator of the bold plan to simultaneously attack Pearl Harbor and Clark Field. It was also Yamamoto who conceived an attack on Midway as a way to complete the job started in Hawaii and finish off the US fleet.

After the Midway disaster, Yamamoto's star was losing its glow. He remained in command of Combined Fleet to avoid a decline in morale, but the naval General Staff was not in a mood to indulge his desire for another 'decisive' offensive strike. Combined Fleet conducted a series of smaller defensive actions, some of which inflicted considerable damage on elements of the US fleet, but the Japanese fleet also suffered losses it could ill afford, and the Imperial Japanese Navy's strength was fading.

Isoroku Yamamoto was no longer seen as a brilliant strategist. To some in the Japanese hierarchy he may even have become a liability. Removing him from the enemy's leadership team was not worth the risk of exposing the degree to which the Allies had penetrated Japan's naval codes. So why did America pursue this imprudent course of action? The name of the operation says it all. The United States was fixated on its failure to anticipate the Pearl Harbor attack. Yamamoto was seen as the mastermind behind that shame. The stain had to be expunged. Operation Vengeance would do that.

— ● —

On 15 April, Admiral Nimitz signalled Admiral Halsey, back in Noumea, to proceed, 'provided all personnel concerned, particularly the pilots, are briefed that the information comes from Australian coastwatchers near Rabaul'. 'Good luck and good hunting,' his message concluded. Bull Halsey passed the order to Pete Mitscher, who was working in his headquarters under canvas near Guadalcanal's Henderson Field, a battered footlocker serving as a desk.

For security reasons, there was no need for pilots to know who the target was or how the command had learned of his whereabouts. They were to be told that their mission was to intercept and engage an important high-ranking officer who would not be named. After the kerfuffle over a press leak following Midway, the military didn't want newspapers reporting that Yamamoto had been the specific target of the mission. If the Japanese became aware of that, they would be asking themselves how the Americans had learned where he would be and when.

The US planes would travel 970 kilometres from Guadalcanal to Bougainville, flying wide to avoid detection by radar on the Solomon Islands. When the mission was completed, participants were to get out of the line of fire as rapidly as possible. The direct return flight of 640 kilometres meant an operation total of 1600 kilometres, beyond the range of the Navy's F4F Wildcats and F4U Corsairs based at Henderson. Instead, the Army's P-38G Lightnings, stationed at Kukum Field, a few kilometres away, were enlisted for the mission, although they would need long-range tanks attached to the fuselage to get them through the full flight path. That introduced another element of risk. P-38s seldom patrolled so far from their base, so their presence could indicate prior knowledge of their target's movements. The Americans hoped the indirect flight path might bolster the cover story that a long-range patrol had chanced upon the Japanese planes.

The USAAF's 339th Fighter Squadron commander, Major John Mitchell, had planned a precise flight path using departure and arrival times from the decrypted Japanese signals, working backwards from the proposed intercept point of the target plane—he had not been told the target was Yamamoto—as it began its descent to Ballale island, off Bougainville. Eighteen P-38s were to take part in the operation. Four were designated as the 'shooter flight'; the others would fly as cover, rising to 5500 metres to engage the escort Zeros and any additional Japanese fighters that might join the fray from Bougainville, where some seventy-five attack planes were thought to be held in reserve.

The day before the mission, John Mitchell and his operations team went through elements of the flight plan with Pete Mitscher and other senior naval officers at the planning table in the 'Opium Den', a ramshackle, smoky, sweltering command bunker on Guadalcanal's Henderson Field. Having an army squadron carry out a naval mission presented difficulties. Mitchell insisted his plane be fitted with a ship's compass to provide the precise dead-reckoning navigation required for a long flight over water, something army planes ordinarily didn't need. Such navigation was beyond the capacity of their 'wet' magnetic compasses. A debate took place about whether it was better to shoot down their quarry's plane or to attack him while he was on the submarine chaser transferring from Ballale. The army man put an end to the debate.

'My men wouldn't know a sub chaser from a sub,' said Mitchell. 'It'll have to be in the air.'

There were 'unknowns' the mission had to accommodate. It was unclear if the single 'medium attack plane' in the itinerary signals meant a 'Betty' (Mitsubishi G4M) bomber or the slower 'Sally' (Mitsubishi Ki-21), or why there was a discrepancy between its flying time from Rabaul to Bougainville and the return flight. Should the mission plan to arrive earlier than the itinerary schedule in case the Japanese had a tail wind? Mitchell didn't have the decrypted itinerary, so he couldn't draw his own conclusions about its details. He worked from a summary provided by his US Navy contacts of what they considered relevant.

The itinerary had the target plane arriving at Ballale at 10 a.m. (local time, two hours ahead of the itinerary's Tokyo time), but with no wind forecast, it was decided to allow for it arriving fifteen minutes early. The descent was calculated to begin ten minutes before landing. Mitchell scheduled his mission to arrive in the vicinity of Ballale at 9.35, twenty-five minutes before the admiral's plane was due to touch down.

Electrical storms the evening before the mission upped the uncertainty. Would Yamamoto's tour be postponed or would it go ahead regardless? But just before midnight, the rain stopped as suddenly as it had started and the cloud cover cleared. Shortly after, Mitchell assembled his pilots in the dark on a hill above Kukum airstrip. Lights were beamed onto a blackboard in front of the briefing tent. There were too many at the briefing for it to be held inside the tent.

The squadron commander announced the names of the pilots who were to participate in the mission and the four who were to make up the shooter group. The formation was to fly over ocean, 'wave-hopping' at altitudes no higher than 15 metres and in radio silence. Wave-hopping was not something army pilots were used to.

'We'll be right on the deck where nobody can spot us,' Mitchell

THE ADMIRAL'S ITINERARY

told his men, 'but watch yourselves. You drop a few feet lower, you're in trouble.'

— ● —

April the 18th dawned on Guadalcanal with clear, bright skies and a slight breeze. The army pilots at Kukum Field downed coffee and a 'chow' of spam and watery scrambled eggs before eighteen P-38 Lightnings started taking off at 7.25 a.m. The engines of the first group of four planes fired up, coughing dark, oily smoke into the tropical air and throttling into a roar. John Mitchell taxied, turned and powered down the runway, followed closely by the rest of his lead group. They circled above the airstrip while the next group, the shooter flight of four, took off, led by Captain Tom Lanphier. Finally, the remaining ten aircraft joined the formation behind Mitchell's group.

Two of the attack planes dropped out soon after taking off, one with a flattened tyre, the other with a fuel blockage from the auxiliary tanks. Of the designated killers only Lanphier and his wingman, Lieutenant Rex Barber, remained. Attack fighters hunted in pairs, one as the prime strike vehicle, the other, the wingman, to provide backup and cover. Lanphier and Barber were a mismatched team, the former brash and ambitious, the latter quietly spoken.

Two planes were brought from the cover group to replace the withdrawn shooters, reducing the cover to twelve fighters. The new attack pilots were Lieutenants Besby Holmes and Ray Hine. Mitchell led the amended formation out to the west at low altitude with the adjusted attack group tucked immediately behind his group of four. Eventually he turned them north towards Bougainville.

Admiral Yamamoto had risen early that morning and put on his black airman's boots, medal ribbons and a belt for a short *samurai* sword given to him by his brother. On the advice of his travelling companion and chief of staff, the admiral wore a plain dark-green field uniform rather than the splendid white uniform of his rank. The choice would imply empathy with the troops he was visiting. It had been arranged for his photo to be taken before departure, but the photographer didn't show up.

Fastidious about punctuality, Yamamoto took off from Lakunai's East Airfield right on the dot of eight o'clock (6 a.m. in Tokyo) in the twin-engined Mitsubishi Betty bomber. Ugaki and other staff officers flew in a second Betty, and the pair were escorted by six Zero fighters. Yamamoto and Ugaki each took the pilot's seat in their respective aircraft, but the 'co-pilots', who were familiar with the area and its flying conditions, took control for take-off. The two bombers climbed to 2000 metres with the escort fighters behind and above in two V formations of three planes. Flying just behind his fleet commander, Ugaki—who was recovering from a bout of dengue fever—soon dozed off. The eight aircraft circled the twin volcanoes at the mouth of Rabaul's Simpson Harbour and headed south-east, unaware of the American mission coming from Guadalcanal to meet them.

The Solomon Sea was glassy but still presented dangers for army pilots flying at very low altitude. One of the wave-hopping P-38s lurched too near the water and was drenched with sea spray across the windscreen, but the pilot managed to ease his craft up safely. A lesson learned! These aircraft were fighters, designed for high-altitude flying, and had no cooling and poor ventilation. At low altitude, the heat and humidity were oppressive. Mesmerised by the drone of his engine and the smooth sea rushing under his plane's nose, Mitchell fought drowsiness as he navigated by flight plan, dead reckoning with his borrowed navy compass. At 9.25 a.m., within 35 kilometres of Bougainville, he turned the formation north-east into a veil of low-level haze.

At the same time, high to the north-west, the Japanese flyers had clear skies, with transport ships and escort destroyers steaming

THE ADMIRAL'S ITINERARY

far below. Running along the coastland's mangrove swamps and palm-lined inlets and past the Japanese air base at the south-eastern end of Bougainville, they began their descent towards Ballale's airfield, the first stop on Admiral Yamamoto's itinerary. Ugaki's pilot handed him a piece of paper with a scribbled note: 'Expect to arrive Ballale at 7.45.'

As the Americans neared Bougainville, they climbed above the shimmering haze to see the cloud-topped peaks of the Crown Prince Range and the scalloped Empress Augusta Bay in front of it . . . but no aircraft. Had there been an error in the calculations somewhere? Mitchell checked his watch, noting the time at 9.34 a.m., a minute ahead of schedule. Just then a shout rang out over the intercom, 'Bogeys! Eleven o'clock high!'

Eight aircraft could be seen descending from a higher altitude in the middle distance, about 5 kilometres up the coastline, apparently not yet alerted to the approaching Americans hugging the water to the south. 'Eight aircraft!' thought John Mitchell. That was one more than he had been briefed to expect. What's more, the additional plane was a second bomber. Which of the two was the target airplane? That was resolved with a snap decision, the practical one: aim to take out both.

'Everybody skin tanks,' Mitchell radioed, meaning drop off the auxiliary fuel tanks, now emptied.

Two of the attack P-38s jettisoned their tanks and turned right onto a course parallel with and towards the Bettys, climbing on full power to intercept them. The tanks on one of the late-addition shooter planes wouldn't detach. Holmes and his wingman turned back towards the sea. Mitchell radioed Lanphier and Barber to engage.

'All right, Tom. Go get them. Get them both.'

By this time, the escort Zeros had spotted the approaching threat and were diving towards the pair of Lightnings rising at the bombers. Lanphier peeled away towards the Zeros, spraying them with machine-gun fire and breaking up their attack. This gave his wingman valuable seconds to chase down the two bomber transports, which dived and passed in front of Barber's nose.

The pilot of Ugaki's plane, having seen the P-38s separate, turned 90 degrees towards the sea, while Barber banked steeply, momentarily losing sight of both planes. When he rolled out of his bank, he found he was behind one of the Bettys and began firing his nose-mounted cannon and four machine-guns furiously into the bomber's right engine and rear fuselage. When he hit the other engine, the plane began to trail smoke and rolled violently. Barber had to take evasive action to avoid a mid-air collision. Looking back, he saw a column of black smoke billowing up from the jungle. He assumed this was from the bomber and that it had plunged into the undergrowth.

Lanphier had rolled out of his engagement with the fighters to report seeing a lone Betty—Yamamoto's—fleeing across the treetops with Barber's Lightning chasing it and three Zeros chasing Barber. Lanphier banked for a desperate extreme-range, almost right-angle burst of machine-gun fire and was surprised to see the Betty's engine flare up. He shook the Zeros off his tail and radioed, 'I got a bomber. Verify him for me, Mitch. He's burning.'

'I see a fire, a column of smoke coming up from the jungle,' Mitchell said, but he had been unable to see who hit the plane. The taciturn Barber didn't utter a word during the whole fight.

Ugaki's plane had made two more evasive turns out over the sea before he spotted Yamamoto's Betty, spewing black smoke and orange flames, brush across the top of the jungle. Later, he recalled thinking, 'Everything is lost now!'

Holmes had finally shed his tanks and he, Hine and Barber chased the remaining bomber over water, raking it with gunfire. The pilot tried to bring his aircraft down on water, but it hit the sea at full speed, rolled over and cartwheeled, breaking into pieces. Only Ugaki and two crewmen survived.

THE ADMIRAL'S ITINERARY

'Mission accomplished,' called Mitchell. 'Everybody get home.'

Japanese fighters at the south Bougainville base could be seen scrambling, too late to change the outcome or even to engage with the attackers. The P-38s headed straight for Guadalcanal. Holmes got only as far as the US forward base in the Russell Islands, where he landed with only four gallons of fuel in his tank. Ray Hine was never seen again. Lanphier and Barber landed at Kukum within minutes of each other, the loquacious Lanphier proclaiming that he had brought down the first bomber.

A Japanese search party found the crash site and the body of Admiral Yamamoto the next day. Army engineer Lieutenant Tomoyuki Hamasuna described finding the admiral's body thrown clear of the plane's wreckage, still upright in his seat under a tree, his white-gloved hand grasping the hilt of his brother's sword, his head lowered as if deep in thought. It's suspected that Hamasuna tidied up Yamamoto's charred remains so they would look as he had described, out of respect for the Combined Fleet's commander. A post-mortem found that Yamamoto had been hit by two bullets, one entering at the back of his left shoulder, the other entering his left jaw and exiting above his right eye. The examining navy doctor determined that the head wound had killed the admiral.

While the Japanese press did not mention Yamamoto's fate for some time, American leaders were forced to sit on the news that they had brought down their Pearl Harbor nemesis. No hint could be given that they knew who was in the downed plane. Finally, on 21 May, five weeks after the event, Japan's Navy Department released a statement announcing that the Commander-in-Chief of the Combined Fleet had died a heroic death in air combat, directing operations from a forward position.

The Japanese apparently smelled a rat. That an American long-range patrol had come across Yamamoto by chance was almost impossible to believe. They investigated and found that although the admiral's itinerary had mostly been circulated in JN-25 code, as directed by Captain Watanabe, it had also been sent in a minor army code. Concerned that the navy code might have been broken, Admiral Kusaka had a decoy message sent out in JN-25 stating that he would make a front-line visit to Munda airbase, in the Solomon Islands, but the Allies recognised the ruse and didn't take the bait. The Japanese concluded that the navy code was secure. If the Americans had known Yamamoto's location, they must have learned about it through an intercept of the army code. It had in fact been an army signal that Keith Falconer had picked up in Townsville, but the gaps had been filled in from naval traffic. JN-25 was not changed.

Just who shot down Yamamoto's plane has been bitterly contested ever since. On returning from Bougainville, Barber landed soon after Lanphier, who was already claiming loudly to have downed the first Betty. Two intelligence officers pushed through the crowd milling around the flyers and asked Barber how it went.

'Great,' he said. 'I got two bombers and a Zero.'

Lanphier protested vehemently, and a short heated argument followed. When it ended, Lanphier reportedly said: 'As long as we live, Rex, we'll never know which one of us got Yamamoto, and that's the way it ought to be.'

No formal intelligence debriefing was held after the mission. The US military credited Lanphier with the downing of Yamamoto's plane, although no one had actually witnessed it, and Holmes with the downing of Ugaki's plane. But because Lanphier reported seeing Barber shoot down another bomber that crashed into the jungle, Barber was credited with a nonexistent third bomber. When, after the war, Japanese records showed that only two bombers were shot down that day, the count was amended to half-credits to Lanphier and Barber for Yamamoto's plane, and to Holmes and Barber for Ugaki's plane. Officialdom has refused to budge from this position even though evidence from surviving

Japanese pilots and forensic examination of the crashed plane throw serious doubts on Lanphier's version of events, set out in a 1966 article he wrote for *Reader's Digest* headed 'I Shot Down Yamamoto'.

This is perhaps merely a matter of pilot vanities and the public record. Of greater concern should have been the risk that the pilots' boasts and the widespread stories that they had shot down Yamamoto might expose a major Allied code-breaking success.

People who say they were there contend that Lanphier emerged from his P-38 yelling, 'I got Yamamoto!', and that celebration of it at the airbase went late into the night. Other accounts of the Yamamoto mission say that during the pre-mission planning at Henderson Field, Lanphier was shown a copy of Frank Knox's cable authorising the mission and even a copy of the decrypted intercept of the admiral's itinerary. Some of these claims strain credulity; others are just troubling. On the other hand, there is no evidence in official archives that commanders expressed concern about this, and if Yamamoto's death was indeed common knowledge in Guadalcanal before Japan announced it, no news outlet picked up the story.

Ten days after the announcement, however, *Time* magazine published an article referring to an unnamed pilot: 'the U.S. will have a new hero'. A second article in the same issue profiled Tom Lanphier as a combat pilot on Guadalcanal who had been assigned to a mission that had shot down some Japanese bombers and had 'wondered if it had nailed some Jap bigwig'. Although the article is full of exaggerated derring-do sourced from its subject, the connection between the two articles seems beyond coincidence. The US Navy reacted angrily to what it regarded as a serious security breach and at one point threatened courts-martial, but settled in the end for downgrading the medals awarded for the mission.

So the public record has the US military concerned about an implication that the target's identity was known in advance after it had already been revealed by the Japanese, but not about this being openly bandied about within its own ranks—unless the latter didn't happen. The most likely conclusion is that those stories arose from poor research, a desire to dramatise the story and Lanphier's desire for fame.

— • —

The US Navy had exacted retribution on Admiral Yamamoto for shaming it at Pearl Harbor, but circumstances had dictated that the army strike the blow. The navy could only handle key coded signals after being alerted to them by the army's Central Bureau, and even then its job was only to tidy up translation of decoded Japanese, fill in gaps and pursue follow-up traffic. Worse, the navy didn't have aircraft available to bring down Yamamoto. That glory had to be subcontracted to the US Army.

FRUMEL had been the intermediary between the initial intercept at Townsville and Admiral Nimitz, but the Melbourne agency was becoming the fringe dweller of code breaking in Australia as the Japanese were pushed back and MacArthur moved his operation north. Rudy Fabian, in command of FRUMEL, was paying dearly for his obstinate insistence on staying put in Melbourne instead of joining the army's commander-in-chief in Brisbane. Now MacArthur was moving his headquarters to New Guinea, with a headquarters echelon already in Port Moresby planning SWPA's drive towards Lae. FRUMEL was left even further away from the main game. The previously effective agency was running out of purpose.

There were then nearly 300 American personnel at the station, although much of the interception work was done by Australian WRANS. With a few IBM tabulators and only Ralph Cook to carry out maintenance, much of the cipher recovery was still done by hand. Otherwise intercepts from Moorabbin and Adelaide River, in the Northern Territory, were photographed and sent to Washington and Hawaii. Film processing in Melbourne was limited, so film was sent undeveloped to Washington to be processed.

With the relevance of their work and Fabian's ability to obtain needed resources both declining, personnel at FRUMEL focused more on his personality. Dislike of Fabian was growing among the Americans under his command as well as the Australians. Promoted to commander, he wielded a heavy hand over linguists who had long held that rank and who saw his behaviour as undermining their operations. The antagonism towards Fabian spilt across to the previously well-regarded 'Honest John' Lietwiler. When Fabian was summoned to Washington for 'talks' in 1943, Lietwiler was not handed leadership of the bureau.

Fabian first went to Washington for the March conference held to resolve tensions between Central Bureau and FRUMEL, which he derailed with his insistence that Japanese army and navy codes were so different there was no need for joint action. In Fabian's absence, Jack Holtwick, a lieutenant-commander recently arrived in Melbourne, was effectively in charge—the higher-ranked Swede Carlson was nominally officer in charge but was fully occupied with translation. Holtwick achieved much that had eluded Fabian. Marine sentries replaced the petty officers who had carried out guard duty for over a year despite Fabian's obsession with security, and a teleprinter link was set up with Townsville.

The Monterey building had become crowded, and local housing authorities were complaining about residential buildings being used for government activities. The head Australian at FRUMEL, Jack Newman, with Holtwick and Lietwiler, looked at alternative accommodation. In the end, they were given a new three-storey brick building on the grounds of Prince Henry Hospital, but it wouldn't be ready until well into 1944.

Also in March, with Bletchley Park discovering the US Navy had held back captured codebooks, the British were looking at operating more independently of the Americans. They moved their Far East operation back to Colombo from Kenya. The US was meanwhile rethinking its own position as more valuable material was starting to come from the British station. Fabian was called back to Washington. The BRUSA (Britain–USA) Agreement on greater cryptography cooperation, signed between Bletchley Park and OP-20-G in May 1943, didn't help his cause. He didn't like the British, and they didn't like him.

Conferences followed at Bletchley. The US Director of Naval Communications, Joe Redman, and the head of OP-20-G, by then Joe Wenger, were there with promises to pass on JN-25 recoveries to the Royal Navy code breakers returning to Colombo in September. They would set up a direct cipher link from FRUMEL to Colombo under an American liaison officer. At one of these meetings, the British complained that a small Royal New Zealand Navy intercept operation under Fabian's control was getting little 'guidance'. New Zealand Wrens, the British said, were remarkably productive with interception, D/F and radio-fingerprinting at sites in the South Pacific as far away as Suva.

In October, a former Bletchley section head toured Allied naval code-breaking centres as an outcome of BRUSA. Commander Malcolm Saunders was impressed with Hypo's operation, seeing it as a model for the re-formed Colombo bureau. He was less impressed with FRUMEL, where he saw Rudy Fabian, back from Washington, as a block to inter-agency cooperation.

'The liaison with Colombo is not nearly as good as it should be,' he reported. 'The security aspect is constantly in mind and there is a constant suspicion of "leakage" to the American Military Authorities in Brisbane.'

The British pressed hard for their participation in the US Navy sigint circuit of FRUMEL, Hypo and OP-20-G, where recoveries were exchanged and code-breaking problems discussed. The outcome was agreement to set up a BRUSA circuit between

THE ADMIRAL'S ITINERARY

Washington, Pearl Harbor, Melbourne, Colombo and Bletchley Park, but an unenthusiastic Admiral Redman insisted that 'the extent to which radio intelligence information and recoveries can be exchanged between the BRUSA stations will continue to be dependent upon communication and other facilities available and on the need for such an exchange'.

Fabian was a marked man, flitting between Melbourne and Washington all through 1943 and always returning empty-handed, as if he'd only been over there to explain himself. Meanwhile, others were left to run FRUMEL. In November, Sid Goodwin arrived to take over from Carlson as officer in charge. An early head of FRUMEL's predecessor, Station Cast in the Philippines, Goodwin had spent two years on sea duty before being returned to this shore command. The writing was on the wall for Rudy Fabian.

A month later, the rejuvenated Colombo code-breaking facility was told its new US liaison officer would be Commander Rudolph Fabian. The head of FECB in Colombo was aghast. Protesting vehemently to Bletchley Park, he was told, 'We must accept the selection made by Admiral Redman, as he particularly dislikes any interference from British authorities and is well aware of the situation.'

Fabian left FRUMEL for Colombo in January 1944 after two years of fractious if sometimes effective leadership. It was not a move that he could have seen as a promotion, nor one that would have been welcomed by the British sigint workers in Colombo. However, it killed two birds with the one stone for OP-20-G and Joe Redman, whom one Englishman in Washington described as 'chock-full of grievances largely because he likes grievances for their own sake'.

Reporting the transfer to his contact in the UK Foreign Office, Mic Sandford commented, 'This is considered by those of us who know him and them as rather funny.'

FRUMEL's staff might have felt relieved at the departure of Fabian, but if they did their enthusiasm was short-lived. It was the beginning of the de-Americanisation of FRUMEL. This was not obvious at first. Jack Newman, the head Australian of the agency, was out of action with an illness that put him in naval hospital for three weeks. Nominally convalescing after that, he came to work daily against doctor's orders.

By the end of the year, Newman was the only survivor of the original senior officers of FRUMEL. Swede Carlson had already left the previous November and Gill Richardson left early in 1944. John Lietwiler went back temporarily to the US in June 1944 and never returned. Visiting Colombo a year later, Newman met Lietwiler, who was looking leaner and fitter. Newman was by then officer in charge of FRUMEL, a position he took up when Sid Goodwin was recalled to Washington at the end of 1944.

Respected by some as a gentleman and derided by others, including some of his 'girls', as weak, Newman had held on to head an Australian-run unit with American lower ranks working under his command. It wasn't a sign of new American respect for the ability of Australians, though. The US Navy had centralised its sigint operation in Washington and personnel there paid scant attention to what the Australians continued to do with their Melbourne bureau. It was doing useful but mostly fairly routine work. Code breaking in Australia had become largely confined to one organisation, the enterprising and expanding Central Bureau.

Chapter 11

Buried treasure

Roosevelt, Churchill and their military chiefs met in Casablanca, Morocco, in January 1943 to map out Allied strategy in the coming year for the European and Pacific wars. The British wanted to extend military operations in the Mediterranean. In 1942, the Pacific strategy had been defensive, to stop the Japanese advancing south from Rabaul towards Australia. By the end of 1942, the scales had been tipped in the Allies' favour by Midway and Guadalcanal. Admiral Ernest King, no admirer of the English, wanted more Allied effort deployed against Japan to continue the momentum established by MacArthur's Southwest Pacific Area and Nimitz's South Pacific Area.

The US Army's Chief of Staff, General George Marshall, argued at Casablanca that the American public would not accept another Bataan—MacArthur's last hold-out in the Philippines—and that sufficient resources had to be kept in the Pacific or 'a situation might arise in the Pacific at any time that would necessitate the United States regretfully withdrawing from commitments in the European Theatre'. Even so diplomatically worded, the threat of the US pulling out of Europe was something the British couldn't countenance. The meeting decided that Europe should take priority but 'adequate' forces should be maintained in the Pacific. 'Adequate' wasn't defined. The overarching strategy remained to defeat Germany first, then concentrate on Japan. This would have repercussions in the level of resources available to the Pacific campaign.

While Japan attempted to regain the initiative during the early months of 1943 by reinforcing the Lae garrison and launching Yamamoto's I-Go air raids in New Guinea and the Solomons, MacArthur's strategists were working on a plan for a two-pronged advance on the Japanese stronghold of Rabaul. Nimitz's commander in the south Pacific, Admiral Bull Halsey, came to Brisbane in April and met MacArthur for the first time. The two established a rapport that would serve them well over the coming campaign.

The outcome of the meeting was an operational plan code-named Cartwheel. Thirteen separate operations were planned over eight months, advancing by stages along two paths and converging on Rabaul. South Pacific naval forces, under Halsey, would move along the Solomon Islands chain, stretching from Guadalcanal to Bougainville, to the east of New Britain and Rabaul. MacArthur's forces would drive along the north coast of New Guinea, seizing Lae, Finschhafen and Madang, then attack New Britain from the south. The two forces would advance in stages staggered so each could provide support to the other in its operations. It was a classic pincer movement designed to put Japan's key southern base of Rabaul out of action.

A key element in Operation Cartwheel was going to be the timely gathering of signals intelligence. Radio units in the field reported to local senior commanders as well as feeding intercepts back to Central Bureau in Brisbane. Each unit would have, in addition to radio operators picking up enemy signals, a team of some thirty traffic analysts, cryptographers and translators to monitor immediate threats and notify field command. No. 2 and

No. 3 Wireless Units were set up by the RAAF outside Darwin, at Coomalie Creek and Batchelor. They would monitor Japanese army air transfers to new airfields from Singapore, China and Java; reconnaissance flights; and naval air movements associated with enemy aircraft carriers.

In January, No. 1 Wireless Unit was transferred from Townsville to Port Moresby to take over monitoring air–ground traffic from the army unit stationed at Fairfax Harbour. A detachment of wireless operators was sent out to the hills near Rouna Falls, where it was better placed to pick up transmissions on the other side of the Owen Stanleys. Set up on the edge of an abandoned rubber plantation, the detachment was able to intercept a large volume of low-grade encrypted messages and front-line signals in plain language. Although static from the frequent thunderstorms often broke up the messages, the Fairfax Harbour station and its detachment in the hills managed to gather enough intelligence to allow General Kenney's planners to gauge movements between Japan's air bases on the north side of New Guinea and guess at their intentions.

By May, Central Bureau's armoury included Japan's Water Transport Code, broken the month before by Joe Richard and others. From it, the cryptanalysts noticed the Japanese were moving troops from the Dutch East Indies and the Philippines to Wewak, in New Guinea, north-west of Madang. Four labour squads were also landed at Wewak and were presumed to be building new airfields nearby. The interceptors could follow the large-transport convoy to Wewak, but the trail went cold after that. Troops were probably moved further east from there to Hansa Bay, Madang and Lae on small barges and trawlers with low-power, short-range radios that the Allies' field stations couldn't pick up. However, Central Bureau's traffic analysis did reveal Japanese planes flying from new airfields at Hollandia, in occupied Dutch New Guinea.

Clearly the enemy was strengthening its defences along the New Guinea coast, building new airfields and enlarging old ones, in the expectation of the Allied counteroffensive pushing towards the region around Lae. An intercept decrypted on 4 June reported that more heavy bombers had been added to the air base at Wewak. An air build-up threatened Kenney's Fifth Air Force from two directions, Rabaul and Wewak, the latter beyond the range of American escort fighters. Unescorted bombers were too risky by day and too inaccurate at night. An air base near Lae would rectify that, but Kenney needed to move quickly.

The first leg of Operation Cartwheel began on 30 June 1943 with landings of a thousand Southwest Pacific Area troops at Nassau Bay, south of Lae and Salamaua. The landing in darkness by PT boats didn't go smoothly. In heavy rain and crashing surf, the first boats landed at the wrong beach and, in turning back, nearly collided with a second wave of PT boats heading for the correct beach. Of the eighteen landing craft, only one avoided being beached or swamped or losing its way. Fortunately, the Japanese had moved troops to Salamaua for an expected landing there. Nassau Bay had fewer than 200 defenders, whose call for air support wasn't heeded because of the weather. They fled to the surrounding jungle when they mistook a bulldozer that was being unloaded for a tank.

Australian troops had pushed forward to near Salamaua after the failed Japanese attempt to take Wau in January, and they held their positions there. The Australian General Blamey had suggested creating the impression that the next step in the Allied drive along the New Guinea coast would be Salamaua rather than Lae so the Japanese would concentrate their defences there at the expense of reinforcing Lae, the actual objective. Blamey had proposed that Operation Cartwheel start at Nassau Bay rather than Lae for the same reason, and that it be used as a staging ground for the attack on Lae while the Japanese were still expecting Salamaua to be the next target. The landing party at Nassau Bay moved north and was met by mortar and machine-gun fire, but by 2 July the beachhead was secured.

On 21 July, General Marshall messaged MacArthur that the US Army could not provide the men and equipment necessary to attack the well-defended base of Rabaul. They were tied up in Europe. He proposed that Operation Cartwheel be cut short and followed by the seizure of Kavieng in New Ireland, north-west of Rabaul, and Manus Island in the Admiralties, further west, isolating Rabaul. MacArthur countered that Rabaul should be captured, not neutralised, as it would make an ideal Allied base, but America's Joint Chiefs of Staff endorsed Marshall's view and ordered his forces to drive on to the Philippines. Rabaul could be left in Japanese hands to wither on the vine, cut off from its supply lines.

— ● —

By the middle of 1943, a change could be sensed in the mood of Central Bureau. Morale and spirits had risen with the ability to read Japan's Water Transport signals, and small but hopeful beginnings were being made on the Japanese army's mainline code. The Bureau's efforts were starting to bite into Japan's attempts to regain the initiative in the Pacific. If traffic analysis suggested a convoy was being assembled, air–ground interceptors would be alerted. Eric Nave's section was breaking naval air operational codes, giving advance warnings of air raids and intelligence on convoys, including overnight shelters with safe anchorages.

One worker in the section described his chief as having 'a sixth sense to sniff out meaning in a jumble of letters or numbers'. Nave found that aircraft sending a litter of numerals were actually reporting to base, 'HAVE TAKEN UP POSITION OVER CONVOY', giving latitude, longitude, course and speed. This information was passed to a US Navy contact to be used for attacks by Allied bombers and American submarines.

Joe Richard was later to comment: 'Fabian's dislike of Eric Nave was very fortunate for us. Nave became an indispensable person.'

At that time, the Admiralty in London was attempting to get Nave returned to its fold, but Mic Sandford stepped in and General Blamey told the British, 'It would be little short of disaster if Commander Nave was removed now.' The matter was dropped and Central Bureau got on with its job.

The timing of Japanese attacks could be anticipated from weather reports sent by air patrols over Allied territory about to be bombed, since the intervals between report and attack were always about the same. The civilian code breaker Gerry Room had been put in charge of weather signals, whose twenty-six-digit code required speedy decryption. Crews of enemy medium bombers on a mission could handle only the simpler air–ground code, so their progress could be tracked. As well, the skills of Japanese radio operators were deteriorating. Many top operators had been killed or isolated, and poorly trained replacements often wanted sections of a message repeated.

Aircraft were moving in August from as far away as the Philippines to Hollandia and then Wewak. Through its field stations, Central Bureau tracked a build-up of Japanese army air power around Wewak's four airfields, but these were out of fighter escort range for any Allied bombing raids. However, moving north from Wau earlier in the year, Australian troops had taken control of the Watut River valley. A site firm enough for an airfield was found downriver near Tsili Tsili, within fighter reach of Wewak. Kenney had the airstrip built secretly. By mid-August, 3000 troops and a fighter squadron were based at the strip, renamed Marilinan because Kenney didn't like one of his bases sounding like 'Silly Silly'.

Marilinan was nearly combat-ready, still undetected by the Japanese, when an enemy patrol spotted it from the air on

BURIED TREASURE

11 August. Dumbfounded, the commander of the Fourth Air Army in Rabaul, General Kumaichi Teramoto, readied his combat units, but the signals of a pre-strike reconnaissance flight were intercepted. When, on 15 August, radar detected Japanese bombers approaching, the alerted Allied fighters drove them off with light losses.

With US patrols confirming the four Wewak airfields were packed with parked aircraft, 200 American planes, B-25 bombers escorted by P-38 and P-39 fighters, headed for Wewak the following morning. Hansa Bay tried to warn Wewak, a twenty-minute flight away, of the attack heading its way, but the phone lines failed. Fragmentation bombs were dropped on the standing planes and fighters strafed the whole complex. Black smoke billowed from oil storage tanks. After a second raid the next day, 18 August, only thirty-eight Japanese aircraft were left intact of the 120 at Wewak. All the airfields were severely cratered. A No. 1 Wireless Unit monitor heard a Japanese pilot trying to contact the four air–ground stations at Wewak. Only one replied.

Air–ground intercepts in the days following the Wewak raids confirmed how devastating the strikes on the crowded airfields had been. Two of particular interest were reported in Central Bureau's daily Special Intelligence Bulletin to the commanding generals of SWPA. 'STRONG EVIDENCE SUGGESTS THERE IS A SERIOUS SHORTAGE OF AVIATION FUEL AT WEWAK,' reported one bulletin. 'THE AIR-GROUND STATION AT HOLLANDIA IS ADVISING INCOMING AIRCRAFT THAT THERE IS NO AVIATION GASOLINE AT HOLLANDIA,' said another. The first shortfall would have been the result of bombing Wewak's oil tanks, the second suggested a supply problem.

— ● —

Although General Blamey was still commander of Allied Land Forces, his role existed only on paper after a 'clean-out' within

SWPA. MacArthur had taken the main American component of Blamey's command, the US Sixth Army, renamed it Alamo Force and placed it under direct command of GHQ, not under Blamey. The balance of Blamey's command, mostly Australian troops, was now called New Guinea Force. It was the beginning of a MacArthur manoeuvre, planned or otherwise, to move Australians away from centre stage of his arena, which would soon be reserved for Americans.

MacArthur ordered New Guinea Force to take Lae with amphibious operations along the New Guinea coast and a coordinated air and overland operation through the Markham Valley, behind Lae. Pressure would continue on Salamaua to maintain the deception that it was the main objective. Kenney, to provide New Guinea Force with air support, wanted fog over New Britain, to keep Rabaul's aircraft away, and clear skies over New Guinea. Such a combination was not unusual, and it was forecast for 4 September.

As the sun rose that day over the beaches east of Lae, 2400 troops of the Australian 9th Division were landed unopposed with supplies after naval bombardment of the beach. Aerial response against the landing was held up by the fog until afternoon when planes from Rabaul arrived and wreaked havoc, damaging landing craft, killing over fifty men and blowing up an ammunition dump. By then the Australians had established a beachhead and were moving slowly in heavy rain along the coast towards Lae.

The 9th Division had been brought back from the Middle East when Japan entered the war. Its men had built a formidable reputation in battles at Tobruk and El Alamein. They were the legendary 'Rats of Tobruk', but here they were grappling with vastly different terrain and climate and a more tenacious enemy. After a few days of sodden trudging, they reached the swollen Busu River, 20 metres wide at the mouth and with Japanese in strength on the opposite bank.

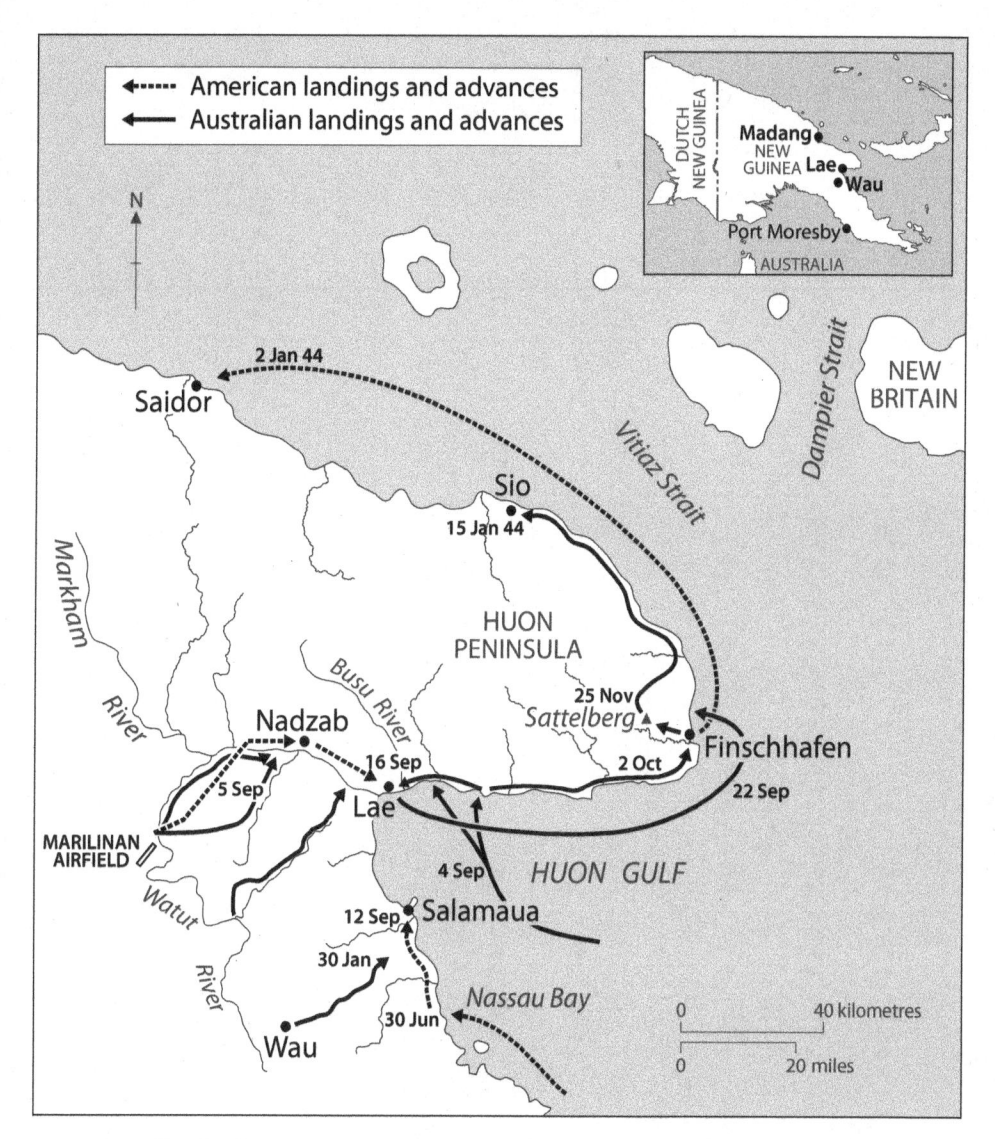

Map 3: Allied advances along the northern New Guinea coast, 1943

The day after the amphibious landing, American paratroopers jumped near Nadzab, 30 kilometres up the Markham Valley. MacArthur and Kenney watched from B-17s high above. Pushing through the tall *kunai* grass, the paratroopers encountered negligible resistance, the main forces having been moved to Salamaua as

Blamey had anticipated. Supply parachutes were dropped during the day, and in the afternoon the Americans were joined by Australian units that had come down the Watut River. American engineers landed the next day to begin building new airstrips. Two weeks later, two 2000-metre runways were ready, with six more being built.

In response to the Allied landings east of Lae, General Hatazo Adachi, commander of Japanese forces in New Guinea, pulled his troops back from Salamaua to Lae. Then, fearing that his 51st Division might be cut off, he ordered a withdrawal from Lae overland across the Huon Peninsula to the north coast. With the Australian amphibious landing approaching Lae from one side and paratroopers and infantry from the other, the Japanese started pulling back on 12 September, desperately short of rations and abandoning their heavy artillery as they dragged themselves over high rivers, around steep mountainous slopes and through the mud in constant pouring rain. They were now fighting the terrain as well as the Allies, and it was sapping their energy.

The Australians had taken a week to cross the Busu River, first by boat in darkness and under enemy gunfire, and eventually hauling up and erecting a box-girder bridge. Volleys of rifle and machine-gun fire from the other side slowed the process. By the time the troops advancing from two directions reached Salamaua, then Lae, the Japanese had melted into the jungle. The only Allied contact with the enemy after that was in sporadic exchanges with units left behind to delay the advance.

Japan's Imperial Headquarters had pulled its perimeter back to a new defence line containing the Dutch East Indies and Japan's western Pacific islands. The Rabaul senior commanders, General Imamura and Admiral Kusaka, were ordered to hold out in New Guinea, New Britain and the nearby islands as long as possible to slow the Allied advance, but ultimately these territories were expendable. Aware of MacArthur's predictable tactics, landing assault forces within 500 fighter kilometres of an Allied air base for a new toehold, the Japanese were determined to hold Bougainville, strengthen Madang and Wewak, and control the straits between New Guinea and New Britain. Finschhafen, on the Huon Peninsula, was a key defensive position and was to be reinforced.

A radio intercept on 21 September indicated that the Japanese were expecting an Allied assault on Finschhafen, which was indeed MacArthur's next objective. Australian troops were landed the next day at the mouth of the Song River, north of Finschhafen, before Japan could move more troops into the area. While Central Bureau could read signals in the Water Transport code, it hadn't broken into the regimental codes used for moving troops overland, but the guess was accurate enough. The Japanese army's 20th Division was bringing reinforcements overland from further west, but they were too late to save Finschhafen.

Landing in the pre-dawn darkness, the first two waves of Australian troops got lost and beached in a small cove south of the planned landing amid scattered enemy gunfire. The third wave was greeted at the intended beach with crossfire from concrete pillboxes. Stiff resistance was eventually forced back and an enclave cleared. Over the next few days frantic messages were exchanged between Finschhafen and Madang. By the 26th, all the Finschhafen stations went dead.

Three Australian battalions attacked the village of Finschhafen on 1 October, occupying it and the harbour by the next morning. General Adachi had ordered defensive positions be set up at Sattelberg, a peak behind Finschhafen with a wide view across the Huon Peninsula. By the time his troops coming overland arrived, Finschhafen was in Allied hands, and the Japanese pulled back towards Sio on the north side of the peninsula. Defences on Sattelberg Heights were strengthened, blocking the Allies' next drive to Sio. Spread thinly along the coastal strip, the Australians had to withstand a determined counterattack that broke through to the coast and for a while split their defensive line. A request for reinforcements was rejected by MacArthur, whose intelligence staff had underestimated the number of enemy soldiers in the area.

Patrols from the two sides fought a series of intense clashes for the next two months, with neither side gaining the upper hand. With very little useful signals intelligence to draw on, MacArthur's advance had slowed to a crawl.

— ● —

A recurring thorn in SWPA's intelligence-gathering was Washington's firm belief that all intelligence should flow through it, to be sent on as it saw fit to commanders in the field. In March, the US War Department proposed that all intercepted messages should be sent to Arlington Hall for translation and analysis; none should be done locally. Pressed by Akin, MacArthur complained to George Marshall about external interference with Central Bureau and the proposal was dropped.

Three months later, the US chief of army intelligence, General George Strong, was offering SWPA direct access to the War Department's decrypted Japanese intelligence in return for the department's officers handling Central Bureau's intercept material. MacArthur responded 'Yes' to the first offer and 'No' to the second. The proposal lapsed again, but by the end of the year, Strong sent Colonel Carter Clarke, who prepared intelligence summaries for US officials, to attach two liaison officers to SWPA. At Akin's behest, Sutherland barred them from contact with Central Bureau; they even required Sutherland's permission to send messages by radio. Central Bureau continued to send signals intelligence directly to SWPA commands without the need for approval from Washington, but MacArthur failed in his attempts to prevent Clarke's Special Security Officers from being attached to his field theatres.

The Americans at Central Bureau resisted Washington's clumsy attempts at control, but they didn't see the need to grant the same licence to their Australian colleagues. The Americans were adamant about how intelligence should flow through the Allied channels of communication, and they didn't like the British using Mic Sandford as their intelligence conduit to and from Australia.

US naval intelligence was strengthening its ties with its British counterparts in Colombo under the May BRUSA Agreement, with Fabian as liaison. Penetration of Japanese army codes was progressing, and the Americans at Central Bureau proposed a regular exchange of results by secure line with the British Army's Wireless Experimental Centre in India. It would consolidate the Bureau's independence from Washington, as well as neutralise Sandford's ongoing contacts outside their control. In September, Joe Sherr flew to Delhi to establish the link between Brisbane and Delhi. On the way home, he was killed when his plane crashed 3 kilometres from Calcutta airfield. It was a shock, but Central Bureau adjusted quickly to his absence. Sherr had spent most of his time in the city centre, anyway. Abe Sinkov took command, remaining at Ascot, and Sandford continued as executive officer. The agency continued without missing a beat and without needing a division head.

For all its importance to the war, work at Central Bureau involved long dreary hours. Much of it was mechanical and repetitive. Numbers filled the workers' brains. They looked for patterns and combinations in phone numbers and on tram tickets, and found release by writing poems, epigrams and 'funnies', which Sandford kept in a large folder in a cabinet for all to read when they needed the distraction.

A news sheet called *Clamor* was put out, with news, poems, interviews, wedding announcements and sports results. Many of the poems were about the differences between Aussies and Yanks, one anonymous American writing about a land 'down under' where things work in reverse:

Where winter comes in summer, and spring appears in fall,
Don't ever ask for 'spirits', the Army has it all.

Where a 'cobber' is a buddy, and a street-car is a 'tram',
Where the favourite word is 'bloody' and it's equal to our damn!
Where a druggist is a 'chemist', and a tavern is a 'pub'
Where a smoogie is a 'kiss' and the food, they call it 'grub'.
Where they always say 'fair dinkum' when they mean a thing's O.K.,
Where they say 'twill be a 'fortnight' when they mean two weeks away.

— ● —

Mic Sandford continued to perform like a man who couldn't stand still, writing to his contacts in British intelligence, explaining the channels by which information was distributed through the Allied structure in the Pacific: where the main code-breaking efforts were being directed and who was getting the results. One moment, he was across in New Guinea trying to expedite movement of forward detachments to places for optimum reception. Then he would be back in Brisbane, writing to his Foreign Office contact about a plan to prepare field units to go straight into the theatre of war with an assault landing party, something they hadn't done before.

That might have been considered indiscreet by the Americans, even if they were prone to the same indiscretions. General Willoughby was insisting all communications with the British Empire should go through General HQ. Sandford was instructed by Akin not to communicate directly with London or India. British intelligence officers had been denied direct access to Central Bureau.

The Australians were unhappy with the restrictions the American visitors placed on them in their own country. Sandford and Australian army intelligence chief John Rogers met with General Blamey, who said that if GHQ and General

Sutherland were adamant on this point, he would recommend that GHQ form its own Central Bureau. He knew that Central Bureau then worked independently of Willoughby—Willoughby was responsible for analysis and interpretation of Central Bureau data, but had no command over the agency—and he also knew about the unimpressive performance of American radio intercept units. Blamey took up cudgels with his colleagues in GHQ, arguing that Australia had to 'retain its individuality', though he acknowledged that 'one show' should serve both their needs. The issue was put to one side, and all continued as if there had never been any suggestion of placing constraints on the Australians.

— • —

By late 1943, Central Bureau had grown beyond Henry Street's capacity to accommodate it. A small park, adjacent to Eagle Farm Racecourse and a few minutes' walk from Henry Street, was requisitioned to take up the overflow. What had been a public park with palm trees around a bandstand gradually filled with demountable wooden huts. A high security fence topped with barbed wire was put up around the perimeter, its two gates guarded by middle-aged Australian militiamen.

The Bureau's administration and the offices of its work unit heads remained in Henry Street when the work areas moved, although over time the heads moved across to join with their teams. Organised along functional lines, the Bureau copied the Bletchley Park 'hut' model, with each demountable on Ascot Park allocated to a particular work area. With few restrictions on movement between huts when the work dictated it, a sense of one big team persisted. In that regard, the Bureau workplace functioned differently from FRUMEL.

Unaware of its source or purpose, neighbours complained about the noise generated by the IBM tabulators in Henry Street's garage, which ran around the clock. The machines were moved to a disused brick fire station in Kitchener Road alongside Ascot Park and their operation continued there. The garage was taken over by No. 11 Cipher Section, which installed Typex encrypting machines for coding traffic to the Australian Army's field units and other Allied sigint units. Workers in the new activity were mostly female cipher clerks working three shifts a day. Baffle screens installed inside the garage door shielded the equipment from outside view and reduced noise levels.

— • —

Traffic analysis by Central Bureau's field units showed in mid-November that the Japanese army's 20th Division in New Guinea had moved its transmitter to Sio, on the north coast. This suggested the start of a withdrawal, even if New Guinea Force was still facing stern resistance from Japanese positions on Sattelberg Heights. On 24 November, the defence finally broke. Sattelberg was overrun, and the Australians pushed on in the relentless monsoon towards Sio, past sick, wounded and dead Japanese soldiers.

As the 9th Division edged its way along 80 kilometres of poorly defined track, slowed—often at creek crossings in the jungle—by a Japanese fighting retreat, the Allied supply chain grappled with the terrain and monsoonal weather. On 2 January, with the Australians nearing their target, the US Alamo Force landed in heavy cloud and rain on a beach defended by fifteen soldiers, and took Saidor, west of Sio. In danger of being cut off by the Americans, the Japanese abandoned Sio, skirting around Saidor and foot-slogging over muddy mountain tracks to Madang, the only escape route still available to them.

Nearly two weeks later, the 9th Division reached Sio. When the Australians had brought their Matilda tanks into the Huon Peninsula campaign, withdrawing Japanese began leaving concealed land mines behind to impede their progress. The advancing New

BURIED TREASURE

Guinea Force routinely swept captured posts for booby traps. On 19 January, an Australian army engineer ran a metal detector around the area the Japanese army had used as its Sio headquarters. Waving the implement over a nearby flooded creek, the sapper was startled by the shrill nervy staccato, like an over-amplified cricket, in his earphones. It might have been a mine, or it might have been some mundane metal object, a biscuit tin perhaps.

Gingerly, the unit's demolition squad pulled up several small steel chests from a deep, water-filled pit. Each was about 70 centimetres long, with carrying handles at each end. They didn't look like mines, but no one was prepared to take the chance. One of the boxes was carefully prised open. The 'land mine' was found to be full of Japanese books. Curiously, each had its front cover torn off.

The unit's intelligence officer was called over to examine them. Their coating of mildew made it difficult to determine what the books were. He knew little of the clandestine world of signals intelligence, so the possibility that they might be codebooks didn't occur to him. They were Japanese, and that was sufficient reason to despatch them to the Allied Translator and Interpreter Section (ATIS) in Brisbane.

The translators there did have an inkling what the books might be. They were filled with tables, some containing numbers and *kana* characters, others just columns of numbers. Someone immediately rang a contact at Central Bureau to check his suspicion.

'Charlie,' he told Captain Girhard, 'some material's come in from New Guinea that we think you might find interesting. Come over and have a look at it. See what you think.'

Girhard went across town to ATIS with Hugh Erskine, head of Central Bureau's translation section. What they saw excited them so much they brought the metal boxes back with them.

'What've you got there, Charlie?' asked Abe Sinkov when he saw the muddy boxes.

'Something come back to ATIS from New Guinea . . . from the

front line there,' Girhard enthused. 'Jap stuff. Looks like crypto. Code books, could be. Ciphers. The works.'

Sinkov and Mic Sandford organised all hands on deck for the task of drying the material Girhard and Erskine had brought back. One by one, the pages of each codebook were carefully separated, and the books were dried individually and meticulously in the oven installed in the new Ascot Park kitchen. Books of additive tables were taken to several of the work huts and dried with electric fans and heaters. In the Brisbane midsummer, it took only a few hours to dry out each of the books, which were printed on strong paper and kept their shape well. Loose pages were taken to Henry Street's garage and hung on clothes lines with electric fans trained on them.

What the workers at Central Bureau found they had at the end of an all-day drying operation was a collection of codebooks, additive tables and other cryptographic paraphernalia. These were mainline codebooks, the Japanese 20th Division's entire cryptographic library, including the high-command ciphers with which the Allied code breakers had been struggling for a year with only modest success. Each recovered page was photographed and sent to Arlington Hall. Sandford ordered copies to be sent as well to his contacts at Bletchley Park and to Delhi.

They had fallen into Allied hands as a result of a dilemma the Japanese soldiers had faced when abandoning Sio. Confronted with hauling their diseased, exhausted and starving bodies over steep muddy tracks in chilly nightly downpours, and crossing swollen rushing rivers on seriously reduced rations, the retreating men had weighed up carefully what they should carry with them and what to leave behind. They were already carrying artillery pieces and other firearms, as well as heavy radio parts. Hauling steel trunks filled with books all the way to Madang was not appealing.

One option was to destroy the books. Army procedure allowed for that, with the proviso that the torn-off covers be retained as 'proof' of the books' destruction. The covers were torn off, but in the relentless rain the books were too wet to burn page by page, the only way to ensure that no legible material survived. The 20th Division's chief signals officer decided they could be safely disposed of by burying them in a rising creek, so that by the time the approaching enemy arrived the buried chests would be deep under water. In time, they'd probably be too water-damaged to read anyway. If the chests had been wooden they would probably have stayed undetected, but they reckoned without the Australians' fear of mines and metal booby traps.

When he reached Madang seven weeks later, the 20th Division's chief signals officer reported that the books had been destroyed and handed over the covers as proof. Later, using the ciphers recovered at Sio, Central Bureau decrypted a signal from a Japanese officer claiming to have overseen destruction of those same ciphers. Japan's army hierarchy had no reason to suspect its high-grade codes had been compromised. In the coming months, that would prove fatal.

Using the captured books, Central Bureau programmed its IBM tabulators to strip off ciphers and print out code values and their *romaji* transcriptions. No 10 × 10 indicator squares, of the type Joe Richard had worked on, were found in the Sio treasure chests, but Arlington Hall had recovered all of the previous square and half of the current square. These were wired to Brisbane, and in a few days the IBM room was pouring out messages decrypted from four different Japanese army code systems.

Overnight the agency had moved from reading a trickle of intercepts to over 20,000 a month, a flow so great the translators couldn't keep pace. Sandford sent FRUMEL a request for a loan of two US Navy linguists. Sid Goodwin, who had taken over from the army-despising Rudy Fabian, obliged, and on 4 February, Tom Mackie and 'Tex' Biard arrived from Melbourne on short-term attachment.

The pair looked critically at Central Bureau's translation operation, making suggestions while they worked through the backlog of untranslated decrypts. They found that some of the Japanese-Americans there were struggling with the idiom used in army messages and with Japanese army radio terminology, but their main task—to attend to the partially decrypted messages—could now be completed. With their help, the agency was transformed by the Sio windfall into a high-quality, high-output cryptographic organisation.

Mackie and Biard found in the pile of recent signals one that had come into Central Bureau on the same day the mine sweeper had detected the buried boxes. It was a thirteen-part message from the high command with a plan to reinforce Wewak and Hansa Bay in anticipation of MacArthur's next move. To shore up the expected Allied targets, the Japanese were weakening the defences at Hollandia, further west, in the belief it was beyond the fuel range of Allied escort fighters.

Intelligence was sent in increasing amounts to the GHQ advance echelon in Port Moresby, where MacArthur and his senior commanders were spending much of their time. The delay between getting coded messages to Brisbane for decryption and translation, and forwarding them to Port Moresby was reducing their effectiveness, leaving little time to act. After being briefed by Mic Sandford, Geoff Ballard was sent to Port Moresby to liaise with GHQ and shortcut the problem.

Japanese strengths, plans and intentions had become virtually an open book. 'They can hardly make a move now without us being aware of it,' Sandford said, 'but it's not much use producing the intelligence unless it can be transmitted immediately to where it's needed and unless there's someone there to interpret it and advise on its limitations.'

'It's going to be a very different game from now on,' he added.

Intercepts through February were able to keep the SWPA planners abreast of Japanese garrison reinforcement. A 6 February decrypt advised that 41st Division at Hansa Bay was having trouble settling into positions because of Allied air raids and the heavy rain. However, an intercept six days later revealed that 2000 troops had been added to both 41st Division and 20th Division, also at Hansa Bay, and that 4500 had reinforced 51st Division at Wewak. According to a coded message sent on 19 February, the projected strength of 20th Division was 15,000 and of 51st Division 10,000.

Based on this information, MacArthur's intelligence chief, the comically Prussian General Willoughby, proposed bypassing Hansa Bay, Madang and Wewak to take the weakly garrisoned Hollandia. MacArthur agreed, but if SWPA was to spring a surprise strike on Hollandia, it first needed to seize the airfields of the Admiralty Islands, west of New Britain, to protect its right flank and extend the encirclement of Rabaul. The prime objective was Momote airstrip on Los Negros, adjacent to Manus, the largest of the Admiralty Islands, but there was a major disagreement between two sources of Allied intelligence on the troop strength remaining on Los Negros.

In early February, two US destroyers had steamed through the Bismarck Sea, between New Guinea and the Admiralties, drawing no response. The Admiralties and Kavieng in New Ireland had been subjected to Allied bombing since the beginning of the year, leaving the airstrips at Momote and at Lorengau on Manus unusable. Anti-aircraft gunfire there had ceased, so it was unclear what defensive positions remained or where, if anywhere, they were.

Later in the month, Kavieng was bombed again with no air response, but this had been a growing trend now that the Japanese were struggling to replace lost aircraft. After General Kenney's raiders softened up Los Negros in preparation for the assault planned for April, three B-25s circled over the islands for 90 minutes, dropping low. No one fired at them and there were no signs of Japanese activity: no soldiers, no trucks, no washing on lines. The airfields were pitted and overgrown with grass.

Kenney was convinced the islands had been abandoned, but Willoughby, drawing on Ultra intelligence from Central Bureau's field intercepts, estimated that a force of some 4000 men were entrenched somewhere on Los Negros. The 19 January signal read by the navy linguists had revealed Imamura's plan to strengthen the island with up to 3000 more troops. Later intercepts revealed that these reinforcements had arrived. Joe Richard was working on messages from the Admiralties at this time. Much of the content he decrypted was about dying for the emperor, but sandwiched between patriotic declamations was the revelation that reinforcements had come from Rabaul. This was an independent task force using a four-digit mainline code that was among those captured at Sio. Had it been in a three-digit regimental code, Central Bureau would have been unable to read it.

Refusing to give Willoughby's sigint-based troop estimates any credence, and with his second-in-command, General Ennis Whitehead, estimating from aerial patrols that there were 300 defenders on Los Negros, General Kenney proposed an immediate landing on the island. On 27 February, a scout party landed by night in rubber boats and reported the area to be 'lousy with Japs'. Still Kenney was unconvinced, refusing to believe his pilots hadn't cleared the island and retorting that '25 Japs in the woods at night' might create that impression.

Despite his air force commander's optimism, MacArthur ordered 'reconnaissance in force'. On the morning of 29 February, after Allied destroyers and cruisers shelled the Los Negros coast, landing craft passed through a narrow harbour entrance on the island's eastern side and came under unexpectedly heavy mortar and machine-gun fire. Three B-25s got through in the overcast conditions to bomb the shore positions, but a second wave of landing craft was turned back by the enemy gunfire. The Americans landed at the next attempt and established a beachhead. By midday, they had overrun Momote field. It was covered with weeds and rusty aircraft parts, and pitted with craters filled with water.

In the afternoon, the Allied assault force was hit by a heavy rainstorm and by a Japanese force clearly nearer to Willoughby's estimate than Whitehead's. Allied bomber support was not possible in the downpour. The front-line troops pulled off the airstrip, returned to the beachhead and dug in. At dusk, a firefight broke out. Japanese infiltrated the invaders' lines, but the Americans held out until morning, when the weather cleared and the Japanese withdrew. Supplies were dropped at the beachhead, and enemy positions were bombarded from the air and offshore.

Unexpected by Kenney, if not by Willoughby, the Japanese response was in anticipation of a large-scale Allied operation in the Admiralties, which they had inferred from increased radio traffic and US submarine activity in the area. Such an operation would be necessary to protect the expected American assault on Hansa Bay or Wewak. As the radio intercepts had shown, Imamura had managed to reinforce defences around the bases. To create the impression that Los Negros had been abandoned, Colonel Yoshio Ezaki, the garrison commander, had ordered his troops to keep all human activity concealed and hold off anti-aircraft fire until the major Allied offensive. The airfields were unusable, so there were no aircraft there, and there was no ground-troop response to American reconnaissance.

The subterfuge had clearly worked well, convincing General Kenney that the island had minimal defenders, but on the assumption there would be a large-scale attack, Ezaki had placed his defences in the north, where the beach was more suited to an operation of that size. Instead, the smaller exploratory force attacked through the narrow harbour entrance to the east; the defence was sufficient to force the assault back from the airstrip, but not to drive it from the beachhead.

The bewildered invasion force built up its beachhead just in time. Four days after it landed, the Japanese returned in waves, reinforced with troops brought across the island. The struggle ebbed and flowed through the night, with high casualties on both sides. In the morning, the Japanese withdrew.

Port Moresby's field station, No. 1 Wireless Unit, with its detachments now across the Owen Stanleys at Lae and Salamaua, intercepted signals from a desperate Japanese garrison at Los Negros. Sent on to Brisbane, they provided insights into its diminishing strength. A 3 March message indicated troop numbers had fallen from 3700 to 2700. By 5 March, Japanese operators were tapping out, 'THE TIMING OF OUR LAST HOUR IS DRAWING NEAR ... WE ARE STRIVING FOR OUR FATHERLAND.'

At that time, three US warships were driven back by heavy fire while trying to force their way into Seeadler Harbour, between the two adjacent islands, Manus and Los Negros. A week later, a strengthened force returned, shelling the area around Lorengau airstrip on Manus and sweeping the harbour for mines. On 15 March, Alamo Force landed on Manus's northern beach and advanced on Lorengau over rain-softened red clay, through heavy rainforest and mangrove swamp. Tanks and flamethrowers were used to overrun Japanese positions, but the advance was faltering in the face of fierce resistance, the Americans getting in the way of their own fire as they tried to manoeuvre around dug-in positions. The only good news was what the exercise revealed about radio intelligence. It had provided accurate insight into the status of the islands' defences. Unfortunately this had been discounted and lives were lost as a result, but greater reliance would be placed on such intelligence in future offensives.

The attacking force took three days to push through to the airfield. By then the Japanese had retreated into the interior of the island. It would take until the end of the month for substantial resistance to be cleared from Manus and Los Negros. On 30 March, No. 1 Wireless Unit intercepted a signal from a disheartened commander to General Imamura in Rabaul: 'WE REGRETFULLY REPORT OUR FORCES ON THE ADMIRALTIES HAVE BEEN OVERCOME WHILE FIGHTING TO THE UTMOST.'

After the capture of the two main Admiralty islands, 400 Japanese bunkers were found, nearly twenty times the estimate from aerial reconnaissance and consistent with the estimates of Japanese strength provided by Central Bureau from sigint. The American assault had been compromised by Kenney's gung-ho reliance on the guesses of the men he saw in the pilot's mess rather than the insights from a secretive and distant facility in Brisbane. That was not a trap MacArthur would fall into. Intelligence garnered from radio decryption by an agency he had probably never visited would be the basis of one of his most daring and significant military operations, the leapfrog to Hollandia that left some 50,000 Japanese troops isolated in Hansa Bay and Wewak.

— • —

At the beginning of March, the Joint Chiefs of Staff had directed MacArthur and Nimitz to submit plans for the advance to the Philippines. MacArthur proposed that two SWPA divisions, supported by Halsey's Pacific Fleet, attack Hollandia on 15 April. The main thrust of his argument was based on high-level signals intelligence, or Ultra.

'The enemy has concentrated the mass of his ground forces forward in the Madang–Wewak area, leaving relatively weak forces in the Hollandia Bay area,' MacArthur reported. 'He is attempting to concentrate land-based air forces in the area of western New Guinea and is developing additional new fields in order to consolidate this area into a bulwark of air defence.'

On 12 March, the Joint Chiefs approved the Hollandia offensive. There would be three simultaneous amphibious landings far behind Japanese lines, with 217 ships moving 80,000 men and supplies 1600 kilometres to bypass the Japanese Eighteenth Army waiting further east. What appeared to be an almost reckless gamble by a vain general was in fact a carefully planned operation against a known Japanese weak point. That weak point was revealed by Ultra.

With the Sio codebooks in its hands, Central Bureau was able to eavesdrop on the Japanese army command in New Guinea as it prepared to meet what it expected to be the next Allied offensive. MacArthur now had the same advantage Nimitz had enjoyed before the Midway naval battle: foreknowledge of the enemy's intentions. He knew from intercepts in mid-March, after Japan's loss of the Admiralties, that General Adachi had moved his headquarters to Wewak from isolated Rabaul, with a forward command post further east at Hansa Bay. A 20 March decrypt notified MacArthur's strategists that 5000 men had been diverted to Madang to counter the anticipated Allied landing. Among the inferences drawn from these messages was that Adachi's forces would be in transition in March and April, not standing by for combat. Earlier in the month, a signal had reported that the Eighteenth Army in the Madang–Hansa Bay area was short of weapons.

An intercept at the end of March contained an estimate of Allied intentions by General Koreiku Anami, the new commander of the Second Area Army, stationed at Davao in the Philippines. He anticipated Allied landings at Madang and Hansa Bay after June. There was no serious expectation of an attack on the more distant Hollandia, with its maintenance workers and small garrison. From Ultra, MacArthur knew not only what the Japanese intended, but what they thought the Allies intended. He also knew where Japan's weaknesses were in the region. It was a gift from heaven—or, more correctly, from a shadowy agency in Brisbane's suburbs.

Thanks to Central Bureau's ability to read the Water Transport Code, Kenney's bombers, and submarines under the new SWPA naval commander, Vice-Admiral Thomas Kinkaid, were able to wreak havoc through March on Japan's efforts to build up its central New Guinea garrison. On 29 February, the sub US *Pelo* sank the transport *Kayo Maru* bringing soldiers from the Palau Islands to Hollandia. An air attack on a barge convoy from Hollandia to Wewak on 15 March sank two barges and drove another aground. On the night of 18 March, B-24s sank the *Yakumo Maru* of Wewak Convoy 21. The remaining three ships rescued the survivors, but all were destroyed by American bombers the next morning. So severe were the losses to Japan's war effort in the region that Imperial HQ suspended large-ship convoys to Wewak. To disguise the source of Allied knowledge, air attacks based on signals intelligence were usually preceded by air patrols. The enemy became so accustomed to these patrols that they didn't suspect their codes had been broken.

The Japanese were building new airfields in central New Guinea to resist the expected Allied strikes. Generals Kenney and Akin, at this stage operating from Port Moresby, were both back in Brisbane for a conference, staying at Lennon's Hotel, when a 25 March intercept revealed that 310 aircraft were on Hollandia's airfields waiting to be delivered to new fields further east. Transfer of these planes was to begin the next morning.

The decoded intercept was taken in the mid-evening from Central Bureau to Akin in his hotel room. Already in pyjamas, he put on his braided general's cap, let the messenger in and read the intercept summary. Still in pyjamas and military cap, Akin immediately caught the lift to Kenney's room.

'This you'll want to see, George!' he exclaimed as he breezed in. 'I think you'll want to move fast on it.'

Indeed Kenney did. He issued an order that night for the Hollandia fields to be attacked as soon as possible before the dispersal of the planes could progress far.

Unknown to the Japanese, who believed Hollandia was beyond the range of Allied escort fighters, Lockheed P-38s had been developed with underwing drop tanks that further extended their range, but these planes had been ordered not to fly beyond their previous range for the time being. On 30 March, sixty B-24 bombers, escorted by the no longer restricted long-range P-38s, attacked Hollandia. Further raids followed on 31 March and 3 April. After the third raid, Japanese reserve air capacity at Hollandia was largely demolished.

On 8 April, the Japanese army changed the key for its four-digit high-level code. For a while, Central Bureau was unable to read these mainline messages and relied on traffic analysis, but thanks to the codes recovered at Sio, the damage to Japan's defence tactics was already done. MacArthur's strategists were already well advanced in planning for the Hollandia offensive.

General Kenney's pilots staged bombing raids on Hansa Bay to reinforce the Japanese expectation of a coming assault there, and flew conspicuous reconnaissance flights over the area. Leaflets were dropped urging Korean and Formosan conscripts to desert, and submarines left empty rafts on nearby beaches suggesting that exploratory patrols had been there. Wewak's airfields were heavily bombed to prevent their use against the coming 'offensive' and to create the belief that the area was being softened for an amphibious landing.

A Japanese naval plane spotted an Allied task force near the Admiralties on 18 April and a transport convoy the next day north of Wewak. It was assumed the ships were heading for Hansa Bay or Wewak, which were put on alert. When American carrier planes made an early-morning strike on Hollandia, the Japanese did not connect it to the approaching invasion fleet because aircraft carriers hadn't been used in any of MacArthur's previous offensives. On this occasion, however, Nimitz had agreed to provide carrier support for the first three days of the operation, withdrawing before Japanese aircraft could get there from further afield. SWPA command decided to seize the airfields at Aitape, 200 kilometres east of Hollandia, to provide air cover for the main assault after carrier support was withdrawn.

BURIED TREASURE

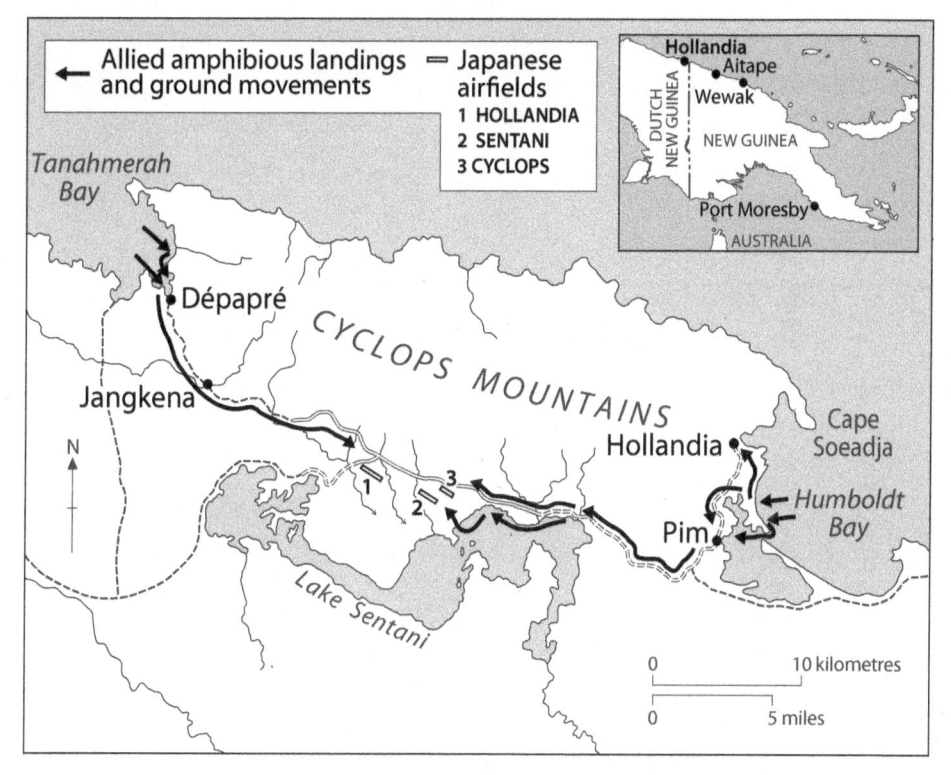

Map 4: Allied assault on Hollandia and its airfields, 22 April 1944

Having steamed west from Manus Island, the assault convoys turned south-west at dusk towards Hollandia. About 120 kilometres from the New Guinea coast, the Eastern Attack Group broke off and turned towards Aitape. Landing there unopposed after bombardment from the convoy's warships, the troops quickly captured the airfield. Caught by surprise and badly outnumbered, its defenders fled to the hills, leaving food and ammunition behind. When they returned to resist the assault force, they were soon overcome. Blamey's New Guinea Force, having taken an abandoned Madang, pressed towards Wewak to prevent the Japanese Eighteenth Army moving west to Aitape, where engineering equipment and materials were being landed by the Americans for speedy airstrip construction.

The main body of the Allied task force steamed up the coast to where the towering Cyclops Mountains dropped steeply to the sea between Humboldt and Tanahmerah bays. Both bays were backed by dense mangrove swamps but provided suitable beaches for an amphibious assault. Over the previous year, the Japanese had built three airstrips on the plain around Lake Sentani, behind the mountains. Large ships unloaded at Hollandia, on Humboldt Bay, with cargo carried down the coast as far as Wewak. Hollandia had grown to a large regional base, second in size only to Rabaul. Serviced by the three airfields, it was still growing, with reinforcements constantly coming in. MacArthur's strategists planned to seize Hollandia before it was developed further, then use it as a major base for the drive to the Philippines.

At seven o'clock on the morning of 22 April 1944, scarlet tracers dashed across the blue-grey overcast sky over Humboldt Bay. Rockets and naval gunfire lit up the shore, and carrier planes roared over at tree level, strafing and bombing whatever happened to be below. Assault troops had breakfast, climbed down nets to small landing craft and waited on rough seas for the sound and light show to conclude. They were further out than planned, the weather obscuring landmarks that were to guide the troop carriers to a closer anchorage.

A regiment landed in light drizzle at Humboldt Bay, and two battalions at Tanahmerah Bay, 40 kilometres away on the other side of the Cyclops Mountains. The battle plan was to push around the mountains from both sides in a pincer movement on the airfields behind. MacArthur's field commanders, not privy to Ultra intelligence, were expecting a bitter fight, but the only resistance was scattered small-arms fire from the flanks of the beach. No enemy aircraft attacked from the Hollandia fields. Only ten days before, Major-General Masazumi Inada had taken command of the local garrison of 15,000 men, mostly pilots without planes and service and signals crew. They were in disarray, uncertain how to respond to such an overwhelming force.

BURIED TREASURE

Beachheads were quickly secured by the attackers. Supplies were landed at a location in Tanahmerah Bay with an impassable swamp behind it. Tanks and artillery mounts got bogged in the mud and had to be pulled out by bulldozer. Boxes were piled on the shore in three-metre stacks. By evening, the beach was covered with supplies, troops, tanks, vehicles and gun emplacements, all with nowhere to go. They had to be shuttled overnight by shallow-draft boat through a reef to another part of the bay, where winding tracks ran back from the shoreline and over the hills to Lake Sentani.

The next day, advancing soldiers and supplies crossing a stream were ambushed by well-concealed Japanese defenders whom air strafing and mortars failed to dislodge. Another day passed, with heavy rain turning the track into a quagmire. The following morning the Japanese were found to have left their positions, but the track had become a sea of mud, parts of it knee-deep in water. The column advanced slowly, hand-carrying what supplies they could. By noon, four days after landing, they reached a hill from which they could see the three airfields that serviced Hollandia.

At the same time as the landing at Tanahmerah Bay, the larger force came ashore unopposed at Humboldt Bay. The intelligence from Central Bureau had served MacArthur well. Rocket fire from the landing craft went unanswered, apart from sporadic rifle fire. A Japanese anti-aircraft gun was found with its canvas cover still on. A sand spit already cluttered with Japanese stores became congested with Allied supplies stacked alongside. Men moved towards Hollandia on one side of the bay, digging in on a ridge overlooking the township while it was bombarded overnight with naval guns and howitzers. A field radio unit intercepted a message from Hollandia to the army command centre on Biak island, 350 kilometres away: 'CODEBOOKS WILL BE BURNED. DESTRUCTION HAS STARTED.' The next morning Hollandia was occupied with no resistance.

Like its counterpart at Tanahmerah Bay, the assault force at Humboldt Bay suffered setbacks. On the day after the landing, three Japanese bombers left the Biak base and arrived at Hollandia in the evening. With the moon in its dark phase, one plane clipped a coconut tree and cartwheeled in a ball of flame, but the other two dropped bombs in the middle of fires lit to illuminate the landing of equipment. They hit a Japanese ammunition dump, exploding near American gasoline drums and spreading to the piled supplies, which burnt out of control through the night and into the next day. Sixty per cent of supplies landed at Humboldt Bay were lost.

An advance patrol started along the road to Lake Sentani with carrier plane support, but heavy rain turned the road to mud and bogged supply transport. The patrol pressed on despite the conditions. With the airfields' defenders aware that the Allies were approaching on both sides, an air–ground station signalled in plain text that 'THE ENEMY IS 2 MILES AWAY' and went off air.

On 24 April, the advance force reached a jetty on the shore of Lake Sentani. Two days later, it took the first of the airfields in the morning without opposition. Together with the force from Tanahmerah Bay, it captured the other two fields by nightfall.

Few enemy soldiers were encountered in mopping-up operations. Had the Japanese been able to attack in force, supply problems caused by the fire, weather and mud would have made holding them off extremely difficult—too much heavy equipment and supplies had been landed too quickly owing to flawed estimates of enemy strength. But the Japanese were never in a position to mount that counterattack.

— ● —

As the Allies pushed along the northern New Guinea coast, intelligence teams searched abandoned airfields for discarded code and cipher material. Worksheets with key and indicator tables had been found in the remains of aircraft at Aitape, but the Japanese had feared a security break in the capture of Hollandia and changed their additives. Analysts were able to decipher the backlog of messages, but not any new ones.

The Japanese Eighteenth Army in New Guinea was supplied with a new additive book in April. The following month, an intercept decrypted at Central Bureau revealed that a barge, the *Yoshino Maru*, which had been set on fire and sunk by the Americans, had on board a current additive book for the Army General Purpose code. It would be hard for the Japanese to recover it, but some at GHQ assumed it had been destroyed in the fire. However, one of the Bureau's analysts was aware that burned books don't disintegrate: ghostly vestiges of print remain in the charred portions and can be made legible. It was worth investigating.

General Akin sent divers to try and retrieve the cipher book from the sunken barge. After several dives, they found a metal box wedged behind a ladder. Inside was a badly charred mass, the remains of a book. It was brought back to Brisbane in a four-engined plane and in the personal custody of an officer sent to the sunken barge. Spencer Akin was taking no chances of losing the prize—if that's what it was.

Robert Holmes, head of Central Bureau's photographic and chemistry section, carefully prised each page from the charred mass using a surgeon's scalpel and mounted it on cotton backing. The pages were dabbed, two cipher groups at a time, with cotton swabs dipped in alcohol. The random number groups appeared plainly for a few seconds until the alcohol evaporated and they disappeared. While they were briefly visible, the groups were copied down and photographed. The separated pages were then packed on cotton in cardboard boxes and sent to Arlington Hall for a repeat reading of the groups.

What Holmes's forensic work had uncovered was the current General Purpose additive book, 500 pages of additive tables and ten pages of indicator ciphers, which denoted the starting point in the additives. It was used to read all mainline Japanese army messages for several months in 1944. Its continued use by Japanese forces cut off in New Guinea was such a boon to the Allies that General Marshall messaged MacArthur:

> So long as 18th Army remains physically isolated and in radio communication with other Jap units it will continue to afford US valuable source of cryptanalytic assistance. To the extent that it will not interfere with your present operations, it is highly desirable that this situation be preserved and fully exploited. Will advise when this advantage to us ceases.

— ● —

A few weeks after the capture of Hollandia, Akin advised Central Bureau that MacArthur wanted his GHQ to move to the base that was now being constructed there. This commander was not a fan of the usual custom of keeping the headquarters in the home country, preferring to move it forward as the front advanced. Sandford wondered how Central Bureau would operate 3000 kilometres from its main client, but first it had to get a field unit operating at the new base.

No. 53 Wireless Section had been set up in Finschhafen early in 1944 and reinforced with No. 55 Wireless Section personnel from Nadzab and Port Moresby, but they were now too far from the action to be greatly effective. In July, the station, with all its paraphernalia and radio gear, was moved to Hollandia on an American ship along with troops to reinforce the garrison at the captured base.

The tank-landing ship scraped up onto the white sand of the Humboldt Bay shore, its great metal doors clanging open for troops, vehicles and supplies to pour out. Jostled by the crowd, the radio men crossed the beach to a narrow isthmus backed by thick jungle. Whirlwinds lifted tents as the men pitched them, but eventually camp was set up.

BURIED TREASURE

The Australians started setting up a temporary radio intercept operation the next day among sago palms and kapok trees. It was like a camping holiday, building fires with driftwood and bathing in the sea. Sometimes wreckage of torpedoed ships drifted onto the shore. Even a case of American K rations was washed up. A sandbag wall was put up to protect the camp from flood tides. Wandering into the derelict town of Hollandia, the men came across a Japanese quartermaster's store with clothing, letter cards and badges of rank, which they sold to Americans for souvenirs.

About that time, a field unit of an American Signal Radio Intelligence Company arrived in Hollandia, direct from training in the US. Two more units followed over the next few months, none with any great experience of operating in war zones.

In August, MacArthur moved his headquarters to the new base. Central Bureau set up a forward echelon there three months later. The bulk of its cryptographic operations and its staff, both Australian and American, transferred to the Hollandia base with the Australian Stan 'Pappy' Clark in charge.

The field units, along with the newly arrived Central Bureau cohort, moved to MacArthur's HQ on the hills overlooking Humboldt Bay. A cipher hut was built on a windy spur, its four Typex encoding machines run with fluctuating power from generators back at the main camp. Meals were taken in a huge mess hall and good quality warm clothes were available from the American quartermaster store. For the Australians this meant a significant improvement in quality of life.

Cecil Corey, a US lieutenant, had worked as a traffic analyst in Brisbane and was paired by Clark with an Australian sergeant, Mos Williams, for further practical training in front-line cryptanalysis. Some of the Americans resented being trained by non-officers, feeling that their nation's troops and resources were winning the war and didn't need Australian help. 'Many of the Americans goofed off in Hollandia,' says Corey. His view was that he learned much from Williams, a veteran of Middle East field radio, and found his enthusiasm for his work infectious. Soon Corey was intercepting Japanese army mainline signals, reconstructing communications nets and looking for new traffic sources.

The Australian government wouldn't allow the women it had trained in cryptanalysis to be transferred overseas. Instead 350 Americans of the Women's Army Corps went to Hollandia, working primarily on the Water Transport Code without the assistance of IBM tabulators. These workers were given a daily quota of messages to decode in the stifling heat of the hut. When they finished, they were free for the rest of the day. Some were fast, others struggled. They had come with various levels of training and those who never caught on were found something else to do.

After the war, MacArthur was quoted as saying the WACs worked harder than men, complained less and were better disciplined. One of their co-workers said they were good workers but talked too much and too loudly.

Central Bureau had separated into two organisations, one at the front very much concerned with the here and now, the other back at home base keeping the show running and, to some degree, looking ahead beyond the end of a war whose outcome now seemed inevitable, even to the enemy.

Chapter 12

The front line and the back room

By mid-1944, Allied forces under General MacArthur's command were only 560 kilometres from the Philippine Islands, near enough to pound Japanese positions with long-range bombers. Admiral Nimitz's naval forces had advanced across the central Pacific, capturing the Gilbert Islands and some of the Marshall and Mariana Islands. Carrier-based warplanes were carrying out strikes against the Japanese in the Philippines. The Imperial Japanese Army in New Guinea and the Admiralty Islands had been either overrun or isolated and bypassed by the US and Australian armies of SWPA. Within bomber range of the southern Philippines, Morotai in the Dutch East Indies had been taken by September.

With signals intelligence informing the Allies of Japanese shipping movements, submarines and aircraft ambushed the enemy's vessels in the western Pacific throughout the year, disrupting its exploitation of resources in the East Indies. Further intercepts in June revealed Tokyo was reinforcing the Philippines defences to counter MacArthur's expected advance north. The Allied high command focused attacks on shipping and flights to the

Philippines, but Japan was still managing to expand its garrison there.

Carrier aircraft from Admiral Halsey's Third Fleet had carried out several successful missions over the Philippines with limited Japanese resistance. Instead of invading the southern island of Mindanao, as originally planned, Halsey recommended a direct strike on the central island of Leyte, whose deep-water approaches and sandy beaches were ideal for amphibious assaults and landing of supplies. The Leyte invasion was planned for October, bringing the Allies' drive towards Tokyo forward by some two months. It would be monsoon season, but they needed to pounce before enemy defences were built up further.

On 6 October, MacArthur's signals chief, Spencer Akin, sent a message to Abe Sinkov at Central Bureau. SWPA wanted a special party of twenty-four from the RAAF's No. 1 Wireless Unit, then stationed on the island of Biak, for a 'highly important commitment in K-2 area'. 'King 2' was military code for the Leyte operation. MacArthur wanted his recapture of the Philippines to be well supported by a signals intelligence unit, and the Australians, with a track record going back to the Middle East, were far more experienced than their American counterparts.

Prompted by his military intelligence chief, John Rogers, General Blamey had initially opposed Australian sigint units going north with the US forces because he thought it would diminish Australia's interception capacity. Blamey had already refused to put other Australian units under American control as part of the invasion force, which MacArthur had probably expected and planned for anyway. Rogers had argued that it was 'high time that the Americans provided their own sections, both signals and intelligence personnel, to care for their own requirements'.

Blamey had already battled with SWPA for Australian personnel to carry out functions in Australia's interests, not just America's, but he changed his mind on this issue after an appeal by the

Americans. They wanted the best, and this unit was the best available. In an invasion force made up almost entirely of US troops and support, the Australian radio intercept unit would stand out as the exception.

On 8 October, a core group of twenty-three interception and intelligence personnel from No. 1 Wireless Unit were flown from Biak to New Guinea for an unrevealed mission. As they approached the coast, the Hollandia anchorage came into view. Spread out widely below them on the sparkling emerald sea were hundreds of ships: warships, transports, oilers and other supply vessels. Something big was afoot.

Now named the Naval-Air Section of No. 6 Wireless Unit and joined by a new unit commander, the Australians were treated like visiting dignitaries. Camping in four-man American tents near the top of Leimock Hill with the elite US Rangers, they had US Army stretchers, mosquito netting, a small table and a view across the majestic Humboldt Bay. For men who had been roughing it in the Australian style for over two years, it was luxury they could barely have imagined.

Told to leave their Australian arms behind in Biak, the men of the new unit were issued with Thompson submachine guns, carbines, .45 revolvers and American jungle knives, but no water bottles. Nor were they shown how to clean, load or use their new weapons. The Americans assumed—incorrectly—that they already knew how to do all that. For the first time, the men were issued with new RAAF clothing: trousers and two shirts each, but no wet weather gear. Given cholera injections by US medics, they knew they were going to a new operational area, but no one had told them where it was. If any of them had overheard the code K-2, it would have meant nothing anyway.

The improvement in their meals was staggering: fresh meat and vegetables, the ubiquitous ice cream, which they had seen Americans eating out of large cartons, bread and coffee, but no tea.

The Australians played baseball with the Rangers, who let them win. They watched movies at night at one end of the beach. And all the while, the men of No. 6 Wireless Unit watched the build-up of shipping in Hollandia's harbour. War? What war? They were soon to find out.

Assembling in a large briefing room, the men were told they would be the nucleus of No. 6 Wireless Unit, supporting operations in the Philippines. They were now seconded to the US Armed Forces. The detachment of twenty-four, made up of twelve intercept operators and twelve intelligence officers (including the commander), would land on Leyte with the invasion force, and the rest of the unit would arrive soon after the island was secured. The mission of the advance party was to monitor army and navy air communications to avoid surprise attacks on the assault force as it rounded Mindanao on the way to Leyte Gulf. They were also to pick up Japanese responses to the US landing, warning of any reinforcements arriving or convoys moving along the Indochina coast.

The unit was allocated three new US-made mobile interception trucks. Equipped with high-powered wireless receivers and frequency meters, the trucks were dimly lit inside so any escaping light couldn't be seen from the air. Metal sides were vented and insect-proofed, as was the inner wire door. There was an aerial on each truck's roof for short-distance receiving, and connections to run aerial lines to tree tops and other high vantage points. A separate trailer-mounted generator, with two petrol motors that could each run for twelve hours, would be towed by the truck to the operating position and detached to stand 50 metres away. Finally, each truck had a power winch at the front to pull it out of bogs. It was the very best of American technological know-how made available to a select unit of Australians.

Back in April, another RAAF field unit, No. 4 Wireless Unit, had experimented with a mobile interception unit mounted on a fleet of vehicles, but these were found to be impractical for island-hopping since transport ships lacked space for them and the trucks were difficult to land across open beaches. These new trucks were going to turn those disadvantages around. The field units were entering a new phase of operation.

— • —

For a year, Mic Sandford had been on a roving commission with the Australian Special Intelligence Personnel as well as with Central Bureau. His job was to facilitate, coordinate and troubleshoot on Australia's behalf across the network of Allied military intelligence, in London, Washington and anywhere else that Australia's interests might lie. His immediate points of contact were Abe Sinkov, the senior American at Central Bureau, and in Australian military intelligence, director John Rogers and his deputy, Robert Little. Sandford also maintained vital links within Britain's GCCS and its operational hub at Bletchley Park.

Sandford and Little were a tag team with contrasting personal styles. The former was expansive and informal, the other, a decorated artillery officer from the First World War, formal and proper. They worked together effectively out of mutual respect. Looking towards postwar geopolitics, the pair had a particular interest in Dale Trendall's D Special Section in Melbourne, which decrypted diplomatic intercepts.

Australia's Department of External Affairs didn't receive a précis of intercepts, but occasionally got intelligence via Britain's Dominions Office with the heading 'information available from a secret but entirely trustworthy source'. When it was clear in one such message that it had actually been intercepted in Melbourne, the department's secretary, William Hodgson, called Little to demand an explanation. Why was the intelligence not being passed to them directly, instead of through London at the latter's discretion? Told of the risk if the source became known to his minister, Hodgson said he would take the matter up officially. Little sensed trouble and warned Sandford.

It was decided that a précis would be sent weekly to Hodgson, who would read it and burn it immediately. If he felt any of the information should be disclosed to the minister, Central Bureau would provide a paraphrased version of the relevant portion, but the very existence of D Special Section would be kept secret from both the secretary and his minister.

The desire to control the distribution of intelligence was contagious, but Sandford was seen by many in the upper echelons as a reliable conduit for it. 'For Sandford from Travis,' cabled the Bletchley Park chief at one time. 'It is requested that L.H.Q. Melbourne [Blamey's military force] in future pass Ultra material through you.'

Sandford told Little that London insisted Australia cease providing diplomatic sigint to the Americans in their region. Any political intelligence in Australian summaries should not be discussed by its recipients with their American counterparts. This was specifically requested by G2 (Special Branch) in Washington. G2's people saw loose cannons wherever they looked, but Sandford was someone they could rely on.

Sandford's written exchanges with his colleague in Military Intelligence became more informal as the partnership grew. They discussed security bushfires and various skirmishes within the Allied military network. One memo to Little was headed 'Dear RAL', Sandford's usual greeting to his colleague, and signed by hand. Its text was in an unconventionally chatty style and ended, 'I have already advised them [London] that we know we are naughty boys and will not do it again.' Another notified Little that Wainwright was en route to Melbourne by train and had been instructed to report to him. Sandford hoped his batman could be given immediate leave, adding: 'There is a very special reason for this and I will explain when I come down or by telephone.' With

Little, Sandford blurred the line between personal and professional, but the older man played a straight bat to it and they got on with the job.

Constantly on the move, Sandford shuttled particularly between Brisbane and Hollandia, his batman with the inexpertly dyed blond hair moving back and forth with him. Homosexuality was seldom considered or mentioned; Colin Wainwright's theatricality was regarded as comical—troops called him 'The Bat-Man'—especially when compared with the somewhat aristocratic demeanour of his senior officer.

Eric Nave remained in Brisbane on doctor's orders, but still oversaw from there the breaking of Japanese air codes as they were routinely introduced. Sandford wrote to General Northcott, the Australian Army's Chief of General Staff, suggesting he prompt Britain's Admiralty to promote Commander Nave to the rank of captain as 'a compliment to themselves, as well as a suitable tribute to Nave'. He pointed out that Nave was on loan to the Australian Army, no longer to the RAN. Thanks to his 'long experience and exceptional technical skill', intelligence got from Central Bureau to Allied Naval HQ with minimal delay so that appropriate action could be taken.

A few months later, Nave was asked to see Captain Edward Thomas, Naval Officer in Charge (Queensland), at his office in a former Brisbane bank building. When he arrived, the secretary said, 'You must excuse Captain Thomas's dress. Our building's air-conditioning has broken down.' Nave entered and was greeted by a bare-chested man seated behind a desk, possibly completely naked for all the visitor could tell.

'I'm to advise you that you are promoted to acting captain,' said Captain Thomas.

Mic Sandford was a frequent visitor to Eric Nave's home. On one occasion, Sandford crooned to Nave's four-year-old daughter as she sat in one of the large frangipani trees in their back yard.

'Don't go climbing that frangipani tree with anyone else but me,' he sang, taking off the popular Andrews Sisters song of the time, 'Don't Sit Under the Apple Tree (With Anyone Else But Me)'. Many years later, Elizabeth Nave could still recall the tall army officer whose visits to their house had left a lasting impression.

Sandford was also a marvellous host. His large, well-appointed Hamilton villa, which had only two occupants when they were in town, developed a reputation for elegant dinners. Sometimes they were gatherings of senior service personnel, contacts from his constant movement around the military network. Sometimes they were a different crowd of social connections he'd built up outside the military, much of it in the city's small world of the arts. Sandford's life was almost in two parts: the busy social life of a gregarious, widely liked young man with a patrician manner; and the equally busy demands on a well-respected contact man in the military who was constantly on the move.

— ● —

On Friday, 13 October, a convoy of nearly 500 vessels of the US Third and Seventh Fleets set out from Hollandia on the 2400-kilometre journey to Leyte. So large was the invasion fleet that it took a day and a half to clear the harbour. Six of the operators from the RAAF's No. 6 Wireless Unit had been scheduled to travel on an assault craft, but when Geoff Ballard attempted to confirm that with the operation's Logistics Unit, he was told there was no room on any vessel.

'It's a CSO order,' Ballard told the truculent American, referring to chief signal officer, General Akin. Half an hour later, Ballard was advised in a surly tone that there was space available on the CSO's communications ship. The Australians were going to have to prove their usefulness to the lower ranks, even if senior command had been made aware of their value. At the intelligence briefing for the mission, Akin had introduced his Australian radio

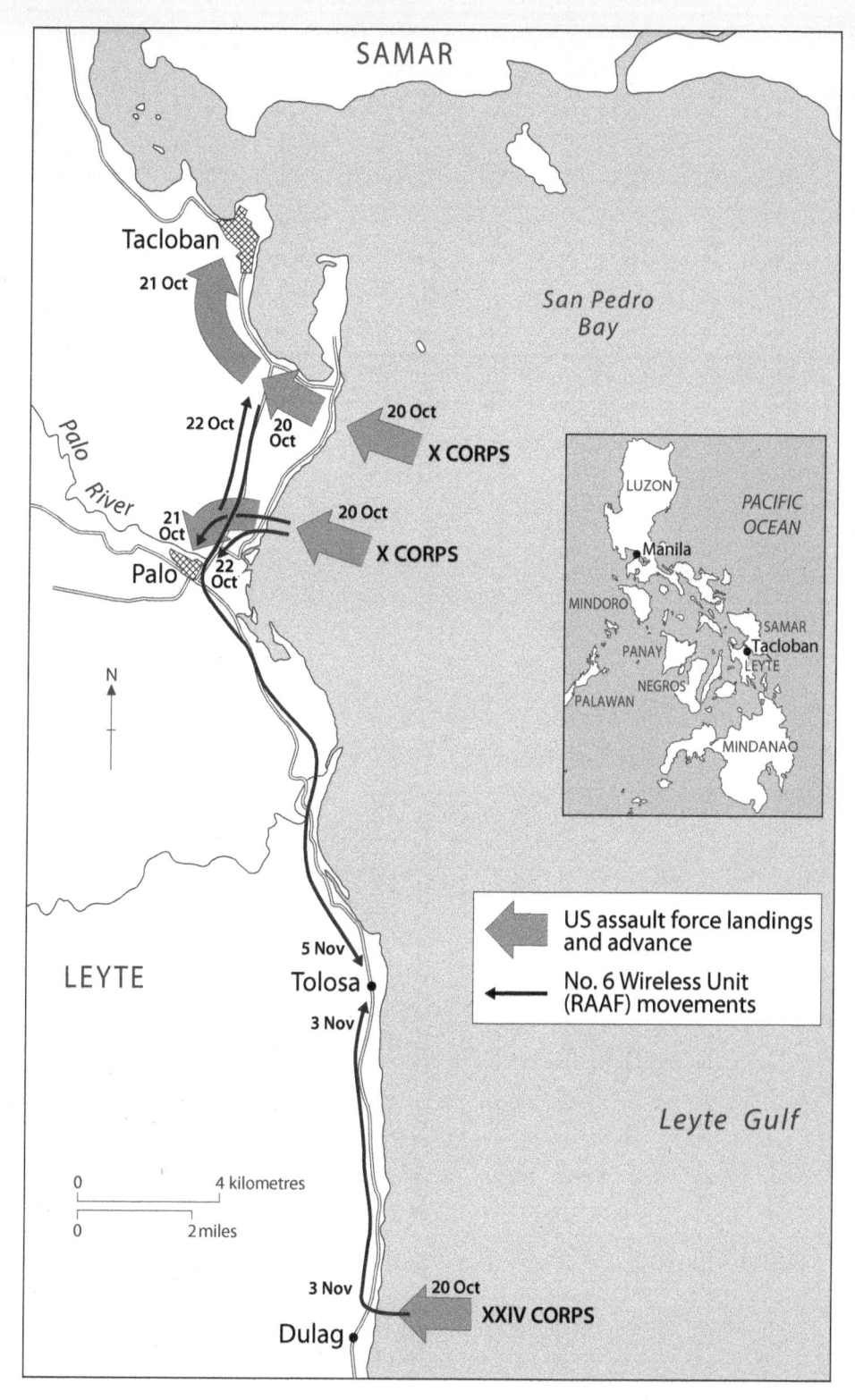

Map 5: No. 6 Wireless Unit landings in support of the Allied invasion of Leyte, 1944

crew as 'the personnel who will be ensuring that no surprise attacks will be made on the convoy during its journey north'.

The six radiomen who were to land with the assault force were taken by launch to *PCE-848*, a 900-ton armed escort and rescue frigate whose hospital space had been turned into a communications centre. The rest of No. 6 Wireless Unit's advance echelon went with their three shiny new interception trucks on the American landing ship *LST-700*. Taken by barge to the ship, with the trucks already on board, they lugged their equipment up a rope net dropped down the ship's side.

A *PCE-848* signals officer took one of the Australians to see the wireless room, telling the operator there he would have to leave the room. He did so, muttering loudly to himself, 'I knew Friday the 13th was going to be a stinker. Now some fucking Aussie thinks he can push me out.' However, it had already been decided the Australians would use a separate, secure room.

The invasion force steamed for six days towards its destination. In any direction, all that could be seen from the deck of *PCE-848* or *LST-700* were ships close together, stretching all the way to the horizon. The heat on the deck by day was unbearable. Inside was no better, with the din of turbines, generators and ventilation fans, and the smell of oil and exhausts. The radiomen slept in triple bunks, four sets to a four-square-metre cabin. A typhoon was reported heading for Leyte Gulf. The gulf was lashed with severe storms, but they would ease by the time the Allied task force got there.

The larger No. 6 Wireless Unit group, quartered on the lower tank deck of *LST-700*, were expected to sleep near their trucks. Not needed for signals work at this stage, they were seconded to other duties on the ship, tasks like loading the Bofors anti-aircraft gun. Naval instructions came intrusively over all decks by loudspeaker, with 'Now hear this! Now hear this!' barked out before each announcement. The sharp American accent sounded alien to the sigint team.

THE FRONT LINE AND THE BACK ROOM

On Akin's communications ship, the six Australians monitored the airwaves to pick up enemy air–ground traffic, with early success. At dawn on the 17th, the convoy was spotted 300 kilometres south of Leyte by a lone reconnaissance plane. Corporal Stan King, in 6WU's radio room beneath a gun turret, picked up a message from the plane's wireless operator, who was transmitting repeatedly and excitedly. He was so worked up that his keystrokes were all over the place, making it hard to get correct readings. King wasn't able to decode the message, but the panicked transmission made it clear the invasion fleet had been sighted.

Despite that, there was no aerial retaliation against the task force. Japan's aircraft stocks were getting perilously low, and Halsey's softening-up strikes the week before, as far away as Formosa, had drawn attack planes away from the Philippines. In fact, the Japanese had amended the reported sighting the next day, uncertain whether it was an enemy convoy or just ships seeking shelter from the violent storms of previous days.

By the late afternoon of 19 October, most vessels of the assault formation had arrived outside Leyte Gulf. The shore they would attack next day, deep inside the gulf, could be seen only dimly in the fading light. The atmosphere on board was tense. Evening prayers, alternately Protestant and Catholic, were broadcast over the ship's speakers, sounding to some on board like last rites. Throughout the night, American and Australian destroyers shelled the Japanese forces on the coastal strip in front of them.

Next morning, the water in Leyte Gulf was glassy calm as the assault vessels steamed into positions offshore in the pre-dawn glow. In the holds, men were dressing under red lights. There was little talking. Some gave their weapons a final check, others lay back and smoked. The small group of Australian wireless operators on Akin's ship were not going ashore with the first attack waves but would be landed after the beaches were cleared of the enemy. They hadn't seen close action so they were feeling the tension.

The communications ship, *PCE-848*, dropped anchor 500 metres astern of the cruisers HMAS *Australia* and HMAS *Shropshire*. At 6 a.m., warships opened fire on the beaches of San Pedro Bay, on the northern side of Leyte Gulf. A Japanese plane appeared, circled the convoy like an inquisitive gull, was fired on and left. The volley was directed randomly but still managed to hit enemy supply dumps and minor installations, sending grey smoke plumes up from the shore. Spasmodic Japanese fire was aimed at Allied spotter planes.

After two hours, the naval bombardment stopped and carrier aircraft roared over the armada to strike further inland. On board, anchor chains started rattling out through portholes. Landing barges were swiftly swung over the sides and lowered into the sea. Voices came from different directions, growing louder and more urgent. Small craft darted around the mother ships as they moved to rendezvous points. Infantry landing craft armed with mortars and rockets slid to the head of assault waves and, at a quarter to ten, raced towards the shore, directing raking fire across the beach. Hundreds of small craft, laden with troops and their equipment, headed for the shore while rockets hit the beaches in front of them in a continuous throaty roar. The brilliant tropical sun burned over the smooth water of San Pedro Bay.

The six Australians waited on the communications ship, one of the *kana* interceptors striving to pick up signals from defenders. Akin stood unperturbed on the deck, fingers in his ears and wearing a fatigue hat as his only protection. He was a military man in his element. A box barrage of flak fired overhead produced a deafening clatter as spent ammunition casings bounced off the ship's metal decks. The racket was too loud to allow conversation, the men too preoccupied with the flow of events to feel fear.

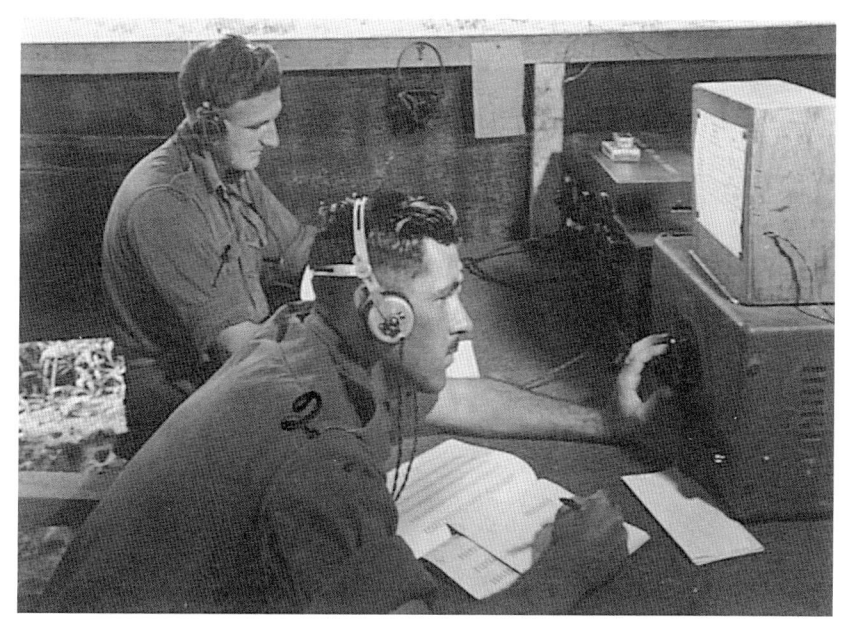

Radio interception at a field unit near Lae, New Guinea.

A mobile intercept unit of No. 1 Wireless Unit, operating in New Guinea.

Senior Australian officers in Central Bureau: (left to right) Roy Booth, Mic Sandford, Bill 'Nobby' Clarke and Jack Ryan.

The weather code team at Central Bureau, led by Gerry Room (centre, front row). To his left is the Bureau's only female cryptographer, Judy Roe; far right, back row, is Donald Friend.

A group of Americans working in Central Bureau: (left to right) Norman Erskine, Abe Sinkov, Larry Clark, Zac Halpin and Joe Richard.

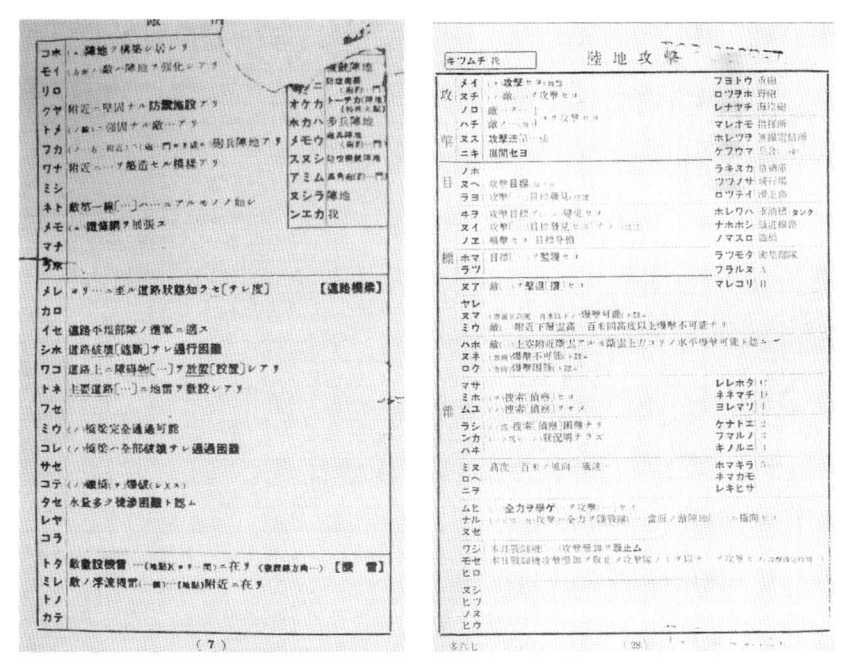

Pages from captured Japanese codebooks: air-ground code (left) and navy air-ground code (right).

Australian assault troops disembarking from American landing ships near Lae.

Japanese aircraft destroyed on the ground by Allied bombers.

Supplies being landed at Aitape, on the New Guinea north coast near Hollandia.

Access road from the beach landing area for the Hollandia assault. The road heads towards the three airstrips near Lake Sentani.

Radio operators working in a cipher tent in New Guinea.

Supplies being landed on Leyte Island in the Philippines.

The advance camp for No. 6 Wireless Unit, near Tacloban on Leyte. A direction-finder is set up centre right, beyond the tents.

The 'Foreign Legion': field operators of No. 6 Wireless Unit at San Miguel, north of Manila.

The Australian camp at San Miguel in the Philippine Islands.

Central Bureau's office at San Miguel.

THE FRONT LINE AND THE BACK ROOM

They watched from the deck as distant amphibious tanks landed first on the long beach fringed with coconut palms. Red Beach, as it had been designated by the SWPA planners, was too shallow for tank landing craft to make a dry landing. Troops following the tanks on foot had to wade with equipment held above their heads, starting thigh-deep in seawater. Hustling across the white coral sand, formless figures could be seen through gently billowing yellow smoke. Behind the beach lay flat marshy ground covered with palm trees and jungle. A small stream had been converted by the Japanese into a wide tank trap running parallel with the beach for 1500 metres. Large, well-camouflaged pillboxes, built of palm logs and compacted earth, were connected by a network of tunnels and trenches. Behind the swamp were open fields and rice paddies, then a low range of hills below jagged mountain peaks.

The landings appeared to be progressing without serious setbacks, but the Japanese defenders had been waiting. After allowing the first five or so waves of landing craft to come in, they opened fire with mortars and artillery on the waves following behind. Still 200 and more metres offshore, four of the landing craft were hit severely, one of them bursting into flames. Three others turned back towards the fleet, carrying the landing force's artillery and most of its tanks. The four hit vessels soon sank with numerous casualties, but the only sounds that reached the Australians on deck were the roars of heavy artillery from both sides. In the deafening noise it was like a silent movie as they watched the beach they were about to be landed on become an inferno.

Troops already on the beach were stunned by the sudden reversal of fortune, torn between pressing on and trying to rescue their comrades. One of the unit commanders who had survived the onslaught took the initiative and, with frantic arm-waving and screaming, mobilised his men to race for the shelter of palm trees. The invasion fleet's artillery started picking out defenders' nests, troops moved onto pillboxes with grenades, and the landings resumed. Soon after midday the beach area was cleared of the enemy. The Americans were able to advance across the open swamp under cover of mortars and heavy machine-guns to a line of trees 150 metres away.

At 1.30 p.m., General MacArthur made a dramatic landing through the surf for the prearranged cameras and announced the liberation of the Philippines.

'People of the Philippines: I have returned! By the grace of Almighty God, our forces stand again on Philippine soil,' he told the cameras. Shortly afterwards, he returned to his flagship.

By the end of the first day, the assault force held firm on a beachhead near the town of Palo and on a strategic hill overlooking the town. In the middle of the night, three Japanese companies under artillery cover enveloped the American flanks and struck at their front positions, killing or wounding all but one of the soldiers there. That one, Private Harold Moon, held off the counterattack for a couple of hours before he was eventually killed, but by then a bayonet charge by backup troops had broken through the Japanese line. The attack continued through the night but was eventually forced back, and by dawn the enemy troops were scattered across rice paddies.

The next day, naval artillery was used to knock out pillboxes dotted around the hills and slopes, fire from the cruisers *Australia* and *Shropshire* being particularly effective. The Australians on *PCE-848* nearby had been monitoring enemy radio traffic since arriving the day before. On pre-dawn duty, Stan King intercepted a message ordering a retaliatory attack on the 'three-stackers'. Both Australian ships had three funnels and were duly notified of the expected attack. Immediately, three Japanese Val dive bombers swooped in.

Surprisingly, the attacking aircraft made no attempt to evade the flak barrage that greeted them; instead they flew straight through it. Pieces of fuselage and wing were torn from the planes, but that

THE FRONT LINE AND THE BACK ROOM

didn't stop them. One plane hit the mast of the *Australia*, spraying burning petrol and smashing into the cruiser's bridge.

Watching from the American frigate 500 metres away, King heard a bang and saw a ball of fire. Burning men ran across the deck. The 21-year-old Australian had trouble making sense of what he saw. Something about the manner of this attack agitated him. It was as if the pilot had no intention of coming out of his dive. The idea of a suicide mission was beyond current comprehension, but in fact the Japanese had launched a new and desperate tactic. HMAS *Australia* was the first target of the dying empire's suicide squad, which operated out of Clark Air Base near Manila. Officially called the Special Attack Unit, it was popularly known as the *kamikaze* (divine wind) unit, invoking the typhoon that had scattered and sunk a Mongol invasion fleet off southern Japan in the 13th century.

At the time, it was just an unsettling incident amid the fury of a major military action. From the shore, assault troops pushed past pockets of determined defenders and across a bridge over the Palo River, entering the town of Palo in the afternoon. At the same time, another squad entered nearby Tacloban, Leyte's provincial capital, to a tumultuous welcome from townspeople who lined the narrow streets, waving American flags and offering gifts of eggs and fruit. By 6 p.m. the capital was in American hands and General Verne Mudge carried out a tour of inspection by tank. A regimental command post was set up in the Leyte Intermediate School for Girls.

Six Australians were ferried to shore in a motorised landing barge in the mid-morning. Japanese aircraft buzzed high in the distance while, overhead, fire from defenders mixed with misdirected fire from American troops. They reached the shore feeling more uncertain than afraid. Directed up a hill to the temporary US Army headquarters, they were met on top by a corpse, a large Japanese soldier with a sign in Japanese hung on one outstretched arm. Someone had had time to make light of the situation. The intercept operators set up their portable receiver and aerial wire to resume interception in the morning. That night, their first on recaptured Philippine soil, they camped in the Chinese section of a local cemetery. In the morning, they heard that a bomber had hit *PCE-848* overnight, killing sixty crew.

There was little time to dwell on that. At midday, *LST-700* pushed up as near to the shore as it could get for the three new interception trucks to trundle through the shallows and the rest of No. 6 Wireless Unit's advance team to wade ashore with their equipment. Racing across the sand beneath shells from bombarding ships and Japanese aircraft, they moved their trucks and gear through shattered palm trees. They were directed to a rotunda in front of Palo's cathedral and given cholera injections at a medical outpost set up there.

The eighteen men who had just landed joined the six already there, moving gear and trucks up the main road towards Tacloban. A few kilometres south of the town, they set up camp near a native village at the foot of some small hills. A creek ran beside the clearing. Along the road, and here and there close to their camp, scattered bodies of enemy soldiers reminded them they were on a battlefield. No one had found time to move the corpses, which still lay where they'd fallen.

The Australians had been issued in Palo with six four-man tents, a tent to use as a working area and a tent for storing supplies. These were pitched, and the rest of the day was spent preparing the interception trucks for immediate operation. Somewhere in the middle distance were the sounds of gunfire as pockets of enemy defenders were prised out of their dug-in positions.

That night the constant gunfire grew steadily louder, sounding as if it had reached the neighbouring hills. An American soldier came running down a slope.

'There's a Japanese company broken through our lines,' he shouted, 'and heading this way. You guys will need to watch out.'

THE FRONT LINE AND THE BACK ROOM

'I'll need to do more than watch out,' thought Corporal Mac Jamieson, who was on lookout alongside the trucks. With two operators already on duty inside the vehicles, he loaded his Tommy gun with a clip of ammunition and put another clip in his hip pocket. Couched tensely behind a clump of coconut palms, he waited for the enemy attack. And waited . . . unsure how he would deal with them single-handed. The *kana* interceptors worked on, unaware of the threat. There was gunfire in scattered bursts nearby, but it wasn't getting any nearer. After two hours, the American finally returned.

'We've shot 'em all,' he said. 'Problem fixed.'

Over the next two days, as the battle for Leyte ground on remorselessly, the Japanese mounted twenty separate air raids over the recaptured area. All three radio trucks were constantly in use, picking up signals so strong the operator could hear them with his headphones hanging around his neck. It was like having loudspeakers in the room. Within a few days, No. 6 Wireless Unit had located all the Japanese strike frequencies, including those of the *kamikaze* missions. Air-raid warnings were passed to Air Formations and Advance Echelon GHQ, MacArthur's forward posting of his headquarters, in Tacloban.

So intense was the battle that the broadcasts never stopped, needing round-the-clock monitoring. With the increasing urgency and desperation of their missions, the Japanese operators lost all rhythm and flow in their message sending, adding to the difficulty of interception. The men from No. 6 Wireless Unit, working in shifts, found it both exhausting and exhilarating. On one occasion, a group relaxing outside between shifts spotted four dive bombers coming in low and assumed they were taking reconnaissance photos before realising this was a *kamikaze* mission. Two of the pilots flew behind a hill, while the other two turned up and away. Immediately an explosion was heard, and smoke rose above the hill. The two aircraft that left must have been escorts sent to spot targets and report the outcome to base.

The Australians made tea with water from the creek flowing past their camp until they found a dead soldier lying in the water 30 metres upstream. After that, they willingly walked over a kilometre to get purified water from a US Army station. Everywhere they roamed in the surrounding countryside, they came across more Japanese bodies. On top of a hill they found two dead soldiers still manning a Juki machine gun. One was wearing a belt of 1000 stitches, a strip of cloth embroidered by village women to protect young men going off to war. On another occasion, they found a corpse that had exploded as gases trapped inside the body heated and expanded. After several days, the stench became so sickening that a bulldozer was brought in to dig a deep hole and push the bodies into a mass grave.

When their paths crossed here and there in Tacloban, Americans and Australians would rib each other about their accents. Distinctive in slouch hats and jungle greens, the Australians were dubbed the 'Foreign Legion' by an American correspondent, but attention from the press was not something Central Bureau welcomed. On 30 October, an article in the Brisbane *Courier-Mail* reported on the unit and its nickname, giving names and states of the twenty-four signallers operating on Leyte, although it didn't reveal what sort of work they did. Keen to match Brisbane's pride, Melbourne and Sydney papers picked up the story, provoking a furious response from Central Bureau.

There were repercussions to follow. For recreation, the Australians would tune into the Japanese propaganda broadcasts by 'Tokyo Rose' on their intercept receivers. They wanted to listen to good music—Glenn Miller's 'In the Mood' was a favourite—and chat that was often witty and entertaining, notwithstanding its origin. One night, they were surprised to hear of an RAAF group in Leyte. The broadcaster went on to give names and home towns and promise swift death to the Australian 'Foreign Legion'. Central Bureau's anger was vindicated.

— • —

The Bureau in Brisbane was becoming a separate world from its forward base at Hollandia and its advance unit in the Philippines. The peripatetic Mic Sandford often liaised between Brisbane and Hollandia in addition to his excursions to London, Washington and Delhi. The role of executive officer in Central Bureau had been handed over to the more stationary Roy Booth, who remained in Brisbane with Abe Sinkov and Eric Nave while younger officers followed GHQ north.

Sinkov, the senior American in the organisation, went to Leyte only once after MacArthur established his forward headquarters there. General Willoughby called a conference with Akin and a US Navy intelligence officer, and Sinkov was flown from Brisbane to attend. Willoughby talked for 45 minutes about signals intelligence functions, then closed the meeting.

'I had to fly 3500 miles to get up there and turn around and fly 3500 miles back,' Sinkov later commented. 'He could just as well have written a letter.'

Generals Sutherland and Akin controlled the flow of intelligence in the Southwest Pacific Area. They kept secret information in the inner sanctum of SWPA, withholding it from Allies, from other service groups, and even from rivals within their own command when they saw fit. Washington and General Willoughby were often sidelined. The Americans continued to press the Australians to restrict their exchanges with the British in both London and Delhi, but as MacArthur's counteroffensive drove north and the command structure spread more widely, the monopoly became more difficult to maintain.

Washington and London had each planted a foot in SWPA's intelligence door. After Colonel Carter Clarke's visit to Brisbane, which had been unsuccessfully resisted by Sutherland, Special Intelligence Bulletins were being circulated from Willoughby's G2 (Special Branch) section. The British had set up a Special Liaison Unit as a result of the BRUSA agreement. At the end of 1944, Bletchley Park sent out a jovial, incorrigible name dropper to head the unit, located on the top floor of Brisbane's AMP Building, where MacArthur's headquarters had been before the general moved north.

Forever describing himself as being 'on the King's business', Squadron Leader S.F. Burley RAF, known affectionately as 'Uncle Bill', was ragged mercilessly by the locals. With his thick-rimmed spectacles and trim moustache, he looked like the bank officer he had once been, but he took the ribbing in good spirit, often playing up to it. The Australians regarded the Special Liaison Unit as quite amateurish, but although the bulk of their information still came from Central Bureau, the British unit offered them another avenue for intelligence and gave them greater independence from the American monopoly.

When the Bletchley Park chief, Sir Edward Travis, visited Brisbane in 1945, it was an opportunity for Burley to demonstrate the extent of his influence in the upper strata. He organised a special dinner for the visiting dignitary at Lennon's Hotel and invited the hierarchy of Central Bureau and the Queensland government, including the state governor, Sir Leslie Wilson. Abe Sinkov and Roy Booth were there, on one side of the head table. Burley arranged to be seated in the middle, beside Travis, but on the distinguished visitor's left was Mic Sandford. Burley might have been on the King's business, but Sandford was Travis's point man in Australia.

— ● —

Donald Friend was an emerging talent in Australia's embryonic art world. After enlisting in the army in 1941, he was posted near

Newcastle, but after a breach of discipline he was moved to a labour battalion in Queensland. Living in an army camp and working on the Brisbane docks, he was told by his friend Bill Beresford that a Colonel Sandford was determined to meet him. Sandford wanted the painter to come to a dinner party at his house in Hamilton. Insouciant and with an air of detachment, Friend had been part of Sydney's bohemian society before the war, as had Beresford, now a captain in the Australian Army.

Friend phoned Beresford from a brothel disguised as a confectionery shop and suggested that he meet with Sandford at 'Major-General Ming's HQ', as they called Brisbane's Cathay Hotel. They would have lunch and 'discuss the matter in hand and go over all evidence available'. Friend's diary is full of such cryptic references.

Private Friend had dinner at Colonel Sandford's house the next night. Sharing similar backgrounds, the two connected. Both were the product of private schools, Sandford of Adelaide's St Peters College, the other of Cranbrook, in Sydney. Friend was from a wealthy grazing family that had been hard hit by the Depression. He was three years older than Sandford, and his dry wit appealed to the urbane young officer. The dinner was an occasion of 'brilliant people, superb food, leisurely talk and a little fine music to listen to, discuss and talk about', according to the diary.

It sounds like a gathering of sensualists, but it was more than that. Mic Sandford, the golden boy of signals intelligence, was a participant in another secret world, as unknown to his colleagues in Central Bureau as the Bureau was to the rest of the world. Sandford was homosexual, but he presented as so thoroughly masculine that few suspected it. With close friends and people who accepted homosexuality, however, he made little effort to pretend. The bohemian set Sandford socialised with were risqué and often reckless, but this was wartime. To a large degree, the rulebook of proper behaviour had been torn up. On one occasion, Friend reports ending up in a taxi outside Sandford's house at 3 a.m., drinking Sandford's beer with his heavily made-up batman. Colin Wainwright had a bottle of Chanel No. 5, though where he got it was anyone's guess.

'Chanel! Chanel! Don't you realise?' he screeched in ecstasy. 'Chanel!'

Sandford was away that night. The taxi driver was drinking with them. They all smelt of French perfume.

'You must stay the night,' said Wainwright.

'Not on your bloody life,' replied Friend. 'I can't stay. I've got a parade at six in the morning.'

Friend thought the officers in the military were uninteresting, but Sandford was perhaps—and only perhaps—an exception, a 'rarity'. Friend ponders in his diary whether Sandford would seem so special in peacetime. 'Presentable, well-educated, a rather witty young man; you'd ask him to dinner occasionally, but he's not in the category of my painter friends, merely an additional gilt curlicue in a rococo boudoir.' This was not a person to get very close to.

Thanks to his contact with Sandford, however, Friend was transferred to Central Bureau. He was glad to be relieved at last from navvy work on the wharves and given a clerical job inside. He was attached to Gerry Room's meteorological unit, but—aware of the importance of the documents he handled—he found the work stressful. No longer in camp but in a room in town, he complained of having to go to bed early, 'exhausted from the mental efforts of the day'. Before long, he was suffering from eye strain.

The painter was a shrewd observer of people, however, sharing insights with Sandford on assorted social occasions. Of MacArthur he noted that most Americans disliked him as an egotist ready to sacrifice lives for self-publicity, but Australians regarded him as a hero.

THE FRONT LINE AND THE BACK ROOM

The Australian intercept group outside Tacloban had been operating for a week when a typhoon hit Leyte. Torrential rain poured down on the campsite, turning it into a muddy swamp. The 100-mile-an-hour gusts blasted the tops off coconut palms, flattened tents, blew away equipment and covered everything with mud. The creek running by the camp flooded, leaving patches of knee-deep mud when it subsided. The direction-finder was destroyed, but the wireless trucks and generators survived the onslaught intact and were able to resume operation the next day.

A few days after the typhoon, the balance of No. 6 Wireless Unit, ninety-four RAAF interceptors, cryptanalysts and linguists, arrived from Hollandia on the USS *Carter Hall*. They were landed at Dulag Beach, down the coast from Palo, along with the US Army's 125th Signal Radio Intelligence Company, and set up in a school building in nearby Tolosa, a cluttered village with a market place and cafes. Cock fighting was popular, and the dirt streets were overrun with children and animals. The men pitched tents in the school grounds and an open shed became their mess hall. They drew water from wells in the grounds and improvised wash basins by setting a helmet on a stand. They even erected a volleyball net on the beach. It was a home away from home of sorts for the Americans and the Australians.

They were soon joined by the advance party, coming down the coast from Tacloban with their intercept trucks and any equipment the typhoon had failed to destroy. Extra receivers were mounted on packing cases in deserted classrooms and a transmitter was installed in a truck. An aerial strung between palm trees was held taut with pulley, rope and sandbag. The men's location in a small village, away from other elements of the invasion force, gave their operation security and secrecy, but as added protection they built a shelter around the trucks to shield them from air raids.

The unit gathered a large volume of intelligence despite the shortage of technical equipment and the loss of the direction-finder in the typhoon. The Japanese staged concentrated air raids from the beginning of November, striking every ten or fifteen minutes day and night from good all-weather bases on the islands around Leyte. The enemy planes flew low over hills to avoid radar, and radio intercepts were often the only way they were detected.

The interceptors also reported sightings of Allied convoys by enemy patrols and passed warnings to the US air controller. The American radio unit concentrated on more distant traffic. From the Philippines it was able, for the first time, to listen in on the internal Japanese circuits in China, Formosa and Japan, gaining foreknowledge of enemy intentions that had previously been beyond the Allies' reach.

— ● —

The Japanese planned a decisive land, sea and air battle to reverse the American gains on Leyte, mounting a succession of air raids on occupied positions and committing nearly their entire surface fleet to a showdown at sea out from Leyte Gulf. Exaggerated reports from their pilots of American losses had engendered an unrealistic hope in Imperial HQ that this could be a turning point in the war.

One of the Japanese task forces contained four aircraft carriers with no aircraft on board as a decoy to lure Halsey's Third Fleet out from the gulf. The plan was to attack and destroy MacArthur's transports and escort carriers, which would be left unprotected as a result. The ruse worked. The super-battleships *Yamato* and *Musashi* moved into the gulf within range of the vulnerable support vessels, but after two and a half hours of desperate fighting the Japanese battle fleet mysteriously broke off the engagement and withdrew from Leyte Gulf.

The Japanese commanders believed they'd annihilated the US carrier force and that MacArthur's ground forces were trapped on Leyte. In fact, they had seriously overestimated the damage they'd inflicted and had lost *Musashi* in the process. The naval battle, fought from 23 to 26 October, was intended to destroy the US

Navy forces supporting MacArthur's Sixth Army, but was instead a decisive defeat for the Japanese. After that, the Imperial Japanese Navy effectively ceased to exist.

While the naval battle played out, the Japanese were moving troops and supplies to Leyte, much of them from the southern island of Mindanao, where they had expected the American invasion to begin. Reinforcements were coming to the port of Ormoc, on Leyte's western coast. The Australian intercept unit located convoys coming down the Indochina coast and others coming across from Luzon, the main island of the Philippines. The first of the convoys set out on 23 October, but initially the SWPA command assumed this was the start of a Japanese evacuation of Leyte, and that the enemy ships were coming to pick up troops, not land them. By the first week of November, it was clear that the Japanese were not withdrawing its garrison at all, but reinforcing it with convoys roughly a week apart. The response to reports from radio intelligence changed, but in the process No. 6 Wireless Unit nearly missed one of the biggest convoys making the journey to Ormoc.

On 11 November, a large convoy of seventeen ships set out from Manila carrying 8000 battle-hardened troops from China and 2500 tonnes of equipment to reinforce the Leyte garrison. The eavesdroppers at Tolosa missed signals that would have alerted them to this imminent mission, but they picked up radio signals sent from escort fighters to their base, continuous chat advising of ship movements and giving estimated times of arrival at Ormoc port. Air Formations were notified and the convoy was attacked as it approached Ormoc Bay, sinking all seventeen ships, including five troop ships and four destroyer escorts.

The Tolosa unit also intercepted messages about a 'special attack unit' created at Clark and Nichols Fields near Manila. Having found the frequency this unit used for its encrypted radio communication, No. 6 Wireless Unit was able to plot its flight patterns through Formosa in the late evening. The planes were brought to the Manila fields to strike first thing in the morning. Realising they were tracking the new *kamikaze* unit, the eavesdroppers notified Allied fighter command of any evening arrivals they detected, and response aircraft were despatched before dawn. The intelligence provided from Tolosa did not eliminate *kamikaze* missions, but it severely blunted their effectiveness.

— ● —

Half of Central Bureau's personnel had moved to Hollandia. One by one, the huts at Ascot Park became silent and empty. The old stagers Eric Nave and Gerry Room remained, however, left largely to their own devices to resolve new air–ground and meteorological codes as they were introduced. Intercepts continued to come in from field stations in Australia by teleprinter and as coded radio messages from New Guinea and the Philippines. Messages from different units enabled gaps in the codes to be filled in and new code values to be sent back to the field.

The Japanese were attempting to coordinate their army and naval air units. Army air sightings were signalled in the army's easily-read three-digit code and re-enciphered in the more difficult naval air code for navy units to use. This process provided Nave with cribs for the harder code. Newcomers to the Bureau marvelled at Nave's instinct for codes and his knack for inferring message content from partial decrypts.

While Nave, always in uniform, was reserved and formal in his dealings with staff, Room was more informal, usually dressed as if he was about to go bushwalking. Among his small team were Ted Holland, a New Zealander who worked only at night when no one else was around, and Judy Roe, a maths graduate from Brisbane and the only female cryptographer in Central Bureau. Australian government policy had not allowed Roe to move to the Philippines with her male colleagues.

THE FRONT LINE AND THE BACK ROOM

Elsewhere in the Bureau, there was concern about security. Intercepts of Japanese coded reports contained material that many believed could only have originated from Allied sources. It looked as if Ultra decrypts were being leaked to the enemy.

In October, MacArthur's security chief, General Willoughby, advised the Australian military intelligence director, John Rogers, that Washington had picked up Japanese broadcasts containing Allied estimates of enemy forces in the Philippines. This information had been traced back to Nationalist China's liaison officer in Australia, Colonel Wang Chih. He was transmitting messages to his own HQ in Chungking using an insecure commercial code that was easily decrypted by the Japanese. Questioned discreetly, Wang said he had got the estimates from Australia's Advance HQ in Hollandia. In fact, he'd seen Japanese locations on a wall map that was usually hidden by a roller blind. Wang had long cultivated the Australians and Americans, and one day he'd walked into the room when the blind was up.

The leaks continued. One seemed to have come from the Australian Military Forces' *Military Intelligence Review*. As Wang had access to part of the *Review*, its publication was suspended. SWPA's General Sutherland told General Frank Berryman, Australia's chief of staff in Hollandia, he was convinced the *Review* was the sole source of the leaks, but Berryman suspected there were other leaks in GHQ. That was fixed when Wang asked to join GHQ in Hollandia and was told it was 'overcrowded'.

In late November, Akin returned to Hollandia for discussions with Sandford and Berryman about the issue. Sandford advised them that in the three months during which Wang received the *Review*, Ultra material had been restricted to an appendix that was not given to him. Eventually Akin accepted that the estimates of Japanese strength hadn't come from Ultra at all. The fuss had been excessive, but it had exposed the weakness in Chinese communications. Sandford, without revealing the reason for his concern, cautioned all recipients of intelligence against sharing it with the Chinese.

In fact, Robert Little had circulated advice to Blamey's forces nearly two years earlier that the Chinese ciphers were defective. He had urged that no information be given to the Chinese that could be detrimental if it fell into Japanese hands. That advice had been ignored, then forgotten. In February, General Northcott ordered that Little's April 1943 memo be reissued to all Allied Land HQ personnel.

At first, Sandford persuaded himself that although the intelligence leaks had come from Chungking, 'the tie-up with the Soviet Embassy [in China] is certain'. He did not indicate how he reached that conclusion, but it was probably prompted by a second, more worrisome leak of Allied intelligence from Australia. In November, a coded Japanese intelligence summary from Harbin, in Japanese-occupied Manchuria, contained details of SWPA operations in the Philippines.

The enemy signal identified the source as the Soviet ambassador in Australia, although it was unclear how the Japanese had got the information from him or how he had obtained it in the first place. However, the message fitted with a growing view that the Soviet Union, officially an ally, was the new enemy. No one seems to have wondered why a communist regime would pass secrets to a militaristic quasi-fascist regime—one with which it would be at war in less than a year—or why the secrets were handed over in Harbin rather than the more convenient Tokyo.

The Japanese had penetrated Soviet codes before the war. Although this project was put aside when the US entered the war, Japanese contact with Finnish code breakers in 1943 furnished a new source of Soviet ciphers. The Japanese may have been able to read the relevant Soviet messages, but there is another possibility. Evidence has been unearthed that intelligence reports from Australia were copied by a Japanese spy working in the Soviet Embassy in Harbin.

THE FRONT LINE AND THE BACK ROOM

The Soviet ambassador in Australia might simply have accessed the information from background briefings for newspaper editors. He was the diplomatic representative of an ally, after all.

Sandford had written to Robert Little in mid-December to let him know he wouldn't be coming to Melbourne as planned. He had things to sort out with Blamey, who had returned to Brisbane the night before. Britain's chief security officer, Group Captain Frederick Winterbotham, was in Australia investigating 'several extremely serious security breaches', namely the Chungking and Harbin leaks. Sandford's friendship with Little had grown to the point where he knew Little's family. The communiqué was signed off with a handwritten, 'Please give my love to Jean and Pep. Yours ever, Mic Sandford.'

Sandford was using Blamey as an excuse to stay in Brisbane, where he had organised what Donald Friend colourfully called a 'Christmas orgy'. It was actually a dinner party in Sandford's other, covert life. Over the meal, the host told a story about another dinner party, this one given by Stalin for Churchill. With vodka circulating freely, Marshal Timoshenko leapt onto a table yelling 'Hoi!' and did a wild Russian dance. With another 'Hoi!', he leapt onto Stalin's lap and kissed him on both cheeks.

'You must forgive the enthusiasm of my old comrade Timoshenko,' Stalin said to Churchill. 'You know how it is. I suppose you must have the same sort of thing with your own General Montgomery.'

After dinner, Donald settled with Mic on the Hamilton verandah and swapped more stories. Sandford recounted the tale of a girl in a French zoo who stood in front of a monkey's cage and goaded the monkey into 'onanistic frenzies' until the keeper begged her to leave, *'parce que, ma'm'selle, vous fatiguez le pauvre singe!'* (because you're exhausting the poor monkey).

— • —

On Christmas Day 1944, General MacArthur announced the end of organised resistance on Leyte, although pockets of Japanese were still fighting in the Ormoc Valley and elsewhere. With more than 50,000 Japanese killed, wounded or taken prisoner, General Eichelberger's Eighth Army relieved the Sixth Army on Leyte. The next SWPA objectives were the main Philippine island, Luzon, and the nation's capital, Manila. MacArthur decided to strike first at Lingayen Gulf, which had sheltered beaches and roads running 180 kilometres south-east across the central plains to Manila. Knowing Luzon would be the next Allied target, and realising he had little air or naval support and insufficient transport and equipment for his 260,000-strong force, General Tomoyuki Yamashita decided to fight a long battle of attrition from three mountain strongholds.

The weather was ideal for the American amphibious landing on 9 January, with lightly overcast sky and a quiet sea. After a preliminary bombardment, the landings began at 8 a.m. with little initial opposition. Over the next few days, the Sixth Army landed 175,000 men along 30 kilometres of beach at the end of Lingayen Gulf.

As with the Leyte landings, a detachment of the Australian No. 6 Wireless Unit was with the invasion force: seven men on General Akin's repaired communications ship, *PCE-848*, and nine on a landing ship with interception trucks and gear. The main body of No. 6 Wireless Unit, still at Tolosa on Leyte, broadcast daily encrypted intelligence reports to their advance party, which was travelling in radio silence while the convoy was in transit. With interference from Japanese signals on the frequencies used, these reports weren't much help, but daily *kamikaze* attacks showed that the convoy's position was known anyway.

The seven operators on *PCE-848* were landed at Dagupan, in the middle section of the beachhead, about twenty minutes after the assault troops, so rapidly was the shoreline cleared of enemy resistance. They set up a rudimentary intercept operation on the

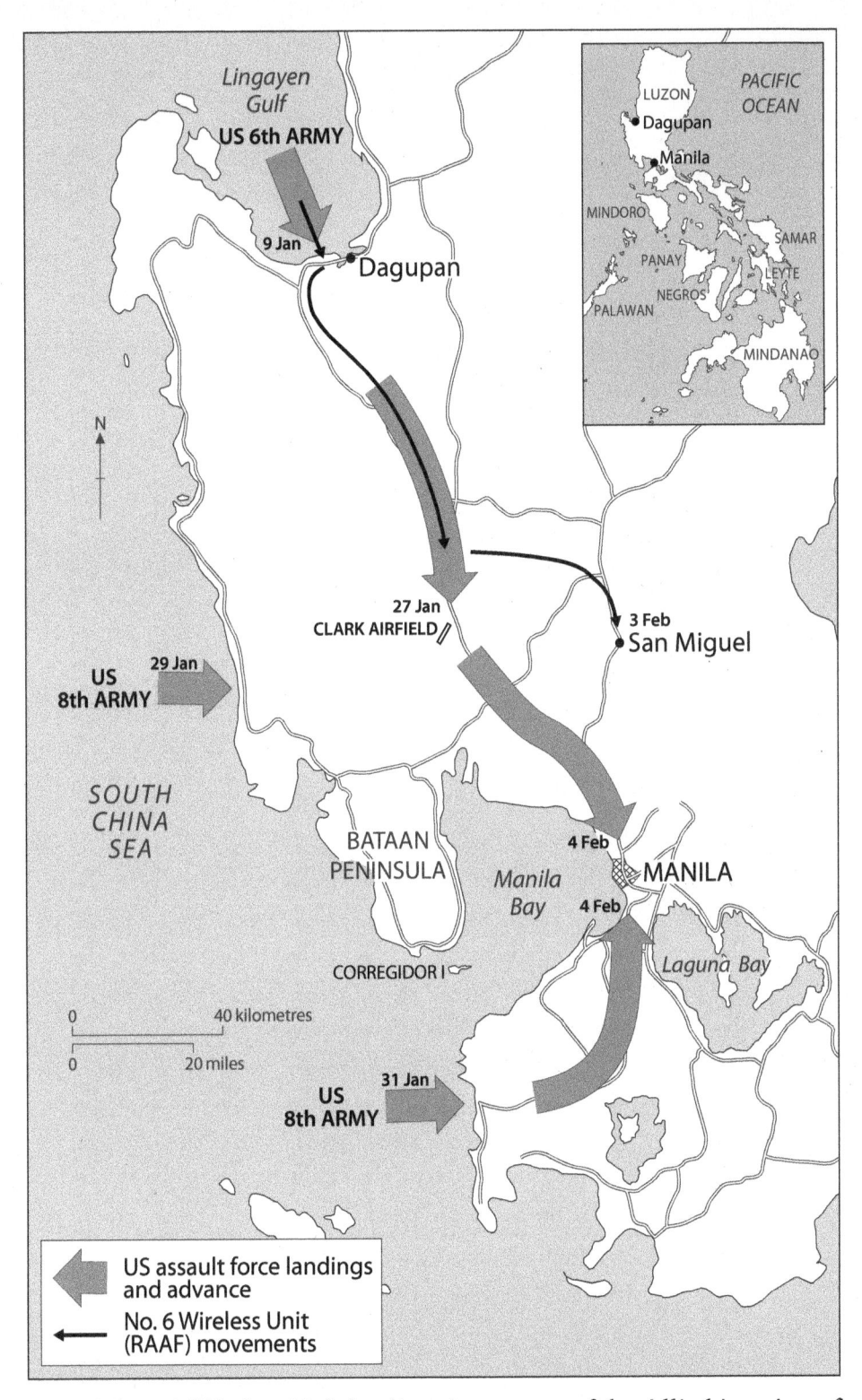

Map 6: No. 6 Wireless Unit landings in support of the Allied invasion of Luzon, 1945

beach until the rest of their detachment was landed with the bulk of the advance equipment. In the event, the other men were landed some distance east of Dagupan. It was several days before they could join their workmates already set up on the shore.

A detachment of an American field unit, 112th Signal Radio Intelligence Company, brought across from Guadalcanal, was also landed at Dagupan with MacArthur's assault force. Unlike the Australians, they were prevented by US Army commanders from getting straight down to work on the tasks they'd been brought to do. Put instead into a labour squad unloading ammunition, fuel and other supplies, they weren't released for their intended duties for several days. By then, a week after landing, two divisions of the invasion force had started moving south down the highway towards Clark Air Field and Manila with only sparse Japanese crossfire to slow them down. The two radio detachments followed closely behind.

On the outskirts of the air base, the advance suddenly met determined resistance and ground to a halt. It took another week of close fighting to capture the base and start the drive further south towards Manila. Meanwhile, the Eighth Army had landed paratroopers south of the capital. They sped untroubled along a paved highway towards the city, cheered by Filipinos along the way. It became a race between forces coming from the north and the south to be the first to enter Manila.

On 3 February, XIV Corps pushed into the northern outskirts of the city. That evening a tank crashed through the walls of Santo Tomas University, liberating 4000 interned civilian prisoners. The guards of the intern camp meekly laid down their arms. Downtown Manila was a different story, however. Its reinforced-concrete buildings and old Spanish stone fortresses provided cover for Japanese riflemen who fought doggedly to stall further movement into the southern parts of the city. An American victory parade had to be postponed. Fighting continued in Manila for a month, with street-to-street and house-to-house combat, until enemy resistance was finally reported as eliminated on 4 March.

The radio detachments, both Australian and American, had stopped following the invasion force before it got to Manila, setting up camp among the sugar fields at San Miguel, 80 kilometres north of the capital. Tents were pitched on an overgrown reserve attached to an exclusive golf club formerly owned by the San Miguel Brewery. The camp had to be built from scratch in muddy ground reeking of human and animal waste, which had been spread everywhere as fertiliser. No. 6 Wireless Unit set up in the local sugar mill, the American unit in a brick office block. As the Allied forces moved on towards Manila, the Australians were able to move to a small room on the top floor of the waterworks building, within earshot of sniper fire.

By now the Japanese air capacity was so depleted there was little air-raid activity for the field units to listen to, but they were able to report enemy sightings of Allied task forces in the South China Sea, and of carriers near Okinawa which came under *kamikaze* attack. The American unit searched for stations operated by troops left behind by the retreating enemy. They found none in the Philippines, but they did find new Japanese stations outside the country.

With much less to do, the units used the time to get on each other's nerves instead. Radio equipment in the vehicles had been configured both to receive—signals from their own command as well as intercepted enemy traffic—and to transmit, so both functions could be performed at the same location. For some reason, the Americans insisted that they should be performed at different locations. Receivers were taken out of the trucks and set up in tents, and the trucks were driven to a designated transmitting area. This led to problems with keying lines and wiring, but with a little ingenuity and scrounging, links could be set up with the main units still on Leyte.

With the separation of Central Bureau into two cohorts, one at the home base in Brisbane and the other overseas near the front line, the intelligence infrastructure began to fray. Personnel were moving in different, sometimes contradictory directions. From time to time, Abe Sinkov and Mic Sandford from Central Bureau and Ath Treweek from the US Navy's FRUMEL in Melbourne visited D Special Section, responsible for intercepting Japanese diplomatic traffic. The navy didn't encourage fraternisation with other cryptographic units, and Treweek had to do it 'under the lap', as he put it. He would go on leave in order to see Sandford and Central Bureau in Brisbane. Clandestinely visiting Dale Trendall at D Section, he passed on material Trendall and his colleagues might find useful, including a message from Tokyo to its overseas posts explaining the Foreign Ministry ciphers. Washington had sent it to FRUMEL.

Sandford was impressed by Treweek, whom he saw as a self-starter. In January 1945, he observed to intelligence director John Rogers that the US Navy had moved 90 per cent of its sigint function out of Melbourne and that 'Newman's party remains a sort of glorified communications channel' where Treweek and others were kept occupied with low-grade codes. When FRUMEL was set up, he pointed out, Treweek was loaned to Rudy Fabian by the Australian Army. With the bulk of the work at Monterey now transferred overseas, an officer of Treweek's calibre would be far better used at Central Bureau. The Australian Military Forces should request his return, and he should be encouraged with advice of the Bureau's impending move to Manila. A handwritten note by Robert Little said that Rogers would follow it up, but the war ended before Treweek could be transferred between the two cryptographic organisations.

Mic Sandford continued to juggle his two worlds. Once while he was away from Brisbane, his fellow officer Bill Beresford, one of Donald Friend's circle, stayed at his Brisbane house. Sandford returned to find his favourite safari jacket missing. Some months later, Friend told Sandford he was sending Beresford a long telegram, to be paid for by the receiver, in retaliation for a perceived slight.

'You'd better tell him to return my safari jacket,' was Sandford's comment. An offended Beresford denied both making the slight and taking the jacket.

A few days later, Friend arrived at work to be told to come to Sandford's Henry Street office.

'Have you heard anything?' Sandford asked the puzzled Friend. He hadn't.

'Well, you're going to get a commission. I've approved it. Soon you'll hear from a Major Dom. He'll interview you. For god's sake, look as though you'll make a good officer.'

Friend was made a temporary captain for six months, the same rank as his erstwhile friend Bill Beresford, and appointed an official war artist with the Australian forces. He was to join immediately the northward migration of servicemen.

Four days later, Sandford invited Friend to dinner to thank him for a gift of an art book. The war artist asked if he could return to Central Bureau as a private when his commission expired.

'Old boy,' said the young colonel, 'wherever I am and whatever I'm doing, you can be sure of a job if you choose to join me.'

— • —

General MacArthur had initially installed his Forward GHQ at San Miguel, but by March, with the lingering resistance in Manila finally cleared, it was moved into the capital and made itself at home in the luxurious Hotel Manila. Two months later, it was announced that a new camp would be constructed at San Miguel. A former Spanish hacienda adjacent to the golf club would become the advance base of Central Bureau, replacing the Hollandia facility. An advance group from the agency went to supervise the work.

By July, the large Hollandia component and much of the rest of Central Bureau in Brisbane had joined them at San Miguel. On 14 June, forty-two men left Hollandia on Akin's command ship, *PCE-848*, for the 4000-kilometre voyage. They spent the first four days without seeing land, on a dull grey sea running a boisterous swell. Many were seasick. On 20 June, they passed Corregidor Island into Manila Bay, full of fishing boats, outrigger canoes and a few motor boats. There were wrecked Japanese ships everywhere, some Allied warships mooching about, and a few rusted hulks of American transports that had been lying there since 1942.

They landed in a city where most of the buildings were partly demolished or burnt out, though some had been patched up for the US Army administration. Rizal Avenue had been roughly rebuilt as a shopping mall, although there was little to buy and prices were high. Girls in gaily coloured dresses walked along streets littered with worthless Japanese money.

The newly arrived personnel were taken north by truck to San Miguel. The golf clubhouse had been converted into a work hut. On the upper level, Typex machines were set up at one end to encode signals back to home bases; the cipher section was at the other end. The American signals centre was below, in a huge room with rows of teleprinters, but Australians were not allowed in there. Large airy huts had been hastily constructed to extend the operations area. With wooden floors, tin roofs and burlap sides, they were so hot in summer that work there was impossible between midday and three.

Staff walked through a forested area to get from work to their living quarters, crossing a creek by stepping gingerly along a log. They were warned to tread noisily because the Filipino guards were known to be trigger happy. American WACs were accommodated in wooden huts behind a high canvas fence. The Americans had brought their female operators to San Miguel, but the highly trained Australian women, many with more than two years' operational experience, were not allowed to join them.

THE FRONT LINE AND THE BACK ROOM

Sandford, through military intelligence director Rogers, had prompted Blamey back in December to press for a loosening of the Australian government's restriction on overseas postings for servicewomen, but the Commander-in-Chief put it off until the women were about to go, saying he expected no objection. He was wrong. Even with the backing of MacArthur's signals chief, General Akin, and adjustments made to the proposed accommodation, the request in May to transfer sixty AWAS and sixty-five WAAAF personnel to Manila was refused. Only the American women, who were generally less experienced, made it to the huts of San Miguel.

Everybody else was in tents, the American and Australian officers in their own tented area. At the centre of this tent city was the Spanish hacienda. Its courtyard, shaded by grapevines over a trellis, became the camp's dining area, cluttered with trestle tables. Next door, a palm-thatched chapel had been built.

Much of the time at the new forward headquarters was spent with sports: tennis, volleyball, softball and 'horseshoe pitching'. If it sounds like a camping holiday in the tropics, it was—despite the heat and the rain. By August 1945, there were 2000 Central Bureau personnel at San Miguel, half of them Australian. As Japan's air activity had ground to a standstill, there was little air–ground traffic to pick up and decode. Instead the intercept operators worked on signal traffic to and from Japan. Sandford advised Blamey that 'through fortunate combinations of breaking and capture, it should be possible for us to read all High Command communications in and out of Tokyo' for the next few months.

This was the calm before the storm. The Allies were planning a final showdown with Japan in November, an invasion of the home islands codenamed Operations Olympic and Coronet. Using the recently captured Okinawa as a staging base, MacArthur's Sixth Army was to launch its assault on Japan's southernmost island of Kyushu. The Australian No. 6 Wireless Unit, was again to be part of the invasion force, listening to the defenders' assessments of what the Americans would do and how they would respond to it. These forces would drive into the heart of the nation they had been at war with for nearly four years. The Australian eavesdroppers would follow on their heels when the invasion took place. But it was never to be.

— • —

At seven in the morning of 10 August 1945, Japan's Foreign Ministry sent a message to the Allies through the neutral governments of Switzerland and Sweden.

'The Japanese Government is ready to accept the terms enumerated in the tripartite joint declaration which was issued on the 26th of last month,' it said, 'with the understanding that the said declaration does not comprise any demand which prejudices the prerogatives of His Majesty as a sovereign ruler.'

At 7.30, the national news agency, Domei, began broadcasting the message to the Allies on shortwave radio.

After the bombing of Hiroshima, the staff at D Special Section in Melbourne were waiting to hear if Japan would surrender. Ronald Bond, who had been with the section since it was part of Eric Nave's SIB, pointed to a heap of traffic in his 'in' tray, including messages from Sweden in machine cipher.

'The answer is in there,' he said.

One of the Australians at San Miguel remembers an American running between the lines of tents in his underpants, shouting, 'The war's over!' It was confirmed ten minutes later by the No. 6 Wireless Unit intercept operator on duty. Cheering broke out among the Australians.

The war had come to a sudden end. The response was one of relief and elation on the one hand, but also of apprehension about what the new postwar world they were entering would look like.

Chapter 13

A new world, a new enemy

The war had been a defining experience for many of the young men and women who participated in it, and it would continue to be for the rest of their lives. In the immediate aftermath of Japan's surrender, however, there was a yawning gap in their daily lives that had to be filled. Instead of decoding, they began dismantling. In the latter part of 1945, the network of teletype circuits was pulled apart piece by piece. This web had linked Henry Street across Brisbane to Somerville House, the girls' boarding school commandeered by the US Army, RAAF Command HQ at Victoria Park, ASWG at Kalinga and Central Bureau's depot at Strathpine aerodrome. IBM tabulators and American SIGIBA encoding machines were packed up and returned to the United States.

The participants in Australia's two joint wartime cryptographic ventures soon parted ways with little fanfare or ceremony. Only a handful of Americans now remained at FRUMEL in Melbourne, and they were quickly repatriated. The US component of Central Bureau had already largely moved north to San Miguel. They went on to Tokyo with the occupation force. The few Americans still in Brisbane packed up and went home. One of the last to go was

Zac Halpin, the American who headed Central Bureau's machine section, with his precious IBM machines.

No longer needed for interception or cryptanalytic work in the Philippines, the Australians waited for arrangements to be made, in the confusion of priorities, to get them home. One officer proposed that the Australians fill the hiatus by building an unwanted road into the San Miguel camp. A few of the men suggested that starting a newspaper would be more productive and put it to Mic Sandford.

'Yes, that's a good idea, but where will you get the news from?' he asked. There were no printed news sources there.

'We can put it together from radio.'

And they did, producing six weekly editions while they waited for word on their departure.

Sandford pointed out that although Japan was in disarray, no one knew what the Soviet Union had in mind once it completed its invasion of Manchuria. Central Bureau might need to intercept Russian traffic, he speculated disingenuously. While they were waiting, some of the translators started learning Russian. Eventually the Australians were repatriated on the American freighter *Francis N. Blanchett*, leaving Manila on 9 October. It was a crowded, miserable voyage of eighteen days, but at least they were going home.

While the men headed back to Australia for demobilisation and a return to civilian life, Sandford hitched a ride on a USAAF flight carrying freight from Clark Field to Tokyo. Driven into the centre of the city, he passed under a banner announcing, 'You are now entering Tokyo, courtesy of 1st Cavalry Division.'

Before leaving Manila, Sandford had written to advise Australian army intelligence chief John Rogers that General Akin had commissioned him, with the help of Abe Sinkov and Roy Booth, to report on flaws in the operation of Central Bureau for future guidance 'on our sins of omission and commission'. In

Tokyo, he would have the 'unwitting assistance of our Japanese counterparts' in preparing the report. The Australian component of Central Bureau would be disbanded on his return.

Sinkov was already in Japan on assignment for TICOM (Target Intelligence Committee) with Hugh Erskine, Central Bureau's Japanese-born chief translator. TICOM was a US–British project whose ostensible aim was to discover enemy capability in signals intelligence. Its brief was to capture German, and later Japanese, cipher systems; its more clandestine purpose was to find out what success the Axis had had in breaking into Soviet systems. TICOM operators from Bletchley Park had moved into Germany with the invasion force and claimed considerable success in seizing keys to Soviet ciphers. Sinkov's attempt to duplicate that in Japan couldn't repeat its success.

Because occupation troops didn't land until a month after the surrender, Japan's cryptographers had time to destroy significant material and disappear. The enemy coders were hard to track down, and little headway was made with those the Allies could find. The Americans were instructed not to disclose their success in penetrating Japanese codes. When the sigint operators they were interrogating said whatever was convenient for them, Sinkov couldn't reveal that he knew they were lying.

After the Japanese navy's decisive defeat at Leyte Gulf, there had been few enemy convoys to track and little need to break into new air–ground codes. Traffic volume was too low for new codes to be solved anyway. Eric Nave had begun compiling the technical records of Central Bureau as a historical account and for future reference. He was instructed to destroy all decrypted signals save fifty messages selected as examples of the Bureau's work. Nave had charge of a multiservice team of twelve that had relocated to 45 Eldermell Terrace, the house Sandford and his batman had vacated in moving to San Miguel in May. The now-empty 21 Henry Street was handed back to its owners. In December,

Nave delivered the completed Central Bureau Technical Records to Robert Little of military intelligence.

After the hostilities came the valedictories. Eleven of the Americans in Central Bureau were awarded the US Legion of Merit. American citations were given to Sandford, Roy Booth and Stan 'Pappy' Clark, although they were kept secret. Sandford wrote to Little proposing nomination of Abe Sinkov, the leader of the American component of Central Bureau, for an OBE in recognition of his 'phenomenal technical capacity, and his untiring cooperation with the Australian component'. Sandford also recommended Mentions in Despatches for Major Geoff Ballard and Captain Charles Inglis, both of Central Bureau, but not for Captain Nave. He'd become disenchanted with Nave in the latter stages of the war.

'Technically,' he wrote to Little, 'Capt Nave is by far the most brilliant officer in the Unit, but he is [so] lacking in initiative and appreciation of changing operational requirements of our forces that his efforts must be constantly guided by Maj Clarke or myself.'

A fairer assessment might have been that breaking ciphers is a young person's game, and Eric Nave was no longer a young person. Sandford did, however, suggest that his pioneering work on Japanese ciphers merited a non-military award. Nave was nominated for an OBE for 'one of the finest contributions to our cryptographic work during the whole of the war in the Pacific'. It was duly awarded.

— • —

When it was clear the war was drawing to an end, Australia's military intelligence leaders had begun to look closely at postwar national security in addition to immediate and ongoing intelligence needs. In September 1944, Sandford and Rogers had flown to England to attend a conference on postwar intelligence strategy chaired by the head of MI6, Sir Stewart Menzies. An item on the agenda was: 'Postwar plans and Australia's intelligence responsibilities in the islands of the Pacific and in the islands north of Australia'. In response to a British proposal that the Australian government establish a Far East Joint Intelligence Bureau after the war, the federal Department of Defence set up a committee to study the idea.

Sandford returned briefly to Manila from Tokyo in November 1945, overseeing the closure of Central Bureau in San Miguel. He then did the same in Brisbane. He was moving on too, telling Blamey's man in Manila, General Frank Berryman, 'The affairs of this unit are being wound up very satisfactorily, and our Magnum Opus, a technical history of our work, is almost complete. I am going to Melbourne in the near future to assist in the formation of the post-war organisation.'

Signals intelligence had been a success story of the war. It became the top priority for the postwar reorganisation of Australian intelligence, building from the residue of FRUMEL and the Australian components of Central Bureau. Sandford moved into Melbourne's Victoria Barracks in December. D Special Section, the highly secret Melbourne unit that had monitored diplomatic traffic during the war, had been disbanded and its personnel returned to civilian life. Sandford and Little had stayed in close liaison with D Section during the war. Now Mic Sandford moved into the office in A Block that had once been Dale Trendall's.

His technical report complete and delivered, Eric Nave also moved to Melbourne and joined the embryonic organisation, which operated without any official imprimatur. In 1944, when FRUMEL had outgrown the Monterey apartment building, Jack Newman had moved with it to the huts of Albert Park Barracks, close to Victoria Barracks. His wireless intelligence group continued delivering material to Victoria Barracks' new occupants. Nothing had changed, yet everything had changed.

During the war, the Australian Army had set up a radio intercept facility at Mornington, on Melbourne's south-eastern fringe. Rhombic directional aerials were erected in the middle of Mornington Racecourse, whose club buildings became operations rooms and messes. Galvanised huts were built as sleeping quarters for the intercept operators, mostly AWAS women. They had been the source of much of the diplomatic traffic that came to D Special Section.

The AWAS personnel at Mornington were discharged in December 1945, and thirty operators, all male, were brought from Kalinga, Queensland, to take over. They were tasked with interception of high-speed Russian traffic. Mostly plain-language messages between individuals or notices about office matters, these were described by one of the eavesdroppers as 'monumentally banal'.

Intercepts were delivered to Mic Sandford in Victoria Barracks, by motorcycle despatch rider from Mornington, just as before the war they had been taken from Melbourne's outskirts to Eric Nave, in the same building. The target of intercepts now, however, was the Soviet Union, an ally in the war so recently ended.

While the Australian military and its government hashed out the structure and objectives of the country's postwar intelligence services, Sandford remained the conduit through which all signals intelligence passed. He distributed incoming messages for decryption and circulated the resulting translations and analyses about the intelligence network. The Americans were no longer a major part of this network. With Japan defeated, they were no longer greatly interested in the Pacific and Asia. Their focus now was on Europe and the intentions of the Soviet Union there. In the geopolitical vacuum this created in the Asia-Pacific, Britain had seen an opportunity to reassert itself, flexing its intelligence muscles in the region with Australia as its proxy.

The British had been closely involved with the development of Australian sigint for many years, with Nave's Special Intelligence Bureau before the war and setting up the Special Liaison Unit late in the war. Following the visit of Rogers and Sandford to Britain in 1944, Bletchley Park's Sir Edward Travis led a British party in pursuit of a multinational sigint alliance. In April 1945, the party came to Australia and visited D Special Section in Melbourne and Central Bureau in Brisbane. With the war over, discussions would continue with Bletchley Park and its head until they crystallised in a new intelligence organisation for Australia.

Back in November 1944, Mic Sandford had ordered IBM tabulators from America for Australian use. The Australians at Central Bureau had been largely excluded from working with the tabulators. He thought that had to change. Computers would be needed in postwar signals intelligence in whatever organisation would take over that responsibility. When Central Bureau moved to San Miguel, it was expected the IBM machines would go with them. That didn't happen, and now they were to be repatriated to the US. They had only ever been on loan to the US Army.

By May 1945, the Australian army section responsible for procuring the machines was still debating details of the order. The request was finally authorised in July by the Minister, who wanted to find the most suitable hire terms 'without further delaying'. However, IBM's agent in Australia began playing hardball on the lease, the operating staff, and training.

In August, with Japan having surrendered and the British and Australians deep in discussion about postwar sigint in the Asia-Pacific region, Sandford advised that the functions allotted to Australia after the war probably meant they would have no need for the IBM machines. At the same time, he thought Australia should stay abreast of developments and acquire tabulators for possible future use. Professor Room had indicated his old department at the University of Sydney would be interested in IBMs and Zac Halpin, the American who had headed Central Bureau's machine section, had offered his assistance.

Nothing came of the idea. By September, all IBM machinery had gone from Brisbane and an opportunity had been lost.

— ● —

The British continued to pursue signals intelligence jointly with other Commonwealth nations. Throughout 1946, Sir Edward Travis was in frequent contact with the Secretary of the Australian Department of Defence, Sir Frederick Shedden. An Australian delegation went to London in February for discussions about Commonwealth sharing of postwar sigint. It was led by Eric Nave. Australia agreed to supply sixty-five operating teams—417 personnel—for global interception operations. Three months later, Travis met with Australia's new Prime Minister, Ben Chifley, who was in London for a conference of Commonwealth prime ministers. He told Chifley that Australia had a Commonwealth duty to set up an ongoing sigint body, but said the British must have significant input into how it should function.

Chifley submitted a proposal to Cabinet in July to establish a 'signals intelligence centre'. With the proposal approved by Cabinet, Defence set about planning the structure and function of the new organisation, to be called the Defence Signals Branch (DSB). In December, Travis returned to Australia with two assistants to discuss the formation of the new organisation and its cooperation with its British counterpart. It was to be based in Melbourne, with associated intercept stations covering the eastern Indian Ocean, parts of East Asia, Southeast Asia and the Southwest Pacific. It was a bold and extensive brief.

Four Australians were under consideration to head up the new organisation: Sandford, Nave, Jack Newman and Hugh Berry, the senior RAAF officer from Central Bureau after Roy Booth, who had returned to his Sydney legal practice. Travis was adamant that a British officer should be chosen. The British, he said, would share material with DSB only if they had 'complete confidence' in its director. In April 1947, Lieutenant Colonel J.E. 'Teddy' Poulden, RN, took up duties as the initial director of the Defence Signals Branch.

There were mutterings in Australian defence circles about the failure to appoint an Australian to the top position. Poulden had spent a short time in Australia during the war and had married an Australian, but he had spent the previous two years at the Royal Navy sigint station near Colombo. Adding to the Australians' scepticism about who really controlled DSB, Poulden was given his own personal cipher to communicate with Travis.

Poulden headed DSB until 1950, when he was succeeded by an Australian. Ralph Thompson had the right pedigree. He had served in the Australian radio field unit, No. 4 Wireless Unit, in Greece, Crete and Syria, and had been put in command of No. 51 Wireless Section, the army field unit set up out of Darwin after Japan entered the war.

Eric Nave stayed with the organisation when it became DSB, in a senior officer position. In 1949, when the more public spy agency ASIO (Australian Security Intelligence Organisation) was formed, Nave moved to it as Senior Officer, C. It was a fairly unremarkable conclusion to a remarkable but under-recognised career. So much for being the pioneer of Australian code breaking.

The golden boy of Australia's wartime intelligence took a different path. Mic Sandford had lost interest in the new Australian unit and either sensed that the wind was changing or was warned by his British contacts about what Travis was proposing. In February 1946, he went to the United Kingdom, from where he joined the British Army of the Rhine, the occupation force in Germany, as an intelligence officer. One of its main purposes became prevention of a Soviet drive into West Germany, although Sandford was primarily keeping an eye out for any resurgence of Nazism. He came back to Melbourne briefly late in 1947 and addressed a weekly intelligence briefing at Victoria

Barracks on the situation in Germany. Then he disappeared back to Europe.

In 1948, Sandford left the military and joined the Anglo-Iranian Oil Company, soon to become British Petroleum (BP), as manager of its Rome office. He lived in Italy for the rest of his life, moving into an ornate stone villa on top of a coastal cliff with his male partner and, later, their adopted son. He came back to Australia from time to time, keeping in contact with family and making no pretence about his sexuality, though he did not reveal it to his mother, who had always thought young Mickey's friends were 'very arty'. Sandford never again lived in Australia.

It's always possible that the executive position in Rome was a cover for continuing intelligence work, but as intriguing as that possibility might be, it is unlikely. Mic Sandford wasn't an undercover man. He was too outgoing and drew too much attention to himself for a clandestine role. He was a highly skilled networker, and that was the secret of his success.

Sandford seems to have had no further contact with his batman after the war was over. Donald Friend tells of a 1947 night out with a mate on the seedy side of Melbourne. They were watching young gay men on the beat being scrutinised when Friend spotted Colin Wainwright among them, 'dyed and painted up like a Matisse houri'.

'Let's get out of here,' Friend said to his mate.

— ● —

The Americans already had. They disappeared from Australia at war's end with minimal farewells and very little fuss. FRUMEL's Fabian and Lietwiler had already gone. Fabian returned to the US in 1945 from the frustration of his Colombo posting, explaining how he'd instructed the British there. When the war was over, he left intelligence and went to sea. Promoted to captain in 1950, he was put in command of an oiler, the *Nebraska*. He retired at the rank of captain in 1961 and went to live in Florida. He never returned to Australia.

John Lietwiler, too, remained in the US Navy and rose to the rank of captain. He kept in contact with Rudy Fabian after the war and, although he lived in Maryland, met up with his former colleague from time to time. Unlike Fabian, Mr and Mrs Lietwiler went back to Australia for a holiday at least once and probably more than once, according to their son.

The Americans at Central Bureau were more inclined to retain their connections with their wartime hosts. Abe Sinkov remained in intelligence, returning from his thwarted mission in Japan to rejoin the Signal Intelligence Service at Arlington Hall. Later, he moved to the newly formed National Security Agency and, in retirement, wrote a textbook on cryptanalysis.

The former personnel of Central Bureau remained silent for some forty years until the High Court and the Freedom of Information Act lifted the prohibition on wartime stories. A Central Bureau alumni association was formed. Sinkov came to Australia to unveil a plaque at the Ascot fire station that had been the IBM machine room, but the American who kept most contact with Australia was Joe Richard. He settled in Silver Spring, Maryland, but Australia was his second home, and he visited the country several times, including for Anzac Day ceremonies.

— ● —

In packing up their equipment and their temporary lives at the end of the war, the workers at FRUMEL and Central Bureau were packing up an extraordinary story in Australian military history. While the Crimes Act kept the story under wraps for four decades, a new war—a Cold War—broke out, with a new generation of ciphers to break. The double-encrypted ciphers that the Japanese had thought impenetrable were succeeded by ever more complex systems. The Soviet VIC triple-encoded system, for example, used a 'straddling chequerboard', a matrix of numbers and letters to code letters as numbers, add a secret key number by non-carrying addition, then code the result back to letters with the matrix. Computer-generated stream ciphers and block ciphers heralded the dawn of a new era of code breaking.

Meanwhile, the men and women who brought the Pacific War to an early close, with a combination of intuition and doggedness, remained without public recognition. Although knowledge of the extent of Japanese penetration of Allied codes is sketchy at best, circumstantial evidence suggests it lagged badly behind Allied signals intelligence and as a result the Japanese paid a high price. That too is generally left out of the general narrative of how the war was won and lost; if Bletchley Park or Alan Turing isn't part of the story, it didn't exist.

The postwar embargo on revealing intelligence activity during the war has meant that much of the knowledge about it has gone. After forty years, personal accounts are prey to faulty memory and to the desire to move into the spotlight or settle old scores.

History can easily be rewritten when there are large gaps in it. Some accounts portray Joe Rochefort as the martyr of Midway, suggesting he single-handedly intercepted, decrypted and translated the Yamamoto message that brought about the Japanese fleet's downfall.

As for Bill Tremblay, he disappeared after the war and this author has been unable to trace him. Yet Tremblay's selection of a sheet from a cardboard box of garbled intercepts was probably as instrumental in bringing about the end of Japan's dream of empire as any act of Douglas MacArthur or Chester Nimitz.

And that's the paradox of the shadow world of signals intelligence: the work done there can reverse the destiny of armies and nations, yet more often than not, those who do it are lost to history.

CODING AND DECODING JAPAN'S MILITARY MESSAGES

Japanese radio operators converted the syllables (*kana*) in their language to Morse-style dots and dashes, each *kana* being represented by a given combination. Japanese messages in Morse could be read by anyone familiar with the code. Each *kana* could be converted to a romanised form (called *romaji*) representing the sound of the kana. Yokohama, for instance, is made up of four *kana*, represented in *romaji* as YO-KO-HA-MA.

Japan's military messages were sent in Morse code, whether between pilot and base, between units or within the command structure. So that the text could not be intercepted and read by the enemy, it was encrypted into a secret text. In the simplest form of encryption, groups of two to four *kana* or numerals were substituted for the characters (or words or phrases where they were frequently used) in the text using a codebook, and the message was sent in that form. The same codebook was used for decrypting the text at the receiver's end.

Diplomatic transmissions were generally coded by a machine whose rotating wheels had *kana* and digits inscribed on them, but these machines—derived from the German Enigma machine—were not used by Japan's military. It used codebooks instead.

Substitute codes were used for pilot–base signals where the message was immediate and speed was essential. Messages within the command structure were of greater strategic importance and their security from the enemy was paramount. Additional security was provided—or thought to be provided—by double encryption.

In the JN-25 series of Japanese naval codes, the text was first encrypted by codebook into groups of five-digit numbers. To these numbers were added a succession of numbers from an additive book of random five-figure numerals set out in rows and columns. The coder started from a unique point in the additive tables and added each successive five-figure number in the book from that point to each successive number in the coded text, using non-carrying addition (see Glossary). The five-figure numbers resulting from these additions were the numbers transmitted as the double-encrypted message.

To decrypt the message, the receiver first subtracted the numbers in succession in the additive book from the numbers in the message, starting from the indicated point in the book. The receiver then used the codebook to decode the resulting numbers and reveal the original text.

The mainline Japanese army code and the Water Transport code were also double-encrypted using additive tables. The starting point in these tables (page, row and column numbers) was encoded using a 10 by 10 matrix known as the indicator table.

The task for code breakers with double-encrypted messages was first to decipher the indicator table that identified the starting point in the additive tables, then to resolve the additive cipher so that additives could be stripped off the intercepted message to reveal the coded message underneath. Lastly, the code had to be broken to reveal the underlying message in plain text. Code breaking was expedited with the advent of tabulator machines that could churn through options by 'brute force' to reveal patterns. Carelessness in sending messages could also provide a window into the code.

Once the additive tables and codebook had been broken, encrypted intercepts could be routinely decoded until the tables or books were replaced with a new version. Then the code-breaking process had to begin all over again.

Glossary of technical terms

additive numbers. Random numbers added successively by non-carrying addition to the groups in a coded message to double-encipher the message.

brute force. Using tabulators to sort code elements in bulk to identify patterns.

cipher, n. A code; more technically, a method of concealing the meaning of a text, usually by direct substitution of letters or numbers.

code, n. A cipher; more technically, a method of concealing the meaning of a text, usually by substituting strings of characters (most often numerals) for letters, numbers, words or common phrases.

cryptanalysis. The art of deciphering codes by analysis; code breaking and/or decoding, depending on who is using the term.

cryptographic system. A system for encryption and decryption via an algorithm, or coding method, and a key, or rules for applying the method.

cryptography. The process of reading and writing codes and ciphers.

cryptology. The study of cryptography and code or cipher systems.

decrypt, decipher. To decode an encrypted message.

encrypt, encipher. To translate a plain-text message into coded form.

indicator table. A coding table, often in a 10 × 10 matrix, used to encrypt the starting point in the additive tables used in a coded message.

Magic. Allied intelligence summaries derived from diplomatic intercepts.

non-carrying (false) addition. Addition where, when the sum is more than 9, the last digit is entered in the sum, but the multiplier of ten is not carried over to the next column—e.g. 5+7 = 2.

plain text. Any text that has not been encoded.

research. Code breaking; pursuit of code and cipher values.

signal. A message sent by radio.

superencryption, double or multiple encryption. The process of encrypting an alre ady coded message.

traffic analysis. The examination of messages to deduce information from aspects of their transmission rather than their content.

Ultra. Allied intelligence summaries derived from military signals.

Cast of characters

Cryptography workers

Archer, Henry (UK: SIB, D Section)—English diplomat evacuated from Manchuria

Ballard, Geoff (Aust: 4SWS, Central Bureau)—Central Bureau officer with Middle East field experience

Bond, Ronald (Aust: SIB, D Section)—young linguist who moved to D Section when SIB disbanded

Booth, Roy (Aust: Central Bureau)—head of RAAF contingent at Central Bureau

Bradshaw, Thomas 'Snow' (Aust: 1WU)—leader of RAAF field unit at Darwin

Brown, Howard (US: Station 6, Central Bureau, 1WU)—gung-ho veteran of Station 6, Manila

Burnett, Malcolm 'Bouncer' (UK: GCCS, FECB)—senior FECB man; close friend of Nave

Carlson, Spencer 'Swede' (US: Station Cast, FRUMEL)—senior linguist, Cast and FRUMEL

Clark, Larry (US: SIS, Central Bureau)—senior cryptanalyst who worked on Purple

Clark, Stan 'Pappy' (Aust: Central Bureau)—headed Central Bureau advance unit in Hollandia and San Miguel

Clarke, Bill 'Nobby' (Aust: 4SWS, Central Bureau)—cryptanalyst with Middle East experience

Cook, Ralph (US: Station Cast, FRUMEL)—IBM's Manila rep, poached by Fabian

Cooper, Arthur (UK: FECB, SIB)—eccentric linguist with pet gibbon; evacuated from Singapore

Erskine, Hugh (US: SIS, Central Bureau)—Japan-born linguist; head of Bureau translation section

Fabian, Rudy (US: Station Cast, FRUMEL)—Cast and FRUMEL leader, at war with US Army and the British

Falconer, Keith (Aust: 1WU)—field operator, intercepted Yamamoto's itinerary

Friedman, William (US: SIS)—US Army cryptography pioneer; head of SIS

Friend, Donald (Aust: Central Bureau)—rising artist, on Central Bureau staff

Graves, Hubert (UK: SIB, D Section)—old-school linguist from British Consular Service

Halpin, Zac (US: Central Bureau)—head of Bureau machine section

Jamieson, A.B. 'Jim' (Aust: SIB, FRUMEL)—linguist, worked 8 years in Japan

King, Stan (Aust: 6WU)—field interception operator, Leyte campaign

Lietwiler, John (US: Station Cast, FRUMEL)—Fabian's offsider, 'good cop' in that leadership team

Lyons, Dickie (Aust: SIB)—mathematician in University of Sydney code-breaking group

Mahrt, Otto (US: Central Bureau)—intuitive code breaker, lived in Japan as youth

Nave, Eric (Aust: China Station (RN), GCCS, FECB, SIB, Central Bureau, ASIO)—seconded to Royal Navy; pioneer of Australian cryptography

Newman, Jack (Aust: FRUMEL)—RAN communications chief; Australian leader at FRUMEL

CAST OF CHARACTERS

Poulden, J.E. 'Teddy' (UK: DSB)—initial head of DSB

Redman, Jack (US: OP-20-G)—section head in Washington, brother of Joe Redman

Richard, Joe (US: SIS, Central Bureau)—cryptanalyst at Central Bureau, broke Japanese army Water Transport Code

Richardson, Gill (US: Station Cast, FRUMEL)—senior linguist, Cast and FRUMEL

Rochefort, Joe (US: Station Hypo)—Station (Hawaii) chief

Room, Gerry (Aust: SIB, Central Bureau)—University of Sydney mathematician, recruited by Nave

Ryan, Jack (Aust: 4SWS, ASWG)—leader of Middle East field unit; head of Bonegilla training unit

Safford, Laurance (US: OP-20-G)—US Navy cryptography pioneer

Sandford, Alastair 'Mic' (Aust: 4SWS, Central Bureau)—with AIF in Crete; executive officer Central Bureau and leader of its Australian Army contingent

Shaw, Harry (UK: GCCS, FECB)—Nave housemate in Japan; senior officer in Far East

Sherr, Joe (US: Station 6, Central Bureau)—unit head in Manila; off-site head in Australia

Sinkov, Abe (US: SIS, Central Bureau)—leader of US contingent at Central Bureau

Thompson, Ralph (Aust: 51WS, DSB)—field unit commander in Northern Territory, with Middle East experience

Tiltman, John (UK: GCCS)—English code breaker, first to break JN-25

Tremblay, Bill (US: Station Cast, FRUMEL)—naval clerk, decrypted Yamamoto's Midway instructions

Trendall, Dale (Aust: SIB, D Section)—classics academic, recruited by Nave

Treweek, Ath (Aust: SIB, FRUMEL)—classics academic, recruited by Nave

Waller, John (UK: FECB)—intelligence officer; as Hong Kong chief clashed with Shaw

Webb, Norman (UK: FECB, Central Bureau)—escapee from Singapore who managed Bureau's traffic files

Wenger, Joe (US: OP-20-G)—senior OP-20-G officer; rival to Safford

Yamagata, Clarence (US: Central Bureau, 1WU)—Manila lawyer who joined Central Bureau

Yardley, Herbert (US: Black Chamber)—pioneer cryptographer with dubious reputation

Others

Akin, Gen. Spencer—SWPA Chief Signal Officer; responsible for Central Bureau

Callahan, Lt-Cdr Fort—chief communications officer in the Philippines

Chapple, Lt Wreford 'Moon'—skipper of US submarine *Permit*, evacuating Cast workers from Corregidor

Clarke, Col. Carter—senior US Army intelligence officer sent to attach liaison officers to SWPA

Colvin, Adm. Ragnar—British naval attaché in Tokyo; later RAN chief of staff

Crace, Adm. John—commander of a joint task force in the Battle of the Coral Sea

Ferrall, Lt-Cdr William 'Pete'—skipper of US submarine *Seadragon* evacuating Cast workers from Corregidor

Fletcher, Adm. Frank—in command of Allied forces at the Battle of the Coral Sea

Halsey, Adm. William 'Bull'—commander of US Navy's South Pacific Area

Hart, Adm. Thomas—commander of US Navy's Asiatic Fleet

Hoeffel, Capt Kenneth—left in charge of Corregidor after Admiral Rockwell's departure

CAST OF CHARACTERS

Imamura, Gen Hitoshi—commander of Japanese Eighth Army, SW Pacific

Inouye, V-Adm. Shigeyoshi—commander, South Seas Force (Imperial Japanese Navy)

Kenney, Gen. George—commander of US Fifth Air Force (SWPA)

Kimmel, Adm. Husband—commander, US Pacific Fleet at time of Pearl Harbor attack

King, Adm. Ernest—Commander in Chief, US Fleet

Knox, Frank—US Secretary for the Navy

Kusaka, Adm. Jinichi—commander of Japan's Southeast Area Fleet

Layton, Lt-Cdr Ed—intelligence officer, US Pacific Fleet; friend of Rochefort

Leary, V-Adm. Herbert—in command of ANZAC Fleet (SWPA); Fabian's favoured recipient of sigint

Little, Lt-Col Robert—deputy to Rogers and confidant of Sandford

Long, Lt-Cdr Rupert 'Cocky'—RAN intelligence chief; instrumental in setting up Nave's unit

MacArthur, Gen. Douglas—Commander in Chief, Southwest Pacific Area

Marshall, Gen. George—Chief of Staff, US Army

Mason, Cdr Redfield 'Rosey'—intelligence officer, US Asiatic Fleet

McCoy, Lt-Cdr Melvyn—deputy to Callahan in Manila

Mitchell, Maj. John—leader of USAAF mission to shoot down Yamamoto

Mitscher, Adm. Marc 'Pete'—commander, US combined air force in Solomon Islands

Nomura, V-Adm. Kichisaburo—Japan's pre-war ambassador in Washington DC; commander of Japanese naval force during 'Shanghai incident'

Northcott, Lt-Gen. John—Chief of General Staff for Australian Army

Redman, R-Adm. Joseph—Director of Naval Communications (US); brother of OP-20-G's Jack Redman

Rogers, Brig. John—Australian Army intelligence chief

Rutland, Fred—English First World War flying ace who spied on America for the Japanese

Short, Gen. Walter—US Army commander in Hawaii at time of Pearl Harbor attack

Sutherland, Gen. Richard—MacArthur's chief of staff

Takagi, Adm. Takeo—commander of Japan's carrier force at the Coral Sea battle

Travis, Sir Edward—head of Bletchley Park in latter part of the war

Turner, Adm. Kelly—head of War Plans Division, US Navy

Ugaki, Adm. Matome—Yamamoto's chief of staff

Wainwright, Pte Colin—Sandford's colourful batman

Watanabe, Capt Yasuji—Yamamoto's staff officer

Willoughby, Maj-Gen. Charles—MacArthur's intelligence chief

Yamamoto, Adm. Isoroku—commander, Imperial Japanese Navy's Combined Fleet

Acknowledgements

This was not an easy book to write. The length of time it has taken for much of the information to be released into the public domain, its fragmented nature and scattered locations, and the complexity of the code systems involved have all contributed to that. But I believe it is an important story, and a fascinating one. I hope I have captured at least some of its allure.

I'm grateful to Richard Walsh of Allen & Unwin for drawing my attention to the subject of this book and having some faith in my ability to do justice to it. If I have succeeded, it's thanks to a number of people who have helped me along the way.

First, I'd like to thank my first port of call on this project, Ian Pfennigwerth, Eric Nave's biographer. His professional background and knowledge of parts of this particular story enabled him to point me in a few promising directions. Few of the personnel of FRUMEL and Central Bureau are still around, but of those who are, Robert Brown, Helen Kenney and Bill Rogers from Central Bureau, and Joan Tourneur and Pat Smith from FRUMEL, have given me first-hand impressions.

I've also received insights into some of the main characters in the story from members of their families, in particular Piers Plumridge (nephew of Mic Sandford—and thanks to Jamie Sandford-Morgan for connecting me with Piers), Elizabeth Neal and Margaret Forbes (daughters of Eric Nave), Charles Lietwiler (son of John), Robin

Room (son of Gerry) and his wife, Gretchen Thomas, and Helen Roberts (née Treweek).

Others who gave me notable assistance have been Peter Dunn (whose website Australia@War is chock-a-block with fascinating snippets), Joe Look (owner of 21 Henry St), David Horner, Des Ball and Peter Dean (Strategic & Defence Studies, Australian National University), Steve Roberts (US Naval Cryptologic Veterans' Association), Karl Muezenmeyer and Damon Collie (assistance with access to the US National Security Agency), Ron Palenski (Sandford in Crete), Robert Stinnett (Lietwiler correspondence) and George Cully (Yamamoto shoot-down).

I'm grateful to my wife, Jan Stretton, and to Helen Ellerker for going through drafts of the manuscript as proxy for the eventual reader, drawing attention to clumsy or ambiguous expression and making suggestions that might bring the story more to life. I've also had the good fortune of help from two mathematicians, Peter Donovan and John Mack, who have considerable expertise in codes and ciphers and who went through the manuscript to eliminate faulty technical description.

Finally, Richard Walsh cast a critical eye over drafts of the early chapters as well as the final manuscript. After the invaluable input of those word police, the copy editor, Liz Keenan, went through the manuscript with the professional scrutiny I would expect and particular expertise in military subject-matter. Keith Mitchell's uncluttered maps have helped clarify some of the action and locations of this story. These people have all combined to produce a far more readable work than the one I wrote.

My thanks to Allen & Unwin, with whom this is my fourth book—they're almost family now—and especially to Rebecca Kaiser, with whom I'm also working for the fourth time, for her feedback and constructive suggestions, and to Angela Handley for shepherding the manuscript through to the bookshop. It's been a difficult journey at times, but that this is here to read means I got there in the end.

Notes

The narrative of this book has been built from a wide and disparate range of sources of varying reliability. The only major character in the story for whom there is a comprehensive detailed source is Eric Nave. Much (but not all) of his story relies on two rough drafts of his unpublished autobiography and on Ian Pfennigwerth's biography, *A Man of Intelligence*, drawn extensively from Nave's manuscript.

Jean Bou's book, *MacArthur's Secret Bureau*, although criticised by former personnel of Central Bureau, provided a useful source about that agency, and there are several memoirs by members of field intercept units, but no comprehensive story of FRUMEL has been written beyond Jamieson's technical report compiled at the end of the war (NAA B5554).

Records of the decryption process are scant as they were routinely destroyed for security reasons. What remains are more commonly reports that summarise the content of these decoded and translated messages. Descriptions by the code breakers and decoders of their method were written over thirty years after the event. They lack consistency, either through poor memory or different methods. The most accurate description of the process is probably Donovan and Mack's reconstruction in *Code Breaking in the Pacific*. Necessarily speculative, it is informed guesswork by two skilled mathematicians who conducted extensive research of context to arrive at their estimation of the process. It's probably the nearest we have to the real thing.

Much of the narrative of this book, therefore, is pieced together from multiple sources, some of them drawing from the same primary sources, reliable or otherwise. In these chapter notes I indicate some of the more detailed and/or reliable sources for the events that the narrative follows.

It's probably useful to note here that although I have used only one name for each code-breaking unit featured in this story, the reality is that their names changed from time to time. So Cast was also called Station C, OP-20-G was also known as Negat, FRUMEL was also called Cast and Belconnen (where its intercept station was located) and Hypo changed to FRUPAC (Fleet Radio Unit Pacific). To minimise reader confusion, I have stayed with the names that were more distinctive.

NAA refers to access code of the National Archives of Australia. Full citations of books and papers, referred in these notes by author's name, can be found in the Bibliography. I have drawn on the narratives in these sources in constructing the narrative of this book, including various pieces of factual information in the sources. Page numbers in the notes following indicate the beginning of that narrative rather than a page in which a particular fact or opinion or piece of speculation can be found. Where there is no page number, the entire source encompassed the narrative of the event in which I was interested.

Chapter 1

The Winds message, as decrypted by Nave, is quoted in his unpublished autobiography, in Pfennigwerth (*A Man of Intelligence*, p. 175) and in Rusbridger & Nave (p. 136). The follow-up with Durnford and Shedden is reported in the same sources. A copy of the Shedden letter of 28/11/1941 is in NAA A5954, 558. Other decrypts of the Winds Message are quoted in several books, including those by Jenkins, Lewin, Prados and Theobald.

The execute weather forecast of the Winds message can be found in various forms in Pfennigwerth (*A Man of Intelligence*, p. 179),

NOTES

M. Smith (*Emperor's Codes*, p. 100), Lewin (p. 74), Prados (p. 168), Theobald (p. 136) and Rusbridger & Nave (p. 147). Nave's decrypt of the Haruna message is quoted in his draft autobiography. The message and its follow-up are reported in Pfennigwerth (*A Man of Intelligence*, p. 176), Bleakley (*The Eavesdroppers*, p. 18) and Jenkins (p. 48).

The quotes from Thomas Schelling are in his introduction to Wohlstetter (p. vii). The early 1941 operational plan for the Pacific Fleet is described in Wohlstetter (p. 22); the 24 September intercept regarding warships in Pearl Harbor is in Wohlstetter (p. 374), Gannon (p. 190) and Rusbridger & Nave (p. 130); and the 1 December intercept regarding observation balloons is in Gannon (p. 195) and Wohlstetter (p. 374). The conversation between Kimmel and Layton is reported in Blair (p. 91) and Gannon (p. 204).

The attack on Pearl Harbor has been described many times and parts of this version have come from several sources, primarily Gannon (pp. 212–24) and the CCH's *Pearl Harbor Review*.

Chapter 2

Much of the material in this chapter comes from Nave's unpublished memoir and the books that draw from it, notably Pfennigwerth (*A Man of Intelligence*) and Rusbridger & Nave.

Miyata's report on Nave's potential is quoted in Funch (p. 29) and Parlett's assessment in Tokyo in M. Smith (*Emperor's Codes*, p. 21).

The 1914 seizure of SS *Hobart* is related in Bou (p. 11) and Winter (p. 4). The story of Nave's life under Admiral Kelly is largely drawn from Pfennigwerth (*A Man of Intelligence*, pp. 95–106). The Y Committee meeting that praised Nave's efforts is described in M. Smith (*Emperor's Codes*, p. 35), the Rutland story in Pfennigwerth (*A Man of Intelligence*, pp. 103–17) and the Kuehn story in Rusbridger & Nave (p. 74).

The Shaw–Weller standoff in Hong Kong is sourced from M. Smith (*Emperor's Codes*, p. 38). The inquisitor at the Rushbrooke dinner and Nave's pursuit of the intelligence leak is drawn from Pfennigwerth (*A Man of Intelligence*, p. 138) and Rusbridger & Nave (p. 75). A description of Tiltman's penetration of the first JN-25 code is in M. Smith (*Emperor's Codes*, p. 58).

How Nave met Helena Gray can be found in Pfennigwerth (*A Man of Intelligence*, p. 138) and M. Smith (*Emperor's Codes*, p. 62).

Chapter 3

Much of the detail about Cocky Long comes from Winter's biography, particularly his role in COIC (p. 70). Menzies' letter to the UK and Lord Cranbourne's response is dealt with in Cain (p. 42), Jenkins (p. 45) and Bou (p. 20). Newman's suggestion that FECB supply high-level codes is in Cain (p. 43), Jenkins (p. 45) and Pfennigwerth (*A Man of Intelligence*, p. 166). FECB's passing on of intercepted Japanese messages from Australia is sourced in Jenkins (p. 45).

Room and Lyons' Sydney code-breaking group and the meeting of Room and Treweek with military personnel in Melbourne are covered in Pfennigwerth (*A Man of Intelligence*, p. 159), Jenkins (p. 46), Bou (p. 22) and Donovan & Mack's article ('Sydney University'). Their decryption of the love letter is described in Pfennigwerth (*A Man of Intelligence*, p. 160). Menzies' letter to the UK, the decrypted love letter and minutes of the Melbourne meeting with Room and Treweek are all filed in NAA A6923, 37/401/425, as are memorandums about the difficulties of transfer of Room and Lyons from academia to the military.

Jamieson's meeting with Nave is reported in Jenkins (p. 45), and Room and Jamieson's visit to FECB and *Kamer* 14 in Pfennigwerth (*A Man of Intelligence*, p. 168) and Jenkins (p. 46). The tension between Nave and Newman comes from Pfennigwerth (*A Man of Intelligence*, p. 173). Wylie's visit to Australia is covered in M. Smith

NOTES

(*Emperor's Codes*, p. 80) and Pfennigwerth (*A Man of Intelligence*, p. 183), with various reports on it in NAA MP692/1, 559/201/989 and MP1185/8, 2021/5/529. The English escapees who arrived in Australia are noted in several places in Ball & Tamura, as well as in Macksey (p. 123) and Ball & Horner (p. 60).

The chronicle of events with No. 4 SWS and Sandford in Crete and the Middle East is primarily in Ballard (*On Ultra Active Service*, p. 71), who was there, with additional material in M. Smith (*Emperor's Codes*, p. 81), Bou (p. 21) and Cain (p. 43). Freyberg's instruction in Crete from Wavell is in Palenski (p. 185). The story of the Darwin RAAF intercept unit and the Darwin raid are in Bleakley (*The Eavesdroppers*, p. 27), with additional detail of the Japanese attack in Grose (p. 71).

Newman's rejection of FECB's request to transfer to Australia is described in Pfennigwerth (*A Man of Intelligence*, p. 183), Ball & Horner (p. 59) and Bou (p. 29), with a copy of Newman's letter in NAA A816, 19/304/330. The US request to evacuate Cast from Corregidor to Australia is reported in Pfennigwerth (*A Man of Intelligence*, p. 185).

Chapter 4

Stimson's response to intercepting diplomatic messages is quoted in M. Smith (*Emperor's Codes*, p. 5) and Rusbridger & Nave (p. 55). The raid on Japan's New York consulate is from Cain (p. 48) and Rusbridger & Nave (p. 62). The Japanese ambassador in Germany's advice is found in Lewin (*American Magic*, p. 55).

Background to Fabian is provided by McGinnis (p. 20), Farley (interview with Fabian) and M. Smith (*Emperor's Codes*, p. 109). Safford's request for Fabian is described in Farley (interview with Fabian). Much of the background to Lietwiler was provided by his son, Charles. Additional information about Fabian and Lietwiler came from their respective entries in the yearbook of the naval college at Annapolis (United States Naval Academy).

A detailed description of the Cast facility at Corregidor is provided in Lewis & Browne (p. 31), Mucklow (p. 51) and Prados (p. 213). The tale of Dowd's recruitment by Mason is from Prados (p. 213). The transfer of Station 6 intercepts to Cast for decoding is from Lewin (*American Magic*, p. 130), Drea (*MacArthur's ULTRA*, p. 11) and Bleakley (*The Eavesdroppers*, p. 24).

Sinkov's comments on his visit to Bletchley Park are in Farley's interview with him. The conversation overheard on a Manila golf course was reported in a Lietwiler letter to Parke, cited in Lewis & Browne (p. 54).

Chapter 5

Much of the content of this chapter has been sourced from articles in Lewis & Browne. This includes Cook's arrival at Corregidor (p. 83), the story of Blackie the dog (Capron article), the evacuated Americans in Java and Exmouth Gulf (Fabian letter), the disputes with Callahan and McCoy (Lietwiler and Fabian letters), the second evacuation on *Permit* (MacKallor article), Lietwiler's advice to Wavell (Chamberlin article) and the later evacuation on *Seadragon* (Burnett, Chamberlin and Cook articles).

Howard Brown's intercepts of Japanese aircraft are described in H. Brown (p. 52) and Maneki (p. 88). The relocation of Station 6 to Corregidor is drawn from H. Brown (p. 52) and Maneki (p. 90).

The first evacuation on *Seadragon* is pieced from Prados (p. 246), Maneki (p. 56), Farley (interview with Fabian) and Blair (p. 173). Setting up in Java is from Prados (p. 247), Farley (interview with Fabian) and Maneki (p. 56), and the stopover in Exmouth Gulf in Farley (interview with Fabian), Winter (p. 146) and Maneki (p. 56).

Lietwiler and Taylor's plan if Cast personnel were captured is detailed in Farley (interview with Whitlock), Whitlock ('Station C') and Prados (p. 269). MacArthur's departure from the Philippines is drawn from Blair (p. 174).

NOTES

The evacuation on *Permit* is sourced from Maneki (p. 3), Prados (p. 267), Farley (interview with Whitlock) and Blair (p. 193). The evacuation of Station 6 from the Philippines is in H. Brown (p. 52), Richard (memoir) and Maneki (p. 5). The third evacuation of Cast is sourced from Chamberlin, Prados (p. 290), Winton (p. 10), Winter (p. 146) and Blair (p. 194), as well as from Lewis & Browne. The stories of Callahan, McCoy and Thompson on capture by the Japanese are from *The Post-Searchlight*, McCoy and Vulcano respectively.

The US Army factions in Melbourne and the Menzies Hotel are set out in Thorpe (p. 91).

Chapter 6

Margin notes by Mason and Fabian on the report to Leary, copied to MacArthur, are quoted in Parker (*A Priceless Advantage*, p. 18). The description of Fabian as a 'tough cookie' is found in Maneki (p. 64). Fabian's attitudes towards Nave are widely commented on, assembled from Bou (p. 44), Pfennigwerth (*A Man of Intelligence*, pp. 189 & 196), Richard (memoir), Pfennigwerth ('Breaking and Entering'), Maneki (p. 70), M. Smith (*Emperor's Codes*, p. 148 & 'An Undervalued Effort') and Donovan & Mack (*Code Breaking*, p. 38). The setting up of the intercept station at Moorabbin is sourced from Huie (p. 177) and Maneki (pp. 56 & 73). The battle between Safford and the Redman brothers is from Budiansky (p. 13), Prados (p. 300) and Blair (p. 260).

The decrypt about *Kaga* with gaps is quoted in Symonds (p. 141) and that about *Kaga* in RZP campaign in Winton (p. 37), Parker (*A Priceless Advantage*, p. 20), Prados (p. 301) and Winter (p. 151). Hara's instruction to two carriers is from Winton (p. 39). The instruction to attack Australia's northern coast is drawn from Bleakley (*The Eavesdroppers*, p. 38), Winton (p. 40) and Winter (p. 152).

Rochefort's desk sign is quoted in Budiansky (p. 3). Nimitz's orders for *Yorktown* and *Lexington* are from Winton (p. 40), Parshall & Tully (p. 60) and Bleakley (*The Eavesdroppers*, p. 36). Intelligence gathered from sigint in the lead-up to Coral Sea is drawn from Prados (p. 302), M. Smith (*Emperor's Codes*, p. 134), Winton (pp. 37 & 52), Blair (p. 220) and Winter (p. 151). The dispute about the code for Aleutians or Moresby is reported in Symonds (p. 147), Prados (p. 300) and Winton (p. 51). The intercept notifying a delay in the new JN-25 is from Bleakley (*The Eavesdroppers*, p. 44) and Lundstrom (p. 76).

The attempts to unload fighters at Rabaul is described in Winton (p. 42) and Parker (*A Priceless Advantage*, p. 24), Takagi's response to the Tulagi air raid is in Winton (p. 43). The intercept of Inouye's order to withdraw is in Winton (p. 46) and Parker (*A Priceless Advantage*, p. 30).

Mackie's decrypt regarding the Port Moresby land assault and MacArthur's assessment of the Kokoda plan are pieced from Bleakley (*The Eavesdroppers*, p. 43), Drea (*MacArthur's ULTRA*, p. 37), Blair (p. 220), A.J. Brown (p. 19), Parker (*A Priceless Advantage*, p. 29), Winter (p. 161) and Huie (p. 174).

Chapter 7

The personal description of Lietwiler is largely sourced from his son, Charles, and in references in memoirs of Cast and FRUMEL personnel. Fabian's security obsession is detailed in M. Smith (*Emperor's Codes*, pp. 148 & 169), Jenkins (p. 157), Pfennigwerth (*A Man of Intelligence*, p. 195), Maneki (p. 79) and Farley (interview with Fabian). The *Washington Evening Star* story comes from Donovan & Mack (*Code Breaking*, p. 320) and M. Smith (*Emperor's Codes*, p. 134).

Sigint reports on war games on *Yamato* are from Parker (*A Priceless Advantage*, p. 39) and Symonds (p. 264). The order to deliver refuelling hose is from Winton (p. 52), and for transmission crystals for the second K campaign from Winton (p. 53) and Lewin (*American Magic*, p. 98). Other early indications of the Midway operations are found in Symonds (pp. 182 & 272), Budiansky (p. 13) and

NOTES

Lundstrom (p. 150). Various intelligence reports connected to the approaching Midway operation are in NAA B5555/4.

Turner's analysis of AF is sourced from Parker (*A Priceless Advantage*, p. 46), as is the antagonism between Turner and Redman. Rochefort's Midway water shortage ruse is drawn from Symonds (p. 184), Winton (p. 56), Prados (p. 138), Lewin (*American Magic*, p. 106) and Maneki (p. 91). The dispute between Hypo and OP-20-G is outlined in Symonds (p. 183), Prados (p. 301), Winton (p. 56) and Budiansky (p. 15).

Halsey allowing *Enterprise* to be spotted is from Parshall & Tully (p. 92). The fast-tracking of repairs to *Yorktown* is in Lord (p. 26), Lundstrom (p. 174) and Parker (*A Priceless Advantage*, p. 55). MacArthur's radio deception is from Parker (*A Priceless Advantage*, p. 51) and Lundstrom (p. 180). The Hypo intercept of the bearing for the Japanese attack is sourced from Winton (p. 56). FRUMEL's incorrect analysis of Yamamoto's command location is in Parker (*A Priceless Advantage*, p. 51).

Tremblay's decryption of the key garbled message is detailed in Maneki (p. 70) and Symonds (p. 387). Wright and Finnegan's work on the gaps and dates is from Symonds (p. 18) and Prados (p. 139). Rochefort's moment of glory is described in Symonds (p. 186), Winton (p. 58) and Budiansky (p. 16).

The standoff in Monterey among the Australians is in Ball & Tamura (p. 2) and Pfennigwerth (*A Man of Intelligence*, p. 200). The background to Treweek is sourced from his daughter, Helen Roberts, and Ball & Tamura (p. 30). Trendall's eye for patterns is quoted in Ball & Tamura (p. 6). Fabian describes his 'bawling out' of Nave in Farley's interview.

Nimitz's praise for Rochefort and the response to the recommendation for Hypo medals is pieced from Budiansky (p. 22), Winton (p. 2) and Blair (p. 262). Rochefort's recall to Washington is from M. Smith (*Emperor's Codes*, pp. 144 & 320), Benson (p. 65), Blair (p. 262) and Budiansky (p. 24).

The recovery of codebooks at Guadalcanal is sourced from Budiansky (p. 257). Nave's decryption of advice that JN-25C will be replaced is in M. Smith (*Emperor's Codes*, p. 142). The overheard tram comment is in Ball & Tamura (p. 134), Pfennigwerth (*A Man of Intelligence*, p. 196) and Huie (p. 183), attributed to different eavesdroppers.

The machinations and flow-on of the Holden Agreement are drawn from Pfennigwerth (*A Man of Intelligence*, p. 202), Donovan & Mack (*Code Breaking*, p. 311), Ball & Tamura (p. 23), Bou (p.44), M. Smith (*Emperor's Codes*, p. 152) and Benson (p. 63).

Chapter 8

The meeting on the *Orcades* is sourced from Bou (p. 49). Roberts' proposal is described in Bou (p. 32) and Ball & Horner (p. 61), and is in NAA A6923/3, S1/2, as are minutes of the 30 March meeting and the 6 April conference. Commentary on the gatherings is in Bou (p. 32) and Ball & Horner (p. 62).

MacArthur's request to Marshall for more staff and equipment is from Drea (*MacArthur's ULTRA*, p. 19) and Bou (p. 31). Willoughby's complaint of selected sigint is noted in Drea (*MacArthur's ULTRA*, p. 24) and Winter (p. 170). Fabian's rules for briefing MacArthur are quoted in M. Smith (*Emperor's Codes*, p. 169). The burning of sigint reports in sight of Willoughby is reported in M. Smith (*Emperor's Codes*, p. 170) and Blair (p. 304), who attributes it to Jimmy Fife, but is a less reliable source than Smith.

The details of Cranleigh and its owner are from Bou (p. 33), as is the attempt to requisition Grosvenor House (p. 34). Nave's training classes are described in Ballard (*On Ultra Active Service*, p. 164).

The journey of 837th Signal Service Detachment to Australia is from Drea (*MacArthur's ULTRA*, p. 19) and Frank. Yamagata's escape from the Philippines is taken from Bleakley (*The Eavesdroppers*, p. 48) and Frank. Profiles of Sutherland, Willoughby and Sinkov are in Drea (*MacArthur's ULTRA*, pp. 16 & 18).

NOTES

Life in No. 51 Wireless Section at Winnellie and Coomalie Creek is pieced from Ballard (*On Ultra Active Service*, p. 182) and M. Smith (*Emperor's Codes*, p. 113), and of No. 55 Wireless Section in New Guinea from Ballard (*On Ultra Active Service*, p. 200), Bou (p. 50) and Pyle (p. 25). Setting up No. 1 Wireless Unit in Townsville is described in Bleakley (*The Eavesdroppers*, p. 32), and the impact of the military on town life in Moore (p. 192). Brown's flight to Townsville is narrated in H. Brown (p. 72) and the drama of his stolen car in Bleakley (*The Eavesdroppers*, p. 58). Description of the intercept station at Stuart Creek is drawn from Bleakley (*The Eavesdroppers*, p. 68) and M. Smith (*Emperor's Codes*, p. 116). The bombing raids on Townsville are from Bleakley (*The Eavesdroppers*, p. 52) and Bou (p. 89). Use of radio fingerprinting (RFP), TINA and 'fist' is drawn from Donovan & Mack (*Code Breaking*, p. 18), Huie (p. 175) and Bou (p. 81).

Ballard's visit to Brisbane is from Ballard (*On Ultra Active Service*, p. 168). The history and description of Nyrambla (Henry Street) is drawn from Bou (p. 35), Pyle (p. 16) and a number of local documents. The move of Central Bureau to Brisbane is detailed in NAA A6923, 16/6/289. The missing IBM shipment that was found in Sydney is from Drea ('Great Patience', p. 29) and Maneki (p. 31).

Operational delays in Willoughby's intelligence reports is sourced from Thorpe (p. 94). Sandford's meeting with Nave is from Pfennigwerth (*A Man of Intelligence*, p. 203). Negotiation of Nave's transfer to Central Bureau is covered in several documents in NAA A6923, 37/401/425, as is correspondence from Archer to Little and the subsequent setting up of D Special Section. The negotiation for Nave is discussed in Pfennigwerth (*A Man of Intelligence*, p. 203) and D Section in Ball & Tamura (p. 23). The offer from Bletchley Park to Room and Lyons is from Pfennigwerth (*A Man of Intelligence*, p. 205). The accidental shooting of Bartlett is sourced from Richard ('The Breaking', p. 295), Bou (p. 37) and Maneki (p. 31).

CODE BREAKERS

Chapter 9

Richard's early life, the St Kilda rented cottage, his appeal to Sinkov, his work on the Water Transport Code, with and without Clark, and the Arlington Hall response are all covered in his *Cryptologia* article ('The Breaking'). His early life is also drawn from Maneki (p. 30), his request to Sinkov for work distraction from Maneki (p. 31) and M. Smith (*Emperor's Codes*, p. 176), and his work on the code in his memoir from Maneki (p. 32) and M. Smith (*Emperor's Codes*, p. 177). Room's input into the process is informed guesswork in conversation with Donovan.

Mahrt's comment is sourced from Richard (memoir). The decrypt of the plan for a convoy from Palau comes from Budiansky (p. 323).

Sandford's letter to Little regarding Nave's work is in NAA A6923, 16/6/289. Details of Sandford's visit to the US and Britain are from M. Smith (*Emperor's Codes*, p. 186) and NAA A6923, 37/401/425 & S1/10. Wenger's quote from Fabian is sourced from M. Smith (*Emperor's Codes*, p. 197) and Benson (p. 88).

The intercept alerting to the convoy bound for Lae, and the Battle of Bismarck Sea are pieced from Bleakley (*The Eavesdroppers*, p. 87), Drea (*MacArthur's ULTRA*, p. 61), Miller (p. 39), Melinsky (p. 31), M. Smith (*Emperor's Codes*, p. 162), Bou (p. 90) and Donovan & Mack (*Code Breaking*, p. 360).

Chapter 10

There are several books written about the shoot-down of Admiral Yamamoto and quite a few items that can be found on the internet. I have drawn the general story primarily from Davis, Glines and Hoyt.

The events with Yamamoto in Rabaul are taken from Davis (p. 100) and Hoyt (p. 241), reports by pilots of the success of I-Go raids are from Davis (p. 102), Glines (p. 244), Bleakley (*The Eavesdroppers*, p. 94), Drea (*MacArthur's ULTRA*, p. 72), Zimmerman

NOTES

('Operation Vengeance'), and Donovan & Mack (*Code Breaking*, p. 367). Discussions among senior Japanese officers, including Imamura's escape from ambush, are sourced from Davis (p. 103), Hoyt (p. 245), Winton (p. 109), Drea (*MacArthur's ULTRA*, p. 73), and Hollway.

The original intercept at Townsville's No. 1 Wireless Unit is sourced from Bleakley (*The Eavesdroppers*, p. 96), A.J. Brown (p. 30), Melinsky (p. 31) and Cain (p. 56); A.J. Brown identifies the operator as Falconer. The subsequent intercept at FRUMEL comes from Glines (p. 7), Maneki (p. 75) and Winton (p. 109).

The decoded and translated intercept central to the operation is in most books on the subject, but with minor differences. I've used the version in Winton (p. 107) and SteelJaw. The discussion between Nimitz and Layton is described in Davis (p. 6) and Glines (p. 5). The meeting with Frank Knox comes from Davis (p. 14) and the president's endorsement of the shoot-down is from Davis (p. 16) and Winton (p. 108). The response from Noumea that the plan is feasible is in Davis (p. 13).

Yamamoto's life story is pieced from Davis (p. 21), Glines (p. 41), Hickman and Chen ('Yamamoto'). His departure for the tour is described in Hoyt (p. 246) and Hollway.

Preparation for Operation Vengeance is covered in Davis (pp. 109–35) and SteelJaw. The operation itself is sourced from Davis (pp. 139–78), Glines (p. 59) and Winton (p. 110). The recovery of Yamamoto's body is from Davis (p. 191), Winton (p. 112) and Chen ('Yamamoto'). Japan's suspicions about the serendipity of the attack is dealt with by Bou (p. 5), Drea (*MacArthur's ULTRA*, p. 73) and M. Smith (*Emperor's Codes*, p. 184). Kusaka's decoy signal is from Bou (p. 6). The controversy about who shot down Yamamoto is dealt with in Davis (p. 179) and Glines (p. 82).

Newman, Holtwick and Lietwiler's search for new accommodation is sourced from Prados (p. 420) and the US National Archive, SRH-275. Saunders' tour of inspection comes from

M. Smith ('Undervalued Effort', p. 148). The Colombo protest at Fabian's appointment is in M. Smith (*Emperor's Codes*, p. 212 & 'Undervalued Effort', p. 217) and Sandford's wry comment on it is in NAA B5435, 360.

Chapter 11

Marshall's argument put at Casablanca is from Miller (p. 7). The description of No. 1 Wireless Unit at Rouna Falls is sourced from Ballard (*On Ultra Active Service*, p. 203), the 4 June intercept of build-up at Wewak from Drea (*MacArthur's ULTRA*, p. 81). The Nassau Bay landings are described in Drea (*MacArthur's ULTRA*, p. 79) and Miller (*Cartwheel*, p. 58). The curtailment of Operation Cartwheel is also from Donovan & Mack (*Code Breaking*, p. 369) as well as Miller (*Cartwheel*, p. 14).

The comment on Nave's sixth sense is in Melinsky (p. 22), Richard's comment on the same subject is in M. Smith (*Emperor's Codes*, p. 171). Blamey's case to the Admiralty regarding Nave is discussed in Pfennigwerth (*A Man of Intelligence*, p. 218).

The intercept of the planned Marilinan strike is drawn from Drea (*MacArthur's ULTRA*, p. 83). The renaming of Tsili-tsili by Kenney is noted in Miller (p. 196) and Drea (*MacArthur's ULTRA*, p. 81). The raid on Wewak airfields is pieced from Drea (*MacArthur's ULTRA*, pp. 6 & 84), Bleakley (*The Eavesdroppers*, p. 104), Bou (p. 93), Miller (p. 198), Melinsky (p. 32), A.J. Brown (p. 31), Pfennigwerth (*A Man of Intelligence*, p. 216) and Donovan & Mack (*Code Breaking*, p. 370). The signals of fuel shortages are in Bou (p. 93) and Melinsky (p. 33). The landings at Lae are drawn from Miller (p. 204) and Drea (*MacArthur's ULTRA*, p. 85); the Finschhafen landings are also drawn from Miller (p. 214) and Drea (*MacArthur's ULTRA*, p. 87).

The proposal for intercepts to be sent to Arlington Hall, Strong's rejected offer and Clarke's visit to Brisbane are in Drea (*MacArthur's ULTRA*, p. 28), Budiansky (p. 325) and Horner (p. 319). Sherr's

NOTES

death is drawn from Bou (p. 41), Horner (p. 321), Donovan & Mack (*Code Breaking*, p. 297) and Richard (memoir). The American's poem in CLAMOR is quoted in Ballard (*On Ultra Active Service*, p. 265). Blamey pressing for Australian independence is sourced from Thomson (p. 175) and NAA A6923, 16/6/289. The move to and setting up in Ascot Park is drawn from Bou (p. 36), Ballard (*On Ultra Active Service*, p. 171), Donovan & Mack (*Code Breaking*, p. 293) and M. Smith (*Emperor's Codes*, p. 166).

The Sio discovery is pieced from Bou (p. 94), Bleakley (*The Eavesdroppers*, p. 111), Budiansky (p. 324), Drea (*MacArthur's ULTRA*, p. 92) Donovan & Mack (*Code Breaking*, p. 296), M. Smith (*Emperor's Codes*, p. 252) and Richard (memoir and 'The Breaking'). The contacting of Central Bureau by ATIS is from Donovan & Mack (*Code Breaking*, p. 299), the drying out of the Sio books from Bou (p. 94), Drea (*MacArthur's ULTRA*, p. 92) and M. Smith (*Emperor's Codes*, p. 252), the loan of two FRUMEL personnel from Drea (*MacArthur's ULTRA*, p. 92).

The decrypt of the weakened Hollandia defence is sourced from Smith (*Emperor's Codes*, p. 252) and Drea (*MacArthur's ULTRA*, p. 105). Sandford's advice to Ballard is quoted in Ballard (*On Ultra Active Service*, p. 238). The supposed evidence of Los Negros being weakly defended is reported in Drea (*MacArthur's ULTRA*, p. 98) and Miller (p. 320), as is the landing at Los Negros (Drea, *MacArthur's ULTRA*, p. 102; Miller, p. 322). Signals at the end of this campaign are from Drea (*MacArthur's ULTRA*, p. 104) and Bleakley (*The Eavesdroppers*, p. 128).

MacArthur's report regarding Hollandia is quoted in Drea (*MacArthur's ULTRA*, p. 105). The intercept of the Anami estimate is in Drea (*MacArthur's ULTRA*, p. 113) and Bleakley (*The Eavesdroppers*, p. 131), that of the aircraft build-up at Hollandia in Bleakley (*The Eavesdroppers*, p. 133) and Melinsky (p. 34). Tactics to reinforce Hansa Bay as an attack objective are outlined in Drea (*MacArthur's ULTRA*, p. 116) and Bleakley (*The Eavesdroppers*, p. 131).

The Hollandia landings are drawn from R.R. Smith (*Approach to the Philippines*, p. 52), Bleakley (*The Eavesdroppers*, p. 141), Drea (*MacArthur's ULTRA*, p. 118) and Pyle (p. 44). The *Yoshino Maru* recovery is sourced from Maneki (p. 36), Richard (memoir), Ballard (*On Ultra Active Service*, p. 196), Drea (*MacArthur's ULTRA*, p. 120), M. Smith (*Emperor's Codes*, p. 256) and Donovan & Mack (*Code Breaking*, p. 299). Corey relates his experience at Hollandia in Maneki (p. 18).

Chapter 12

The selection of No. 1 Wireless Unit to join Operation King 2 is sourced from Ballard (*On Ultra Active Service*, pp. 221 & 246), Bou (p. 99), Bleakley (*The Eavesdroppers*, p. 171) and Melinsky (p. 44). Rogers' opposition to Australian sigint units under US control is from Horner. The activities of No. 6 Wireless Unit in Hollandia is drawn from Bou (p. 99) and A.J. Brown (p. 75), including detail of the American intercept trucks. No. 4 Wireless Unit's experiment with trucks is sourced from Bou (p. 53).

Hodgson's complaint is from NAA 6923, 37/401/425. The Travis cable to Sandford is in NAA A6923, S1/10, as is a Sandford letter to Little, the other being in NAA A6923, 37/401/425. Sandford's letter to Northcott regarding promotion for Nave is in NAA A6923, 16/6/289. Nave's meeting with Thomas is in Pfennigwerth (*A Man of Intelligence*, p. 224). Sandford's crooning to Elizabeth Nave (now Elizabeth Neal) was described by her and told also in Pfennigwerth (*A Man of Intelligence*, p. 220).

The preparation of No. 6 Wireless Unit for Leyte is described in Bou (p. 75). The intercept of a Japanese patrol is noted in Ballard (*On Ultra Active Service*, p. 221), Bou (p. 100), A.J. Brown (p. 79), Melinsky (p. 44) and M. Smith (*Emperor's Codes*, p. 262). The US assault on Leyte draws particularly from Cannon and Anderson. MacArthur's staged landing is sourced from A.J. Brown (p. 80). The intercept regarding 'three-stackers' is sourced from Bou

NOTES

(p. 101), Bleakley ('US chiefs') and Jinman ('Front-row seat'). The incident with approaching Japanese soldiers is from Bou (p. 101) and A.J. Brown (p. 83). The Australians as the 'foreign legion' and its repercussions are drawn from Bou (p. 102), A.J. Brown (p. 87) and Melinsky (p. 44).

Sinkov's comments on the Willoughby conference are in Farley (interview with Sinkov). The arrival of Burley is from Ballard (*On Ultra Active Service*, p. 284 & letter) and Ball & Horner (p. 85). The involvement of Friend with Sandford and Central Bureau is sourced from Hetherington (p. 138).

The typhoon damage, the arrival of the rest of No. 6 Wireless Unit at Leyte and working at Tolosa is described in Bou (p. 103). The typhoon is also noted in A.J. Brown (p. 105) and Tolosa operations in Bleakley (*The Eavesdroppers*, p. 222), Melinsky (p. 45) and M. Smith (*Emperor's Codes*, p. 263). The convoy from Manila that was nearly missed is from A.J. Brown (p. 104) and Melinsky (p. 45). Interception of the special attack unit is in A.J. Brown (p. 85), Melinsky (p. 45) and M. Smith (*Emperor's Codes*, p. 263).

The incident with Colonel Wang is in Ball & Horner (p. 73). The Harbin leak is sourced from Ball & Horner (pp. 86 & 114), Christos and Horner, and the Japanese penetration of Soviet codes is covered in Army Forces Far East and National Institute for Defense Studies.

The Luzon assault is drawn primarily from Andrade. The landing of No. 6 Wireless Unit is from Ballard (*On Ultra Active Service*, p. 222), Bou (p. 103) and M. Smith (*Emperor's Codes*, p. 266). Activity of the cryptographic units at San Miguel is drawn from Bou (p. 104) and Ballard (*On Ultra Active Service*, p. 222).

Sandford's lobby for Treweek is in NAA A6923, 16/6/289. The non-transfer overseas of Australia's female operators is sourced from NAA A6923, S1/2. The story of Bond's intray is told in Ball & Tamura (p. 122).

Chapter 13

The field unit newspaper was related in the interview with Rogers. Sandford's visit to Tokyo is sourced from Laidlaw (p. 82) and NAA A6923, S1/2, and Sandford's letter to Rogers is also in the latter file. The story of TICOM is from Maneki (p. 84), Bamford (p. 7) and Parrish (p. 271). The end-of-war citations are from Donovan & Mack (*Code Breaking*, p. 305), Pfennigwerth (*A Man of Intelligence*, p. 226) and NAA A6923, 16/6/289.

The conference for postwar strategy at MI6 is sourced from Ball & Horner (p. 164), Thomson (p. 179), Horner (p. 325) and Pfennigwerth (*A Man of Intelligence*, p. 228). Sandford's letter to Berryman is from Ball & Horner (p. 164), as is the story of the Mornington intercepts, which is also found in Ball & Tamura (p. 150). The fate of the IBM machines is drawn from documents in NAA A6923, S1/2. The setting up of Defence Signals Branch is in Ball & Horner (p. 166) and Pfennigwerth (*A Man of Intelligence*, p. 234).

Sandford's postwar life is sourced from Ballard (letter) and the interview with his nephew. Friend's night out in Melbourne is related in Hetherington (p. 518). Fabian and Lietwiler's postwar careers are sourced from the interview with Lietwiler's son and Maffeo (p. 78).

Bibliography

Primary sources

INTERVIEWS
Farley, Robert D. (1979), Oral History Interview with Dr Abraham Sinkov, May, NSA-OH-02-79 to NSA-OH-04-79, National Security Agency/Central Security Service, Fort George G. Meade MD
——(1983), Oral History Interview with Capt Duane L. Whitlock, 11 February, NSA-OH-05-83, Center for Cryptologic History, National Security Agency, Fort George G. Meade MD
——(1983), Oral History Interview with Capt Rudolph T. Fabian, 4 May, NSA-OH-09-83, Center for Cryptologic History, National Security Agency, Fort George G. Meade MD

INTERVIEWS WITH THE AUTHOR
Desmond Ball, Strategic and Defence Studies, Australian National University
Robert Brown, Central Bureau
Peter Donovan and John Mack, authors of *Code Breaking in the Pacific*
David Horner, Strategic and Defence Studies Centre, Australian National University
Helen Kenny, Central Bureau
Charles Lietwiler, son of John Lietwiler
Elizabeth Neal, daughter of Eric Nave
Ian Pfennigwerth, author of *A Man of Intelligence*
Piers Plumridge, nephew of Mic Sandford
Helen Roberts, daughter of Ath Treweek
Bill Rogers, Central Bureau
Robin Room and Gretchen Thomas, son and daughter-in-law of Gerry Room
Pat Smith, FRUMEL
Joan Turnour, FRUMEL

LETTERS

Ballard, Geoff (1982), letter to Julian Frisby, 8 October, courtesy of Piers Plumridge

Fabian, R.J. (1942), letter to Captain Safford, Melbourne, 13 June, cited in Graydon A. Lewis and Jay R. Browne (eds) (2003), *Intercept Station 'C': From Olongapo Through the Evacuation of Corregidor, 1929–1942* (2nd edn), Naval Cryptologic Veterans Association, Pensacola FL, pp. 125–32

Lietwiler, Lieutenant John (1941), letter to Lieutenant L.W. Parke, 16 November, accessed through Robert B. Stinnett (2002), 'Pearl Harbor Document: Letter from Lietwiler to Parke', in Independent Institute, www.independent.org/issues/article.asp?id=1432

——(1942), letter to Captain L.F. Safford, Melbourne, 9 June, cited in Graydon A. Lewis and Jay R. Browne (eds) (2003), *Intercept Station 'C': From Olongapo Through the Evacuation of Corregidor, 1929–1942* (2nd edn), Naval Cryptologic Veterans Association, Pensacola FL, pp. 118–24

Snezwell, Major B. (1982), letter to Piers Plumridge, 16 June, Central Army Records Office, Melbourne

MEMOIRS, AUTOBIOGRAPHIES AND ORAL HISTORIES

Ballard, Geoffrey St Vincent (1991), *On Ultra Active Service: The Story of Australia's Signals Intelligence Operations during World War II*, Spectrum Publications, Melbourne

Bleakley, Jack (1992), *The Eavesdroppers*, AGPS Press, Canberra

Brion, Irene (1997), *Lady GI: A Woman's War in the South Pacific*, Presidio, Novato CA

Brown, A. Jack (2006), *Katakana Man: I Worked Only for Generals*, Air Power Development Centre, Canberra

Brown, Howard W. (1988), 'Reminiscences of Lieutenant Colonel Howard W. Brown', in Ronald H. Spector (ed.), *Listening to the Enemy: Key Documents on the Role of Communications Intelligence in the War with Japan*, Scholarly Resources, Wilmington, DE

Byrnes, Matthew (ed.) (1995), *Wartime Recollections*, Australia Remembers 1945–1995, Moreton Commemorative Committee, Brisbane

Frank, George, Grodin, Richard, Mayer, John et al. (eds) (1946), *Special Intelligence Service in the Far East, 1942–1946: An Historical and Pictorial Record*, SIS Record Association, New York

Hetherington, Paul (ed.) (2003), *The Diaries of Donald Friend*, Volume 2, National Library of Australia, Canberra

Hillier, Jean (1995), *No Medals in This Unit*, self-published, Mundulla, South Australia

BIBLIOGRAPHY

Laidlaw, D.H. (2001), *Anecdotes of a Japanese Translator, 1941–1945*, self-published

Layton, Edwin T. (with Roger Pineau and John Costello) (1985), *'And I Was There': Pearl Harbor and Midway—Breaking the Secrets*, William Morrow, New York

Levett, Robin (1997), *The Girls*, Hudson, Melbourne

Maneki, Sharon A. (1996), *The Quiet Heroes of the Southwest Pacific Theater: An Oral History of the Men and Women of CBB and FRUMEL*, Center for Cryptological History, National Security Agency, Fort George G. Meade MD

Melinsky, Hugh (1998), *A Code-breaker's Tale*, Larks Press, Dereham UK

Nave, Eric (n.d.), 'Codebreaker Extraordinary', unpublished memoir, courtesy of Elizabeth Neal

Nimitz, Chester W. [1941–45] (2012), 'The Nimitz Graybook', in Chester W. Nimitz Papers, Naval Historical Collection, US Naval War College, Newport RI, usnwc.edu/ Academics/Library/Naval-Historical-Collection.aspx#items/show/849

Paterson, Michael (2007), *Voices of the Code Breakers: Personal Accounts of the Secret Heroes of World War II*, David & Charles, Cincinnati OH

Penglase, Joanna and David Horner (1992), *When the War Came to Australia: Memories of the Second World War*, Allen & Unwin, Sydney

Petty, Bruce M. (2004), *Voices from the Pacific War: Bluejackets Remember*, Naval Institute Press, Annapolis MD

Pyle, Nell (told by Doug Pyle) (2006), *The Ultra Experience: Service with the Central Bureau Intelligence Corps*, Australian Military History Publications, Sydney

Richard, Joseph E. (n.d.), unpublished memoir, Australian War Memorial, Canberra

Spector, Ronald H. (ed.) (1988), *Listening to the Enemy: Key Documents on the Role of Communications Intelligence in the War with Japan*, Scholarly Resources, Wilmington DE

Thomas, Gretchen (n.d.), 'High Walden', unpublished memoir

Thompson, Joyce (1984), oral history interview with Joyce Linnane, 24 August, Accession No. S00227, Sound Collection, Australian War Memorial, Canberra, static.awm.gov.au/images/collection/pdf/S00226_TRAN

Whitlock, Duane L. (n.d.), '"And So Was I" (A Gratuitous Supplement to "And I Was There")', unpublished notes

Wyatt, Ray A. (1999), *A Yank Down Under: From America's Heartland to Australia's Outback*, Sunflower University Press, Manhattan KS

CODE BREAKERS

NATIONAL ARCHIVES OF AUSTRALIA

A571, 1944/4124	Enlistment of Canadian Nisei interpreters in AIF
A705, 151/1/746	Directorate of Works and Buildings—Number 1 Wireless Unit
A705, 201/23/453	Chief Cypher Officers—Second Conference of at RAAF Hqrs
A816, 19/304/330	Misc. cables—Intelligence Assessment of Japanese Army
A816, 43/302/18	Cryptographic Organization
A816, 48/301/92	RAAF Mobile wireless units
A816, 66/301/232	Proposed Awards of US Decorations to Sandford, Clark & Booth
A1196, 3/501/15	Machinery for Inter-Governmental Consultation in event of Japanese Aggression, 1941–42
A5954, 530/2	Naval operations in Pacific: Midway Is & Aleutian Is actions, June 1942
A5954, 558	Far Eastern Crisis—November–December 1941
A5954, 2334/18	Circulation of messages received from secret sources
A6923, 1/REFERENCE COPY	Special Intelligence Section report—Japanese diplomatic ciphers
A6923, 12/7/123	Wireless (radio) stations carrying intercepted enemy traffic
A6923, 16/6/289	Australian Military forces—Central Bureau
A6923, 37/401/425	CGS Branch—Military Intelligence—Special Intelligence Section
A6923, SI/2	Australian Military Forces—Y Organisation in Australia
A6923, SI/5	Technical—Signals—Intelligence Report No. 2
A6923, SI/8	Australian Military Forces—DMI—Central Bureau— Special Intelligence, ULTRA, related to the interception of enemy wireless traffic and Harbin spy reports
A6923, SI/10	Australian Military Forces [DMI—Central Bureau]— Special Intelligence, ULTRA
A9695, 489	RAAF participation in the Coral Sea battle
A10909, 1	FRUMEL WWII Diplomatic intercept (German/Japan)
A11093 311/236G	RAAF Command Headquarters—Y Signals Communications
A11093 320/5K5	RAAF Command Headquarters—Central Bureau
B5435, 222	Correspondence with General Akin
B5435, 360	London—GCCS, 24 May 1943 – 31 January 1944
B5436	Central Bureau Technical Records
B5554	Volume of technical records containing actual codes and cipher

BIBLIOGRAPHY

B5555/3   FRUMEL records (incomplete) of Communications Intelligence relating to the Coral Sea Battle

B5555/4   FRUMEL records (incomplete) of Communications Intelligence relating to the Midway Battle

MP692/1, 559/201/989 Recommendations and suggestions for the increase of DSC staff

MP721/1, W205/18 Radio receiving station No. 1 Wireless Unit near Townsville

MP1185/8, 1937/2/126 Southwest Pacific Area—ABDA Organisation

MP1185/8, 1937/2/415 Establishment of a Cryptographic Organization in Australia

MP1185/8, 2021/5/529 Intelligence problems discussed with Capt F.J. Wylie RN

MP1185/8, 2026/10/1854 Report on the capture of SS 'Nankin' by a German raider

OTHER ARCHIVES AND RECORDS

Army Forces Far East (1955), 'Anti-Soviet Operations of Kwantung Army Intelligence, 1940–41', in *Japanese Intelligence Planning Against the USSR*, Central Intelligence Agency, www.cia.gov/library/center-for-the-study-of- intelligence/kent-csi/vol6no2/html/v06i2a08_0001

Central Bureau Intelligence Corps Association newsletters (1982–2015)

Directorate of Military Intelligence (1941), 'Operational Planning Directive No. 1 for Guidance in the Formulation of Detailed Plans', in 'Coordinated Plans for the Defence of Australia, Sept–Oct 1941', AWM347, 237, Department of the Army (Australia), October

Laffan, B.R. (1941), 'Accommodation from AHQ Signals: Park Orchards: Ringwood', Board minute on Military Board Agendum, No. 341/1941 (28 November)

McCoy, Melvyn H. (1943), 'Escape of Lt. Cdr. Melvyn H. McCoy, USN, from a Japanese prison camp in the Philippines', NARA 4697018/38, Office of Naval Records and Library, College Park MD, www.fold3.com/document/270731924

Menzies, Douglas (1941), 'Special Intelligence Organisation', Defence Committee minute paper 169/1941, 29 November

National Institute for Defense Studies (NIDS) (2009), 'Japanese Intelligence and the Soviet-Japanese Border Conflicts in the 1930s', NIDS, Tokyo, www.nids.go.jp/publication/senshi/pdf/200803/09.pdf

Nave, Commander T.E. (1942), 'Special Intelligence Organisation', Department of the Navy, minute paper, 12 November, NAA A816, 43/302/18

Office of Naval Intelligence (US) (1943), *The Battle of the Coral Sea, May 4–8, 1942*, US Navy Department, Washington DC (transcribed and formatted by Jerry Holden, HyperWar Foundation, 2002), www.ibiblio.org/hyperwar/USN/USN-CN-Coral

Robertson, J.K. (1940), Report: 'Park Orchards' Property, Ringwood-Mitcham, 26 August

Safford, Captain L.F. (1946), 'Statement Regarding Winds Message' (before the Joint Committee on the Investigation of the Pearl Harbor Attack, 25 January), in Naval History and Heritage Command, Washington DC, www.history.navy.mil/library/online-reading-room/title-list-alphabetically/s/statement-regarding-winds-message

Safford, Laurance F. (1952), 'A Brief History of Communications Intelligence in the United States', National Archives (US), SRH-149

Sandford, A.W. (1947), 'An Australian Looks at Intelligence Division', typed report, private communication (March)

Sissons, D.C.S. (1987), 'NSA/CCS Cryptologic Documents Series: File SRMN-006 Declassified 6 June 1985: Analysis of Contents/Provenance' (24 April)

United States National Archives, NARA SRH-275, OP20G File of Fleet Radio Unit Melbourne Frumel, 28 June 1943–23 Sept 1945, National Archive and Records Administration, Washington DC

Secondary sources

BOOKS, MONOGRAPHS AND ARTICLES

Aldrich, Richard J. (2000), *Intelligence and the War Against Japan: Britain, America and the Politics of Secret Service*, Cambridge University Press, Cambridge

Arakaki, Leatrice R. and John R. Kuborn (1991), *7 December 1941: The Air Force Story* (1991), Pacific Air Forces Office of History, Hickam Air Force Base HA

Ball, Desmond (1978), 'Allied Intelligence Cooperation Involving Australia During World War II', *The Australian Outlook*, 33, pp. 299–309

Ball, Desmond and David Horner (1998), *Breaking the Codes: Australia's KGB network, 1944–1950*, Allen & Unwin, Sydney

Ball, Desmond and Keiko Tamura (eds) (2013), *Breaking Japanese Diplomatic Codes: David Sissons and D Special Section during the Second World War*, ANU E Press, Canberra

Bamford, James (2001), *Body of Secrets*, Doubleday, New York

Bath, Alan Harris (1998), *Tracking the Axis Enemy: The Triumph of Anglo-American Naval Intelligence*, University Press of Kansas, Lawrence KA

BIBLIOGRAPHY

Bauer, Craig P. (2013), *Secret History: The Story of Cryptology*, CRC Press, Boca Raton FL

Benson, Robert Louis (1997), *A History of US Communications Intelligence During World War II: Policy and Administration*, monograph, United States Cryptologic History, Series IV, World War II, Volume 8, Center for Cryptologic History, National Security Agency, Fort George G. Meade MD

Biard, Forrest R. (1998), 'Wartime Melbourne: Heaven or Hell', *Cryptologia* 19, 1 (Winter)

——(2006), 'Breaking of Japanese Naval Codes: Pre-Pearl Harbor to Midway', *Cryptologia*, 30, 2 (April), pp. 151–8

Blair, Clay Jr (1975), *Silent Victory: The U.S. Submarine War Against Japan*, J.B. Lippincott, Philadelphia

Borrmann, Donald A., William T. Kretkas, Charles V. Brown et al. (2013), *The History of Traffic Analysis: World War I—Vietnam*, monograph, Center for Cryptologic History, National Security Agency, Fort George G. Meade MD

Bou, Jean (2012), *MacArthur's Secret Bureau: The Story of the Central Bureau, General MacArthur's Signals Intelligence Organisation*, Australian Military History Publications, Sydney

Bradley, John H. (2002), *The Second World War: Asia and the Pacific*, Square One, West Point NY

Budiansky, Stephen (2000), *Battle of Wits: The Complete Story of Codebreaking in World War II*, Free Press, New York

——(2000), 'Closing the Book on Pearl Harbor', *Cryptologia*, 24, 2 (April), p. 119

——(2001), 'Codebreaking with IBM machines in World War II', *Cryptologia*, 25, 4 (October), pp. 241–55

Cain, Frank (1999), 'Signals Intelligence in Australia during the Pacific War', in David Alvarez (ed.), *Allied and Axis Signals Intelligence in World War II*, Frank Cass, London

Campbell, Douglas E. (2016), *Save Our Souls: Rescues Made by U.S. Submarines During World War II*, self-published

Cannon, M. Hamlin (1993), *Leyte: The Return to the Philippines*, Office of the Chief of Military History, Department of the Army, Washington DC

Carlson, Elliot (2011), *Joe Rochefort's War: The Odyssey of the Codebreaker Who Outwitted Yamamoto at Midway*, Naval Institute Press, Annapolis MD

Chamberlin, Vince (1992), 'Corrigedor: The Final Days', *Cryptolog*, U.S. Naval Cryptologic Veterans Association, Pensacola FL, www.usncva.org/clog

Chan, Wing On (2007), 'Cryptanalysis of SIGABA', Project Report to Department of Computer Science, San José State University, San José CA

Clark, Chris (2005), 'Code War', *Wartime*, 31, pp. 48–51

Davis, Burke (1969), *Get Yamamoto*, Arthur Barker, London
Donovan, Peter (2004), 'The Flaw in the JN25 Series of Ciphers', *Cryptologia*, 28, 4 (October), pp. 325–40
——(2006), 'The Indicators of Japanese Ciphers 2468, 7890, and JN-25A1', *Cryptologia*, 30, 3 (July–September), pp. 212–35
——(2014), 'Alan Turing, Marshall Hall, and the Alignment of WW2 Japanese Naval Intercepts', *Notices of the AMS*, 61, 3 (March), pp. 258–64
Donovan, Peter and John Mack (2014), *Code Breaking in the Pacific*, Springer, New York
Drea, Edward J. (1992), *MacArthur's ULTRA: Codebreaking and the War against Japan, 1942–1945*, University Press of Kansas, Lawrence, KS
——(1993), '"Great Patience is Needed": America Encounters Australia, 1942', *War and Society*, 11, 1 (May), pp. 21–51
Ephron, Henry D. (1985), 'An American Cryptanalyst in Australia', *Cryptologia*, 9, 4 (October), pp. 337–40
Erskine, Ralph (1999), 'The Holden Agreement in Naval Sigint: The First BRUSA?', *Intelligence and National Security*, 14, 2 (Summer) pp. 187–97
——(2000), 'What did the Sinkov Mission receive from Bletchley Park?', *Cryptologia*, 24, 2 (April), pp. 97–109
Evans, Harold (1998), *The American Century*, Alfred A. Knopf, New York
Farago, Ladislas (1967), *The Broken Seal*, Arthur Barker, London
Funch, Colin (2003), *Linguists in Uniform: The Japanese Experience*, Japanese Studies Centre, Monash University, Melbourne
Gannon, Michael (2001), *Pearl Harbor Betrayed: The True Story of a Man and a Nation Under Attack*, Henry Holt, New York
Glines, Carroll V. (1990), *Attack on Yamamoto*, Orion Books, New York
Gordon, John (2011), *Fighting for MacArthur: The Navy and Marine Corps' Desperate Defence of the Philippines*, Naval Institute Press, Annapolis MD
Green, Irvine and Beatty Beavis (1983), *Park Orchards: A Short History*, Doncaster-Templestowe Historical Society, Melbourne
Grose, Peter (2009), *An Awkward Truth: The Bombing of Darwin, February 1942*, Allen & Unwin, Sydney
Gugliotta, Bobette (2014), *Pigboat 39: An American Sub Goes to War*, University Press of Kentucky, Lexington KY
Hannan, Agnes (1995), *Victoria Barracks Melbourne: A Social History*, Australian Defence Force Journal, Canberra
Hanyok, Robert J. and David P. Mowry (2008), *West Wind Clear: Cryptology and the Winds Message Controversy—A Documentary History*, Center for Cryptologic History, National Security Agency, Fort George G. Meade MD

BIBLIOGRAPHY

Haufler, Hervie (2003), *Codebreakers' Victory: How the Allied Cryptographers Won World War II*, New American Library, New York

Hirschfeld, J.W.P. and G.E. Wall (1987), 'Thomas Gerald Room, 10 November 1902–2 April 1986', *Biographical Memoirs of Fellows of the Royal Society*, Vol. 33, Royal Society Publishing, London

Holmes, W.J. (1979), *Double-Edged Secrets: U.S. Naval Intelligence Operations in the Pacific during World War II*, Naval Institute Press, Annapolis MD

Horner, D.M. (1978), 'Special Intelligence in the South-West Pacific Area in World War II', *The Australian Outlook*, 33, pp. 310–27

Hoyt, Edwin P. (1990), *Yamamoto: The Man Who Planned the Attack on Pearl Harbor*, Lyons Press, Guilford CT

Hughes, Robert (1965), *Donald Friend*, Edwards & Shaw, Sydney

Huie, Shirley Fenton (2000), *Ships Belles: The Story of the Women's Royal Australian Naval Service in War and Peace, 1941–1985*, Watermark Press, Sydney

Isom, Dallas Woodbury (2007), *Midway Inquest: Why the Japanese Lost the Battle of Midway*, Indiana University Press, Bloomington IN

Jacobsen, Philip H. (2003), 'Foreknowledge of Pearl Harbor? No!: The story of the U.S. Navy's efforts on JN-25B', Cryptologia, 27, 3 (July), pp. 193–205

Jenkins, David (1992), *Battle Surface! Japan's Submarine War Against Australia 1942–44*, Random House Australia, Sydney

Jordan, Donald A. (2001), *China's Trial by Fire: The Shanghai War of 1932*, University of Michigan, Ann Arbor MI

Kahn, David (1996), *The Codebreakers: The Story of Secret Writing*, Scribner, New York

Lewin, Ronald (1978), *Ultra Goes to War: The Secret Story*, Penguin, London

——(1982), *The American Magic: Codes, Ciphers and the Defeat of Japan*, Farrar Strauss Giroux, New York

——(1982), *The Other Ultra*, Hutchinson, London

Lewis, Graydon A. (1998), 'Setting the Record Straight on Midway', *Cryptologia*, 22, 2 (April), pp. 99–101

Lewis, Graydon A. and Jay R. Browne (eds) (2003), *Intercept Station 'C': From Olongapo Through the Evacuation of Corregidor, 1929–1942* (2nd edn), Naval Cryptologic Veterans Association, Pensacola FL

Lockwood, Charles A. (1951), *Sink 'Em All: Submarine Warfare in the Pacific*, E.P. Dutton, New York

Lord, F.E. (1932), 'Brisbane's Historic Homes: Nyrambla', *The Queenslander*, 24 March, p. 35

Lord, Walter (1968), *Incredible Victory: The Battle of Midway*, Hamish Hamilton, London

Lukacs, John D. (2010), *Escape from Davao*, Simon & Schuster, New York

Lundstrom, John B. (1976), *The First South Pacific Campaign: Pacific Fleet Strategy, December 1941—June 1942*, Naval Institute Press, Annapolis MD

McGinnis, George P. (ed.) (1996), *U.S. Naval Cryptologic Veterans Association*, Turner Publishing Co., Paducah, KY

McKenzie-Smith, Graham (2012), 'The Other Dick Smith and the Sio Code Books', *Sabretache*, 53, 1 (March), pp. 13–16

McKernan, Michael (1999), *Beryl Beaurepaire*, University of Queensland Press, Brisbane

Mack, John (2012), 'Codebreaking in the Pacific: Cracking the Imperial Japanese Navy's Main Operational Code, JN-25', *Rusi Journal*, 157, 5 (October/November), pp. 86–92

Macksey, Kenneth (2003), *The Searchers: How Radio Interception Changed the Course of Both World Wars*, Cassell, London

Maffeo, Capt. Steven E. (2016), *U.S. Navy Codebreakers, Linguists, and Intelligence Officers Against Japan, 1910–1941*, Rowman & Littlefield, Lanham MD

Manchester, William (1978), *American Caesar: Douglas MacArthur, 1880–1964*, Little Brown, Boston

Maslowski, Peter (1995), 'Military Intelligence: Unmasking Those Fearsome Apparitions', in Gabor S. Boritt (ed.), *War Comes Again: Comparative Vistas on the Civil War and World War II*, Oxford University Press, New York

Mellen, Greg (ed.) (1982), 'Rhapsody in Purple: A New History of Pearl Harbor' (Part 2), *Cryptologia*, 6, 4 (October), pp. 346–67

Mercer, Charles (1977), *Miracle at Midway*, Putnam, New York

Miller, John Jr (1959), *CARTWHEEL: The Reduction of Rabaul*, Office of the Chief of Military History, Department of the Army, Washington DC

Moore, John Hammond (1981), *Over-Sexed, Over-Paid and Over Here: Americans in Australia 1941–1945*, University of Queensland Press, Brisbane

Morison, Samuel Eliot (1948), *The Rising Sun in the Pacific, 1931—April 1942*, Little Brown, Boston MA

Morris, Eric (1982), *Corregidor: The Nightmare in the Philippines*, Hutchinson, London

Morton, Louis (1962), *Strategy and Command: The First Two Years*, Office of the Chief of Military History, Department of the Army, Washington DC

Odgers, George (1968), *Air War Against Japan, 1943–1945*, Australian War Memorial, Canberra

O'Neill, Sharon (2006), *We Missed Out on Our Teen Years*, self-published, Frankston, Victoria

BIBLIOGRAPHY

Palenski, Ron (2013), *Men of Valour: New Zealand and the Battle for Crete*, Hodder Moa, Auckland

Parker, Frederick D. (1993), *A Priceless Advantage: US Navy Communications Intelligence and the Battles of Coral Sea, Midway, and the Aleutians*, Center for Cryptological History, National Security Agency, Fort George G. Meade MD, www.nsa.gov/about/_files/cryptologic_heritage/publications/wwii/priceless_advantage

——(1994), *Pearl Harbor Revisited: United States Communications Intelligence, 1924–1941*, Center for Cryptological History, National Security Agency, Fort George G. Meade MD

Parrish, Thomas (1986), *The Ultra Americans: The U.S. Role in Breaking Nazi Codes*, Stein & Day, New York

Parshall, Jonathan B. and Anthony P. Tully (2005), *Shattered Sword: The Untold Story of the Battle of Midway*, Potomac Books, Washington DC

Pfennigwerth, Ian (2006), *A Man of Intelligence*, Rosenberg, Sydney

——(2012), 'Breaking and Entering', *Wartime*, 57, pp. 22–8

Prados, John (1995), *Combined Fleet Decoded: The Secret History of American Intelligence and the Japanese Navy in World War II*, Random House, New York

Prange, Gordon W. (ed.) (1950), *Reports of General MacArthur*, Volume 1, *The Campaigns of MacArthur in the Pacific*, Office of the Chief of Military History, Department of the Army, Washington DC

——(1981), *At Dawn We Slept: The Untold Story of Pearl Harbor*, Penguin, New York

Richard, Joseph E. (2004), 'The Breaking of the Japanese Army's Codes', *Cryptologia*, 28, 4 (October), pp. 289–308

Rusbridger, James and Eric Nave (1991), *Betrayal at Pearl Harbor: How Churchill Lured Roosevelt into World War II*, Summit, New York

Simpson, Edward (2010), 'Bayes at Bletchley Park', *Significance*, The Royal Statistical Society (June), pp. 76–80

Smith, Michael (2000), *The Emperor's Codes: The Breaking of Japan's Secret Ciphers*, Arcade, New York

——(2001), 'An Undervalued Effort: How the British Broke Japan's Codes', in Michael Smith and Ralph Erskine (eds), *Action This Day*, Bantam Press, London

Smith, Robert Ross (1953), *The Approach to the Philippines*, Office of the Chief of Military History, Department of the Army, Washington DC

——(1963), *Triumph in the Philippines*, Office of the Chief of Military History, Department of the Army, Washington DC

Stanley, Peter (2003), 'New Guinea Offensive', *Wartime*, 23, Australian War

Memorial, Canberra, www.awm.gov.au/wartime/23/new-guinea-offensive

Straczek, Jozef (2001), 'The Empire is Listening: Naval Signals Intelligence in the Far East to 1942', *Journal of the Australian War Memorial*, 35 (December), www.awm.gov.au/journal/j35/straczek

Stripp, Alan (1989), *Codebreaker in the Far East*, Frank Cass, London

Symonds, Craig L. (2011), *The Battle of Midway*, Oxford University Press, New York

Theobald, Robert A. (1954), *The Final Secret of Pearl Harbor: The Washington Contribution to the Japanese Attack*, Devin-Adair, New York

Thomson, Judy (2000), *Winning with Intelligence*, Australian Military History Publications, Sydney

Thorpe, Elliott R. (1969), *East Wind, Rain*, Gambit, Boston

Toland, John (1961), *But Not in Shame: The Six Months After Pearl Harbor*, Anthony Gibbs & Phillips, London

Van Der Rhoer, Edward (1978), *Deadly Magic*, Charles Scribner's Sons, New York

Watson, Richard L. (1947), 'Pearl Harbor and Clark Field', in W.F. Craven and J.L. Cate (eds), *U.S. Army Air Forces in World War II*, Volume 1, *Plans and Early Operations, January 1939 to August 1942*, HyperWar Foundation, ibiblio.org/hyperwar/AAF/I/AAF-I-6

Weintraub, Stanley (2011), *Pearl Harbor Christmas: A World at War, December 1941*, Da Capo Press, Cambridge MA

West, Nigel (2010), *Historical Dictionary of Naval Intelligence*, Scarecrow Press, Plymouth UK

Whitelaw, J. (2002), 'Simpson, Colin Hall (1894–1964)', *Australian Dictionary of Biography*, Melbourne University Press

Whitlock, Duane L. (1995), 'The Silent War Against the Japanese Navy', *Naval War College Review*, 48, 4 (Autumn), pp. 43–52

Wilford, Timothy (2002), 'Decoding Pearl Harbor: USN Cryptanalysis and the Challenge of JN-25B in 1941', *The Northern Mariner/Le marin du nord*, 12, 1 (January), pp. 17–37

Willmott, H.P. (1983), *The Barrier and the Javelin: Japanese and Allied Pacific Strategies February to June 1942*, Naval Institute Press, Annapolis MD

Winter, Barbara (1995), *The Intrigue Master: Commander Long and Naval Intelligence in Australia, 1913–1945*, Boolarong Press, Brisbane

Winterbotham, F.W. (1974), *The Ultra Secret*, Weidenfeld & Nicholson, London

Winton, John (1993), *Ultra in the Pacific: How Breaking Japanese Codes and Cyphers Affected Naval Operations Against Japan, 1941–45*, Leo Cooper, London

Wohlstetter, Roberta (1962), *Pearl Harbor: Warning and Decision*, Stanford University Press, Stanford CA

BIBLIOGRAPHY

Worth, Roland H. Jr (2001), *Secret Allies in the Pacific: Covert Intelligence and Code-Breaking Prior to the Attack on Pearl Harbor*, McFarland & Co., Jefferson NC

Yoshihara, Lt Gen Kane (2007), 'The defence of Hollandia and the withdrawal from Hollandia', in *Southern Cross* (trans. Doris Heath), Australia–Japan Research Project, Australian War Memorial, Canberra, www.ajrp.awm.gov.au/ajrp/ajrp2.nsf/pages/NT000019EE?openDocument

Young, Desmond (1963), *Rutland of Jutland*, Cassell, London

NEWSPAPER AND MAGAZINE ARTICLES

The Advertiser (1942), 'I Came Through; I Shall Return', Adelaide, 21 March

——(1948), 'US awards to Australians: Three Recipients in S.A.', Adelaide, 16 April

——(1971), 'Well-known SA identity dies in Italy', Adelaide, 6 January

The Age (1942), 'Japan's threat to America: Raids on Alaska', Melbourne, 5 June

——(1942), 'Attack on Midway: Japanese Warships Hit', Melbourne, 6 June

——(1942), 'Smashing blows on Japanese fleet: Carriers sunk; heavy ships damaged; great battle in progress', Melbourne, 8 June

——(1942), 'Japanese withdraw: Midway Battle Broken Off', Melbourne, 9 June

Bleakley, Jack (1994), 'US chiefs tapped into decoders', *Weekend Australian*, supplement 'D-Day in the Pacific', 22–23 October, p. 6

Bravin, Jess (2013), 'Echoes From a Past Leak Probe: Chicago Tribune Reporter Targeted After World War II Scoop on Japanese Codes', *Wall Street Journal*, New York, 7 August

Bromby, Robin (1994), 'Overpaid, oversexed, and over here . . . ', *Weekend Australian*, supplement 'D-Day in the Pacific', 22–23 October, p. 8

Forbes, Cameron (1994), 'Ordinary Men Re-live First Kamikaze Attack', *Weekend Australian*, 22–23 October, pp. 1–2

Jenkins, David (1993), 'Man of Compulsive Secrecy Blew the Cover of Others', *Sydney Morning Herald*, 28 June, p. 11

Jinman, Richard (1994), 'A Front-row Seat in Bombing Barrage', *Weekend Australian*, supplement 'D-Day in the Pacific', 22–23 October, p. 6

Lyons, Leonard (1946), 'The Lyon's Den', *The Amarillo Daily News*, Amarillo TX, 19 September, p. 6

Norton-Taylor, Richard (2000), 'British Flying Ace was Spy for Japan', *The Guardian*, 10 November

The Post-Searchlight (2010), 'Fort Callahan and the Last Cable', Bainbridge GA, 28 May, www.thepostsearchlight.com/2010/05/28/fort-callahan-and-the-last-cable

Time (1943), 'Thank You, Mr. Yamamoto', 31 May, p. 28
——(1943), 'The Younger Generation', 31 May, p. 66

WEBSITES, BLOGS AND ONLINE PUBLICATIONS

Air Power Development Centre (2012), 'The Bombing of Darwin, 19 February 1942: The RAAF Experience', *Pathfinder*, No. 171, February, airpower.airforce.gov.au/Publications/List/4/Pathfinder.aspx?page=3

Anderson, Charles R. (n.d.), 'WWII Campaigns: Leyte', US Army Center of Military History, Fort McNair, Washington DC, www.history.army.mil/brochures/leyte/leyte

Andrade, Dale (n.d.), 'WWII Campaigns: Luzon', US Army Center of Military History, Fort McNair, Washington DC, www.history.army.mil/brochures/luzon/luzon

Azzole, Pete (1995), 'Afterthoughts', U.S. Naval Cryptologic Veterans Association, Pensacola FL, www.usncva.org/clog

Bowen, James (2009), 'The Pacific War from Pearl Harbor to Guadalcanal', Pacific War Historical Society, www.pacificwar.org.au

Brisbane City Council (2014), 'Gallivant Through Ascot and Hamilton', www.brisbane.qld.gov.au/sites/default/files/20140703_-_gallivant_through_ascot_and_hamilton_heritage_trail

Budge, Kent G. (2010), *The Pacific War Online Encyclopedia*, pwencycl.kgbudge.com

Burke, Arthur (2015), 'Front-line Townsville 1942', in Anzac Day, Anzac Day Commemoration Committee of Queensland Inc., www.anzacday.org.au/history/ww2/bfa/townsville

Center for Cryptologic History (CCH) (2016), 'Pearl Harbor Review', National Security Agency-Central Security Service, Fort George G. Meade MD, www.nsa.gov/about/cryptologic-heritage/center-cryptologic-history/pearl-harbor-review

Chen, C. Peter (n.d.), 'FJ Rutland', in World War II Database, ww2db.com/person_bio.php?person_id=531

——(n.d.), 'Isoroku Yamamoto', in World War II Database, ww2d.com/person_bio.bhp?person_id=1

——(n.d.), 'Raids into the Indian Ocean, 31 Mar 1942—9 Apr 1942', in World War II Database, ww2db.com/battle_spec.php?battle_id=7

Christos, T. (2012), 'Japanese codebreakers of WWII', in Christos Military and Intelligence Corner, chris-intel-corner.blogspot.com.au/2012/07/japanese-codebreakers-of-wwii

Cribbin, John (1995), 'The Secrets of Chesterville Road', in Kingston Historical Website, City of Kingston, Melbourne, localhistory.kingston.vic.gov.au/htm/article/195

BIBLIOGRAPHY

Donovan, Peter and John Mack (2002), 'Sydney University, T.G. Room and Codebreaking in WW II', www.maths.usyd.edu.au/u/ww2codes/gazette

Dunn, Peter (2006), Australia@War, www.ozatwar.com

Gough, Michael (2007), 'Failure and Destruction, Clark Field, the Philippines, December 8, 1941', in MilitaryHistoryOnline.com, militaryhistoryonline.com/wwii/articles/failureanddestruction.aspx

Hackett, Bob and Sander Kingsepp (2013), 'IJN Submarine I-1: Tabular Record of Movement', in Sensuikan!, www.combinedfleet.com/I-1

Hickman, Kennedy (2016), 'World War II: Operation Vengeance—Death of Yamamoto', in About.com, militaryhistory.about.com/od/aerialcampaigns/p/operation-vengeance

Hollway, Don (2012), 'Death by P-38', in HistoryNet, World History Group, www.historynet.com/death-by-p-38

Jacobsen, Philip H. (n.d.), 'The Codebreakers: Intelligence Contributions to U.S. Naval Operations in the Pacific', in The Pacific War: The U.S. Navy, www.microworks.net/pacific

——(2010), 'Navy Cryptology and the Battle of Midway: Our Finest Hour', in Naval History Blog, US Naval Institute and Naval History & Heritage Command, www.navalhistory.org/2013/06/04/navy-cryptology-and-the-battle-of-midway-our-finest-hour

James, Karl (2013), 'Remembering the War in New Guinea', Australian War Memorial, Canberra, awm.gov.au/blog/2013/09/09/remembering-war-new-guinea

Lokker, Brian (2013), 'U.S. Coffee Rationing in World War II', in Coffee Crossroads, www.coffeecrossroads.com/coffee-history/u-s-coffee-rationing-in-world-war-ii

MacGarrigle, George L. (2003), 'Aleutian Islands: The U.S Army Campaign of World War II', in U.S. Army Center of Military History, www.history.army.mil/brochures/aleut/aleut

Miller, J. Michael (1997), 'Bombing of Cavite', in *From Shanghai to Corregidor: Marines in the Defense of the Philippines*, Marines in World War II Commemorative Series, Marine Corps Historical Center, Washington DC, www.nps.gov/parkhistory/online_books/npswapa/extContent/usmc/pcn-190-003140-00/sec5.htm

Millikin, Donald B. (1942), 'The Japanese Morse Telegraph Code', in RF Café, Kirt Blattenberger, Kernersville NC, www.rfcafe.com/references/qst/japanese-morse-telegraph-code-sep-1942-qst

Ministry for Culture and Heritage (NZ) (2012), 'Royal NZ Navy's Bird-class ships: *Moa* and *Kiwi* bag a sub', in New Zealand History, History Group of the New Zealand Ministry for Culture and Heritage, www.nzhistory.net.nz/war/bird-class-minesweepers/moa-and-kiwi-bag-a-sub

Morton, Louis (1952), 'The Siege of Corregidor', in Remembering Corregidor, Corregidor Historical Society, www.corregidor.org/chs_army/morton_01

Mucklow, Timothy J. (2011), 'The Navy Tunnel STATION CAST: Tip of the Lance', in Federal History 2011, pp. 52–65, shfg.org/shfg/wp-content/uploads/2012/01/4-Mucklow_Layout-11-final

National Security Agency: Central Security Service (NSA: CSS) (n.d.), 'Cryptologic Hall of Honor', in NSA: CSS website, Fort George G. Meade MD, www.nsa.gov/about/cryptologic_heritage/hall_of_honor/1999

Pelvin, Ric (2006), 'Battle of the Coral Sea, 4–8 May 1942', Encyclopedia, Australian War Memorial, www.awm.gov.au/encyclopedia/coral_sea/doc.asp

Pfennigwerth, Ian (2012), 'No Contest! The US Navy Destroys Australia's Special Intelligence Bureau', Military History and Heritage Victoria, mhhv.org.au/?p=2754

Rickard, J. (2014), 'Operation Cartwheel: The Reduction of Rabaul (30 June 1943–January 1944)', in HistoryOfWar.org, www.historyofwar.org/articles/operation_cartwheel

——(2015), 'Second World War: Wars, Campaigns and Treaties', in HistoryOfWar.org, www.historyofwar.org/subject_ww2

Rough, Brian et al. (2015), 'Queensland Historic Places', Queensland Government www.ww2places.qld.gov.au

Schorreck, Henry F. (2015), 'The Role of COMINT in the Battle of Midway', in website of Naval History and Heritage Command, Washington DC, www.history.navy.mil/library/online-reading-room/title-list-alphabetically/r/the-role-of-comint-in-the-battle-of-midway

Smith, Alan H. (2003), 'Operation "Potshot"—Exmouth Gulf, 1942–44', *Sabertache* (1 June) and in The Free Library, Farlex inc., Huntingdon Valley PA, www.thefreelibrary.com/Operation+'Potshot'--Exmouth+Gulf+1942-44.-a015370859

Spinetta, Lawrence (2007), 'Battle of the Bismarck Sea', in *World War II*, www.historynet.com/battle-of-the-bismarck-sea

SteelJaw (2009), 'The Solomons Campaign: Operation Vengeance—the Shootdown of Yamamoto', on US Naval Institute, blog.usni.org/2009/10/12/the-solomons-campaign-operation-vengeance-the-shootdown-of-yamamoto

Stephens, Alan (2014), 'The Battle of the Bismarck Sea', Battle for Australia Association, www.battleforaustralia.org.au/BBBismarckSea

Stinnett, Robert (2002), 'Pearl Harbor Document: Letter from Lietweiler to Parke', www.independent.org/issues/article.asp?id=1432

BIBLIOGRAPHY

——(2003), 'The Pearl Harbor Deception', on www.Antiwar.com, www.antiwar.com/orig2/stinnett1

——(2006), Message 3 of 5 in 'Conversations' 519 (Re: Pearl Harbor), 6 January, 'Market Liberalism', Yahoo! Groups, groups.yahoo.com/neo/groups/marketliberal/conversations/messages/517

Straczek, Jozef (n.d.), 'Listening for the Empire', on Royal Australian Navy website, www.navy.gov.au/sites/default /files/documents/Straczek_-_Listening_for_the_Empire

——(n.d.), 'Battle of the Coral Sea', on Royal Australian Navy website, www.navy.gov.au/history/feature-histories/battle-coral-sea

United States Naval Academy (1932), Lucky Bag Yearbook (Annapolis MD) Collection, edition on *E-Yearbook.com*, www.e-yearbook.com/yearbooks/United_States_Naval_Academy_Lucky_Bag_Yearbook/1932/Page_136

Vulcano, Mario (ed.) (2015), 'Fleet Radio Unit Melbourne (FRUMEL) closed 70 years ago today on November 1, 1945', on Station HYPO website, stationhypo.com/2015/11/01/fleet-radio-unit-melbourne-frumel-closed-70-years-ago-today-on-november-1-1945

Weadon, Patrick D. (2009), 'The Battle of Midway', on National Security Agency/Central Security Service (USA) website, www.nsa.gov/about/cryptologic_ heritage/center_crypt_history/publications/battle_midway

Whitlock, Duane L. (1995), 'Station C, Corregidor as I Remember It', on Corregidor, Then & Now: Echoes in Time, Corregidor Historical Society, corregidor.org/crypto/chs_whitlock/station_c and corregidor.org/crypto/chs_whitlock/ whitlock_2

Whitman, Paul F. (1999), 'Cryptography: One Story is Good Until Another is Revealed—Breaking Purple', on Corregidor, Then & Now: Echoes in Time, Corregidor Historical Society, corregidor.org/crypto/chs_crypto1/purple

——(1999), 'Cryptography: One Story is Good Until Another is Revealed—JN-25D', on Corregidor, Then & Now: Echoes in Time, Corregidor Historical Society, corregidor.org/crypto/chs_crypto1/jn25

Wright, David (ed.) (n.d.), 'United States Asiatic Fleet: Order of Battle, December 1941', on The United States Asiatic Fleet website, www.asiaticfleet.com/orbat

Zimmerman, Dwight Jon (2013), 'Operation Vengeance: The Mission to Kill Admiral Yamamoto', on Defense Media Network, Faircount Media Group, www.defensemedianetwork.com/stories/operation-vengeance-the-mission-to-kill-admiral-yamamoto

——(2013), 'Operation Cartwheel: The Start of the Island-hopping Campaign', on Defense Media Network, Faircount Media Group, www.defensemedianetwork.com/stories/operation-cartwheel

Index

9th Division (AIF) 254–8, 262–3
20th Division (IJA) 257–8, 262–5, 267
21 Henry Street 190–4, 201, 204, 208, 210–11, 261–2, 264, 321, 323
112nd Signal Radio Intelligence Company (US) 314–15
125th Signal Radio Intelligence Company (US) 305–6
837th Signals Service Detachment (US) 174

Adachi, General Hatazo 256–7, 272
Admiralty 22–5, 29, 36, 166, 197–8, 214, 252, 289
AF location 139–42, 146, 161
Aircraft Warning Service, Manila 83–4
Aitape 274–5, 278
Akin, Spencer 71, 84, 96, 106, 169, 173, 186, 194–5, 214, 258, 260, 273, 279–80, 284, 290, 292–3, 301, 309, 318–19, 322
Alamo Force 254, 262, 270
Aleutian Islands 124, 142–3, 145, 147–9, 153–4, 159
Alexander-Sinclair, Admiral Sir Edwyn 24

Allied Translator and Interpreter Section (ATIS) 263–4
Anami, General Koreiku 272
Archer, Henry 60, 111–12, 198–200, 216
Arlington Hall 195, 206–9, 212–14, 216, 258, 264–5, 279, 331
Ascot Park 261–2, 264, 308
Asiatic Fleet (US) 77–8, 84, 86, 89, 91, 95, 105
ASIO 329
Australian Naval Board 27
Australian Women's Army Service (AWAS) 179–80, 319, 326

Ballard, Geoff 53, 190–1, 266, 290, 324
Bandung 90–2
Barber, Lieutenant Rex 235, 237–40
'barium meal' 38
Bartlett, John 201, 204, 214
Bataan Gang 107, 164, 169
Bataan Peninsula 76, 88–9, 94, 97, 101–3, 247
Batangas 89, 100
Battle of the Bismarck Sea 218–21
Battle of the Coral Sea 128–34, 136, 150, 194

INDEX

Battle of Jutland 23
Battle of Leyte Gulf 306–7, 323
Battle of Midway Island 150–1, 153–8, 160, 194, 231, 247, 272, 332
  newspaper reports 159–60
Battle of Savo Island 162–3
Beresford, Bill 303, 316–17
Berryman, General Frank 309, 325
Biard, Forrest 'Tex' 265–6
Black Chamber 65–6
Blackie 87
Blamey, General Thomas 107, 169, 250, 252–6, 260–1, 284–5, 288, 310–11, 319
Bletchley Park 39, 51, 53, 78, 112, 164, 166, 169, 173, 196, 199–200, 207, 212, 215–16, 243–5, 260–1, 264, 287–8, 302, 323, 327
Bond, Ronald 112–13, 320
Bonegilla 178–9, 199–200
Booth, Roy 170, 178, 183, 195, 301–2, 322, 324, 328
Botchan 21
Bougainville 223, 226, 232–4, 236–40, 257
Bradshaw, Thomas 'Snow' 54–5, 61–3
Bratton, Colonel Rufus 14
British Embassy, Tokyo 19–20
British Far Eastern Fleet 101, 121, 166
Brown, Howard 82–4, 99–100, 185–6
BRUSA Agreement 244–5, 259, 302
'brute force' 72, 335
Burley, Squadron Leader S.F. 302
Burnett, Malcolm 'Bouncer' 40, 78, 152, 164

Burnett, Sid 102
Busu River 254, 256
Butte 75–6, 138

Callahan, Fort 85–6, 88, 95, 101–2, 104
Carlson, Spencer 'Swede' 78, 90, 93, 243, 245–6
Carpender, Admiral Arthur 164
Carpenter, Walter 43
Cast *see* Station Cast
Cavite 75–6, 83–5, 87, 90, 100
Central Bureau ix, 169, 171–9, 182–3, 186, 190–7, 199–201, 203–4, 206–18, 222, 225, 227, 242–3, 246, 248–9, 251–3, 257–74, 277–82, 284, 287–301, 303, 308, 316–25, 327, 331
Chamberlin, Vince 84, 102
Chapple, Lieutenant Wreford 'Moon' 97–9
Chifley, Ben 328
China Station 21, 23–9, 32, 38, 44
Chungking 4, 309–11
Ciano, Edda 38
Cipher Bureau 65
Clamor 259–60
Clark Airfield 76, 82, 231, 297, 307, 313–14, 322
Clark, Larry 174, 192, 209–11
Clark, Stan 'Pappy' 281, 324
Clarke, Colonel Carter 258, 301–2
Clarke, Bill 'Nobby' 225, 324
Clarke, William 'Nobby' 25–6
Colvin, Admiral Ragnar 21, 43, 45, 47
Combined Operational Intelligence Centre (COIC) 55–7, 171
Cook, Ralph 84–6, 101–2, 145–6, 242

381

Coomalie Creek 181–3, 249
Cooper, Arthur 59–60, 111, 199–200
COPEK channel (US Navy) 79, 137
Coral Sea *see* Battle of the Coral Sea
Corey, Cecil 281–2
Corregidor 64, 75–6, 78–9, 84, 87–9, 94–6, 100–4, 318
cover story 71, 220, 232–3, 273
Crace, Rear-Admiral John 128, 133–4
Cranbourne, Lord 44–5
Cranleigh 173, 176–8, 191, 197, 203
Crete defence 52, 190
Curtin, John 1, 5, 138

D Special Section ix, 198–200, 216, 287–8, 316, 320, 325–7
Dagupan 312–14
Darwin attack 62–3
Darwin base (RAAF) 54–5, 61–3
Defence Signals Branch (DSB) 328–9
Del Monte 96, 99–100
Denniston, Alistair 24, 216
despatch riders 1–2, 6, 73, 115, 121, 139, 199, 326
direction-finder antenna 60, 90, 186–8, 244, 305
District Censor (Australia) 48–9
Dockyard Code (Japan) 39–40
Dominions Office (UK) 43–5, 287
Doolittle air raid 122
Dowd, Robert 77
Driscoll, Aggie 80
Durnford, Commodore John 5, 7–8
Dutch Harbor 153–4, 159
Dyer, Tom 72–4

Eldermell Terrace 192, 290, 303–4, 311, 316, 323
Enigma cipher machine 34, 78, 206, 212, 333
Erskine, Hugh 174, 263–4, 323
Exmouth Gulf 92–4
Ezaki, Colonel Yoshio 269

Fabian, Rudy 75–8, 80–1, 84–6, 88–95, 105–6, 109–12, 116, 119–20, 124, 126, 136–8, 144, 152, 164–5, 170–3, 176–7, 199, 215, 242–6, 252, 259, 265, 316, 330–1
Fairfax Harbour 183, 249
Falconer, Keith 224–6, 240
Far East Combined Bureau (FECB) ix, 5, 33–4, 37–41, 43–46, 50, 56–7, 59, 65, 73, 78, 87, 112, 137, 152, 164, 166, 170, 174, 215, 243, 245, 259
Ferrall, Lieutenant-Commander William 'Pete' 90, 103–4
Finschhafen 248, 255, 257, 280
'fist' 189–90
Fletcher, Admiral Frank 123, 127, 129, 131–4, 155, 157
Foley, Captain James 5, 197
Forde, Frank 176
'Foreign Legion' (nickname) 300–1
Foreign Office (UK) 24, 29, 43, 198–9, 214, 245, 260
Fort McKinley 76, 79
Fort Shafter 14–16
French Frigate Shoals 140
Freyberg, General Bernard 53
Friedman, William 66–7, 70–2
Friend, Donald 302–4, 311, 316–17, 330

INDEX

FRUMEL ix, 108–11, 115–17, 120–6, 133–4, 136, 139–41, 143–53, 158–60, 164, 166, 171–2, 177, 196, 198–200, 214–16, 218, 226–7, 242–6, 261, 265, 316, 321, 325, 330–1
Fuchikami, Tadeo 15

Girhard, Charlie 263–4
Glassford, Admiral 92
Goggins, William 162
Goodwin, Sid 245–6, 265
Government Code and Cipher School (GCCS) ix, 24–6, 28, 33–6, 39, 45, 216–17, 287
Graves, Hubert 60, 111–12, 198–200
Greater East Asia Co-prosperity Sphere 5
Greece defence 52
Grew, Joseph 71
Grosvenor House 175–6
Guadalcanal 126–8, 162–3, 217, 221–2, 228, 232–5, 239, 241, 247

Hakone 20–1
Halpin, Zac 193, 209, 322, 327
Halsey, Admiral William 'Bull' 142–3, 228, 232, 248, 271, 284, 293, 306
Hamasuna, Lieutenant Tomoyuki 239
Handelsverkehrsbuch 22
Hansa Bay 249, 253, 266–7, 269, 271–2, 274
Harbin 310–11
Hart, Admiral Thomas 78, 84–6, 91, 105
'Haruna' message 6–7, 9, 56
He'eia 73

Henderson Airfield 232–3, 241
Hine, Lieutenant Ray 235, 237–9
Hirohito, Emperor 25, 222, 230
HMAS *Australia* 294, 296–7
HMAS *Shropshire* 294, 296
HMAS *Sydney* 23
HMS *Hawkins* 21, 25
HMS *Kent* 27–31, 35
Hodgson, William 287–8
Hoeffel, Captain Kenneth 97, 101, 103–4
Holden Agreement 166, 196, 198, 212
Holland, Ted 308
Hollandia 249, 252, 266–7, 271–8, 280–2, 285–6, 289–90, 301, 308–9, 317–18
Holmes, Lieutenant Besby 235, 237–40
Holmes, Robert 279
Holtwick, Jack 243
Hong Kong 33, 39
Hori, Admiral Yugoro 30
Hull, Cordell 5, 13
Hyakutake, General Harukichi 134
Hypo *see* Station Hypo

IBM tabulators 71–2, 75, 77, 79, 81, 85, 101, 110, 118, 144, 192–3, 202, 208–9, 242, 261, 265, 321–2, 327–8
Imamura, General Hitoshi 217, 223–4, 227, 256, 268–9, 271
Imperial Japanese Navy 28
Inouye, Vice-Admiral Shigeyoshi 120, 123, 128–9, 132–3
intercepts
    Admiralty Islands defenders 270–1
    Coral Sea aftermath 134

intercepts *continued*
  Coral Sea preparation 121, 123
  Hollandia defenders 277–8
  Midway preparation 141, 143
  New Guinea airfields 253
  Pearl Harbor preparation 10, 12–14
  US reading codes 70
  Yamamoto itinerary 226

Japanese aircraft carriers
  Akagi 145, 149, 153, 156, 159
  Hiryu 157–8
  Junyo 154, 157
  Kaga 118–21, 123, 156, 158
  Ryujo 154, 157, 159
  Shoho 123, 125–6, 128–32
  Shokaku 122–3, 126–7, 130–3
  Soryu 156, 158
  Zuikaku 122–3, 126–7, 130–3, 151

Japanese codes
  Army Air Force General Purpose 205, 207, 279–80
  D *see* JN-25
  Flag Officers 33, 39, 41, 69, 73
  J-18 56
  J-19 3, 6, 12, 56
  JN-1 26–7
  JN-4 56, 111
  JN-20 56, 163
  JN-25 39–41, 46, 50, 65, 69–70, 72–3, 77–9, 81, 86–7, 111, 115, 117–21, 125, 137–8, 145, 148, 151, 161, 163–4, 177, 206, 218, 223, 225, 227, 239–40, 244, 334
  LA 48
  Orange 34–5
  PA-K2 12
  Purple 6, 65, 69–70, 79–81, 95–6, 112, 195, 209

Water Transport 193, 205–14, 216–17, 220, 249, 251, 257, 272, 282, 334

Jack, Dorothy 173
Jamieson, A.B. 'Jim' 49–51, 57, 112, 120, 124, 152, 198
Jamieson, Mac 299
Japanese consulates, Australia 46
Japanese consulate, New York 67
Japanese Embassy, London 26, 36
Japanese surrender 320
Java invasion 59, 61, 91
Jellicoe, Lord 23
Joshima, Rear-Admiral Takaji 224

Kamer 14 ix, 5, 50, 56, 89–91, 105, 110
kamikaze attack 296–7, 299–300, 307–8, 312, 315
kana 3, 23, 34, 54, 56, 82, 114, 173–4, 189, 201, 225, 333
kana typewriters (RIP-5) 68, 75, 90, 114
kanji 3
Kavieng 251, 267
Kelly, Vice-Admiral Sir Howard 27–32
Kenney, General George 217–18, 249–50, 252, 254–5, 267–9, 271–4
Kimmel, Admiral Husband E. 10, 12–13, 15–16, 72
King, Admiral Ernest 89, 96, 116, 122, 141–3, 161–2, 164, 247
King, Stan 293, 296–7
Kingsley radio receiver 52, 54–5
Kinkaid, Vice-Admiral Thomas 272
Knox, Frank 14, 228, 241
Kokoda 134–5, 217
Kondo, Admiral Nobutake 144

INDEX

Kramer, Commander Al 14
Kranji 40
Kuehn, Otto 37
Kukum Airfield 232, 234–5, 239–41
Kurusu, Saburo 5
Kusaka, Vice-Admiral Jinichi 222, 224, 240, 256
Kwantung Army 29

Lae 119, 123, 217–21, 242, 248–50, 254–6, 270
Lakunai Airfield 221–2, 236
Lanphier, Captain Tom 235, 237–42
Layton, Ed 13, 72–3, 122, 140–1, 148, 227–8
'Leaping Lena' 54
Leary, Vice-Admiral Herbert 105, 110–12, 117, 134, 137–8, 164, 172, 174
Leyte 284, 286, 290–301, 305–8, 312, 315
Leyte invasion 293–300
Lietwiler, John 80, 85–7, 89, 94–5, 97, 101–2, 117, 121, 136–8, 144, 152, 243, 246, 330–1
Lingayen Gulf 88, 312–3
Little, Lieutenant-Colonel Robert 196–9, 214, 216, 287–9, 311, 316, 324–5
London Naval Conference 1934 229–30
Long, Rupert 'Cocky' 42–44, 51, 55–7, 59–60, 106–7, 124, 137, 170–1, 197–8
Longfield Lloyd, Ian 49
Lorengau airstrip 267, 270
Los Negros Island 267–71
LST-700 292, 298

Luzon 312
Lyons, Dickie 47, 50, 164, 200

MacArthur, General Douglas 79–80, 86, 88, 96, 106–7, 110–11, 121, 127, 129, 134, 137–8, 142–3, 151, 162, 170, 172, 190, 195, 197, 218, 242, 247–8, 251, 254–8, 266–8, 271–2, 274, 277, 280–3, 296, 301, 304, 306–7, 312, 317
McCoy, Melvyn 95, 102, 104–5
McDaniel, C. Yates 138
Mackie, Tom 134, 265–6
MacRobertson Girls High School 106, 169
Madang 248, 249, 257, 262, 265, 267, 271–2, 275
Magic intelligence reports 10–11, 335
Mahrt, Otto 213
Malinta tunnel 84–6, 88
Mandated Territories 45–6, 55, 61, 111, 122, 124, 152
Manila
  Allied advance on 312–15
  Japanese advance on 87–9
Manila Bay 90, 96, 103–4, 318
Manus Island 251, 267, 270–1, 275
Marilinan airstrip 252–3, 255
Markham Valley 254–5
Marshall, General George 14, 137–8, 170, 247, 251, 258, 280
Mason, Redfield 'Rosey' 77, 90–2, 105–6, 111
Menzies Hotel 106–7
Menzies, Robert 43–5, 55
Merry, Alan 111–12
MI5 35–6
MI6 24, 33, 36, 43, 324
Midway invasion preparation 139, 141–52, 231

Midway Island 140–1
Miles, General Sherman 14
Mitchell, Major John 233–9
Mitscher, Admiral Marc 'Pete' 228, 232–3
Miyata, Mineichi 19
Momote airstrip 267–9
Monkey Point tunnel 75, 85–8, 90, 95, 101, 325
Monterey 107, 109–13, 120, 125–6, 128, 131, 139, 152, 165, 243
Moon, Private Harold 296
Moorabbin 107, 114–15, 121, 124–5, 127–8, 139, 144–5, 242
Mornington 325–6
Musashi 306

Nadzab 255, 280
Nagumo, Admiral Chuichi 121, 144–5, 147, 150, 153–7
Nassau Bay 250–1, 255
Naval Academy, Annapolis 76–7, 80
Nave, Elizabeth 289–90
Nave, Eric 2–9, 18–41, 44–6, 49–51, 54–7, 59–60, 68, 105, 107, 111–14, 117, 119–20, 124, 126, 137–8, 152, 163–7, 170–1, 176–7, 192, 196–201, 214, 251–2, 289, 301, 308, 323–6, 328–9
Nave, Helena (née Gray) 39–41, 44, 113, 200
Navy Office (Australia) 44
New Guinea Force 254, 262–3, 275
Newman, Jack 43–6, 56–9, 64, 105–7, 111, 114–5, 124, 166, 170, 174, 176–7, 196, 243, 246, 316, 325, 328

Nichols Airfield 76, 82–3, 307
Nimitz, Admiral Chester 122–3, 126, 129, 134, 140–3, 147–51, 153, 155, 158–62, 226–8, 232, 242, 271–2, 274, 283
Nomura, Kichisaburo 5, 31, 70
Northcott, General John 197–9, 289, 310
Nyrambla *see* 21 Henry Street

Olongapo 75–6
On-the-Roof Gang 68
OP-20-G ix, 56, 68–71, 73, 77–8, 87, 105, 116–17, 120, 124, 139–43, 147, 150, 161, 165–6, 215, 244–5
Operation Cartwheel 248, 250–1
Operation I-Go 221–3, 248
Operation King 2 284–5
Operation MO 122, 124–9, 133–4
  preparation for 120–5
Operation Vengeance 228, 232–9, 242

Palo 291, 296–8
Panay 230
Park Orchards 1–3, 6, 54, 57, 114, 179
Parlett, Harold 19–20, 22
PCE-848 292–8, 312, 318
Pearl Harbor attack 8–10, 15–16, 31, 58, 73, 82, 84, 116, 135, 229, 231–2, 242
Port Moresby 119, 121–3, 125, 127–30, 134–5, 139, 143, 190, 266, 273, 280
Poulden, Lieutenant-Colonel J.E. 'Teddy' 329

Quezon, Manuel 88, 96

INDEX

Rabaul 119–21, 123–7, 130, 133–4, 163, 187–9, 217–27, 232, 234, 247–8, 251, 254, 267–8, 272, 276
radio fingerprinting 189, 244
Red Book 67
Redman, Jack 116–17, 140, 143, 150, 161
Redman, Rear-Admiral Joseph 116, 161, 177, 244–5
Richard, Joe 202–12, 214, 216–17, 249, 252, 265, 268, 331
Richardson, Gill 78, 90, 95, 147, 226, 246
Roberts, Colonel Caleb 169–71, 196
Rochefort, Joe 12, 16, 72–4, 116, 120, 122, 124, 140–1, 148–51, 160–3, 227, 332
Rockwell, Rear-Admiral Francis 86, 95–7
Roe, Judy 308
Rogers, Brigadier John 196, 199, 260, 284, 287, 309, 316, 319, 322, 324, 327
romaji 56, 225, 333
Room, Gerry 47, 49–51, 164, 200, 206, 211, 252, 304, 308, 327
Roosevelt, Franklin 8–9, 228, 247
Rouna Falls 249
Royal Australian Navy 2, 8, 19, 23
Royal Navy 2, 8, 18, 24–5, 27, 59
Royle, Admiral Sir Guy 8
Rushbrooke, Captain E.G.N. 38
Rutland, Fred 35–7
Ryan, Jack 51–3, 64, 168–9, 179

Safford, Laurance 67–8, 70, 72, 77, 116–17
Saidor 255, 262
Saito, Vice-Admiral Shichigoro 23, 37
Salamaua 119, 123, 250, 254–6, 270
San Miguel 313, 315, 317–23, 325, 327
Sandford, A.W. 'Mic' 52–4, 64, 167–71, 173, 176, 178, 190, 192, 195–7, 214–17, 245, 252, 259–60, 264–6, 280, 287–90, 301–4, 309–11, 316–17, 319, 322–30
Sandford, Sir Wallace 52–3
Sattelberg 255, 257–8, 262
Saunders, Commander Malcolm 244
Schelling, Thomas 9, 11
Secraphone 8
Shanghai 30–1, 48, 78, 89
Shaw, Harry 20–2, 25–6, 33–4, 37, 40, 50, 164
Shedden, Frederick 5, 328
Sherr, Joe 79, 83, 96, 106, 170–1, 173, 177, 186, 197, 214, 259
Shinkawa 35–6
Shizuoka 19–21, 45
Short, General Walter 10, 14–16
Signal Intelligence Service (SIS) ix, 10, 66–71, 78, 202–3, 207, 331
Simpson, Brigadier Colin 168–70
Sinclair, Admiral Sir Hugh 33, 36
Singapore 24, 28, 40, 45–6, 58–9, 87, 89
Sinkov, Abe 66–7, 78, 178, 192, 194–6, 204, 206–12, 259, 263–4, 284, 287, 301–2, 316, 322–3, 331
Sio 255, 262–6, 268, 272, 274
Smart, General Ken 197–8
South Pacific Area 226, 247–8
Southwest Pacific Area (SWPA) command 106, 134–5, 171, 174, 190, 198, 214, 242, 247–8, 258, 260–1, 266–7, 274, 280–1, 284, 301, 307, 312

Soviet Union 310–11, 322–3, 326, 329, 331–2
Special Intelligence Bureau (SIB) ix, 2, 45, 49–50, 54, 56–7, 59–60, 105, 107, 111–12, 114, 124, 137, 152, 166, 196, 198, 200, 216, 326
Special Liaison Unit 302, 326
Special Wireless Section; *see also* Wireless Section
  No. 1 51
  No. 4 51–4, 64, 329
SS *Hobart* 22
Stark, Admiral Harold 14
Station 6 ix, 79–84, 88, 96, 170, 174
  evacuation from Corregidor 99–100, 184–5
Station Cast ix, 56, 64, 71, 73–5, 77–82, 84–8, 91, 94–5, 100–1, 105, 109, 116, 139, 245
  evacuation from Corregidor 89–94, 96–9, 101–4, 107, 115, 118, 136
Station Hypo ix, 56, 69–74, 116, 120, 122–5, 139–40, 142–3, 147–51, 158, 160–3, 218, 227, 244
Stimson, Henry 66
Stonecutters Island 33–4, 39–40
Strong, General George 258
Stuart Creek 186–7, 224–6
substitution codes 3
Surabaya 90
Sutherland, General Richard 79, 82, 96, 172, 190, 195, 198, 258, 261, 301–2, 309
SWPA *see* Southwest Pacific Area

Tacloban 291, 297–301, 305
Takagi, Admiral Takeo 128–9, 131–3
Taylor, Rufus 94

Tertius 59, 200
Theobald, Admiral Robert 153–4
Thomas, Captain Edward 289
Thompson, Arthur 88–9, 105
Thompson, Ralph 181, 329
TICOM 323, 331
Tiltman, John 39–40, 215
TINA 189–90
Tjilatjap 92
Togo, Shigenori 13
Tojo, Hideki 231
Tokyo, occupation 321–3
'Tokyo Rose' 300–1
Tolosa 291, 305–8, 312
Townsville 183–9, 226, 243
  bombing raids 187–9
traffic analysis 51, 60–1, 81, 87, 100, 125, 159, 163, 217, 251, 262, 274, 335
Travis, Sir Edward 288, 302, 327–9
Tremblay, Bill 145–7, 332
Trendall, Dale 47, 50, 60, 112–13, 152–3, 198–200, 216, 287, 316, 325
Treweek, Ath 47, 49–50, 112–13, 120, 124, 152, 196, 198, 316
tropical sprue 2, 41, 44
Tulagi 122–3, 125–9, 142, 162
Turner, Admiral Kelly 140, 143, 150

Ugaki, Vice-Admiral Matome 223–4, 236–8, 240
Ultra 53, 194, 268, 272, 276, 288, 309, 335
University of Sydney cryptography group 47–50, 54, 60, 171
US Pacific Fleet 8–11
USS *Enterprise* 122–3, 142, 144, 150, 155–7

INDEX

USS *Hornet* 122–3, 142, 144, 150, 155–6
USS *Lexington* 123, 127, 129–32
USS *Permit* 97–9
USS *Seadragon* 90, 101, 103–4
USS *Snapper* 92
USS *Swordfish* 96
USS *Yorktown* 123, 127–32, 142, 144, 150, 156–7

Victoria Barracks 1, 6–7, 44–5, 54–5, 58, 105, 107, 114, 170, 173, 198–9, 325–6, 329–30

WAAAF *see* Women's Auxiliary Australian Air Force
Wainwright, Colin 192, 288–9, 304, 323, 330
Waller, John 34
Wang Chih, Colonel 309
Wanigela 183
War Cabinet (Australia) 1, 8
Washington Naval Conference, 1921 66, 229–30
Watanabe, Captain Yasuji 222–5, 240
Watut River 252, 255–6
Wau 217–18, 250, 255
Wavell, General Archibald 53, 101
Webb, Norman 174, 204, 211, 216
Wenger, Joe 116, 215, 244
Wewak 249–50, 252–3, 267, 269, 271–6
Whitehead, General Ennis 268–9
Whitlock, Duane 94
Williams, Mos 281–2
Willoughby, General Charles 96, 106, 172, 195, 260–1, 267–9, 301–2, 309

Windemere Road 200
'Winds' message 4–7, 9, 56–8
   execute message 6
Winnellie 180–1
Wireless Experimental Centre (WEC) ix, 196, 206–7, 215–17, 259–60, 264
Wireless Section; *see also* Special Wireless Section
   No. 51 180–3, 329
   No. 53 280–1
   No. 55 183, 280
Wireless Unit
   No. 1 54–5, 61–2, 184–9, 218, 224–5, 249, 253, 270–1, 284–5
   No. 4 286–7, 329
   No. 6 285–6, 290–301, 305–8, 312–15, 319–20
Women's Army Corps (WAC) 282, 318
Women's Auxiliary Australian Air Force (WAAAF) 174–5, 319
Women's Royal Australian Naval Service (WRANS) 114–15, 126, 165–6, 242
Wylie, Captain 59
Wyndham 63–4

Yamagata, Clarence 175, 184
Yamamoto, Admiral Isoroku 11, 124, 135, 139, 141, 143–4, 149–50, 153, 157–9, 221–42, 332
Yamashita, General Tomoyuki 312
Yamoto 139, 150, 157, 306
Yardley, Herbert 65–6
Yoshino Maru 279

Zachariah, Captain Ellis 228